S0-AHI-646

THE
CARIBBEAN

Survival, Struggle and Sovereignty

By
Catherine A. Sunshine

An EPICA Publication

FROM REVIEWS OF THE FIRST EDITION:

"The best single introductory source published on the topic in the last decade."

— Manning Marable, *Christianity & Crisis*

"Cathy Sunshine's new book is far and away the best, the most comprehensive and the most progressive survey history of the region to come on the scene in recent years. For the general reader who knows little about the Caribbean, here at last is an accessible source that is easy to read."

— Milton Benjamin, *The Guardian*

"There is, to date, no other book which sets out to do what Cathy Sunshine attempted here for so many countries . . . A fine job."

— Neville C. Duncan, *Caribbean Contact*

"Few stones are left unturned in this study, which includes overviews of individual countries, alliances, and a hard look at the region's historic fragmentation. It also examines unofficial bridge-building efforts among diverse countries, seen in women's and rural workers' organizations, among development workers and in the churches."

— *Latinamerica Press*

"A forward-looking book, concerned with the issues facing the contemporary Caribbean. It is as densely packed with factual information as Jenny Pearce's *Under the Eagle*, and its great achievement is in making that information available to the general reader."

— *Race & Class*

"Written with vigor and clarity."

— *Caribbean Insight*

Typesetting: Grimwoods'

Front cover photo: Grenadian fishermen, © 1973 by Flora Phelps

Back cover photo: Trinidadian workers on strike, © 1980 by Transport and Industrial Workers Union of Trinidad and Tobago

Copyright © 1985, 1988, 1994, 1996 by EPICA.
Fourth edition, first printing, 1996.

All rights reserved. No portion of this book may be reprinted, except for review purposes, without written permission of EPICA.

ISBN: 0-918346-07-X

Printed in the United States of America

Ecumenical Program on Central America and the Caribbean
1470 Irving Street, N.W.
Washington, D.C. 20010

Contents

BERMUDA
Hamilton
Col. U.K.
Crown Colony
Pop. 72,000

BAHAMAS
Nassau
Col. U.K.
Ind. 1973
Pop. 241,000

CUBA
Havana
Col. Spain
Ind. 1898
Pop. 9.8 million

CAYMAN ISLANDS
Georgetown
Col. U.K.
Crown Colony
Pop. 20,000

JAMAICA
Kingston
Col. U.K.
Ind. 1962
Pop. 2.2 million

BELIZE
Belmopan
Col. U.K.
Ind. 1981
Pop. 152,000

NETHERLANDS ANTILLES
1. Curacao
2. Aruba
3. Bonaire
4. St. Maarten
5. Saba
6. St. Eustatius
Willemstad
Col. Holland
Self-governing
 colony
Pop. 260,000

FRENCH GUIANA
Cayenne
Col. France
French overseas
 department
Pop. 77,000

SURINAME
Paramaribo
Col. Holland
Ind. 1975
Pop. 376,000

KEY

JAMAICA	Name of country
Kingston	Capital
Col. U.K.	Former colonizer (at time of independence)
Ind. 1962	Date of independence
(Status)	(Political status if not independent)
Pop. 2.2 million	Population

GUYANA
Georgetown
Col. U.K.
Ind. 1966
Pop. 700,000

TRINIDAD AND TOBAGO
Port-of-Spain
Col. U.K.
Ind. 1962
Pop. 1.1 million

GRENADA
St. George's
Col. U.K.
Ind. 1974
Pop. 110,000

BARBADOS
Bridgetown
Col. U.K.
Ind. 1966
Pop. 256,000

ST. VINCENT & THE GRENADINES
Kingstown
Col. U.K.
Ind. 1979
Pop. 123,000

TURKS & CAICOS
Grand Turk
Col. U.K.
Crown Colony
Pop. 8,000

HAITI
Port-au-Prince
Col. France
Ind. 1804
Pop. 5.2 million

DOMINICAN REPUBLIC
Santo Domingo
Col. Spain
Ind. 1844
Pop. 6.3 million

PUERTO RICO
San Juan
Col. Spain/U.S.
U.S. possession
Pop. 3.2 million

BRITISH VIRGIN IS.
Road Town
Col. U.K.
British dependency
Pop. 13,000

U.S. VIRGIN IS.
1. St. Thomas
2. St. Croix
3. St. John
Charlotte Amalie
Col. U.S.
U.S. territory
Pop. 103,000

ANGUILLA
The Valley
Col. U.K.
British dependency
Pop. 7,000

ANTIGUA & BARBUDA
St. John
Col. U.K.
Ind. 1981
Pop. 77,000

ST. KITTS/NEVIS
Basseterre
Col. U.K.
Ind. 1983
Pop. 45,000

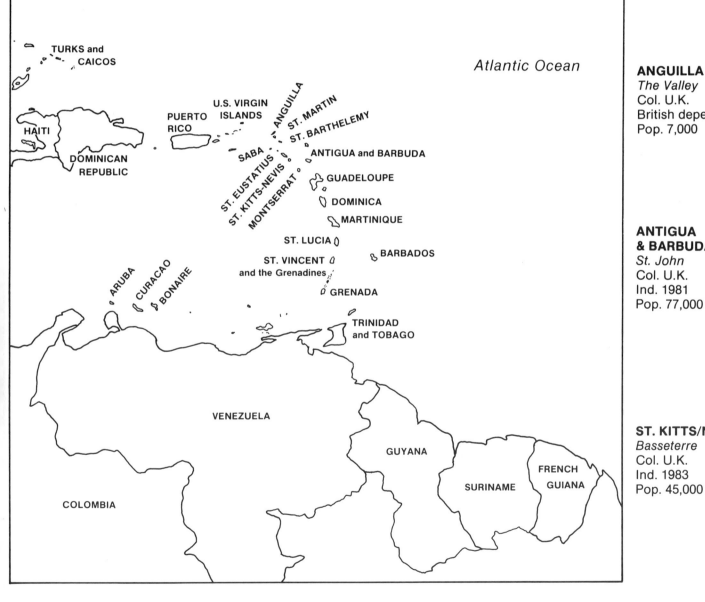

The Caribbean

Atlantic Ocean

ST. LUCIA
Castries
Col. U.K.
Ind. 1979
Pop. 119,000

MARTINIQUE
Fort-de-France
Col. France
French overseas
   department
Pop. 303,000

DOMINICA
Roseau
Col. U.K.
Ind. 1978
Pop. 74,000

GUADELOUPE
Pointe-à-Pitre
Col. France
French overseas
   department
Pop. 328,000

MONTSERRAT
Plymouth
Col. U.K.
Crown Colony
Pop. 12,000

Preface to the Second Edition

The Caribbean embraces some 27 island and mainland territories, four major linguistic groups and a kaleidoscope of races and cultures. This makes writing about the region as a whole a difficult task. We have not tried to cover every country in equal depth, but rather to give a sense of the broad picture.

The book's structure is basically thematic. To illustrate these themes we have drawn examples from the English, Spanish, French/Creole and Dutch-speaking territories. We have included the Atlantic coast of Central America because of its historic and cultural ties to the Caribbean islands.

The original edition of *The Caribbean* was published in 1985. This book follows the same format, but includes substantial updating, additions and rewriting throughout. Readers familiar with the first edition and professors using the book as a text may find helpful the following guide to organizational changes.

Part Two: Has been substantially revised to deal with major developments of the 1960s and '70s. Includes new chapters on the U.S. invasion of the Dominican Republic, the rise of the Duvalier dictatorship, and the New Jewel Movement in Grenada.

Part Three: The chapter on Brooklyn has been incorporated into a new chapter on Caribbean migration to the United States, "Moving North."

Part Five: Analysis of Reagan administration policies, previously found in Part Seven, has been moved to Part Five under the title "Invasion Aftermath: Reagan's New Caribbean Order."

Part Six: Profiles of the Bahamas, Dominica, Grenada and Suriname have been added.

Part Seven: This section has been revised to focus on grassroots organizing and positive alternatives. "Caribbean Women: Old Burdens, New Voices" is a new addition.

Appendix: Includes recommended books, periodicals and audiovisual resources; a list of U.S. organizations working on Caribbean issues; and an index.

A note on terminology: Among the various territories there are many instances of inconsistent usage. People of African descent, for example, are generally called *Creole* in Belize, Nicaragua and Suriname; *Afro-Guyanese* or *African* in Guyana; *Afro-Caribbean* in England; and *black* in most other places. Persons from the United States are usually called *Americans* in the English-speaking Caribbean and *North Americans* in the Spanish-speaking countries. Our general practice in this book is to use the term employed most commonly in the country under discussion.

Acknowledgements

We are indebted to many people who helped make this book possible, and our acknowledgements must remain incomplete. In every country we visited, we were assisted by friends who shared their ideas, opened their files, arranged interviews and provided hospitality. To all of them, we express our deep appreciation, and hope that our work may contribute in some way to the success of their efforts.

Organizations we wish to thank include the Caribbean Conference of Churches at its Barbados headquarters and subregional offices. Also, the Center for Ecumenical Action and Planning (CEPAE) in the Dominican Republic; the National Ecumenical Movement (PRISA) in Puerto Rico; the Social Action Centre in Jamaica; the Small Projects Assistance Team (SPAT) in Dominica; the Grenada Community Development Agency (GRENCODA); and the Working People's Alliance and People's Progressive Party in Guyana.

Special thanks for their help and hospitality go to Chandra Binnendyke in Suriname, Linda Rupert & Richenel Ansano in Curacao, Karen de Souza in Guyana, Sr. Marcelle Wachter in Guadeloupe, and Nicki Kelly in the Bahamas.

Many persons read and critiqued portions of the manuscript, among them Tony Bogues, O. Nigel Bolland, Hopeton Dunn, Todd Jailer, Kim Johnson, Karen Judd, Roy Neehall, James Phillips, Charles Roberts, Rickey Singh, Claudio Tavarez, Chiqui Vicioso, and Katherine Yih.

Philip Wheaton, director of EPICA, conceived the original idea for the book and helped guide its initial evolution. EPICA interns Leslie Wade, Janet Theiss and Dan Furman provided research assistance and helped in many ways. Vicky Surles created the drawings which begin each section, and James True assisted with the maps. William Minter provided overall editorial advice, along with hope and cheer when the task seemed endless.

We gratefully acknowledge assistance in publishing the original edition from:
National Community Funds, the Funding Exchange
United Church of Canada
Women's Division, Board of Global Ministries, United Methodist Church
Jesuit Centre for Social Faith and Justice, Toronto

For assistance in publishing the revised edition:
World Council of Churches, Human Rights Resources Office for Latin America
National Council of Churches USA, Committee on the Caribbean and Latin America
Church of the Brethren
Agricultural Missions, Inc.
Maryknoll Fathers, Justice and Peace Office
Susan Turits

Catherine Sunshine
September 1988

Introduction

by Philip E. Wheaton

The subtitle of this book—**survival, struggle and sovereignty**—reflects themes which dominate the history of the Caribbean and its present reality.

For many Caribbean people, **survival has become the overriding concern as the region-wide economic crisis tightens its grip.** Unemployment rates of 30% and higher, soaring food prices, and deep cuts in social services have caused a steady decline in living standards. Highlighted by riots in the Dominican Republic and Jamaica, regionwide strikes and protests reflect the deepening discontent.

Struggle refers to that thread of hope and meaning which runs through Caribbean history. Resistance to slavery and colonialism set the stage for today's struggles. These include the effort to define new models of development and a common vision of a united Caribbean.

Sovereignty was supposed to have been won with independence from the colonial powers. But it has been fragile, and today is threatened by the growing regional dominance of the United States. Successive U.S. governments have claimed the Caribbean as their own "backyard." Their attempts to militarize the region have frustrated Caribbean peoples' desires for self-determination, non-alignment and peace.

Many North Americans visit the Caribbean as tourists or on business, but few go beyond the invisible walls which surround the tourist and transnational enclaves in the islands. Posh hotels, private beaches and yachts, limbo dancers and pseudo-Voudou performances—the essence of Caribbean tourism is artificiality and isolation from the real lives of Caribbean people. Decades of such tourism have barely scratched the surface of American ignorance about the region.

In the past decade, however, it has become more difficult for Americans to view the Caribbean simply as a tropical playground. Presidents Carter and Reagan made the Caribbean "basin" a foreign policy priority, an arena where the United States would pursue a renewed Cold War. U.S. military aggression, centered in Central America, cast its shadow over the Caribbean as well. The U.S. invasion of Grenada in 1983 signalled the Reagan administration's return to the "big stick" tactics of the gunboat diplomacy era.

The crisis in Central America has prompted many Americans to examine that region's history and present realities for the first time. The same process must begin for the Caribbean—not in the self-serving ways which followed the Grenada invasion, but out of a desire to build a new relationship with the region. While the Caribbean is not an arena of armed conflict, suffering is so acute that protest is bound to increase. This challenges Americans to develop solidarity with the Caribbean, a movement which has begun but is still limited. The Black community in the United States has led the way in this expanded interchange between North Americans and Caribbean people.

The Caribbean: Survival, Struggle and Sovereignty draws on EPICA's more than twenty years of work on Caribbean and Central American issues. It reflects contact with a wide range of Caribbean organizations, including church and ecumenical groups, trade unions, women's organizations, peasant associations and grassroots development groups. In modest yet effective ways, they are carrying out the heart of the struggle for social justice in the region.

Our work also reflects cooperation with North Americans working for justice and peace in the United States and the Third World. This book was written with them in mind. We believe that only through north-south dialogue and solidarity can the injustices of the past be challenged and new relationships created for the future.

In the long view of Caribbean history, one is struck by the unbroken domination of foreign powers in the region—yet also by the fact that, one by one, these powers have declined or left the region, leaving Caribbean people to deal with colonialism's legacy. We affirm that the Caribbean is "nobody's backyard" in spite of North American presumptions. We also affirm that only the people of the Caribbean can forge alternative models of development, justice and peace in the region.

The Rev. Philip E. Wheaton is director of the Ecumenical Program on Central America and the Caribbean (EPICA).

The stone had skidded arc'd and bloomed into islands:
Cuba and San Domingo
Jamaica and Puerto Rico
Grenada Guadeloupe Bonaire

curved stone hissed into reef
wave teeth fanged into clay
white splash flashed into spray
Bathsheba Montego Bay

bloom of the arcing summers . . .

The islands roared into green plantations
ruled by silver sugar cane
sweat and profit
cutlass profit
islands ruled by sugar cane

Excerpted from "Calypso"
by Edward Braithwaite, Barbados

PART ONE
Caribbean Peoples' Unity
History and Culture

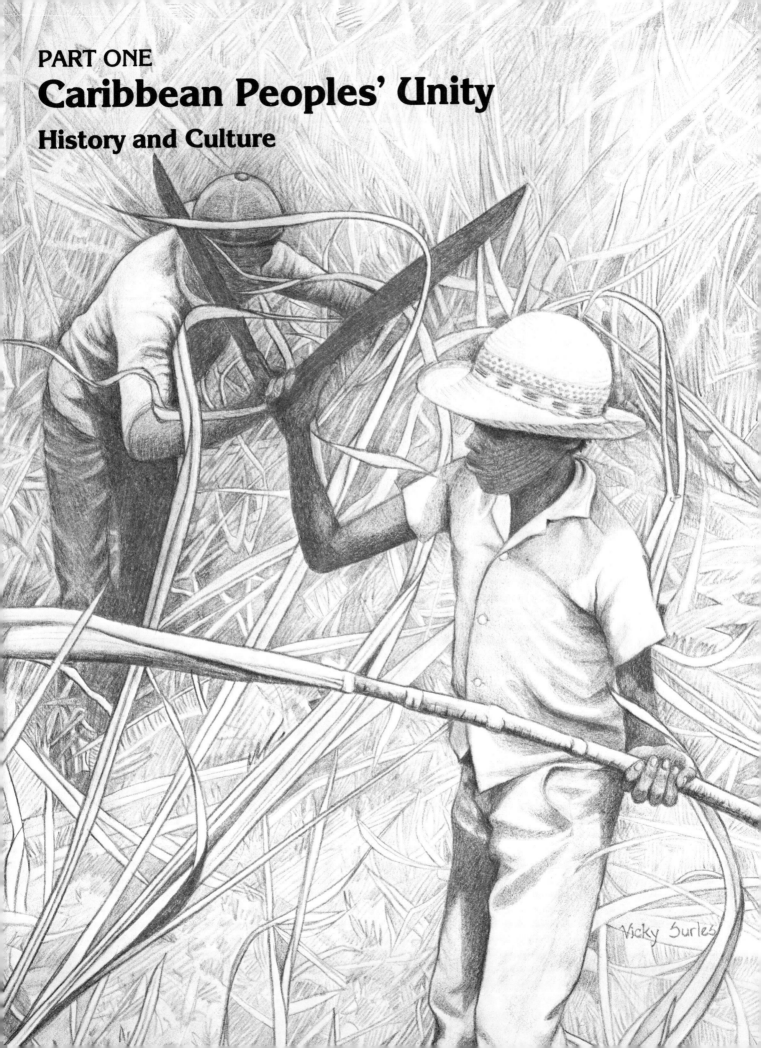

Brief History of the Caribbean Through Emancipation

When Queen Isabella of Spain sent Christopher Columbus across the Atlantic Ocean in 1492, his official mission was to discover a new trade route to Asia and Christianize the "heathens" who lived there. But Columbus and the Spanish *conquistadores* who followed him made little secret of their real interest: gold. When Columbus landed in the Bahamas and saw the native Arawaks adorned with gold trinkets, he was convinced that mythical "El Dorado"—the Golden Land— must be nearby. For years, the conquistadores pushed farther and farther into the Americas, driven by their greed for precious metals.

They were driven also by a lust for power. Many were *hidalgos,* or knights, who hoped to grab enough land and wealth in the New World to join the Spanish ruling class. Once the land had been claimed for Spain through conquest, the Spanish monarchy awarded them *encomiendas*—rights to rule—over areas of land inhabited by Amerindians.[1] The Spaniards forced the Indians into slavery in gold mines and on their colonial farms and ranches.

Destruction of the Arawaks by the Spanish; Carib Resistance to the British and French

When the Spanish arrived in the Caribbean, there were two Amerindian peoples living there: the Arawaks, centered in the Bahamas and the Greater Antilles, and the Caribs, in the Eastern Caribbean. Both had come from the tropical rain forest areas of northeastern South America, with the more aggressive Caribs gradually pushing the Arawaks northward.

The Indians were subsistence farmers and fishermen, growing corn, cassava, sweet potatoes, cotton and tobacco. They navigated among the islands in dug-out canoes capable of holding up to 80 people, which they used for inter-island trade, and in the case of the Caribs, to raid the Arawaks for goods and slaves.

The Arawaks whom Columbus encountered included three major subgroups: the Lucayanos, living in the Bahamas; the Borequinos in Puerto Rico; and the Tainos in Cuba, Jamaica and Hispaniola (now Haiti and the Dominican Republic). Though not warriors like the Caribs, the Arawaks made a brave effort to oust the Spanish from the Greater Antilles. Their resistance was crushed by the Spaniards' superior weaponry, vicious fighting mastiffs and armor-covered horses. The Spaniards' system of forced labor completed the destruction of the Arawaks, who died from starvation, abuse, and new European diseases, especially smallpox. Unable to successfully enslave the Amerindians, the Spanish turned to African slaves supplied to them by Portuguese traders.

England, France and Holland refused to recognize Spain's claim to "ownership" of the entire Caribbean,[2] and in the early 17th century, after years of warfare with Spain, the French and British began to colonize the Lesser Antilles. The Caribs living on those islands put up a fierce and prolonged resistance to the European invaders. Early attempts to colonize Grenada and St. Lucia had to be abandoned because of Carib ferocity, and later settlements on St. Kitts, Antigua, Montserrat, Grenada and St. Lucia were attacked repeatedly by the

DEATH OF HATUEY

Hatuey, an Arawak chief on the island of Hispaniola, fled to Cuba where he was captured by the Spaniards and burnt alive as an example to other Indians who resisted colonization.

From Bartolome de las Casas, *Very Brief Account of the Destruction of the Indies, 1552.*

Caribs. In Grenada, the Caribs fought the French for three years and finally hurled themselves into the sea rather than submit to French domination.

By the mid-17th century, the Europeans' superior firepower had forced the Caribs back into Dominica and St. Vincent. These mountainous islands were natural fortresses, and the Europeans recognized them as under Carib control in a treaty signed in 1660. From their strongholds, the Caribs continued to raid the European settlements for the rest of the century.

From Small Farms to Sugar Estates: The Big Planters Take Over

Barbados was uninhabited when the Europeans arrived, and a British colony there quickly grew and flourished. The colonists originally tried to make their fortunes growing tobacco, as pipe-smoking was a new fashion in Europe. Even these small farms required a cheap labor force, so the colonists brought in white indentured laborers from Europe. These were often convicts or debtors who signed themselves into servitude with the hope of some free land after a few years' bonded labor.

By the 1640s tobacco was no longer very profitable, so the settlers on Barbados turned to growing sugar cane, setting a pattern that was soon to be followed in all the French and British islands. The turn to sugar transformed the colonies and signalled the start of an era of exploitation which was to bring misery to hundreds of thousands of people. Unlike tobacco, sugar had to be grown on large plantations and required costly investment in buildings, equipment, and labor. Wealthy entrepreneurs steadily bought out or drove out the small farmers and consolidated their holdings into large sugar estates. Many of these big planters became "absentee landlords" who left the running of their estates to attorneys and overseers while living luxuriously in England on the profits from sugar.

The plantations required an endless supply of labor. Plantation work was so grueling that few people would voluntarily sign themselves into this kind of servitude; so the governments of Britain and France forcibly transported to the colonies thousands of convicts, paupers, and political or religious dissidents. But even these were not enough. Because the white laborers were Europeans, it was harder for the planters to rationalize the use of cruelty to keep them subdued. Africans, on the other hand, were a non-European race, and had already been slaves on Spanish and Portuguese plantations. Spain, France and Britain readily embraced the idea of an enslaved African workforce kept in submission by barbarous and inhuman methods.

The Dutch initially controlled the slave trade. From commercial bases on the islands of Curaçao and St. Eustatius, Holland kept the Spanish, British and French colonies supplied with slaves as well as food and other goods. After the ocean journey in the hold of a slave ship, the Africans were held in walled-in slave camps on Curaçao before being reshipped to other colonies. At the height of Holland's "Golden Age" in the mid-1600s, these camps often held more than 15,000 people at a time.[3]

African Resistance to Slavery

The dominant theme throughout the slavery era was the continuous struggle between the planters' coercive power and the slaves' determined resistance. Everything was pitted against the Africans: cruel torture devices on board the slave ships, the whips and guns of the planters and overseers, posses of soldiers and dogs sent out after runaway slaves. By 1700, slaves greatly outnumbered Europeans in most Caribbean colonies, and the planters lived in constant fear of a slave insurrection. They thus resorted to horrible punishments and executions of "troublemakers" to keep the slaves from rising against them.

But the slaves did revolt, repeatedly and often violently. There were hundreds of mutinies or attempted mutinies by slaves during the "middle passage" across the Atlantic. On the islands, especially Jamaica, slaves organized large-scale uprisings in which plantations were burned and the slave-masters killed. Some of the leaders of these revolts are remembered in

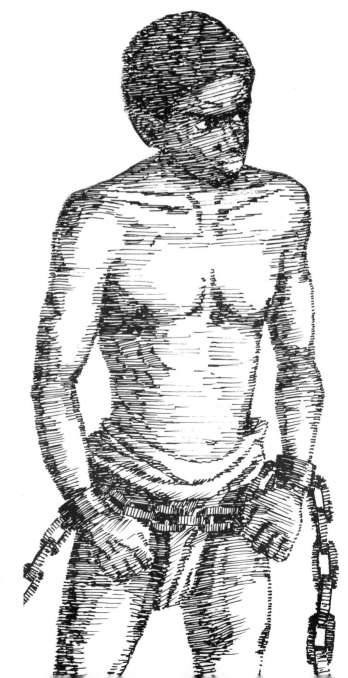

Courtesy Belize Government Information Service

the Caribbean for their daring: Cuffy in Guyana, Nanny and Tacky in Jamaica, and Morales in Cuba, among others.

In certain colonies, large numbers of slaves escaped from the plantations and set up independent communities beyond the reach of the planters. This was possible only where the terrain provided protection for the runaways, as did the mountainous interiors of Jamaica, Dominica, and St. Vincent, and the jungles of Guyana and Suriname. In Jamaica, the Maroons—as the rebels there were called—waged two long wars against the British, forcing the colonists to strike treaties recognizing them as free men. In Guyana and Suriname, they were called "Bush Negroes" since they lived in the wild interior:

> . . . Their villages were built on circular pieces of ground cleared of bush. The huts were hidden by planting fruit trees, yams and plantains and the whole area was defended by a wide ditch filled with water which covered sharp stakes. False paths were laid to lead enemies away from the underwater firm paths into the village.
>
> From their hidden homes the Bush Negroes raided the European plantations and forced the Dutch to send expeditions into the interior to attempt to crush them. These expeditions were costly in soldiers' lives and probably helped future runaways, for the Europeans took slaves with them who thus learned of the pathways through the bush. Rather than continue with the wars the Dutch Governor made treaties in 1761 and 1767 with the two main groups of Bush Negroes. The treaties were modeled on those with the Jamaican Maroons and gave the Bush Negroes freedom in return for an agreement to return any new runaways.[5]

Mercantilism: Consolidation of the Colonial System

In the mid-17th century, France and Britain had little interest in the moral niceties of the slavery issue because the economic logic for slavery was so strong. The transportation of slaves to the Americas formed one side of a three-legged "triangular trade." Slave ships would load up with guns, ammunition, and manufactured goods in British and French ports, then sail to Africa where the cargo was exchanged for slaves. Then came the middle passage across the Atlantic, and the sale of the Africans in the Caribbean and North American colonies. Finally, the ships loaded up with colonial sugar, cotton and tobacco and sped back to England and France, where the raw produce was refined and re-exported to other countries.

The triangular trade was one aspect of the mercantilist system of economic policy becoming the dominant view in England and France.[6] According to mercantilist theory, a nation could accumulate wealth by controlling colonies which would supply raw materials for industry, and also provide a captive market for the goods produced. Mercantilism depended on monopoly. For instance, the British colonies could buy only British goods and had to ship all their produce in British ships. In return, they were given a monopoly of the sugar market in England.

The system produced enormous profits for the colonial planters, the slave traders, and the merchants who financed the

trade and processed the sugar. Many spin-off industries also profited: shipbuilders, iron-mongers (who made the handcuffs and leg irons), and the industrialists who manufactured the goods sent to Africa. In both Britain and France, these interests used their wealth to buy political influence, keeping the colonial system entrenched for over 100 years.

The Caribbean became an arena for imperialist rivalry. France and Britain first fought three wars to drive the Dutch out of the Caribbean and reserve the lucrative slave trade for themselves. Then they turned on each other. Disputes which began in Europe were fought in the Caribbean with the colonies as pawns. French and British warships would attack and ravage each other's colonies, or seize and occupy them; in the latter part of the 18th century many of the islands flip-flopped back and forth between French and British ownership. Tiny Dominica, an extreme example, changed hands twelve times.

Revolutionary Surge at the Turn of the Century: Slave, Maroon, and Carib Revolts and the Haitian Revolution

For over a century, France and Britain exploited their colonies to extract every last cent of sugar profits. The results, by the end of the 1700s, were depleted soils, an enraged slave population, and prohibitively expensive sugar. As France and Britain were swept up in the Industrial Revolution, West Indian sugar lost its economic importance. The colonies entered a period of economic and social crisis, culminating in the Caribbean's only successful slave revolt, the Haitian Revolution.

HORRORS OF THE MIDDLE PASSAGE

The slaves were collected in the interior, fastened one to the other in columns loaded with heavy stones of 40 or 50 pounds in weight to prevent attempts at escape, and then marched the long journey to the sea, sometimes hundreds of miles, the sickly and weak dropping to die in the African jungle ...

On the ships the slaves were packed in the hold on galleries one above the other. Each was given only four or five feet in length and two or three feet in height, so that they could neither lie at full length nor sit upright. Contrary to the lies that have been spread so pertinaciously about Negro docility, the revolts at the port of embarkation and on board were incessant, so that the slaves had to be chained, right hand to right leg, left hand to left leg, and attached in rows to long iron bars. In this position they lived for the voyage, coming up once a day for exercise and to allow the sailors to "clean the pails." But when the cargo was rebellious or the weather bad, then they stayed below for weeks at a time. The close proximity of so many naked human beings, their bruised and festering flesh, the foetid air, the prevailing dysentery, the accumulation of filth, turned these holds into a hell. During the storms the hatches were battered down and in the close and loathsome darkness they were hurled from one side to another by the heaving vessel, held in position by the chains on their bleeding.

... They died not only from the regime but from grief and rage and despair. They undertook vast hunger strikes; undid their chains and hurled themselves on the crew in futile attempts at insurrection. What could these inland tribesmen do on the open sea, in a complicated sailing vessel? To brighten their spirits it became the custom to have them up on the deck once a day and force them to dance. Some took the opportunity to jump overboard, uttering cries of triumph as they cleared the vessel and disappeared below the surface.

— C.L.R. James, *The Black Jacobins*[4]

The French colony of St. Domingue (now Haiti) was the biggest sugar producer in the Caribbean. It epitomized the repressive and decadent plantation societies found all over the region, and was rigidly stratified according to skin color. As elsewhere in the Caribbean, the planters had made a practice of sexually using the slave women on their plantations. The mulatto or "colored" children of these unions were born into slavery, but often were freed by their fathers and sometimes inherited property. Especially in the French colonies, some free colored became relatively wealthy, owning estates and even slaves. Despite this, however, they were still denied full social and political equality by the white ruling class.

The French Revolution of 1789, with its promise of freedom and equality for all men, sent shock waves through the Caribbean—most of all in St. Domingue. The uprising began as a revolt by the free colored to gain full equality, but soon escalated into an island-wide slave revolution under the dynamic leadership of the slave named Toussaint L'Ouverture. Toussaint's black troops first soundly defeated a large British army sent out from Jamaica to seize St. Domingue. Next, the slave army defeated and massacred the mulatto military forces who wanted to set up a separate colored republic. In 1799, France recognized Toussaint's total control over St. Domingue and made him Governor-General of the island.

Toussaint, about 1801 or 1802, came to a conception for which the only word is genius. He wrote a constitution for San Domingo and he didn't submit it to the French government. He declared in the constitution that San Domingo would be governed by the ex-slaves. French officials asked him: what is the place of the French government in this constitution? He replied, "They will send commissioners to talk with me"—and that was all he would say.[7]

Meanwhile, however, the French Revolution had fallen into the hands of Napoleon Bonaparte, who plotted an invasion to restore slavery in St. Domingue. Toussaint was captured and killed by Napoleon's trickery, but the momentum of the Haitian Revolution continued. In 1803 slave armies led by Dessalines and Christophe defeated Napoleon's fever-ravaged army and set up the first independent republic under black control.

The success of the Haitian insurrection gave courage to subjugated peoples all over the Caribbean. Revolts broke out, incited in some cases by agents of the French Revolution, but drawing their force from the volcanic uprising of the black and colored masses. In Guadeloupe and St. Lucia, the slaves helped repel British invasions so as to keep the islands under French revolutionary control. In Grenada and Dominica, the slaves, free colored, and resident French joined in a struggle to overthrow the British rulers of the islands. There was a major slave revolt in the Dutch colony of Curaçao. On St. Vincent a group known as the "Black Caribs" revolted under the leadership of their chief Chatoyer. The British defeated the uprising and deported the surviving Black Caribs from St. Vincent to the Bay Islands off the coast of Honduras.

The revolutionary surge in the Eastern Caribbean coincided with a second major war by the Jamaican Maroons against the British. Although the Maroons were finally subdued and many deported to Nova Scotia, they exhausted the British forces and thus contributed to the British defeat by Toussaint in St. Domingue. Several years later the Maroons on Dominica joined the Dominican slaves in revolt. While all of these rebellions were eventually defeated, the cost to Britain was high. From then on, the British stood on notice that the viability of the slave system was nearing its end.

Declining Profits and Rising Violence Force the Emancipation of the Slaves

The idea that the moral pressure of the British abolitionists alone ended slavery is a myth. The slaves in the French and British colonies were emancipated when the slave system became unprofitable—and not until then.

As the Trinidadian historian Eric Williams argues in *Capitalism and Slavery,* it was the wealth the slaves created which finally destroyed the slave system.[8] The profits from the West India sugar trade had been steadily reinvested in British banking, finance, and industry. By the end of the 18th century, the Industrial Revolution was in full swing and new British industries were mass-producing goods for export around the world. Britain traded these manufactures for raw materials—cotton from the United States and India, coffee from Brazil, and most of all, *sugar,* from huge new producers like Brazil, India, and Cuba. Obviously, this system could not work if the West Indies kept their monopoly making them the only ones who could sell sugar to Britain.

It was also a question of price. The West Indian islands were small, their soils exhausted and production costs were high. Meanwhile the world market was flooded with cheap sugar from the new producers and from beet sugar, a growing industry in France. Powerful industrial and financial interests in Britain who had previously supported slavery now wanted to put the West Indian planters out of business so that Britain could buy this cheaper sugar. To attack the West Indian monopoly, Britain abolished the slave trade (but not slavery) in 1807. With the West Indian colonies no longer profitable, the way was cleared for the abolitionists to turn public opinion against slavery for moral and humanitarian reasons.

The second crucial factor was the slaves themselves, whose increasingly violent demands for freedom left the slave owners little choice but to get off the "powder keg" they were sitting on.[9] The slaves were acutely aware of the abolition debate in England and of the planters' resistance to ending slavery. Many slaves in fact believed that the French and British governments had already ordered emancipation, and that the planters were illegally withholding freedom.

Britain and France tried to defuse the situation through a reformist strategy: improving treatment of the slaves, sending money and missionaries to the colonies, liberalizing the system slightly. It failed. The West Indian slaves refused to wait any longer and the islands exploded one by one in revolt. In Guyana, 12,000 slaves on fifty plantations rose up demanding unconditional emancipation. Slaves on Barbados angrily claimed that "the island belonged to them, and not to white men." Sam Sharpe's Montego Bay revolt in Jamaica was crushed by British troops, leaving hundreds dead. There were four major rebellions on previously placid Martinique in the space of eleven years. In the Danish Virgin Islands, the slaves delivered an ultimatum: freedom by four o'clock or they would burn the capital to the ground. Freedom was granted. Finally,

Members of the plantocracy out for a stroll with their servants on the grounds of a private estate in Barbados. Note the Victorian style of dress which was stifling in the tropical heat.

Moorland-Spingarn Research Center, Howard University

on August 1, 1834, all the slaves in the British colonies were declared free, followed by emancipation in the French islands in 1848.

The Planters Turn to Immigrants to Avoid a Free Labor Market

After emancipation, the planters tried every possible scheme to keep the ex-slaves tied to the plantations. The slaves were not actually freed in 1834; instead, they became "apprentices" obliged to perform 40½ hours of unpaid labor each week. The slaves were outraged by this hypocrisy and rioted violently in some colonies, and by 1838 the impractical apprenticeship system was abandoned. As soon as the slaves were released the local island assemblies passed laws aimed at keeping them on the plantations by making "vagrancy" and unemployment punishable crimes.

Everywhere, the freed slaves looked for ways to leave the hated plantations and become economically independent, but this was only possible in some colonies. In Barbados, Antigua, and St. Kitts, which are flat, virtually all the land was under sugar cane and there was nowhere for the ex-slaves to go. They stayed on or near the sugar plantations, working for a small wage.

In the mountainous Windward Islands the situation was different. These islands had never been ideal for growing sugar, and many of the smaller estates were abandoned when the market for West Indian sugar collapsed. Thousands of ex-slaves left the plantations to buy, rent, or squat on abandoned estates or idle land in the hills. They formed the beginnings of an independent peasantry which pioneered the introduction of new export crops to replace sugar: cocoa and nutmeg in Grenada, arrowroot in St. Vincent, limes in St. Lucia and Dominica, cotton in Nevis and Montserrat. They also grew food crops which they sold to the estates or to neighboring islands.

Jamaica and Guyana, where land was relatively abundant, saw the fullest development of the free peasant society. Under pressure from the planters, the British government would sell land only in large tracts so as to keep the ex-slaves from buying. But the freed slaves circumvented this restriction by pooling their savings and buying land jointly, either forming cooperatives or parceling out individual plots to families. Missionary societies also purchased land for the ex-slaves, especially in Jamaica. By 1865, two-thirds of Jamaica's freed slaves had left the sugar plantations and were living in free villages.

These villages had their own internal governments which built and maintained roads, settled disputes, and helped to market crops. In some cases former slaves took over the entire operation of abandoned sugar estates. In a radical departure from the plantation system in which almost all food was imported, the free peasantry concentrated on growing food for local consumption. The surplus was sold to nearby estates in order to have money to pay taxes. They also grew crops for export, so that within several generations, Jamaican peasant farmers were producing a large portion of the island's national income.

The sugar planters liked to wail to the British government that the ex-slaves had deserted the plantations and brought about the financial ruin of the colonies. In fact, the best arable land remained under planter control, and many freed slaves had no choice but to remain on or near the estates as tenant farmers or sharecroppers. By charging steep rents for houses and house lots, the planters kept the ex-slaves in perpetual debt and ensured that those who remained in their homes on plantation land would have to perform wage labor on the plantation.

The planters could not use rents to extract labor from the residents of the free villages, so they used taxes. The colonial government greatly feared the growth of a self-reliant peasant economy, and levied punitive taxes to keep it in check. To pay these taxes, most of the villagers had to perform some wage labor on nearby estates. But their base of independent production gave them considerable latitude in deciding when and where to work, and the planters furiously resisted negotiating on a basis of equality with the ex-slaves for their labor.[10]

To avoid a "free" labor market where the workers could bargain for better wages and terms, the planters brought in indentured laborers from India, Asia, Africa, and Europe. Although most of them signed limited indentureship contracts voluntarily, these laborers were under the control of the planters once they arrived in the West Indies, and could be used as a weapon against the demands of the free workers.

Indentureship had the greatest impact in Trinidad and Guyana, where the sugar industry continued to flourish after it had declined in other islands. In Guyana, the freed slaves formed work gangs which moved from estate to estate, negotiating for short-term labor. They sought the best-paid, most highly skilled tasks, and bargained hard for favorable wages and terms, not hesitating to withhold their labor at crucial points in the crop cycle. When the Guyanese planters actually *reduced* wages in the 1840s, corresponding to a fall in the price of sugar, the free workers backed up their demands with strikes.[11]

The Guyanese planters used indentured labor to break the strikes. In 1845 and 1846, they brought in 6,000 Portuguese from the Madeira Islands, 4,000 laborers from India, and 2,000 Africans captured from foreign slave ships. With this new labor force, the planters were able to break the second and more serious sugar strike in 1848.[12]

Except in Haiti, Santo Domingo, Puerto Rico, and Barbados, the Caribbean islands underwent a demographic revolution in the 1800s as a result of this new immigrant labor. To the old black/white/colored structure were added East Indians, Chinese, Javanese, Portuguese, Africans, poor Europeans, and even a few Japanese. East Indians dominated the influx: more than half a million of them came to the Caribbean, primarily to Trinidad and Guyana. These two societies became biracial, with populations nearly evenly divided between people of African and East Indian descent. Not surprisingly, the planters' use of immigrants to control the free laborers left a legacy of animosity between the two groups, despite the fact that all were victims of the same exploitative system. ■

Collaborative Role of the Colonial Church

... and challenge from the Afro-Christian cults

Christianity came to the Caribbean as part and parcel of Spanish, French, British, Dutch, and finally, North American colonialism. The Church went on to assist these powers in building colonial societies: it endorsed slavery, and helped to entrench racial and class divisions after emancipation. Neither the prophetic role of a few church leaders nor the individual sincerity of the faithful altered this long history of religious collaboration with the colonial system.

Spanish colonization of the Caribbean had as its double weapon the sword and the cross. Its very justification for conquest was to convert indigenous peoples from their "heathen" beliefs. Fray Bartolome de las Casas, the Spanish priest, tried to defend the Amerindians from the Spanish onslaught, but his belated appeal for a few thousand Indians came after tens of thousands had already been killed or died of foreign diseases. It was not the Church which prevented the total genocide of the Indians, but the fact that the Spanish turned to importing African slave labor.

The Church gave its blessing to slavery. In 1685, the Council of the Indies in Spain decreed that the slave trade was lawful "where there was no danger of the Faith being perverted."[1] Meanwhile, Catholicism was imposed with almost complete disregard for the bloody crimes being committed against the Church's new converts. This produced a faith which was hardly more than skin-deep for the vast majority of its enslaved "converts."

The Church explained slavery as the result of a "divine judgement" or curse on the black race; or alternatively, as part of a divine plan for the betterment of mankind through the Christianizing of heathens and the enrichment of the planters. A French intellectual writing in 1675, for example, defended the slave trade on grounds that . . .

> inhuman though it might appear, the Christian merchants were enabled by its means to retrieve from a cruel slavery in Africa people who were idolaters or Muslims, to transport them to a milder servitude in the West Indies, and to confer upon them there a knowledge of the true God and the way of salvation by the teachings of priests and ecclesiastics who took pains to make them Christians.[2]

The Catholic Church actively assisted in institutionalizing slavery in the Spanish and French colonies. The French *Code Noir,* or Black Code, served as a means of enforcing both Church strictures and social control of the slaves:

> The Code, like the Spanish legislation of the preceding century, was permeated with the spirit of Roman Catholicism. All slaves were to be baptized, only Roman Catholics could have charge of slaves, slaves were not to be worked or go to market on Sundays or holy days, marriages among them were to be encouraged, consent of father and mother being replaced by consent of the owner.[3]

In the case of the British colonies, where Anglicanism and Protestantism were dominant, the Church's role focused on subduing and assimilating the Africans. Originally, there was little interest in Christianizing the slaves, and the few early missionary efforts which did reach out to blacks were marked by racism and elitism. Count Zinzendorf, a Moravian leader, said in 1739:

> God punished the first Negroes by making them slaves, and your conversion will make you free, not from control of your masters, but simply from your wicked habits and thoughts, and all that makes you dissatisfied with your lot.[4]

This led to an ironic situation in which those blacks who became Christians often prayed for their white oppressors, saying in one case: "Father, forgive them, for they know not what they do . . . Buckra (the master) left him God in England, and the devil in Jamaica stir him up to do all this wickedness. Poor thing! Him eye blind, and him heart hard."[5]

In fact, the impact of this early Christian teaching remained superficial, since African religious beliefs and practices continued to dominate the plantation until the 1830s. In the slave world people turned to African religions such as Shango and Kumina, or to *obeah* (sorcery) for spiritual and practical help. Through the dances and drumming, masks and rituals, the slaves realized a link to their ancestral home. At the same time, these practices were used to provide protection against the planters. The obeah-man or woman could give the slave a charm to be worn to protect him against the cruelty of the overseer. Charms and potions could also be used to take revenge on fellow slaves who collaborated with the Europeans. The planters' fear of obeah magic was one reason they finally allowed the slaves to be Christianized:

> In short, I know not what I can do with him, except to make a Christian of him! This might induce the negroes to believe that he [the obeah-man] has lost his infernal power by the superior virtue of the holy water . . .[6]

Kumina or myalism, strongest in Jamaica, stemmed from an ancient Ashanti ancestor possession cult. Through a ritual dance, the spirit of the ancestor takes control of the dancer's body to communicate hidden knowledge to the living. By the 1780s, Kumina had incorporated some Christian elements as a result of the coming to Jamaica of black Baptists from the southern United States. As these "Native Baptists" spread their faith, Kumina absorbed key elements of the Baptist religion, including belief in possession by the Holy Spirit—similar to the African belief in ancestor possession—and baptism by immersion in water. For the next 40 years, membership in the cult grew rapidly, so when missionaries in Jamaica in the 1830s tried to convert the slaves to Christianity, they had to compete with the powerful and entrenched Kumina/Native Baptist complex.

Baptist missionaries baptizing Jamaicans in the sea in 1843.

National Library of Jamaica

When it became clear that emancipation was inevitable, the colonial authorities encouraged the churches to help assimilate the blacks. The Anglican, Dutch Protestant, and French Catholic churches were favored for this role over the non-conformist Moravian, (English) Baptist, and Methodist churches.* By 1830-31, the churches were allowing blacks into their worship and had begun to open up parochial schools to teach them to read and write. The goal of this education was not enlightenment toward social freedom, however, but preparation for servile roles in the colonial church and planter-dominated society. The ruling class . . .

demanded and obtained [an agreement] that the school would not be used to affect adversely the supply of manual labor on the plantation, nor to encourage the coloured people to wish to rise too quickly up the social ladder.[7]

The Baptists, Methodists and Moravians played a more positive role, forming an alliance with the freed slaves to help them become independent from the planters. In Jamaica, where a majority of the ex-slaves left the plantations and moved to the hills, the non-conformist churches provided thousands of acres of land bought with church money. As a result, these denominations were initially seen as "liberators." The Methodist Church in Jamaica doubled its membership between 1831 and 1841, while the Baptists' tripled from 10,000 to 34,000 during the same period.[8]

Even among these churches, however, the white leadership made clear that its task was not to arbitrate between master and former slave. The Church was forbidden to meddle in "social and political questions," its task being to pacify the rebel spirit in the blacks through education and Christian

*Called "non-conformist" because they refused to conform to the rules and practices of the Church of England (Anglican Church).

teaching.[9] Thus just a few years after emancipation, missionaries reported with pride that:

cunning, craft, and suspicion—those dark passions and savage disposition before described as characteristic of the Negro—are now giving place to a noble, manly, and independent, yet patient and submissive spirit.[10]

Rise of the Afro-Christian Cults

Such "success" blinded the missionaries to the real process taking place: black disenchantment with the white churches and the steady growth of Afro-Christian syncretic religions. Mistaking church attendance for assimilation, the missionaries failed to realize that the blacks were merely allowing the practice of Christianity to co-exist and blend with their African religious beliefs.

The racial, class and color bias of colonial society was scarcely affected by emancipation. The failure of the mission churches to challenge these social attitudes drove many blacks away within a decade after emancipation. For one thing, the churches discouraged the baptism of illegitimate children, which meant that at least 70% of the population was barred from full privileges of membership in the Church. Governed by a Victorian, white European morality, the missionaries regarded the reluctance of the blacks to marry as evidence of "deep cultural defects which would take a long time to remove."[11]

Also disturbing to many blacks who converted to Christianity was that the training of black leaders—primarily in the non-conformist churches—did not mean oversight of a congregation, much less denominational leadership. Rather, blacks became deacons (servants), teachers and preachers *within* the congregation. These new positions had a social impact in terms of providing jobs, but they were confined to service roles in support of the white missionaries. The training

17

of native leaders and lay agents within these churches facilitated the entry of blacks into service occupations in the larger society, such as clerks, subordinate estate managers, and school teachers.

This gradual social integration was not accompanied by a lessening of racist attitudes, but by their intensification, as blacks moved closer to whites in the social spectrum. As in the post-reconstruction period in the U.S., it became common in the Caribbean to hear blacks referred to as "niggers." As late as 1870 the West Indian Anglican Church was publicly asserting that blacks had the right to "spiritual equality" with whites, but not cultural equality.[12]

As a result of these attitudes and practices, between 1842 and 1865 the mission churches in Jamaica lost up to half the members they had gained since 1831. Black children dropped out of the church schools. Many blacks trained as native ministers (especially Baptists) left to pastor their own African and Afro-Christian churches.

While the European churches preached deference to the system, the essence of the black religions was resistance. Native Baptists figured prominently in the Montego Bay revolt just before emancipation, and afterward, the Kumina/Native Baptist movement became the core of resistance to the hardship of the post-emancipation years. In 1841-42, the connection of the cult to plantation work stoppages led the planters to outlaw Kumina, and the movement went underground.

As with other elements of West Indian mass culture, however, the attempt to suppress Kumina only led to its resurgence in a stronger, if altered form. In the early 1860s, the mission churches in Jamaica launched a united assault on black religion, aimed at a sweeping conversion to "pure" Christianity. But their attempt to stir up a Christian religious frenzy in Jamaica produced unexpected results: the revival turned African in form, with oral confessions, trances, dreams,

prophecies, spirit seizures and wild dancing. This marriage of myalism and Christianity came to be called Pocomania—the strongest of the Jamaican native religions until the emergence of Rastafarianism in the 1930s.

A similar syncretic process produced Haitian *Vodou.* Many Haitian slaves came from the Dahomey region of Africa, where they had worshipped gods called *voduns.* The French planters suppressed this practice through the Catholic Church, which held total control over the slaves' religious life according to the French Code Noir. To get around this, the slaves used Catholicism as a cover for the practice of Vodou. Latin liturgical rituals meshed with the traditional rites of dancing and drumming until Vodou became an Afro-Christian religion, widespread at all levels of Haitian society as a form of popular resistance to domination by the European/Christian value system.

A third example of syncretism is the Shango/*santería* complex, variants of which exist in Trinidad, Cuba, Puerto Rico, the Dominican Republic, and Brazil. It is based on the polytheistic religion of the Yoruba, who were transported to the Spanish and Portuguese colonies in great numbers. The Yoruba believed in multiple gods called *orishas.* As the dominance of the Catholic Church in the colonies gradually transformed the religion, the Yoruba gods merged with the Catholic saints. "During the course of their captivity," explains a Puerto Rican writer, "the Yorubas started to recognize their gods behind the white facade of the Catholic images."[13] Thus the orisha Chango (Shango), god of fire and storms, is identified with Saint Barbara. Olorun-Olofi, the creator, represents the Crucified Christ. Oggun, god of iron and war, is Saint Peter; and so on. The orishas are credited with supernatural powers, and followers of santeria practice a complex magic with herbs and ritual objects for the purpose of healing or casting spells. Although it originated as an Afro-Christian cult, many of the white Spanish and Portuguese settlers also became involved with santería, and today it is widespread throughout the Spanish-speaking Caribbean.

* * *

As if floating on a higher plane, the colonial Church remained aloof and defensive toward these challenges. Its contributions to justice and liberation were minimal, while its collaboration with the power structure of colonial society was a self-conscious and chosen role. It was as if the Church couldn't see the forest of its own biblical revelation for the trees of its forms, fashions, and filial relationship with the colonial system.

It was the black majority which constantly called out for the Church to hear and respond. The emergence of the Afro-Christian religions was the first major challenge to the colonial Church. It set the stage for the 1920s and 30s, when black religiosity would be a seminal influence in the explosive popular rebellion against the Church, the colonial powers, and the established social order. ∎

Batá drums of Cuba, used in ceremonies worshipping Yoruba orishas.

Unifying Themes in Caribbean Cultures

The overwhelming cultural characteristic of the Caribbean, taken as the sum of its parts, is diversity. In race, in culture, in language and religion, it is one of the most heterogeneous areas in the world. This stems from the complex population movements which created Caribbean societies: forced and voluntary migrations from Africa, Europe and Asia into the Caribbean, and the continuing migration within the region itself.

A cultural map of the Caribbean reveals rigid barriers and omnipresent interconnections. The main barriers are the ones imposed by colonialism, which carved the region into Spanish, British, French and Dutch empires. These divisions have persisted into the era of political independence. Thus the English-speaking Caribbean forms a community, the "Commonwealth Caribbean," with political and economic ties among its members. The Spanish-speaking peoples of Cuba, the Dominican Republic and Puerto Rico consider themselves part of Latin America, although U.S. control has blurred this identity for Puerto Rico. The French Antilles and French Guiana, still under colonial rule, look only toward France. The Netherlands Antilles are part of the Kingdom of the Netherlands, while Suriname, formally independent, retains strong ties to Holland.

The linkages are more subtle. Despite the colonial divisions, Caribbean histories are parallel and intertwined. What unity there is rests on this shared experience: of African or Asian origins (for the majority), of slavery and indentured servitude, of colonization by the European powers. This history sometimes links people in a way which transcends the colonial barriers. During the 1700s, runaway slaves moved between French-held Martinique and St. Lucia, forming rebel communities. When St. Lucia passed to British ownership in 1814, formal ties with the French colonies ended, but links of language, culture and migration continued. Today the official language of St. Lucia is English, but the mass vernacular remains French Creole, virtually identical to that spoken in neighboring Martinique and Guadeloupe.[1]

In the former French and British colonies, which knew plantation slavery for 150 years, the majority of the population traces its roots to Africa. This is a force for unity, although colonial ideology and education long conspired to deny its importance. While the Jamaican nationalist slogan—"Out of many, one people"—suggests an equal contribution from numerous groups, in reality Jamaica is Afro-Caribbean, with 95% of its people black or brown.

In Guyana and Trinidad & Tobago, Indian indentureship

Dancing the merengue in the Dominican Republic: Afro-Latin roots.

El Nuevo Diario

on a large scale led to biracial populations almost evenly divided between people of African and East Indian descent. Suriname follows a similar pattern, with the addition of a significant third group, the Indonesians.

The Spanish-speaking Greater Antilles stand somewhat apart from this variant of the Caribbean experience. They had plantation slavery, but it developed on a large scale only after two centuries of Spanish settler colonialism. During this time the Spanish, some African slaves, and the surviving Arawak Indians mingled, forming racially blended populations sharing a common Spanish language. In Puerto Rico, where slavery was not extensive, a mainly light-skinned peasantry emerged. In Cuba, by contrast, the development of a huge sugar industry meant a large slave population, with less racial mingling. Many Cubans are Spanish in appearance, but many others are clearly of African descent. Blending was greatest in the Dominican Republic, due in part to continuous contact with the black population of neighboring Haiti. The Dominican Republic today is predominantly a mulatto nation.[2]

The Spanish-speaking countries have a cultural unity arising from their own historic links. The ties between Cuba and Puerto Rico were particularly strong. Their independence struggles were jointly planned in the 1860s, and many Puerto Ricans fought and died in Cuba's war against Spanish control. The U.S. takeover of Spain's colonies in 1898 created a barrier to this unity, but the nearly identical flags of the two countries testify to the closeness which once existed.

The struggle against colonial Spain did not mean a rejection of Spanish culture. Rather, nationalist movements stressed Latin identity as a counter to North American cultural and political pressures. In addition, the middle and upper classes emphasized their Spanish antecedents in order to downplay the reality of an African heritage. The most extreme example occurred in the Dominican Republic, where the dictator Trujillo promoted Latin culture and anti-black racism as a way of rejecting the country's experience under Haitian rule.

The African roots of the Afro-Latin cultures, and indeed of all Caribbean cultures, are most evident in music and religion. Santeria, the popular religion of Cuba, Puerto Rico and the Dominican Republic, is based on West African Yoruba beliefs. It is closely linked to Shango in Trinidad and Candomble in Brazil, two other countries which received many Yoruba slaves. Black Puerto Ricans in rural areas still perform the traditional African dances of *la bomba* and *la plena*. La bomba has Ashanti origins, and resembles dances in Jamaica and Haiti. Dominican peasants do drum dances called *los palos;* a festival involving the dance was outlawed by Trujillo in his campaign to de-Africanize the country. African influences permeate contemporary music as well. Cuban *son* and *rumba,* Dominican *merengue* and Puerto Rican *salsa* all feature the strong drum rhythms of Africa.

The one thing all Caribbean societies have in common is a colonial past. Through its components of migration, racism and class oppression, colonialism gave rise to three themes woven throughout the cultural tapestry. They are the **class basis** of Caribbean cultures, their use of creative **synthesis,** and **culture as resistance.**

The Class-Color-Culture Triangle

The correlation between skin shade and class has become a truism of Caribbean life. White (with admixtures of Middle Eastern and Chinese) equals upper-class; mulatto or "brown" is middle-class; while the African and East Indian majority occupies the base of the social pyramid. These broad divisions, however, underlie a more complex stratification resulting from social mobility through education, politics, property ownership and marriage.

The class-color correlates of the West Indian social structure are real. But they are not the absolutes of a rigid caste system. Skin color determines social class; but it is not an exclusive determinant. There are many fair-skinned persons who are not upper-class, and many dark-skinned persons who are. The real divisions of the society are the horizontal ones of social class rather than the vertical ones of color identification.[3]

Puerto Rican farm worker, 1945.

Rosskam, courtesy of Centro de Estudios Puertorriquenos, City University of New York

20

Racial perceptions in the Caribbean differ somewhat from those in Europe, and, especially, the United States. In U.S. society persons are generally defined as either "white" or "black," unless they are Hispanic or Asian. The slightest trace of African ancestry usually qualifies even a light-skinned person as "black." In the Caribbean, by contrast, skin color is seen as part of a continuum in which small variations become socially important. Brown-skinned persons are distinguished from those who are black; indeed there has traditionally been a world of social distance between them.

These color/class divisions carry with them cultural implications. At the top of the pyramid, the white elite waves the banner of its European origins—the English mores of Jamaica's upper class, or the Frenchness of Martinique's native white *bekes*. This sets the standard for the society, becoming the goal toward which the brown and black middle class aspires. Historically, Caribbean societies have idealized the culture of the colonizer and looked down upon the culture of the mass. Yet ironically, it is from the original and vibrant mass cultures—not the imitative culture of the elite—that a Caribbean identity has emerged.

For if there is a common West Indian culture, it has been created, first and foremost, by the social classes at the bottom... They, more than any others, have been the culture carriers, for the higher rung groups have been inhibited by the hybrid form of European culture they have imbibed from playing that role.[4]

Use of language is a case in point. The Caribbean is a region of tremendous linguistic diversity, in which the division into "English-speaking," "French-speaking," "Spanish-speaking" and "Dutch-speaking" obscures a far more complex reality.[5] Only in the Spanish-speaking Antilles is the official language also the language of all the people.

Elsewhere, French, English and Dutch compete with the far more widely spoken Creole languages. These originated when Africans speaking related languages of the Niger-Congo family in Africa came to the Caribbean. To make slave revolts more difficult, slave owners mixed Africans of different ethnic groups on their plantations, and they forbade the speaking of African languages. To communicate, the slaves preserved the grammatical core of their related mother tongues and infused into this structure vocabulary from the colonizers' European languages.[6]

In the French colonies, *Kreyol* based on French words and African syntax emerged as the national language. Some 85% of Haitians speak only Kreyol. Yet the official language of Haiti has always been French; French is used in the schools, the government, and courts of law. In Haiti more than elsewhere, language has become part of a vicious class system which discriminates against the black, Creole-speaking majority.

The situation differs somewhat in the anglophone Caribbean. Here a similar historical process produced *Patwa*, an English Creole. But in contrast to the clear separation between French and Kreyol, standard English and Patwa are two ends of a continuum, with many intermediate forms in between. The less education a person has, the more his or her speech will likely tend toward the Patwa end of the scale and vice versa.

Yet even this is too simple: in a country like Jamaica, where the Patwa tradition is strong, everyone, including the middle and upper classes, can and does speak it. They simply adapt their speech to the social context of the moment. Thus a West Indian politician will use standard English for policy discussions, then go out on the soapbox and regale the crowd with jokes in Patwa.

Colonial ideology defined the Creole languages as inferior "corruptions" of European languages, and for a long time most Caribbean people accepted this view. That image has changed somewhat in recent years, with language coming to be seen as important to national identity. This is particularly so in Haiti and the French Antilles, where political movements have made Kreyol a symbol of popular empowerment. Throughout the region there are efforts to systematize the writing of Creoles, enabling the growth of a Creole literature and strengthening their image as legitimate languages.

This process has gone farthest in the Netherlands Antilles, where the mass vernacular is a Portuguese-based Creole called Papiamentu. While Dutch remains the official language and is used throughout the school system, Papiamentu has virtually replaced it as the spoken language of daily use. This is true not only for the popular majority, but for all classes. No longer stigmatized, Papiamentu is increasingly the language of national literature and the press.

Religion is another area closely linked to class. Jamaican author Leonard Barrett tells of the division in his own family between his mother's relatives, who belong to the brown middle class, and his father's family, black Jamaicans from the peasantry. The former are Christian church-goers, while the latter follow the Afro-Christian Pocomania cult.[7] As people move up the social ladder, they tend to leave the African syncretic religions in favor of mainline denominations such as the English Baptists, Methodists and Presbyterians. Each country also has its high-status denominations historically associated with the colonial ruling class: Anglicanism in territories colonized by Britain, Catholicism in those colonized by the French and in the Dominican Republic, U.S. Protestantism in Puerto Rico, and Dutch Protestantism in the Netherlands Antilles.

The "official" view of popular culture has changed somewhat in recent years. With political independence, the new black and brown leadership has turned to the people's culture as a reservoir of authenticity in the struggle to create a national identity. A major factor has been the international commercial success of Caribbean art forms. Reggae and steelband music, born in the poverty of Kingston and Port-of-Spain slums, are now highly commercialized. Carnival, likewise, was a working-class "bachannal," scorned as vulgar and rowdy by the middle class. But when its colorful pageantry started drawing thousands of tourists to Trinidad, the government gave Carnival official sponsorship and a new respect, which also served to bring the festival under closer control.

Synthesis and Resistance

A second theme which marks Caribbean cultures is **synthesis:** the blending of diverse cultural elements into new, original forms. The merger of Africa and Europe is at the root of Caribbean cultures. Other strong influences include India, Latin America and the United States.

Carnival provides a rich example of this process. In colonial Trinidad, the French Catholic elite celebrated the pre-Lenten season with masked balls and parades. Black Trinidadians had their own "Canboulay" celebrations commemorating emancipation from slavery. Eventually these traditions merged into the Carnival of today.

> From its opening moment of *jour overt* and the "ole mas" costume bands to its finale, forty-eight hours later, in the dusk of Mardi Carnival, the Trinidadian populace gives itself up to the "jump up," the tempestuous abandon of Carnival . . . Port-of-Spain becomes a panic of mob art: the Sailor Bands, sometimes of five thousand or more . . . the Seabees groups, mocking their original United States Navy inspiration with their exaggerated high-ranking officer titles and overblown campaign ribbons . . . impertinent personifications of, variously, Texas Rangers, French Foreign Legionnaires, British Palace Guards and Nazi High Command officers . . . [8]

And underneath it all runs "a powerful undercurrent of Shango, bamboo-tamboo, canboulay"—the African traditions in Caribbean culture.[9]

The West Indian music known as calypso provides another example of creative synthesis. Originating in Trinidad in the 1800s, calypso has roots in the African oral tradition. Early lyrics were in French Creole, then shifted to English toward the end of the century. Musical influences on calypso included French and Spanish music (from those colonial periods in Trinidad), East Indian drumming, and black Revivalist spirituals. During World War Two, with hundreds of U.S. troops in Trinidad, calypso absorbed influences from rhythm and blues, swing and bebop, along with an increasing degree of commercialism.

The same blending process underlies the Afro-Latin cultures. The *merengue* of the Dominican Republic was originated by the peasantry using drums and other African instruments. Middle and upper class Dominicans scorned the merengue, preferring to dance the waltz. But gradually, a change occurred: Spanish instruments such as the *tres* and *cuatro,* the accordion and the *bandeón* were incorporated into merengue alongside the drums. This Europeanized merengue was called *merengue de salón*—parlor merengue—and was popular with town-dwellers. Merengue is now a national passion spanning all classes in the Dominican Republic.

Closely connected to the theme of synthesis is the theme of **culture as resistance** which runs through Caribbean history. By borrowing elements of culture and transforming them, Caribbean people fought back against cultural domination. This often is expressed in satire, as in the ribald parodies of Carnival. The Jonkonnu parade which once flourished in Jamaica, Belize and the Bahamas combines African elements such as the horsehead, cowhead and devil costumes with grotesque masked caricatures of British royalty. Such ir-

reverent humor has its roots in the slavery era, when one form of slave resistance was subtle mockery of the ruling class.

In West Indian cultural resistance, the drum has always held pride of place. Drums were used in Africa for long-distance communication, and slaves on the plantations continued this practice. Fearful of slave revolts, the planters outlawed the drum. After emancipation, the planters and missionaries banned drumming as subversive and an obstacle to the assimilation of the blacks. But they could never totally suppress it. In 1884 riots broke out in Port-of-Spain when the colonial authorities banned the use of drums for Carnival.

The ban on drumming gave rise to a substitute known as *bamboo-tamboo,* the practice of beating out rhythms on the ground with cured sticks. In the late 1930s, young men in the urban slums of Trinidad turned to using metal biscuit tins and old oil drums, and the modern steelband—"pan"—was born. ∎

PAN RECIPE

*First rape a people
simmer for centuries*

*bring memories to boil
foil voice of drum*

*add pinch of pain
to rain of rage*

*stifle drum again
then mix strains of blood*

*over slow fire
watch fever grow*

*til energy burst
with rhythm thirst*

*cut bamboo and cure
whip well like hell*

*stir sound from dustbin
pound handful biscuit tin*

*cover down in shanty town
and leave mixture alone*

when ready will explode

— John Agard, Guyana

Links to Central America: The Atlantic Coast

Most North Americans think of Honduras, Nicaragua, Costa Rica and Panama as Latin or mestizo nations—as indeed, in terms of their population majorities, they are. But the traveler who journeys to the isolated, sparsely-populated Caribbean or Atlantic coast of Central America is in for a surprise. Spanish place names are interspersed with towns like Bluefields, Nicaragua; Brewers, Honduras; Livingston, Guatemala; and Stann Creek, Belize. Goods imported from England line store shelves and cater to the tastes of a population more West Indian than Spanish in its cultural identification. The coastal population is primarily of African and Amerindian descent; people speak more English than Spanish, and Protestant religion dominates over Catholicism.

Early British Colonization

Although Spain laid claim to all of Central America in the 16th century, the absence of precious metals, the lack of a large indigenous work force, and the difficult climate and topography kept the Spanish from maintaining a physical presence along the Atlantic coast of the isthmus. But for British pirates, the swampy coastal lagoons and rivers were perfect supply and refuge sites; and there were valuable timbers to be harvested. In 1655, after capturing Jamaica from Spain, Britain moved into the Atlantic coast to challenge Spain's nominal claim. Based at Providence Island and Cape Gracias a Dios, the British founded settlements all along the coast as far north as British Honduras (present-day Belize).

English colonization of the Atlantic coast took on two distinct forms. With the Indians living along the Miskito Coast of Nicaragua, the British traded firearms and metal tools for turtle meat, lumber and fish. They formed alliances with the Miskito Indians, using them as guerrilla forces to counter Spain's occasional attempts to regain control. The British even set up a Miskito monarchy of British-educated "kings" who presided over the area, loyal to the British Crown.[1]

In Belize, Bluefields, and the Bay Islands off Honduras, on the other hand, English settlers cut logwood and mahogany or grew indigo, sugar and bananas. These industries required a large labor force, so the British brought in African slaves captured from the Spanish or purchased in Jamaica. In Belize, slaves accounted for 71% of the settlement population by 1745, leading to many slave revolts and escapes requiring intervention from the British naval forces based in Jamaica.[2] In these areas, then, the Caribbean colonial/slavery model dominated.

Garífuna drummers in Belize.

Belize Government
Information Service

23

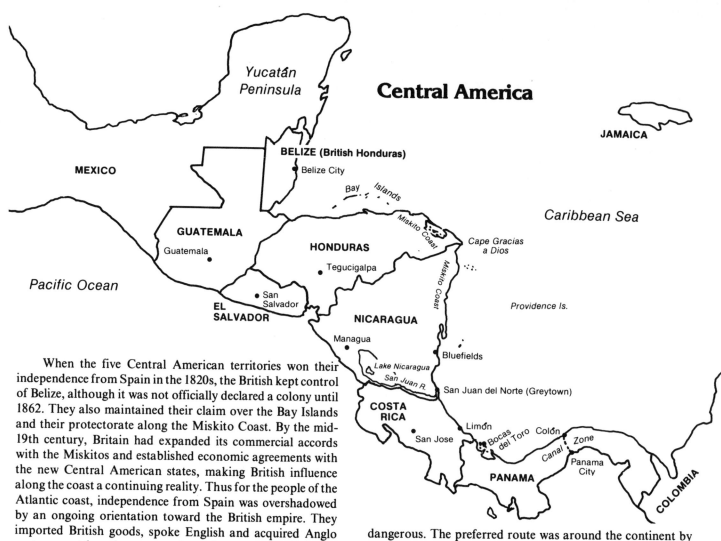

Central America

When the five Central American territories won their independence from Spain in the 1820s, the British kept control of Belize, although it was not officially declared a colony until 1862. They also maintained their claim over the Bay Islands and their protectorate along the Miskito Coast. By the mid-19th century, Britain had expanded its commercial accords with the Miskitos and established economic agreements with the new Central American states, making British influence along the coast a continuing reality. Thus for the people of the Atlantic coast, independence from Spain was overshadowed by an ongoing orientation toward the British empire. They imported British goods, spoke English and acquired Anglo customs, setting them apart from the dominant Spanish-mestizo cultures in the central regions and on the Pacific side of the isthmus.

Yet this British influence represented not a fully developed colonialism, but a limited, *enclave* model of foreign domination. It laid the basis for a continuing exploitation by foreign governments and corporations (mostly British and North American) which occupied areas of Central America with little regard for either the sovereignty or boundaries of states. This model led to both the underdevelopment of the enclave areas and their isolation from larger national societies, contributing to the historic impoverishment of the Atlantic coast region.

The Trans-Isthmian Enclave

The British presence was soon to be challenged by the emerging power to the north, the United States. In 1823, President James Monroe announced what came to be called the Monroe Doctrine, warning the European powers against further colonization in the western hemisphere, while leaving the way open for future U.S. expansion.

By the 1840s, the United States had reached its western continental limit, California. Beginning in 1846, Americans stampeded west to claim land in the Oregon territory, and in 1848 the California Gold Rush began. Both made it profitable for business interests to provide a fast route to the west coast, as the overland crossing by covered wagon was slow and dangerous. The preferred route was around the continent by steamship, requiring a passageway across the Central American isthmus.

One such route was through Panama, then a department of Colombia. U.S. financiers first provided passage across Panama by horse-drawn carriage, and in 1855 completed the construction of the Panama Railroad. The presence of the railroad and of North American travelers required protection along the passage strip, so a Texas Ranger named Ran Ruggles was hired to organize a police force, while U.S. Marines intervened in Panama five times between 1856 and 1865 to put down protests or strikes along the route.[3]

A shorter route lay to the north in Nicaragua. Here a traveler could board a boat at Greytown (San Juan del Norte) on the Atlantic coast, sail up the San Juan River into Lake Nicaragua and across the lake, leaving only a twelve-mile trip over land to reach the Pacific. This passage was controlled by the Accessory Transit Company owned by U.S. railroad magnate Cornelius Vanderbilt.

But the mouth of the San Juan River was part of the British protectorate over the Miskito coast, and Britain quickly challenged the right of the U.S. to monopolize transit through the area. The issue was temporarily resolved by the Clayton-Bulwer Treaty of 1850, in which it was agreed that neither the U.S. nor Britain would unilaterally build a canal through Central America. The treaty also prohibited either side from attempting to occupy or rule any part of the isthmus, so Britain eventually gave up its protectorate over the Bay Islands and the Miskito Coast.

In Nicaragua too, the presence of U.S. interests encouraged bids for political control. This was temporarily realized in the 1850s by a North American filibuster (adventurer) named William Walker, who was invited into Nicaragua by the Liberals to aid in their fight against the Conservatives. Heading a small mercenary army and backed by the Accessory Transit Co., Walker gained control over all of Nicaragua and became president in 1856.

The slave states of the U.S. South, fearing that their plantation days were numbered, saw Walker's activities as a beachhead for the expansion of slavery into all of Central America and thus a way to bolster their weakening position. Walker did reinstitute slavery in Nicaragua, hoping for southern support to counter the U.S. government's rising opposition to his role. But he was defeated on May 1, 1857 by the combined armies of other Central American states (who feared the filibustering model) and by an epidemic of cholera among his troops.[4]

The Panamanian and Nicaraguan passageways represented a continuation of Britain's enclave approach by the U.S., which sought to control limited strips of territory for specific economic and political ends. Once they had served their purpose, however, these enclaves and their inhabitants often were abandoned without a second thought. When the first transcontinental railroad across the United States was completed in 1867, the Panama Railroad fell into bankruptcy. San Juan del Norte on the Miskito coast became a backwater, undeveloped and forgotten for a hundred years.

The Banana Company Enclaves

By the 1890s, U.S. interests had moved into the Atlantic coast region to begin large-scale banana exports, along with lesser exports of cocoa, sugar and timber. One of the first was a U.S. railroad magnate, Minor Keith, who acquired land in Colombia, Panama and Costa Rica to plant bananas. Keith's holdings in Bocas del Toro, Panama and Limón, Costa Rica formed a single large operation and later led to disputes between Costa Rica and Panama as to where the border between them actually lay.

In Honduras, the hundreds of small traders exporting bananas to the United States between 1870 and 1890 shrank to twenty as the great fruit trusts began expanding overseas. By 1894, their number was reduced to three: the Boston Fruit Company, which also had holdings in Cuba, Jamaica and Puerto Rico; the Cuyamel Fruit Company; and Vacarro Brothers (later Standard Fruit). In 1899, Keith merged his holdings with those of the Boston Fruit Company to form the United Fruit Company, which came to control 80% of the U.S. banana market.[5]

United Fruit built its Honduran operation into a vast infrastructural enclave. Honduras, seeking a railroad to improve internal transportation, agreed to give the company 15,000 acres of land in exchange for building the Tela Railroad. But the railroad did not link the capital of Tegucigalpa to the coast, nor even the coastal towns to one another; rather, each segment linked a banana plantation to an Atlantic coast port. In thirty years, only 50 miles of "national" railroad was completed, while United Fruit built 900 miles of crisscrossed rails connecting its land holdings.[6]

The Canal Enclave

Competition between the United States and Great Britain for control of the Caribbean temporarily slackened during the last quarter of the 19th century. England's imperial might was waning, and the U.S. was bogged down with its Civil War and postwar reconstruction. Into this vacuum stepped the French, fresh from their successful completion of the Suez Canal. In 1878, France obtained a concession from Colombia to build a canal, and in 1880 the digging began.

But the narrow strip of land turned out to be far more formidable than anyone had imagined: a "geologist's nightmare" of volcanic bedrock, mountains, jungle and swamp. The French attempt was a costly failure, with thousands of deaths among the West Indian contract laborers who did the digging. The French bid spurred the United States to undertake a canal quickly lest some European power establish such a crucial foothold in the U.S. "backyard." The canal also was seen as essential to the United States' continued commercial expansion, including a link to the markets of the Orient. President Rutherford Hayes said in 1880:

> The objective of this country is a canal under American control. The United States cannot consent to turning over this control to some European power nor to some combination of European powers . . . Our commercial interest in the canal is greater than that of other countries, while its relationship to our means of defense, our unity, peace and security is a matter of primary importance for the people of the United States.[7]

The Spanish-American War of 1898 provided the final motivation for the canal: a strategic defense rationale based on the need to move U.S. warships from the Pacific to the Atlantic without sailing around Cape Horn. The U.S. first attempted to negotiate with Colombia for rights to build and control a canal. When this was rejected, the U.S. orchestrated a Panamanian revolt against Colombian control and promptly concluded a "treaty" with the newly-independent state. The treaty was signed on Panama's behalf by a Frenchman, Bunau-Varilla, a representative of the bankrupt French Canal Co. which hoped to recoup some of its losses by selling the remaining French interests in the canal to the U.S. No Panamanian signed the Panama Canal Treaty of 1903.

The great majority of construction workers on both the Panama railroad and the canal were contract laborers from the West Indies. During the French attempt to build the canal, some 38,000 workers were brought to Panama, including 18,000 Jamaicans and 8,000 Haitians.[8] When the U.S. took over the project, the Panama Canal Company recruited another 45,107 workers, of whom 31,071 came from the Caribbean. Most of these came from Barbados, Guadeloupe and Martinique.[9] Because these migratory waves arrived in a sparsely populated, primarily campesino society, the Panamanian working class essentially developed as a result of this foreign immigration.

Belize: The British Enclave

The exception to this pattern of expanding U.S. influence was British Honduras, the only formal British colony in Central America. Renamed Belize in 1966, the colony developed along lines which largely paralleled the history of the British West Indies, but with important differences. The basis of the Belizian economy was timber, which was less important to Britain than its sugar production in the Caribbean. Also, there was a large indigenous population of Mayan Indians which was not, as in the West Indies, completely destroyed. Instead, the foreign settlers pushed the Indians farther and farther into the interior, where they lived isolated from the settler economy along the coast.[12]

Within the slave-based colonial society, however, there were many parallels. As in the West Indies, the Africans in Belize continuously resisted their servitude. Slave uprisings in the 1760s culminated in a large revolt in 1773 which was put down by a British naval force from Jamaica. The last revolt

occurred in 1820 under the leadership of two slaves named Will and Sharper. There was also a continuous movement of runaway slaves into remote areas of interior Belize and neighboring Mexico, Guatemala and Honduras.

Another link to the islands were the Black Caribs, known in Belize as the Garífuna. They were descendents of Carib Indians who intermarried with escaped African slaves on St. Vincent. After they rebelled in 1795, about 5,000 Garífuna were exiled by the British to the Bay Islands off Honduras, from which some migrated to Belize. The settlers used the Garífuna as another source of slave labor in the mahogany camps.

After emancipation in 1838, Belizean blacks, like their West Indian counterparts, entered a new period of hardship. The situation of land ownership and wage labor paralleled that in the West Indies. The mahogany cutters owned the best land; in fact, most of the privately-owned land in Belize belonged to an elite group of twelve families. Through anti-squatting laws

WEST INDIAN WORKERS ON THE PANAMA CANAL

The construction of the Panama Canal is commonly depicted in history books as a North American achievement, the fruit of U.S. engineering and medical advances. Those were important factors, but it was the people of the Caribbean, along with other foreign laborers, who actually built the Canal between 1881 and 1914. Driven by economic need, they labored and died in the Panamanian jungle so the United States could realize its grandiose dream.[10]

Many of the workers during the French period of construction came from Jamaica, but there were also Cubans, South Americans, Europeans, Chinese, and blacks from the United States. This ill-fated group labored under horrifying conditions. Before the canal could be dug, the men had to hack their way through thick tropical jungle and swamps infested with poisonous snakes and stinging vermin. Panama's oppressive heat and humidity made the work a nightmare, especially during the rainy season, which lasted eight months of the year. There was little fresh food or pure drinking water, and the terminal towns of Colon and Panama City became sinkholes of diseases including dysentery, pneumonia, tuberculosis, typhoid, yellow fever and the bubonic plague. Once the digging began into the mountainous core of the isthmus, landslides added a new element of danger. It is estimated that 20,000 workers died during the disastrous French attempt to dig the canal.

After the United States took over the project, the government of Jamaica refused to allow any further recruiting of canal workers. But recruits flooded in from the other depressed, overcrowded islands of the British and French West Indies, especially Barbados, where the lack of available land and high unemployment made many people desperate for income. Some 20,000 Barbadians left for work on the canal during the construction years—40% of the

adult male population of the island.

The workers were given free passage to Panama and guaranteed repatriation after 500 working days. Wages were 10 cents an hour for heavy labor such as digging out rock with a pick and shovel. While the black workers thus made about $24 a month—considered good money at the time—salaries for the white Americans working as overseers and technicians averaged $87 a month. The black laborers received their pay in Panamanian silver coins, the North Americans in gold.

A caste system permeated every aspect of life in the Canal Zone. Housing, schools, hospitals and mess halls were segregated into "silver" and "gold," which became code words for black and white. While the North American workers lived comfortably in modern housing provided for them, the West Indians were crowded into the slums of Colon and Panama City, or lived in makeshift jungle camps.

Due to improved sanitation and the eradication of disease-carrying mosquitos, only about 5,600 deaths occurred during the U.S. phase of the project. However, black workers died at a rate four times that of the white workers. Many others were maimed by accidents or disease. Visiting a black hospital ward, one observer wrote:

> Some of the costs of the Canal are here. Sturdy black men in a sort of bed-tick pajamas sitting on the verandas or in wheel chairs, some with one leg gone, some with both. One could not help but wonder how it feels to be hopelessly ruined in body early in life for helping to dig a trench for a foreign power that, however well it may treat you materially, cares not a whistle-blast more for you than for its old worn-out locomotives rusting away in the jungle.[11]

and high land prices, the British kept the freed slaves from forming independent farming communities, leaving them with no choice but to perform contract labor in the mahogany camps.

Meanwhile, the Mayan Indians underwent the final phase of their subjugation by the British. In 1848, the Indians in the Yucatan peninsula in Mexico rebelled against the Spanish, and in the resulting chaos, thousands of Indians and mestizos fled south to Belize. These refugees formed farming communities which grew rice, corn, vegetables and sugar for subsistence and export. In fact, Indian sugar production was so successful that the big landowners of Belize decided to take it over. With their land and capital, they set up sugar plantations using steam machinery on which they forced the Indians to work as wage laborers.

By 1866, some Mayan refugees had migrated into central Belize where they founded independent villages near the mahogany works. In 1867, three hundred British soldiers invaded the principle Mayan village and burned it to the ground, along with the Indians' crops. The Mayan chief, Marcos Canul, fought the British for five years but was finally defeated in 1872. From then on, the Indians were incorporated into the colonial structure as a dispossessed and dominated minority.

Because of this resistance in the interior, the British focused their attention on the coast, with most of the population concentrated in Belize City. However, the spirit of resistance was strong among the blacks as well. In 1894, a group of mahogany workers demanded higher wages and upon being refused, looted the properties of the merchants and contractors. Troops from a British warship stationed off the coast were landed to quell the rebellion, and most of the leaders of the uprising fled into the interior or into Mexico. Belize entered the 20th century a stagnant colonial enclave, with the majority of its people living in poverty along the coast or isolated in the undeveloped interior. ∎

Laborers loading holes with dynamite at the Culebra Cut, October 10, 1913.

National Archives

Roots of U.S. Imperialism in the Greater Antilles

Decline of Spanish Colonialism Leads to U.S. Penetration

Following the "horror and the glory" of the Spanish conquest, the Spanish Caribbean took a back seat to the riches of Mexico and Peru, falling into more than two centuries of controlled neglect. This stagnation was interrupted in 1799 by the Haitian Revolution, the first major challenge to colonial rule in the Caribbean. Not only was Toussaint L'Ouverture's slave army powerful enough to defeat the French and British forces; but once independent, Haiti went on to seize the western part of Hispaniola from Spain in 1822.

With this challenge to European domination came the first bid by the United States to exert its influence over the region. The U.S. coveted the Caribbean trade, but was not ready to overtly challenge the European powers. Opportunity appeared with the sudden independence of Haiti and then Santo Domingo, which freed itself from Haitian control and became the Dominican Republic in 1844. Haiti, facing economic isolation, needed North American markets to survive. Toussaint therefore signed two agreements, one with the U.S. and another with England, granting them commercial and maritime rights that opened up Haiti to economic penetration.[1] In the Dominican Republic, the emerging middle class, anxious to secure its weak independence, turned over Samana Bay to the U.S. as an economic base and finally attempted to annex the whole country to the United States in 1877, a motion which failed in the U.S. Senate by only one vote.[2] Economic necessity in the case of Haiti and middle-class opportunism in the Dominican Republic thus opened the door to the United States long before the U.S. was strong enough to take over the islands by force.

During the 19th century, Spain tried everything to hold on to its restless Caribbean empire: troops, treaties, settlers. Ironically, the influx of Spanish settlers into Cuba, Puerto Rico and Santo Domingo after 1815 led to the formation of a nationalist middle class on each island which eventually challenged Spanish control.[3] In Cuba, the *autonomistas* joined with freed Cuban slaves to fight for independence in a decade-long war (1868-78) spearheaded by the black brigadier-general Antonio Maceo. Spain was steadily forced to yield ground to these internal independence movements, granting autonomy to Cuba and Puerto Rico in 1897.

Proximity and a vastly larger market made the United States a far more advantageous trading partner for the Spanish Caribbean than was Spain itself. U.S. firms moved steadily into the Greater Antilles during the 1870s and 1880s to grow and export sugar and bananas. By 1877, exports from Puerto Rico to Spain totalled only 709,000 pesos, while those to the United States were valued at 4,702,000 pesos.[4]

U.S. flag raised over San Juan, Puerto Rico on October 18, 1898.

National Archives

It was within this context that the United States forced Spain to sign the Commercial Treaty of 1891, facilitating U.S. trade with Cuba and Puerto Rico and in effect handing over economic supremacy in the Spanish Caribbean to the U.S. This agreement was the handwriting on the wall which virtually guaranteed some form of U.S. military challenge to Spain. The Spanish-American War broke out only seven years later.

The Expansionist Dream

Until the 1870s, most North Americans were anti-colonialist and anti-imperialist in spirit, believing themselves morally superior to the colonial exploiters of Europe. This was

28

to change, however, as the United States' evolving capitalism began producing more goods than the domestic market could absorb. By the 1880s, this overcapacity had led to economic depression, and U.S. business interests began searching for ways to acquire new markets and areas for investment abroad.

In government, business circles, and the press, many influential voices argued for a southward expansion. "The day is not distant," one senator proclaimed, "when the dominion of the United States will be extended . . . to every part of the American continent—British America, Mexico, Cuba, Central America, and the islands on our coast."[5] U.S. businessmen and politicians organized the American Annexation League in 1878 to push for the annexation of territories in Latin America and Canada.

This drive toward empire was cloaked, however, in pseudo-scientific and moralistic rationalizations. One such concept evolved out of Charles Darwin's *Origin of the Species* and came to be called Social Darwinism. According to this

thesis, if the United States was not to perish in the struggle for survival of the fittest, it must compete fiercely with other nations, taking over or controlling weaker lands. Reinforcing this theory was blatant racism—belief in an inherent Anglo-Saxon superiority which supposedly gave the United States the right and duty to "bring civilization" to other lands. One newspaper declared:

> The miserable republics of Central America, peopled by a degraded half-race of humanity, will yet bow to the rule of the Anglo-American . . . [and Americans will carry] moral and material well-being to the disintegrating communities and decaying races of Spanish America.[6]

These ideas all formed part of the credo known in the U.S. as "Manifest Destiny," meaning that God had intended white North Americans to take over and control the entire hemisphere.

A second rationalization arose from Captain Alfred Mahan's famous *Influence of Sea Power on History* (1890) which defined naval power as the key to national supremacy. Mahan stressed the relationship between overseas expansion and U.S. economic growth: "Whether they will or no, Americans must begin to look outward. The growing production of the country demands it . . . "[7] Mahan made clear that this expansion depended on a strong U.S. Navy and on control of the strategically located Caribbean territories of Cuba, Puerto Rico and Panama.[8] His ideas had a major impact on leaders such as John Hay, Theodore Roosevelt, and Henry Cabot Lodge, as well as on the North American public, paving the way for direct U.S. intervention in the Caribbean Basin over the next thirty years.

Shifting Caribbean Paramountcy: From Great Britain to the United States

Before this expansionist dream could be put into practice, the dominant Caribbean power—Great Britain—had to be somehow edged out of the region. Despite the Monroe Doctrine of 1823, the Caribbean was still basically considered a British lake. The West Indies were studded with British strongholds, and British warships outnumbered the American fleet by seven to one. The United States hardly dared challenge England on the high seas, but by the 1840s, the U.S. was signing treaties with Britain which politely signaled America's imperialist intent.

The issue of the British presence came to a head in 1895 in relation to a boundary dispute between Venezuela and the colony of British Guiana. The British stronghold at the mouth of the Orinoco River in Venezuela was strategically placed to control the Amazon and the entrance to the Caribbean at the southern tip of the Windward Island chain. It was here that the U.S. chose to make a decisive challenge. Venezuela wanted the British out, and the United States, while not openly siding with Venezuela, delivered a powerful message to the British literally ordering them to resolve the matter. When the British refused, the issue of the Monroe Doctrine was drawn, implying the ominous possibility of war with the United States.

The crisis was resolved when the United States softened its terms slightly and the hesitating British backed down. An Anglo-American agreement was signed setting the terms for a treaty between Great Britain and Venezuela. In effect, England had given in peacefully to U.S. pressures and yielded paramountcy in the region. As one historian wrote:

> In the Caribbean, Britain's surrender of 1896 proved to be only the beginning of a process which within a decade converted the hitherto British-dominated sea into a primary defense zone of the United States.[10]

The Spanish-American War of 1898

By the 1890s the independence struggle in Cuba was far advanced, drawing its ideological leadership from the Cuban nationalist intellectual José Martí. In 1894 the United States imposed a duty on Cuban sugar exports, which until then had been duty-free by agreement with Spain. This blow to the island's economy triggered renewed armed rebellion within the context of the Cuban independence movement. Insurgents roamed freely through most of the country, while Spain controlled Havana, the seaports, and the larger towns. Some of the property held by the insurgents was U.S.-owned and the rebels began setting fire to sugar cane fields, hoping to provoke an American intervention on their behalf.

North American business interests were by then entrenched in Cuba with around $50 million in investments, mainly in sugar production. They hoped for a peaceful settlement of the crisis, since the war was hurting profits. In 1894, U.S. exports to Cuba were worth $20 million, but by 1898 they had fallen to $10 million. U.S. imports from Cuba sank from $76 million to $15 million in the same period.[11]

The Liberals in Cuba replaced the Conservatives in 1897 and seemed to offer a chance for compromise. Spain granted "autonomy" to Cuba and Puerto Rico, hoping to defuse the issue. But the Spanish loyalists in Havana, furious about the grant of autonomy, rioted on January 12, 1898, crushing U.S. hopes for a quick end to the conflict. To the United States it now seemed that Spain could no longer keep control in Cuba; and conversely, that the Cuban rebels could not win independence from Spain without a prolonged and costly war.

At that moment, an event occurred which changed the course of history: an explosion sank the battleship *USS Maine* in Havana harbor, killing 260 crew members. Stunned American reaction turned on Spain as responsible. At the time, an investigation indicated that the *Maine* had been blown up by a Spanish submarine mine. The U.S. Congress immediately approved a defense fund of $50 million to be used at the discretion of President McKinley.

The destruction of the *Maine* coincided with a shift in opinion on the part of the U.S. business community, which had come to see U.S. intervention as the quickest way to resume business as usual in Cuba. For these interests, the blowing up of the *Maine* was suspiciously opportune. One of the most influential protagonists of war with Spain, newspaper magnate William Randolph Hearst, sent a reporter to Havana to cover

MARTI'S WARNING

José Martí, the Cuban poet-journalist who led his country's independence movement from Spain, warned Latin Americans against trading Spanish colonial control for dominance by the United States. While Martí admired many traits of the North American people, whom he came to know during his years in New York, he clearly saw the road down which the growth of monopoly capitalism was taking the United States in the crucial decade of the 1880s. On the eve of the U.S.-controlled "Pan-American Congress" in 1889, Martí repeated his dark predictions of North American imperialism masquerading as Pan-Americanism, and made a futile call for the Latin nations to demand a true and unified independence:

Dangers must not be recognized only when they are upon us, but when they can be avoided. In politics the main thing is to clarify and foresee. Only a virile and unanimous response, for which there is still time without risk, can free all the Spanish American nations at one time from the anxiety and agitation—fatal in a country's hour of development—in which the secular and admittedly predominant policy of a powerful and ambitious neighbor... would forever hold them . . .[9]

a "big story." Shortly before the explosion, the reporter cabled back: "Everything is quiet . . . there will be no war. I wish to return." Hearst replied, "Please remain. You furnish the pictures and I'll furnish the war."[12]

More recently, an investigation by Ret. Rear Admiral Hyman Rickover has concluded that the explosion was caused by a bomb placed inside the hull of the *Maine* in an intentional act of sabotage. Whatever the truth of the matter, the blowing up of the *Maine* triggered a decisive shift in public and Congressional opinion in favor of war. On April 13, Henry Cabot Lodge stated:

> All men in this country are agreed today . . . that this situation must end. We cannot go on indefinitely with this strain, this suspense, this uncertainty, this tottering on the verge of war. It is killing to business.[13]

Days later, Congress passed a resolution declaring the people of Cuba "independent" and ordering Spain to evacuate the island. War was declared on April 25, 1898. Under the battle cry "Remember the *Maine!*", U.S. Marines invaded Spain's remaining overseas colonies—Cuba, Puerto Rico, and the Philippines—and took control of all three countries. Puerto Rico and the Philippines became U.S. possessions, while a puppet government was established in nominally independent Cuba. Under the "Platt Amendment" which the United States wrote into Cuba's constitution, the U.S. retained the right to intervene militarily in Cuba and to maintain the Guantanamo naval base on the island until the year 2000. The United States, born in revolution and anti-colonialism, had itself become an imperial power.

Gunboat Diplomacy and Economic Expansion

The War of 1898 opened a new era in the Caribbean Basin as the full might of North American imperialism descended like a tempest upon the countries of the region. Military interventions and corporate land takeovers became commonplace as the United States now assumed the role of regional policeman, judge and executioner.

> Chronic wrongdoing, or an impotence which results in the general loosening of the ties of civilized society . . . in the Western hemisphere . . . force the United States, however reluctantly . . . to the exercise of an international police power.
>
> — President Theodore Roosevelt, 1904

In the name of "prosperity" and "order," U.S. Marines invaded independent countries of the Caribbean 33 times in as

Cartoon from around 1910 portrays President Theodore Roosevelt and his "Big Stick" of American military intervention. The U.S. invaded independent countries of the Caribbean dozens of times during the gunboat diplomacy years.

many years, remaining in five countries—Cuba, Nicaragua, Panama, the Dominican Republic, and Haiti—for prolonged periods. The official justifications for these interventions fell into several categories:

- To protect American property and interests or American lives
- To "promote peace and government stability"
- To prevent revolution
- To create or maintain neutral zones or cities.

Officially, President Roosevelt's justification for intervention was to maintain "law and order"; President William Taft's goal was to contain the "malady of revolutions that produce financial collapse"; while President Woodrow Wilson's stated purpose was to reform and educate "backward" societies in the image of America.[14]

These ideals notwithstanding, the cold reality of U.S. interventions involved extensive corporate land takeovers. Under the protection of the Marines and the new laws they imposed, U.S. corporations moved in and seized peasants' lands, turning them over to export production. Before 1898 the invaded countries had grown much of their own food; now they became dependent on imported foreign products.

To better organize this empire-building, the U.S. government and business leaders held a hemispheric "economic planning conference" in 1915 in Washington, D.C. To get the edge on the British, the conference was deliberately held at a time when England was tied down by its involvement in the First World War. Financial initiative shifted from London to New York, and by 1929, the United States had taken over economic leadership in the hemisphere.[16]

U.S. Marine Interventions in the Caribbean Basin Between 1899 and 1934[15]

Cuba 1898, 1906-09, 1912, 1917-1933
Puerto Rico . . . . .1898 and thereafter
Nicaragua 1898, 1899, 1910, 1912-25, 1926-33
Colombia 1902, 1904, 1912, 1903-14
Honduras 1903, 1907, 1911, 1912, 1919, 1924, 1925
Dominican Republic 1903, 1904, 1914, 1916-24
Haiti 1914, 1915-34
Mexico 1913, 1914-17, 1918-19
Guatemala 1920
Panama. 1921, 1925

The Human Impact: Examples from Cuba, Puerto Rico, and Panama

There were three principal consequences of the U.S. expansion:

- The takeover of large tracts of land and removal of local property holders through force, cheap payoffs, or legal trickery;
- The elimination of tens of thousands of subsistence farms which fed local populations;
- U.S. government and business alliance with the conservative sectors of national bourgeoisies against the working-class and peasant majority.

Cuba. The United Fruit Company entered Cuba in 1901, as soon as the U.S. conquest was complete. The company quickly acquired large tracts of land through the implementation of U.S. Military Order No. 62, which legalized *de facto* occupation of land by North American corporations. United Fruit's technique was to draw up a possession lien on a given property and then use that lien or actual occupancy against legal challenges in the Cuban courts. To carry out this occupation, the company had to first remove the peasants who had lived on and worked the lands for years.

One such case involved an area called El Cristal in the municipality of Mayari. Cuban authorities, unable to counter United Fruit or in collusion with the company, ordered the police to clear the land of its inhabitants. The peasants expelled from El Cristal appealed their case in court, declaring:

> We protest before said judges and authorities the threats, charges and repressive acts to which we have been subjected . . . they (the UFC) have made charges against us for the crime of "usurping land and damaging property and products" . . . Even after we managed to get free under bond, the authorities detained us illegally and we have been held prisoner for 72 hours . . .[17]

After the removal and arrest of peasants, United Fruit would then bring in Haitians to cut the sugar cane on the plantations, so that the dispossessed peasants could not even secure wage labor on their former farm plots.

Puerto Rico. In 1898, Puerto Rico had a balanced agricultural economy: 41% of the total arable land was used for coffee cultivation, 32% for edible foods, 15% for sugar, and 1% for tobacco. Puerto Rican farmers owned 93% of the existing farms, and a large number owned their own homes.[18]

Immediately after the 1898 invasion, U.S. companies arrived in Puerto Rico to set up large-scale sugar and tobacco industries. Four U.S.-owned sugar mills were established: Central Aguirre in 1899, South Porto Rico Sugar Company in 1900, Farjardo Sugar Company in 1905 and Loiza Sugar Company in 1907. Puerto Rico's small farms were swallowed up, and the peasants lucky enough to get work on the plantations received at most 80 cents per day during the six months of cane cutting. Once a self-reliant agricultural country, in the space of a decade Puerto Rico had become a foreign-owned, foreign-run plantation.

Courtesy of Centro de Estudios Puertorriquenos, City University of New York

Puerto Rican rum on San Juan docks awaiting shipment to the United States.

By 1929, the situation of Puerto Rican peasants, called jíbaros, was desperate. Luis Muñoz Marín, future governor of Puerto Rico, wrote an angry indictment of U.S. colonial rule:

> By now the development of large absentee-owned sugar estates, the rapid curtailment in the planting of coffee—the natural crop of the independent farmer—and the concentration of cigar manufacture into the hands of the American trust, have combined to make Puerto Rico a land of beggars and millionaires, of flattering statistics and distressing realities. More and more it becomes a factory worked by peons, fought over by lawyers, bossed by absentee industrialists, and clerked by politicians. It is now Uncle Sam's second largest sweatshop.[19]

Panama. Between 1904 and 1925, the United States virtually ran Panama. North Americans held key posts in bureaucracies such as the National Police, the Public Works, and General Education. A Panamanian petty bourgeoisie was developing, but they had very little capital and sought to acquire more power as landlords of slum housing in Colon and Panama City. To bolster their position, in 1925 they pushed through a new law raising taxes by 5% on all property in the two port cities. This increase was then used as an excuse to raise rents by 25-50%. The tenants revolted in what has become famous in Panama as the Gesta Inquilinaria (Renters' Protest).

The tenants formed a Renters' League under the leadership of the General Workers' Union, and rallied people through a series of public meetings which were finally outlawed by the mayor of Panama City. The League then called for a

THE CHURCH AND THE "AMERICANIZING" OF PUERTO RICO

The historic Protestant churches based in the United States played a key role in socially legitimizing and institutionalizing North American domination over Puerto Rico after 1898. Shortly after the Marines took over, six Protestant denominations began working in Puerto Rico, dividing up the island into separate geographic areas reserved for exclusive evangelization by each church body.

Encouraged by U.S. officials and facilitated through "freedom of worship" statutes, the new churches quickly gained access to the rural areas where the Catholic Church had weak roots. The Protestants grounded their evangelistic efforts in social action by founding schools—virtually taking over public education at the primary level—as well as hospitals, orphanages, medical clinics, small agricultural projects and technical training centers. In this way they undercut the Catholics' social base and established strong ties to the people, although their leadership and funding was almost entirely North American.

The end of Spanish control and the shift to U.S. colonialism produced a deep dislocation within the Roman Catholic Church as its official recognition and privileges came to an end. To compensate, Rome replaced Spanish prelates with Irish Catholic bishops from New England, who brought with them North American clergy, customs, catechism, hymnology and theological attitudes. This new Catholic leadership also helped to Americanize Puerto Rico. However, many Spanish priests and nuns stayed and resisted this "foreign" process, remaining sympathetic to Puerto Rican autonomist or independence forces. This produced a split within the Puerto Rican Catholic Church between pro-American and pro-Hispanic tendencies which intensified over the years.

But it was the Protestant churches which expanded rapidly while the Catholic Church struggled merely to hold its own. The new denominations promoted baptism and membership as a sign of Puerto Ricans' becoming "good Americans" and "true Christians"—reflecting both their colonizing role and the competitiveness which developed in relation to the Catholic Church.[24]

mass meeting on October 10, 1925, but attempted to cancel it at the last moment when it became evident that the police planned to provoke violence. But the leadership could no longer stop the hundreds of Panamanian workers who poured into Santa Ana Park to demand lower rents. The first speaker at the rally was shot by police when he rose to urge the crowd to go home. This triggered a barrage of gunfire from the surrounding police, resulting in three deaths and ten injuries. On October 12, U.S. troops entered Panama City to "guarantee independence and sovereignty of the Fatherland"—thus beginning the U.S. practice of siding with Panama's upper class.[20]

Training U.S. Surrogates: The National Guard Model

The practice of gunboat diplomacy met with resistance everywhere. Charlemagne Peralte of Haiti led a people's army which held one-fifth of the country before being defeated by U.S. Marines in 1919. In the Dominican Republic, resistance in the eastern flatlands was continuous between 1916 and 1924, when it was finally crushed by Rafael Trujillo's brutal repression under Marine supervision. The uprising of Sandino's peasant-worker army in Nicaragua was never defeated, even after five years of fighting the Marines (1927-1932).

Other opposition was non-violent, such as the workers' strikes in Honduras and El Salvador during the 1920s. A growing middle-class protest emerged through the national congresses of the region, weak and elitist as they often were. An Anti-Imperialist League created by middle-class businessmen in Central America and the Spanish Caribbean found sympathetic support in Europe and even in the United States itself.

The unpopularity and injustice of gunboat diplomacy gradually penetrated North American consciousness. In 1928, the Clark Memorandum attempted to eliminate interventionism as a principle from the Monroe Doctrine, while preserving the ability of the U.S. to intervene in practice. President Hoover opposed the idea of a global American empire; yet his warning about the "specter of Bolshevism" signaled the new propaganda that would rationalize U.S. interventions in the future.[21] Financier Thomas Lamont was less theoretical and more pragmatic, and it was his argument which finally convinced the United States to change its tactics. He said: "The theory of collecting debts by gunboat is unrighteous, unworkable, and obsolete."[22]

But the United States could not maintain its empire without some means of controlling local resistance in the exploited countries. So began the process, in the late 1920s, of training and installing local militias and national guards as U.S. surrogates. The first example of this new strategy appeared in the Dominican Republic when the Marines set up a National Guard and prepared Generalisimo Rafael Trujillo to lead it. Another occurred in Nicaragua where the U.S. created and trained a National Guard and placed Anastasio Somoza García in charge. In Haiti, the Marines trained the "Guarde d'Haiti" to take over when they left. These forces were not intended to be independent national armies, but praetorian guards of the United States.

It was only when these surrogates were in place that President Franklin D. Roosevelt could introduce his non-interventionist diplomacy called the "Good Neighbor" policy. The United States, he said, would now return to its "traditional Jeffersonian *de facto* recognition" of the independence of other states. The Marines left Nicaragua on January 2, 1933, and on March 4, President Roosevelt stated:

> The essential qualities of a true Pan-Americanism must be the same as those which constitute a good neighbor, namely, mutual understanding, and . . . a sympathetic appreciation of others' point of view.[23]

While Roosevelt was willing to forego the practice of armed intervention in the Caribbean—and withdrew the last Marines from Haiti in 1934—he also admitted subsequently of Nicaraguan dictator Somoza that while "he is an S.O.B., he's *our* S.O.B." The same was initially true of Trujillo, whose cruelty had become legendary after only four years in power.

Despite rumblings of internal revolt in the Caribbean and war abroad, the United States sailed into the 1940s on the lofty words of good-neighborly Pan-Americanism. Under this banner, a General Maximiliano Hernández Martínez could murder 30,000 peasants in 1932 in El Salvador, and Trujillo could murder 20,000 Haitians in the Dominican Republic in 1936 while Washington hardly blinked an eye. The Marines had come home, but the U.S. corporations and their new gendarmes remained in tight control. ∎

U.S. Marine officer inspecting rifles of the Haitian National Guard, 1919.

The West Indies: Middle-Class Ambivalence, Workers' Revolt

The extreme poverty and exploitation of West Indian workers led to the upsurge of Marcus Garvey's black nationalist movement after World War I and, subsequently, to the organized labor movement in the West Indies. For a while, from 1919 through the early 1930s, the two movements were closely linked. As the confrontation between the ruling class and the people intensified, however, it was middle-class leaders who were able to mediate and speak "on behalf" of the masses. This opened the way for a middle-class cooptation of the labor movement and the eventual abandonment of its more revolutionary goals. Garvey's radical Pan-Africanism, excluded from this process, helped inspire Rastafarianism, a religion rooted in social protest but one which refused to play an active part in formal "politics."

Rise of the Middle Class

The Sugar Equalization Act of 1846, which revoked the West Indies' monopoly of the British sugar market, meant bankruptcy for many planters. Many left the islands, and their lands were taken over by London firms and banks. But planters, their attorneys, and rich merchants still dominated the political life of the colonies, occupying all the seats in the local legislative assemblies. This led to a struggle by the native-born middle class for the political power they felt was rightfully theirs.

This emerging class was formed of two strands. On the one hand were the mulatto (or "brown-skinned") descendents of the unions between planters and slaves. They rose by inheriting property, often using their assets to go into business as merchants. On the other hand, a substantial number of blacks moved up through education, with the most successful leaving the colonies to study abroad on scholarship. They rose socially through the professions, becoming doctors, lawyers, teachers, journalists, and clergy. The more affluent individuals from these two groups began to stand for election to the local assemblies, where they challenged the entrenched position of the planter class.

Meanwhile, the British were becoming alarmed that the dwindling white plantocracies could no longer control the black majority in the colonies. These fears were confirmed by a riot in Jamaica in 1865 led by Paul Bogle, a black Native Baptist preacher, and George W. Gordon, a colored Baptist leader. The freed slaves in Jamaica, as elsewhere, had suffered decades of harassment since emancipation: arbitrary evictions, high taxes, and harsh penalties for "trespassing" were all used to deny the ex-slaves access to land. The Morant Bay rebellion was an outburst of pent-up anger by the Jamaican peasantry against these conditions. The governor overreacted to the riot and his colonial troops killed 439 blacks, flogged another 600, and burned more than 1,000 homes to the ground. Bogle and Gordon were arrested and hanged.[1]

Convinced that the planters were losing control of the situation, the British government persuaded a willing Jamaican Assembly to give up its authority and allow Jamaica to become a Crown Colony. By 1870, all the British colonies except Barbados had followed Jamaica's lead. Crown Colony government meant a return to direct imperial rule. Instead of local assemblies which made laws, each colony was to be ruled by a governor who answered directly to the Colonial Office in Britain. The governor was "assisted" by two local councils which essentially served to rubber-stamp his decisions.[2]

The middle class was dismayed by this turn of events, since it cut short their growing political influence. Through their professional organizations and local newspapers, they agitated for "self-government" in which they would play a leading role. Especially after 1920, this campaign often took the form of protest to the colonial authorities over the plight of the poor. T.A. Marryshow of Grenada and Arthur Cipriani of Trinidad were leading spokesmen for this liberal tendency.

The petty reforms won by the middle class—allowing themselves to be elected to the powerless councils—were all but meaningless to the masses. The middle class wanted to speak *for* the poor, but recoiled in horror from the idea of a universal suffrage which would allow the poor to speak for themselves. Like the ruling class they emulated, the middle class viewed the poor black majority from a paternalistic, color-conscious perspective heavily conditioned by two hundred years of colonial rule.

The Marcus Garvey Movement

This societal racism and complacency was soon to be challenged by a rising social movement, one with roots both in the intellectual tradition of Pan-Africanism and in black religion [see pp. 38-39].

Even before the turn of the century, West Indians had put forth new concepts of Africa which refuted the racist theories of the day. Edward Blyden, born in the Virgin Islands in 1832, emigrated to Liberia and became a high official in the Liberian government. He focused on West Indian-African historical links, urging West Indians to emigrate to Africa. J.J. Thomas, a Trinidadian scholar, wrote a book refuting the racist opinions of the Englishman J.A. Froude, and emphasized the need for black unity to accomplish the "true purposes" of the African race. H.S. Williams, also born in Trinidad, convened the first Pan-African Conference in London in 1900 which formed a Pan-African Association with branches in many countries.

All these figures were overshadowed by the fame of one man, Marcus Garvey, who successfully consolidated Pan-Africanism as a dynamic mass movement. Garvey was born in Jamaica of humble peasant origins. In 1910, he traveled up the Atlantic coast of Central America, where he was outraged by the exploitation of black workers on the banana plantations and railroads and on the Panama Canal. Between 1912 and

Jamaica Journal

Members of Garvey's Universal Negro Improvement Association line the streets of Harlem for the parade preceding their annual convention in 1924.

1914, Garvey lived in London and worked on the *Africa Times and Orient Review,* a Pan-Africanist paper. Upon returning to Jamaica he formed the Universal Negro Improvement Association (UNIA), aimed at uniting "all the Negro peoples of the world into one great body to establish a country and Government absolutely their own."[3]

Garvey's formation of the UNIA coincided with the period of the first serious labor organization in the West Indies. After 1900, labor disturbances had become frequent on the estates and in the towns, but they were generally spontaneous and unorganized. World War I marked a turning point. Some 15,000 West Indian men served in the West India Regiment of the British Army, and many returned home radicalized by their first exposure to the outside world and by their experience of discrimination in the segregated military. After the soldiers came home in 1919, a wave of strikes and riots swept the region. The uprisings drew their philosophical inspiration from the new racial consciousness of Garvey's UNIA, and UNIA members figured prominently in the disturbances.

The returning soldiers also gave a strong push to the formation of trade unions. But except for Hubert Critchlow's British Guiana Labour Union—recognized in 1919 with the help of the British Labour Party—the fledgling unions remained unrecognized and unprotected through the 1930s. Picketing was illegal, and employers could sue strikers for damages or simply call on troops and police. Strikes were quickly crushed by the colonial forces.

Garvey ultimately met with frustration in Jamaica, where colonial ideas of white superiority were deeply ingrained. The middle class hated and feared him, and even many of the workers and small farmers were not yet ready for Garvey's open affirmation of their blackness. He moved to the United States, where his ideas caught fire among thousands of blacks driven by poverty into the slums of the northern cities in a massive post-war migration. The UNIA took root as a grassroots movement in New York City's Harlem section, and soon expanded to include branches in 40 countries and an estimated 2 million dues-paying members.

> The UNIA's impact on West Indian affairs was almost immediate. Garvey's agents traversed the area establishing branches and spreading the word of nationalism and anti-colonialism. Some were deported from, and/or refused permission to land in certain territories.
>
> (It was) a genuine Pan-Caribbean mass movement, cutting across political and linguistic barriers. Cuba had more branches (52) than any other territory in the West Indies, and indeed more than any country other than the United States. Trinidad had at least 30 branches, Jamaica had 11, British Guiana 7, and the Dominican Republic 5.[4]

At its height, the UNIA ran a far-flung network of centers called Liberty Halls which provided social services and credit

Marcus Garvey

to black communities. Garvey also started a visionary but financially unsuccessful steamship venture, the Black Star Line, in order to link black peoples around the world and carry blacks who wished to repatriate back to Africa.

The theme of repatriation was a powerful element of Garvey's message. His slogan, "Africa for the Africans, those at home and those abroad," resounded around the world as the colonial powers completed their scramble for Africa. Garvey defied the whole system of white domination, at the same time challenging blacks to build themselves up as a self-reliant, proud people. His movement soon incurred the enmity not only of white America but also of the black intelligensia, which feared the strength of his openly race-based appeal. He was arrested by U.S. federal marshalls on trumped-up mail fraud charges, imprisoned for two years in Atlanta and deported to Jamaica in 1927.

1930s: The People Revolt

Conditions had worsened in the Caribbean during the years of Garvey's absence. While the middle class was politely pursuing constitutional reform, the workers were becoming desperate over their low wages, unemployment, and the near starvation of their families. Wages for unskilled workers ranged from 28¢ to 60¢ per day throughout the West Indies.[5] Where sugar was still "King," as in Barbados, so little local food was grown that laborers and their families had to subsist on imported rice and cornmeal.[6] Living conditions for the poor were typified by this report from Jamaica:

> At Orange Bay the Commissioners saw people living in huts the walls of which were bamboo knitted together as closely as human hands were capable; the ceilings were made from dry crisp coconut branches which shifted their positions with every wind. The floor measured 8 feet by 6 feet. The hut was 5 feet high ... In this hut lived nine people, a man, his wife, and seven children. They had no water and no latrine. There were two beds. The parents slept in one, and as many of the children as could hold on in the other. The rest used the floor.[7]

The people's health and strength were sapped by malnutrition and diseases like hookworm, tuberculosis, and malaria. In Barbados—patronizingly called "Little England"—217 of every 1000 babies died before their first birthday, compared to 58 of every 1000 in "Big England."[8]

Garvey returned to a triumphant hero's welcome from Jamaican workers. "No denser crowd has ever been witnessed in Kingston," proclaimed the *Daily Gleaner* upon his arrival.[9] He formed the People's Political Party, the first anti-colonial party in Jamaica's history. It contested the 1929 council elections on a platform which included a minimum wage, an 8-hour work day, workmen's compensation, land reform, rural housing construction, and judicial reform.[10] He also started a trade union, the Jamaica Workers and Labourers Association.

Even before he arrived back in Jamaica, the colonial authorities had mounted a campaign to suppress Garvey's influence. His newspaper *Negro World* was widely banned, and Garvey was denied visas to visit other islands. Active Garveyites were persecuted under obsolete laws. Garvey's failure in Jamaican electoral politics, however, had more to do with the fact that he needed the support of the black and brown petty bourgeoisie—since the poor could not vote and had no money—but this group remained ambivalent, excluded from the power structure but still unwilling to upset the system.

The Great Depression severely eroded the financial base of Garvey's movement. He left in 1935 for England, where he died five years later. But the hardship of the Depression had just begun to have its impact on the Caribbean. As production fell off in the U.S. and England, imports from those countries became expensive and scarce. The world market for sugar and bananas collapsed, meaning higher unemployment, falling wages, and increased taxation for Caribbean workers. To make matters worse, the United States stopped admitting West Indian emigrants in 1927, and countries where many West Indians were working—Cuba, the Dominican Republic, and Central American countries—began deporting the migrants, who swelled the ranks of the impoverished in their home countries.

As the Depression deepened, a wave of mass strikes and violent demonstrations erupted across the region. The first was in St. Kitts, where all the land was under sugar cane and cane cutters earned at most 36¢ per day.[11] The planters' refusal to raise wages in 1935 led to a widespread strike and violent police reaction which left three workers dead. In St. Vincent, where wages averaged 28¢ per day, riots broke out when the government attempted to raise taxes on imported food. In the coaling port of Castries, St. Lucia, coal stokers were joined in protest by the unemployed. In Belize, a labor revolt closed down the sawmill owned by the Belize Estate and Produce Company, which was by then the largest employer in the colony. All of these uprisings were swiftly crushed by armed colonial police and British Marines.

As the riots spread, contradictions emerged between the desperate actions of the starving workers and the reformist strategies of the middle-class politicians. In 1933, oilfield workers in Trinidad organized a hunger march to protest their starvation wages, but the march was called off by Cipriani because the government promised to pass a minimum wage bill. The bill was passed but never enforced, leaving the workers worse off than before and disillusioned with liberal strategies for change. They had only two years to wait before a leader emerged from their own ranks. In 1935 Tubal Uriah Butler, a Grenadian-born oilfield worker, led a ragtag band of 120 poor people on a hunger march from the southern oilfields straight into the Trinidadian capital of Port-of-Spain. Butler's dynamic leadership gave Trinidadian workers a self-confidence and unity they had never known before. On June 19, 1937, every Trinidadian oil worker laid down his tools, and the strike quickly spread to the other major labor sectors, the sugar cane cutters and the urban workers. This was too much for the government, and it foolishly tried to have Butler arrested as he addressed a public meeting. The crowd reacted with fury, and in the resulting violence both workers and police were killed. As elsewhere, the uprising was finally quelled when the governor called in a British destroyer and a contingent of British Marines.

Middle-Class Takeover: Adams, Bustamante, and Manley

As the uprisings spread, a pattern emerged which was to have a definitive impact on the future of West Indian politics. The strikes which were initiated and sustained by the workers were used by middle-class leaders to win a popular following.

In Barbados, for instance, the deportation of a radical Butlerite, Clement Payne, sparked riots in which hundreds of workers were arrested and imprisoned. Many of them were defended by a liberal lawyer named Grantley Adams, who emerged as the champion of the people. From this base, Adams went on to form the Barbados Labour Party and the Barbados Workers Union: labor-based organizations under middle-class control. From them emerged the two parties which dominate Barbadian political life to the present day.

It was the famous Jamaican uprising of 1938, however, which illustrated this process most clearly and became a symbol of the region-wide upheaval. In 1935, unemployment in Jamaica stood at 11%, while another 50% were employed only part of the year. Employers followed a system of "rotational employment" in which they would take on a worker for two weeks, then fire him to make way for another.[12] By 1936, Jamaican workers were organizing under the leadership of Hugh Buchanan, an ex-Garveyite and the first Jamaican Marxist, and G.S. Coombs, a union leader. Throughout the next year "the whole country rumbled with huge marches and strikes" involving banana workers, sugar workers, ex-servicemen, dockworkers, and other groups.[13] By 1938 things had come to a head. Estate after estate went out on strike, protesting not only low wages but also the burden of rents, and thus zeroing in on the key question, control of land. In May, workers struck at Frome, the largest sugar estate in the

Banana workers in rural Jamaica around the turn of the century. The United Fruit Company gained a virtual monopoly over the Jamaican banana trade after 1900, forcing many independent peasants off their lands to become wage laborers on the company's plantations. The poverty in rural Jamaica under the thumb of United Fruit made banana workers the most militant group in the 1938 strikes.

Moorland-Spingarn Research Center, Howard University

Photos facing page: National Library of Jamaica

LABOUR
LEADERS
IN COURT

country, which was owned by the British company Tate & Lyle. Colonial police crushed the strike by charging into the crowd with fixed bayonets.

As demonstrations rippled across the island, a leader emerged in the person of Alexander Bustamante, a near-white member of the lower middle class (he was a petty money-lender) who had assisted Buchanan and Coombs. Together with a leading Garveyite, St. William Grant, the charismatic "Busta" thrust himself to the head of the workers' movement.

<blockquote>
Early next morning, the 23rd of May, the city of Kingston was in the hands of the working population. Groups of workers moved from place to place and dislodged others from their stations. Street cleaners, power station workers, pumping station employees and municipal workers joined the throng of people who surged through the street. Traffic was halted, business places closed. Shops were invaded. Passing cars were stoned.

As the military moved in on the crowd, Bustamante in a dramatic gesture bared his chest and declared, "Shoot me if you want, but spare the poor defenseless people." The police drew nearer. Bustamante called upon the audience to sing the national anthem. As the strains of "God Save the King" were raised, the Police were forced to stand at attention, and could advance no further. Bustamante then moved away with the large crowd following him.[14]
</blockquote>

Bustamante was the man of the hour. His arrest and imprisonment by the authorities triggered a public fury which paralyzed Kingston. But his cousin, a lawyer named Norman Manley, arranged for Bustamante's release, and the two men proceeded to negotiate a settlement between the workers, the employers and the government. While this settlement had some favorable provisions, it was by no means revolutionary. The outcome was clear: middle-class leaders had assisted the workers in their struggle but compromised on their demands.

BUSTAMANTE And St. William Grant, The Arrested Labour Leaders, Looking Fit And Well As They Left The Central Police Station Yesterday Under Guard For The Court.

Never before had Jamaican workers tried to organize at a national level to negotiate with the ruling class for change. It was this inexperience, in part, which led them to eagerly accept the leadership of Bustamante, who brought the resources of his class into the fight on the people's behalf. But while he was dedicated to winning immediate gains for the workers, Bustamante lacked a political strategy for structural change. Norman Manley, on the other hand, had a clear anti-colonial perspective, but his nationalism did not include radical social change within Jamaica.

The 1938 revolt laid the basis for Jamaica's future political system. In the aftermath of the strikes, the popular movement came under the umbrella of two new organizations: the Bustamante Industrial Trade Union (BITU), headed by Busta, and the People's National Party (PNP) headed by Manley. The colonial authorities feared the militancy of a working class which could not be divided by race (as had been done in Trinidad and Guyana), and they feared the radical anti-colonialism of Marxist leaders within the PNP. They therefore contrived to split the movement. Under the influence of the colonial governor, Sir Arthur Richards, Bustamante broke from Manley in 1943 and formed the Jamaica Labour Party (JLP) to compete for the loyalty of the workers.

Although the PNP and the JLP were ideologically different at first, the groundwork had been laid for a "Tweedledum-Tweedledee" two-party system. Each party was dominated by one politician, a "big man" whose influence was overwhelming. Over the next ten years, external forces worked on Manley to persuade him to force the radicals from the PNP, culminating in the expulsion of the four leading Marxists from the party executive in 1952. Over the next two crucial decades, the JLP and the PNP moved steadily closer in ideological terms. But the working class was split into two warring political "tribes" which blocked popular unity on real social issues. ■

RASTAFARIANISM

The refusal of the colonial Church to bend on its commitment to a white, middle-class value system, and its failure to challenge the racism of the larger society, continued to fuel the growth of black religion. The Revivalist and Native Baptist churches welcomed anyone: black and poor, married or unmarried, legitimate or illegitimate. Moreover, poor people felt that the black church was with them in their historic and continuing search for freedom from slavery, poverty, and oppression. This search is the source of the eschatological fervor which marks black religion in all its Caribbean variants: the belief in a coming "redemption" as a means of enduring the pain of the present.

The religious basis for this hope is found in the Old Testament, particularly in the story of the Exodus, and in the Book of Revelations of the New Testament.

> The comparison of African traditional religion and the Old Testament indicates a link between black religion and biblical religion. The search for freedom in history runs like a black thread between both worlds.[1]

To the Revivalists there was no contradiction between biblical religion, including a belief in Jesus, and the West African myalist belief in a world peopled by spirits who have the power to help the living. The Bible was the most important element of the Revival service. These services were held in house yards, where a pole would be erected with a banner attached and an ark (of the covenant) placed on top. The "mother" of the service wore a belt with a pair of scissors (to "cut clean") evil spirits, a whistle (to warn the spirits) and a key (to open the door of salvation). The drum was central to the ceremony, which also included Bible readings, prayers, spirit possession, public testimonials and baptism by immersion.[2]

Alexander Bedward, the "Father of Revivalism," was a poor estate laborer in Jamaica who became a founder of the Native Baptist Free Church. In 1920, Bedward declared himself to be the incarnation of Jesus Christ. Thousands of Jamaicans sold their lands and houses and traveled to Kingston to see the Messiah:

> Bedward gave to the people a hope that in him a deliverer had emerged for blacks. Addressed at first as "Shepherd" by his followers, he changed his title to "Incarnation of Jesus Christ" in 1920, with the promise that he would ascend to heaven on December 31, 1920, thereby destroying the rule of white people and establishing the kingdom of Bedwardism on earth.[3]

The messianic focus of Bedwardism set the stage for Marcus Garvey, whose vision of the liberation of Africa from colonialism and a world-wide empire of black people was a new incarnation of the continuing search for societal deliverance. Garvey linked this search to the biblical

...and the search for freedom in black religion

doctrine of creation, asserting that since God had created all equal and provided space for all peoples, Africans must claim the continent God had given them.[4] He backed this apocalyptical promise with concrete action in the historic present in the form of his attempt to build a world-wide black organization, the United Negro Improvement Association.

Garveyism also found its theological basis in the Old Testament, equating the enslaved Israelites with the black race and the promised land with Africa.

> As children of captivity we look forward to a new, yet ever old, land of our fathers, the land of God's crowning glory. We shall gather together our children, our treasures, and our loved ones, and as the children of Israel, by the command of God, face the promised land, so in time we shall also stretch forth our hands and bless our country.[5]

Garveyism in turn provided the theological and philosophical base for the new movement which emerged among the Jamaican poor in the 1930s. Garvey is reputed to have said, "Look to Africa where a black king will be crowned, for the day of deliverance is near." When King Ras Tafari of Ethiopia was crowned Emperor Haille Selassie I in 1930, he was proclaimed by a growing cult of Jamaican followers to be divine, a messiah sent by God to liberate Africans from colonialism. Selassie was the "Lion of the tribe of Judah, the Root of David" (Rev. 5).

Echoing the anthem of Garvey's UNIA, "Ethiopia, Thou Land of Our Fathers," the Rastafari asserted that Ethiopia is the real Zion referred to in the scriptures. At the same time, they point out that Ethiopia is the only African country never under colonial domination (except for a brief incursion by Italy). This joining of the biblical with the concrete historical extends to their interpretation of the entire New Testament. For the Rastafari, the true children of Israel are the blacks, and the exile their diaspora to the New World; and the exodus will be a return to Ethiopia, the promised land.

> Within the Bible itself, and particularly in the Old Testament, there were gifts of tongue and a conception of the life and history of the black people of Jamaica. Were not African enslavement and plantation cruelty the same as The Scattering of the twelve tribes of Israel and the Exile in Babylonian captivity? Surely, then, the Return to the Promised Land for the Jews must be the Return to Africa for the Jamaican Blacks![6]

Some of the early Rastafari had been active Garveyites, and the Rasta movement regarded Garvey himself as a prophet, sometimes identified with John the Baptist. Garvey's dream of black repatriation to Africa was also the focal aim of the Rastafarian movement. As one Rasta said:

We say repatriation is redemption. We come and say it is a redemption for us, not black people alone, but the *world*.[7]

The Rastas argue that each race was given a continent of its own, and that by enslaving other peoples and seizing their lands, the white race has brought misery to the world. This can only be erased when each people returns to its rightful home. Unlike Garvey, however, who saw this deliverance as the fruit of determined human effort and organization, the Rastafari believe that it will come by divine intervention of Selassie, and that their role is to believe and wait.

> Repatriation will come, though I don't know the time. Not even the birds that fly high knoweth the time appointed by His Majesty.[8]

Taken on its own terms, therefore, Rastafarianism is an apocalyptical faith rather than a political movement. Yet its political impact on the Caribbean and on Jamaica in particular has been immense. By giving biblical and religious underpinnings to the Pan-African themes of black pride and unity, Rastafarianism called into question the entire structure of white-dominated colonial society.

The Rastafari regard the white Church as an integral part of the structures which hold them in captivity, and thus the movement challenges the Church directly.

> We don't business with religion! A colonial thing that! That is what the white man bring down here to enslave the black man![9]

From a theological standpoint, the Rastas denounce the Church for teaching that God is outside man or "in the sky," rather than on earth in man. They accuse the Church of a preoccupation with death and the afterlife rather than life on earth. Indeed, at the heart of the challenge posed by black religion to white church/society is the idea that deliverance and salvation are not individual and in the afterlife, but rather, *collective* (societal) and *in the foreseeable future*. When the slaves in the U.S. south sang "Swing low, Sweet Chariot," they were referring to escape northward, not heavenly ascent.[10] According to Jamaican theologian Noel Erskine, this joining of the concrete historical and the eschatological underlies the role of black religion in the struggle for black freedom and equality.[11]

The reaction of the Church to Rastafarianism, not surprisingly, was one of social rejection and religious belittlement. Any possibility of a prophetic message in the Rastafarian creed was summarily dismissed. But the marriage of black religion, black nationalism, and anti-colonialism continued to disturb and challenge the Caribbean Church until the 1960s, when the thunderbolt known as the Black Power movement finally forced the Church to come face to face with the social realities it had helped create.

Political Independence Without Economic Independence After World War Two

The Second World War effectively brought a halt to the labor revolts of the 1930s. England demanded, and received, full cooperation from her West Indian colonies in the war against Nazi Germany. The colonial authorities also used the war to suppress radical elements of the labor movement. The more forceful leaders—Bustamante, Butler—were jailed on the pretext that they "hindered the war effort."

After the war, England turned to a strategy of social reform based on the recommendations of the Moyne Commission. The commission toured the West Indies in 1938-39, denouncing the awful poverty of the West Indian masses and recommending palliative measures in health care, housing, education and wages. This welfarism was one element contributing to the weakening of labor's more radical demands.

Anti-colonial politicians close to the labor movement, such as Norman Manley, did use their new power to win certain concessions from England. These included universal suffrage, giving all adults the right to vote without regard to color or property ownership. Trade unions also won the crucial right to legal recognition and protection. As a result, strong unions sprang up all over the British West Indies in the 1940s and joined the new regional labor body, the Caribbean Labour Congress (CLC).

Britain also gave approval for a Federation of the West Indies, which would group ten English-speaking Caribbean territories into a new nation within the British Commonwealth. At conferences in 1945 and 1947, the Caribbean Labour Congress agreed to push for a strong federation which could implement socialist planning on a regional basis.[1] Britain, however, favored a federation for entirely different reasons, basically as a means of streamlining the administration of its colonies.

Most of the new unions included a "political committee" which became the nucleus of a party closely linked to the union. Thus the Belize General Workers Union, formed in 1939, gave birth to the People's United Party in 1950. The St. Kitts-Nevis Trade and Labour Union, formed in 1940, gave rise to the St. Kitts-Nevis Labour Party in 1951. From the Dominica Trade Union emerged the Dominica Labour Party; from the Antigua Trades and Labour Union came the Antigua Labour Party; and so on all over the English-speaking Caribbean. When Britain granted universal suffrage in the early '50s, working-class voters going to the polls for the first time swept these labor-based parties into power.

World War Two created powerful pressures on Britain to relinquish its hold over its colonial empire. At U.S. insistence, British prime minister Winston Churchill joined U.S. president Roosevelt in signing the 1942 Atlantic Charter calling for "sovereign rights and self-government [to be] restored to those who have been forcibly deprived of them."[2] As soon as the war ended, strong nationalist movements in Britain's eastern colonies—particularly India and Egypt—demanded independence. This signaled the imminent breakup of the empire and prompted Britain to seek a more gradual and controlled independence process for her West Indian colonies.

Accordingly, the British Labour Party government which came to power in 1945 promised to "guide" the West Indies to "self-government." Britain's strategy was really a delaying process aimed at establishing a neocolonial structure in the islands before granting full independence. During the 1940s and '50s, the colonies received new constitutions setting up governments on the Westminster model—with a Parliament, a governor representing the Crown, and a premier, who would become prime minister upon independence. During this transition colonial administrators still controlled key areas such as finance and the police. Middle-class West Indians schooled in the British system gradually took over most posts in the civil service.

Key West Indian leaders—notably Norman Manley of Jamaica and Grantley Adams of Barbados—placed their trust in the British Labour government and its brand of Fabian socialism. Rather than demand immediate independence, they went along with the gradual transition to self-rule. They also cooperated with Britain and the U.S. to isolate Marxist elements of the labor movement, including Cheddi Jagan in Guyana and left-wing members of Manley's People's National Party in Jamaica.

France and the Netherlands, meanwhile, also faced pressures from their colonial possessions around the world. But unlike Britain, they had no intention of giving up their Caribbean colonies, especially given the nationalist struggles building in the more important colonies of Algeria and Indochina (France) and Indonesia (the Netherlands).

Instead, they sought to "decolonize" their empires by integrating the colonies more closely with the metropolitan center. France created the myth of the "French Union" in which the colonies were no longer called colonies, but became overseas provinces of France. In 1946 Guadeloupe, Martinique and French Guiana became *départements d'outre mer,* French overseas departments, an option pushed by conservative white and mulatto groups in the Antilles. Similarly, the Dutch in 1954 created a tripartite Kingdom of the Netherlands in which Holland, the Dutch Antilles and Suriname became self-governing, supposedly equal partners.

The U.S. and the Puerto Rican Model

The Spanish-American War and the First World War had provided the United States with a military foothold in the Greater Antilles of Cuba, Puerto Rico and Hispaniola. To guard access to the Panama Canal, the U.S. had also purchased the Virgin Islands from Denmark in 1917 and established a naval base at St. Thomas harbor.

The Second World War expanded this military presence as the U.S. enlarged its existing bases. But the war also meant U.S. expansion into a new area: the English-speaking Carib-

A U.S.-run sweatshop in Puerto Rico in the 1950s.

Library of Congress Collection

bean. Under a "land-lease agreement" with Britain, the United States traded 50 old destroyers to the British Navy in exchange for 99-year leases of land for military bases on Antigua, St. Lucia, Jamaica, Guyana and Trinidad. The largest base was built at Chaguaramas, Trinidad. West Indian governments, especially Trinidad's, strongly opposed the U.S.-British deal.

U.S influence rose also in the economic and social spheres, corresponding to Britain's gradual withdrawal. In 1942 the United States helped set up an "Anglo-American Caribbean Commission," an event which signalled Britain's willingness to let the U.S. become involved in the affairs of British colonies. In those islands where the U.S. built bases, the presence of thousands of U.S. soldiers brought a Yankee cultural invasion. American pop music, clothing styles and foods became wartime fads. This was especially true in Trinidad, both on account of the huge Chaguaramas base and because of U.S. oil companies which moved into Trinidad during the war. The bases and their spin-off activities drew

many people off the land to seek high-wage work with the Americans. At the same time, social contradictions were reinforced as many of the white U.S. troops treated West Indians with open racism.

The end of the war saw the newly-powerful United States restructure the international economic system, with the U.S. dollar replacing gold as the new world currency. At the Bretton Woods conference in 1944, the World Bank and the International Monetary Fund (IMF) were set up to provide support to post-war Europe and supervise an international free trade system necessary to U.S. economic expansion.

In this context, the United States introduced in the late 1940s what it touted as a new model of development for the Caribbean. Launched in Puerto Rico in 1947, the plan was for U.S. corporate investment to create new industries in the region to replace the moribund plantation system. Led by investment in minerals, manufacturing and tourism, whole new sectors appeared in Caribbean economies.

In Puerto Rico, the model was initially based on manufacturing consumer goods like shoes and clothing. U.S. firms were offered generous incentives to set up branch plants on the island. These so-called "screwdriver factories" brought in all of their raw materials, machinery and pre-fabricated parts from the United States, then used cheap Puerto Rican labor to assemble the parts into finished goods. These were then shipped back to the U.S. for export to world markets.

One believer in the Puerto Rican model was Sir Arthur Lewis, a St. Lucian-born economist. Lewis urged the English-speaking Caribbean territories to copy the model on a regional, cooperative basis. During the 1950s, the larger territories of Trinidad and Jamaica did attempt to industrialize by offering investors tax-free periods and other incentives—what Lewis called "a period of wooing and fawning upon" foreign capitalists.[3] However, they did not do so on a regional basis as Lewis had proposed, but individually, competing against each other.

The 1950s and 60s saw Caribbean economies transformed as North American firms moved into the region on a large scale. With the U.S. economy booming, capital was going "transnational"—seeking low-wage labor, cheap raw materials and new markets around the globe. U.S. and Canadian aluminum multinationals arrived to mine the rich bauxite ore of Jamaica, Guyana and Suriname. Tourism controlled by American investors mushroomed in Jamaica, Barbados and the Dominican Republic, and became important to the economies of the smaller islands, especially Antigua. In manufacturing, U.S. firms sought to transfer their labor-intensive operations to the Caribbean to escape minimum wage laws and other workers' gains in the U.S.

Industrialization went farthest and fastest in Puerto Rico, Trinidad and Jamaica. The latter have the largest domestic markets in the English-speaking Caribbean, and some of the goods produced could be sold locally. On the other hand, the smallest islands such as Grenada, St. Vincent and Dominica had little infrastructure and were ill-positioned to attract foreign investment. They remained heavily dependent on agricultural exports, especially bananas.

Proponents of the Puerto Rican model argued that although the strategy depended on low wages, the firms' profits would be reinvested locally and industrial skills and technology transferred to the region. The results were not so glowing. As it turned out, the multinationals repatriated their profits and invested hardly anything back into the local economies. The firms brought in North Americans to fill most technically skilled jobs, while West Indian workers received low wages for routine assembly-type work.

The multinationals made clear that to come into the Caribbean they required guarantees of labor peace. Many refused outright to deal with unions. To satisfy the companies, governments passed repressive legislation curtailing the rights of workers to strike—for example, the Industrial Stabilization Act (ISA) in Trinidad, which workers dubbed "Is Slavery Again." Despite these concessions, firms frequently packed up and left as soon as their ten or twelve-year tax holiday expired, or if wages rose.

The new industries were integrated not with the economies of Caribbean host countries, but with the economies of their home countries where their headquarters were based.[4] They depended on duty-free imports of machinery and parts from abroad. Decisions were made in foreign corporate boardrooms with concern only for profits, not for the development needs of the Caribbean. Even Caribbean governments could exert little influence over the decisions of their powerful guests. Often the investors literally wrote their own package of incentives which was then relayed to the appropriate minister to sign.

The other side of this process was a growing Caribbean dependence on imported food and consumer goods. Prime agricultural lands were turned over to the multinationals for manufacturing, mining and tourism. At the same time, advertising by foreign firms helped shift people's tastes away from local foods and toward imports. The result was a steadily climbing food import bill. The Caribbean became dependent on the U.S. for virtually all of its wheat flour and corn, and for much of the meat, milk and other foods consumed in the region.[5]

Despite the introduction of new industries, the Puerto Rican model did little to alter the economic relationships of colonialism. The Caribbean countries were still gearing their production to the needs of the developed countries. As on the old sugar plantations, the management, capital and technology for production were still imported from the industrialized countries, and all the products and profits returned there.

Anti-Federation propaganda of the Jamaica Labour Party claimed that Jamaica would have to subsidize the smaller islands.

44

Political Independence and the Failure of Federation

The labor movement's vision of a strong West Indies Federation ran headlong up against these new political and economic trends. The original plan as set out by the CLC called for a strong central government which could plan development on a regional basis. But by the late 1950s, many of the labor heros held political office, and were now reluctant to agree to anything that would weaken their power. In Trinidad and Jamaica, the largest members, the rush was on to industrialize. Not only were their governments competing for investments, but they viewed with dismay the prospect of a link to the weak economies of the smaller islands.

Negotiations leading up to the formation of the Federation gradually stripped it of all but token powers over the member states. Key to this process was Norman Manley, who took office as Jamaican premier in 1955 and promptly yielded to British pressures for changes in the Federation's constitution. Richard Hart, then secretary of the Caribbean Labour Congress, describes Manley's role:

> The reason for this change of policy was that Mr. Manley's whole conception of how to industrialize had changed. He now saw industrialization not as a process to take place under local ownership and against the interests of imperialism, but as a process actually to be performed by foreign investors . . . He therefore no longer wanted a strong federal government with power to control investment in the entire area. Instead he wanted a weak central government, so that he would have the right to pursue an independent policy of attracting foreign capital by tax and other incentives to Jamaica.[6]

A similar mentality prevailed in Trinidad, while the smaller islands were willing to accept federation on any terms. The result was that the strong central government was scrapped. When finally launched in 1958, the Federation was barely a shadow of the united and progressive new nation which the labor movement had envisioned in the 1940s.

Jamaica and Trinidad received internal self-government from Britain in 1959. After this, the idea that West Indian unity was a precondition for self-government lost its mystique. The politicians of each territory began looking toward national independence, and Manley pulled back from the Federation in order to prepare for his role as prime minister of an independent Jamaica. Meanwhile, the Jamaica Labour Party headed by Bustamante whipped up a propaganda campaign against the Federation, claiming that Jamaica would have to subsidize the smaller islands. Finally, in a referendum held in 1961, Jamaicans voted to pull out.

As soon as Jamaica left, Trinidad premier Eric Williams made his famous pronouncement that "One from ten leaves zero," and Trinidad followed Jamaica in abandoning the regional body. The Federation thereupon collapsed, and with it the hopes of many Caribbean people for a strong and united West Indian nation. Many people, at least in retrospect, blamed the politicians for allowing selfish insularity to destroy the Federation. The Trinidadian calypsonian Mighty Sparrow captured these feelings of scorn and disappointment in his "Federation" calypso:

Federation boil down to simply this
It's dog eat dog, and survival of the fittest
Everybody going for independence
Singularly, Trinidad for instance
And we'll get it too, boy, don't bother
But I find we should all be together
Not separated as we are
Because of Jamaica.

But the reasons for the collapse were complex, and went beyond the actions of individual leaders. West Indian insularity has deep roots, based in the colonial system in which lines of communication and trade went from each island to London, not from island to island.[7] And unlike Cuba, Haiti or Puerto Rico, the English-speaking territories had no history of anti-colonial struggle on which a concept of unified nationhood could be built.

The break-up of the Federation left each island facing independence weak and alone. Foreshadowed by the United States' refusal to yield its Chaguaramas military base in Trinidad for the Federation's capital site, the failure of West Indian unity opened the door to U.S. domination of a weak and quarreling region.

Beginning with Jamaica and Trinidad in 1962, Britain's Caribbean colonies became independent one by one. But political independence did not bring economic independence, as ties to colonial Britain gave way to increasing dependence on North America. Former labor leaders now held political power, but economic power remained in the hands of local elites and foreign firms. The next decades would be ones of upheaval as a new generation rose to challenge these structures and the legacy of colonialism. ∎

NOTES TO PART ONE

Brief History of the Caribbean

1. *Amerindians* refers to those peoples who inhabited the Americas before the arrival of the Europeans. *West Indians* are people born in the West Indies in the post-Columbus era. *East Indians* trace their ancestry to India.
2. Spain based its claim on a Papal Bull which divided the world between Spain and Portugal along an imaginary line west of the Azores. Spain was to rule everything west of the line and Portugal everything east of it.
3. J. Hartog, *Curacao: Short History* (Aruba: De Wit Stores, 1979), p. 17.
4. C.L.R. James, *The Black Jacobins* (New York: Vintage Books, 1963), pp. 2-3.
5. William Claypole and John Robottom, *Caribbean Story* (Essex: Longman Group Ltd., 1980), Book One, p. 148.
6. Mercantilism was associated with the rise to power in England of Oliver Cromwell, who represented the interests of the emerging commercial bourgeoisie. Under Cromwell's "Western Design," Britain attempted to seize Spain's Caribbean possessions, capturing Jamaica from Spain in 1655.
7. C.L.R. James, *Spheres of Existence* (London: Allison & Busby Ltd., 1980), p. 182.
8. Eric Williams, *Capitalism & Slavery* (New York: University of North Carolina Press, 1964).
9. *Ibid.*, p. 207.
10. Walter Rodney, *A History of the Guyanese Working People, 1881-1905* (Baltimore: Johns Hopkins University Press, 1981).
11. *Ibid.*, Chap. 2.
12. *Ibid.*, p. 33.

NOTES TO PART ONE *(continued from previous page)*

Collaborative Role of the Colonial Church

1. Eric Williams, *From Columbus to Castro: The History of the Caribbean 1492-1969* (New York: Harper & Row, 1970), p. 203.
2. *Ibid.,* p. 203.
3. *Ibid.,* p. 183.
4. Idris Hamid, *Troubling of the Waters* (Trinidad: Rahaman Printery, 1973), p. 63.
5. James M. Phillippo, *Jamaica: Its Past and Present State* (London: Unwin Brothers, 1843), p. 158.
6. M.G. Lewis, *Journal of a West Indian Proprietor* (New York: Houghton Mifflin, 1929), p. 124.
7. Keith D. Hunte, "The Church in Caribbean Development," in David I. Mitchell, *With Eyes Wide Open* (Barbados: CADEC, 1973), p. 143.
8. Philip D. Curtin, *Two Jamaicas: The Role of Ideas in a Tropical Colony 1830-1865* (New York: Atheneum, 1970), p. 162.
9. Noel Leo Erskine, *Decolonizing Theology: A Caribbean Perspective* (Maryknoll, NY: Orbis Books, 1981), p. 74.
10. Phillippo, p. 253.
11. Lilith M. Haynes, *Fambli* (Guyana: CADEC, 1971), p. 40.
12. *Ibid.,* p. 36.
13. Migene Gonzalez-Wippler, *Santeria: African Magic in Latin America* (New York: Julian Press, 1973).

Unifying Themes in Caribbean Cultures

1. Morgan Dalphinis, *Caribbean & African Languages: Social History, Language, Literature and Education* (London: Karia Press, 1985), chapter 2.
2. H. Hoetink, "'Race' and Color in the Caribbean," in Sidney W. Mintz and Sally Price, eds., *Caribbean Contours* (Baltimore: Johns Hopkins University Press, 1985), pp. 56-58.
3. Gordon K. Lewis, *The Growth of the Modern West Indies* (New York: Monthly Review Press, 1968), p. 20.
4. *Ibid,* p. 28.
5. Mervyn C. Alleyne, "A Linguistic Perspective on the Caribbean," in Mintz and Price, p. 155.
6. Dalphinis, pp. 1-2.
7. Leonard Barrett, *The Sun and the Drum: African Roots in Jamaican Folk Tradition* (Jamaica: Sangster's Book Stores Ltd., 1976), pp. 11-12.
8. Gordon K. Lewis, pp. 30-31.
9. *Ibid,* pp. 31-32.

Links to Central America: The Atlantic Coast

1. Center for Research and Documentation of the Atlantic Coast, *Trabil Nani: Historical Background and Current Situation on the Atlantic Coast of Nicaragua* (New York: Riverside Church Disarmament Project, 1984), p. 12.
2. *The Road to Independence* (Government of Belize, 1981), p. 7.
3. Dalva Acuna de Molina, "Repercusiones de la Trajada de Sandia," in *Relaciones entre Panama y los Estados Unidos* (Panama: Ministry of Education, 1974), pp. 136-139.
4. Robert E. May, *The Southern Dream of a Caribbean Empire* (Baton Rouge: Louisiana State University Press, 1973), pp. 85-110.
5. Humberto E. Ricord et al., *Panama y la Frutera: Una Batalla Contra el Colonialismo* (Panama: Editorial Universitaria de Panama, 1974), p. 11.
6. "Banana Diplomacy: The Development of U.S.-Honduran Relations," *El Salvador Bulletin,* Vol. 2, No. 7, May 1983 (Berkeley, CA: U.S.-Salvadoran Research and Information Center), p. 4.
7. EPICA, *Panama: Sovereignty for a Land Divided* (Washington, DC: EPICA, 1976), p. 12.
8. Luis A. Diez Castillo, *Los Cimarrones y Los Negros Antillanos en Panama* (Panama, 1981), pp. 71-72.
9. *Informe de la Comision del Canal Istmico, 1914.* Cited in Xabier Gorostiaga, "La Zona del Canal y su Impacto en el Movimiento Obrero Panameno," *Tareas* (Panama), #32, July-Aug. 1975, p. 34.
10. The main source for this section was David McCullough, *The Path Between the Seas: The Creation of the Panama Canal 1870-1914* (New York: Simon & Schuster, 1977).
11. *Ibid.,* p. 582. Quote is from Harry Frank, *Zone Policeman 88, A Close Range Study of the Panama Canal and Its Workers* (Century, 1913).
12. The main source for this section was *The Road to Independence, op. cit.*

Roots of U.S. Imperialism in the Greater Antilles

1. Jose L. Franco, *Historia de la Revolucion de Haiti* (Havana: Instituto Cubano del Libro, 1966), pp. 272-274.
2. Juan Bosch, *Composicion Social Dominicana* (Santo Domingo: Impresora Arte y Cine, 1970), Chs. 19 and 20.
3. Gordon K. Lewis, *Puerto Rico: Freedom and Power in the Caribbean* (New York: Monthly Review Press, 1963), p. 58.
4. Juan Angel Silen, *Historia de la Nacion Puertorriquena* (San Juan: Editorial Edil, 1973), p. 112.
5. Philip S. Foner, ed., *Inside the Monster: Writings on the United States and American Imperialism by Jose Marti* (New York: Monthly Review Press, 1975), p. 40.
6. May, p. 5.

7. Alfred T. Mahan, "The U.S. Looking Outward," *Atlantic Monthly* LXVI (1890), p. 816.
8. Alfred T. Mahan, "The Strategic Features of the Gulf of Mexico and the Caribbean Sea," *Harper's New Monthly Magazine,* Vol. XLV (October 1897), pp. 680-691.
9. Jose Marti, "The Washington Pan-American Congress," in Foner, p. 340.
10. Arthur Whitaker, *The United States and Latin America: The Northern Republics* (Cambridge, MA, 1948), p. 160.
11. U.S. Bureau of the Census, *Historical Statistics of the United States, Colonial Times to 1957* (Washington, 1961), pp. 550-552.
12. Hugh Thomas, *Cuba: The Pursuit of Freedom* (New York: Harper & Row, 1971), p. 340.
13. *Congressional Record,* 55th Cong., 2nd sess. (April 13, 1898), p. 3781.
14. William Appleman Williams, *Empire As A Way of Life* (Oxford: Oxford University Press, 1980), pp. 130-136.
15. *Ibid.,* pp. 136-142.
16. Norman Bailey, *Latin America in World Politics* (Walker & Co., 1967), p. 50.
17. *United Fruit Company: Un Caso del Dominio Imperialista en Cuba* (Havana: Editorial de Ciencias Sociales, 1976), p. 54.
18. Manuel Maldonado-Denis, *Puerto Rico: A Socio-Historic Interpretation* (New York: Vintage Books, 1972), p. 75.
19. Cited in *American Mercury,* Vol. XVI, No. 62, February, 1929.
20. EPICA, *Panama: Sovereignty for a Land Divided,* p. 14.
21. William A. Williams, p. 153.
22. *Ibid.,* p. 155.
23. J. Lloyd Mecham, *United States-Latin America Relations* (New York: Houghton Mifflin Co., 1965), p. 115.
24. Moises Rosa Ramos, "Analysis of the Church in Puerto Rico" (Church and Theology Project of the National Ecumenical Movement of Puerto Rico, 1985).

The West Indies: Middle-Class Ambivalence . . .

1. EPICA, *Jamaica: Caribbean Challenge* (Washington, DC: EPICA, 1979), pp. 21-23.
2. Patrick Emmanuel, *Crown Colony Politics in Grenada 1917-1951* (Barbados: ISER, University of the West Indies, 1978).
3. Amy Jacques-Garvey, ed., *Philosophy and Opinions of Marcus Garvey* (New York: Atheneum, 1969), p. 126.
4. Tony Martin, "Marcus Garvey—A Caribbean, Not Jamaican Hero," *Caribbean Contact,* April 1979.
5. Eric Williams, *From Columbus to Castro,* p. 444.
6. *Ibid.,* p. 449.
7. *Ibid.,* p. 453.
8. *Ibid.,* p. 454.
9. *Daily Gleaner,* December 12, 1927. Cited in Rupert Lewis, "Political Aspects of Garvey's Work in Jamaica 1929-35," *Jamaica Journal,* Vol. 7, No. 1-2, p. 32.
10. *Ibid.,* p. 34.
11. Eric Williams, *From Columbus to Castro,* p. 444.
12. *Ibid.,* p. 446.
13. Trevor Munroe and Don Robotham, *Struggles of the Jamaican People* (Jamaica: Workers Liberation League, 1977), p. 110.
14. BITU, *Jamaica 1938: The Birth of the Bustamante Industrial Trade Union* (Jamaica: BITU, 1968), pp. 7-8.

Rastafarianism

1. Erskine, p. 38.
2. *Ibid.,* pp. 99-100.
3. *Ibid.,* p. 98.
4. *Ibid.,* p. 108.
5. Jacques-Garvey, p. 121.
6. Joseph Owens, *Dread: The Rastafarians of Jamaica* (Jamaica: Sangster's Book Stores Ltd., 1976), p. xiii.
7. *Ibid.,* p. 195.
8. *Ibid.,* p. 190.
9. Owens, p. 82.
10. Erskine, p. 55.
11. *Ibid.,* p. 55.

Political Independence Without Economic Independence

1. Gordon K. Lewis, pp. 346-347.
2. Samuel B. Bemis, *A Diplomatic History of the United States* (New York: Henry Holt & Co., 1942), pp. 863-864.
3. W. Arthur Lewis, "Industrialization of the British West Indies," *Caribbean Economic Review,* Vol. 2, 1950.
4. Ransford W. Palmer, *Caribbean Dependency on the United States Economy* (New York: Praeger Publishers, 1979), p. 41.
5. *Ibid,* p. 38.
6. Richard Hart, "Trade Unionism in the English-speaking Caribbean: the Formative Years and the Caribbean Labour Congress," in Susan Craig, ed., *Contemporary Caribbean: A Sociological Reader,* Vol. II (Trinidad: Craig, 1982), p. 89.
7. C.L.R. James, "Parties, Politics and Economics in the Caribbean," in *Spheres of Existence,* pp. 151-156.

Two Turbulent Decades: 1959-1980

Introduction

The two decades between 1959 and 1980 saw events largely reshape the political landscape of the Caribbean. The twin dictators of the Greater Antilles, Cuba's Batista and the Dominican Republic's Trujillo, fell after 30 years of rule. The Cuban revolution became a symbol, or rather, several conflicting symbols: of justice to the poor, of independence and nationalism to Latin America—and to the U.S. leadership, of an intolerable challenge to the existing order.

Fear of "another Cuba" became a U.S. obsession, leading successive administrations into ill-conceived acts. First came the Bay of Pigs, the attempt to invade Cuba with a proxy force of anti-Castro exiles. Its failure pointed up the difficulty of overthrowing a popular government without the use of foreign troops. So when a popular revolt erupted in the nearby Dominican Republic, demanding a return to democratic government, the Johnson administration sent in 23,000 Marines. Both invasions earned the U.S. hostility in Latin America and the rest of the Third World.

While unwilling to coexist with socialist Cuba, U.S. leaders offered tolerance and support to a murderous dictatorship in neighboring Haiti. Francois Duvalier and his son Jean-Claude tortured, jailed and killed tens of thousands of Haitians. But to Washington, Haiti's largest source of economic aid, the Duvaliers offered anticommunist "stability" at Cuba's door.

In Puerto Rico, a U.S.-sponsored development model based on foreign investment proved a short-term economic success but a long-term social failure. Copied in other countries of the region, especially Jamaica and Trinidad, the Puerto Rican model produced economic growth but also more unemployment and inequality. The widening gap between the black majority and a small elite of foreigners, local whites and mulattos sparked a wave of protests at the decade's end.

The pressure of unrest led political leaders in Jamaica and Trinidad & Tobago to shift direction, sharply increasing national control over their economies. In Trinidad, state control was a largely bureaucratic move. By contrast, "democratic socialism" in Jamaica was an attempt to respond to demands for justice and dignity for the poor. It foundered on economic problems, upper-class and foreign hostility, and the Manley government's own ambivalence about radical change. But it succeeded in raising the political awareness and expectations of Jamaicans, leaving a deep mark on the country and the region.

While change in Jamaica and Trinidad came within the framework of established political parties, tiny Grenada provided a different model. The dictator Eric Gairy offered no reforms, only repression. The lack of an effective opposition to Gairy created an opening for younger, radical leaders schooled in the Black Power movement. The Grenada revolution which closed the decade brought the left to power in an English-speaking country, posing a sharp symbolic challenge to Washington. ∎

Revolution in Cuba

After the Haitian Revolution of 1795, Cuba replaced Haiti as the sugar bowl of the Caribbean. "King Sugar" absorbed the human labor, exhausted the soil, and razed the island's forests. A Havana-based sugar aristocracy lived in luxury, while the peasants were thrown off their plots and a half-million slaves labored on the plantations.

When most of Latin America gained independence in the 1820s, the Cuban upper class clung to colonial Spain as protection against slave revolts. But a nationalist movement grew gradually, resulting in a Ten Years' War against Spain from 1868 to 1878. Freed slaves made up a large part of the armies fighting for Cuban independence and the abolition of slavery. The war failed, but in 1886 slavery ended in Cuba.

U.S. companies meanwhile were investing heavily in the country, buying up land and sugar mills. Cuban *independentistas* launched a new offensive in 1895. But the United States soon entered the war, and in 1898 Spain surrendered— to the United States, not to the Cubans who had been fighting Spain for thirty years. Cuba became independent in 1902, after Washington had written the Platt Amendment into its constitution, giving the U.S. the standing right to intervene in the country.

Mario García Joya, courtesy of Center for Cuban Studies

"We are Cubans, and today more than ever, proud to be. Now or never, long live Free Cuba. Forward, Cubans!"

Over the next decades Cuba became "in every sense of the term an American colony."[1] U.S. interests owned banks, cattle ranches, mines, ports, railways, and the telephone and power companies. Washington helped install the dictator Gerardo Machado in 1925, and when a revolt erupted against him in 1933, maneuvered Fulgencio Batista into power as army chief of staff.

Batista forged an early alliance with U.S. organized crime. After he lost power and fled to Florida in 1944, the Cuban's powerful friends came to his aid. In 1952, syndicate boss Meyer Lansky bribed the president of Cuba to let Batista back into the country. Batista promptly seized power in a coup and proceeded to realize Lansky's dream of turning Cuba into the hub of a Caribbean Mafia empire.

> Havana in the fifties became the capital city of organized crime, an anything-goes Disneyland run by the mob and a major conduit for narcotics flowing into the United States. Alongside the rocketing casino trade, fueled by mob-organized junkets from the mainland, the satellite rackets—prostitution, narcotics, and wholesale abortions—spun in profitable orbit.
> Batista kept the mob in the driver's seat, and Washington kept Batista in power through economic and military aid. In Washington two of Batista's most devoted supporters were Florida senator "Gorgeous George" Smathers and his good friend and later vice president Richard Nixon.[2]

Prerevolutionary Havana glittered with expensive hotels and casinos, many of them, like the luxurious Havana Riviera, joint ventures between Lansky's syndicate and the Batista government. This was the Havana North Americans knew. In the countryside, Cuba was a stagnant backwater, where there was one doctor for every 2,000 people; where less than 10% of dwellings had electricity and only 15% running water; where only 4% of the peasantry ate meat regularly, and only one family in ten could give their children milk to drink.[3]

The July 26 Movement

Batista's second regime was more brutal than his first. Opposition grew steadily, rooted in the alliance of labor unions, university students and intellectuals that had opposed Machado. The movement contained numerous ideological currents—liberalism, socialism, nationalism and populism among others—joined in opposition to the dictatorship. Labor unions organized by the Communist Party played a key role. But the party itself sought co-existence with Batista and did not initially back the struggle.[4]

Fidel Castro, a young lawyer from a landowning family, had been a student leader at the University of Havana. A year after Batista's coup, on July 26, 1953, he and a group of companions attacked the Moncada Barracks in the eastern city of Santiago, hoping to spark a general uprising. The attack failed: Castro and his followers were taken prisoner and many were tortured and shot by Batista's police. The brutal murders of so many young people provoked a public outcry and strengthened the image of the opposition movement.

The survivors were imprisoned until 1955, when they were released in an amnesty. They left immediately for Mexico to prepare a second attempt. In December 1956, Fidel, his brother Raúl, the Argentinian Che Guevara and 80 companions returned to Cuba aboard the yacht Granma. They were met by Batista's troops, who slaughtered all but 12. From strongholds in the Sierra Maestra mountains, the handful of survivors launched a guerrilla war that would last two years.

Batista reacted to the insurgency by torturing and killing hundreds of people. The United States supplied him with weaponry, including tanks, armored cars and B-26 bombers. Despite the regime's abuses, the Eisenhower administration viewed Batista as a loyal anticommunist ally, along with Somoza in Nicaragua, Duvalier in Haiti and Trujillo in the Dominican Republic. Even after halting arms shipments in 1958, the U.S. continued military training and other links with the regime.[5]

While well supplied, Batista's army was hopelessly corrupt, incompetent and demoralized. Many peasants joined or aided the guerrillas, while trade unions and students mobilized support in the towns. By 1958 opposition had spread to the middle class and even some businessmen and landowners. The regime crumbled rapidly, and in the early hours of Jan. 1, 1959, Batista fled to exile.

Revolution's Early Years

While imprisoned on the Isle of Pines after the Moncada assault, Fidel Castro had penned his defense, History Will Absolve Me. In it, he described the plight of the poor:

> Eighty-five percent of the small farmers in Cuba pay rent and live under the constant threat of being dispossessed from the land they till. More than half of the most productive land belongs to foreigners. In Oriente, the largest province, the lands of the United Fruit Company and West Indian Company join the north with the south coast. There are two hundred thousand peasant families who do not have a single acre of land to till to provide food for their starving children. On the other hand, nearly three hundred thousand caballerias of cultivable land owned by powerful interests remain uncultivated.[6]

The new government of Castro's July 26 Movement moved quickly against corruption and economic injustice. On March 6, 1959 all rents in Cuba were reduced by 50%. The First Agrarian Reform Law in May nationalized lands held by foreigners, and limited private land holdings by Cubans to 400 hectares (about 1000 acres). Peasants received title to plots they rented or sharecropped.

Many of Batista's henchmen were tried in public tribunals, and 483 were executed. But many other Batista collaborators escaped to the United States. There they formed the nucleus of a militant exile community, soon to be swelled by disaffected members of the Cuban upper and middle class.

While insisting on freedom from foreign control, Castro initially sought an accommodation and trade relations with the United States. In April 1959 he visited Washington and met Vice President Nixon. Nixon, who had ties with Batista's empire through such individuals as Bebe Rebozo and Howard Hughes, reported to the CIA that Castro had communist sympathies and recommended training an exile force to overthrow him.[7]

Fidel Castro meets Vice-President Nixon in 1959.

Through the long months of preparation, the American planners and their Cuban exiles had accepted unquestioningly the assumption that Castro ruled by force and fear. Given a clear alternative, they believed, the Cuban masses would unite behind a revolutionary movement aimed at overthrowing Castro. In the tense days of mid-April 1961, Castro proved he had the loyalty of the Cuban people.[12]

The failed invasion exposed the U.S. to harsh criticism all over the Third World. It hardened the breach between Washington and Havana and accelerated Cuba's turn toward the Soviet bloc. Castro declared the revolution socialist on the eve of the assault, and afterwards, made clear that the Soviet Union was to be Cuba's primary ally. A week after the invasion Washington imposed a permanent trade embargo, cutting Cuba off from vital supplies of food, medicine and machinery.

The Bay of Pigs fiasco did not end U.S. hopes of overthrowing Castro. From their base in Miami the CIA, right-wing exiles and organized crime elements joined forces to wage a "secret war" against Cuba. As described in a 1981 study, *The Fish is Red:*

> The Cuba Project was an overreaching program of clandestine warfare, offhanded military adventures, sabotage, and political and economic subversion. It ran the gamut from counterfeiting to biological warfare to assassination. It began in 1959 during the Eisenhower administration, reached its paramilitary heights under the brothers Kennedy, slumbered under Lyndon Johnson, and was reawakened with a vengeance under Richard Nixon. Vestiges remain operational.[13]

As Cuba cemented ties to the socialist world, U.S. propaganda focused on the Soviet connection and on Cuban attempts to foment revolution in other Third World countries. That practice, which reflected Cuban policy in the 1960s, ended by the end of the decade with the death of its main advocate, Che Guevara, and pressures from a disapproving Soviet Union.

Cuba did influence political movements throughout Latin America and the Caribbean. But it was an influence which stemmed more from the power of example than from its attempts at active intervention, all of which failed. The revolution's achievements—health and education for all, social egalitarianism, an end to exploitation—stood as proof that justice was possible once a country freed itself from foreign control.

For more than 50 years, Cuba, Hispaniola and Puerto Rico had been outposts of U.S. capitalism, controlled directly through military occupation or indirectly through U.S.-backed dictators. Cuba's revolution was the first break in this control. U.S. officials portrayed it as the result of Soviet expansionism. At the same time, some did recognize acute poverty as a motor force for revolution in Latin America. This gave rise to a double thrust in the 1960s of counterinsurgency, to crush leftist movements, and developmentalism, to ease poverty through economic growth. The Kennedy administration's Alliance for Progress was conceived in direct response to the Cuban revolution as a program of U.S. aid that supposedly would preempt the need for radical change. ∎

Although the Cuban Communist Party had belatedly allied itself with the July 26 Movement, the revolution initially had no defined Marxist ideology. During 1959 and 1960, however, the new government began undertaking more radical social reforms than most middle-class Cubans had expected. It also began diplomatic overtures to the Soviet Union. The flight to Miami of the well-to-do became an exodus.

Tension between Washington and Havana meanwhile escalated as the revolution chipped away at U.S. holdings in Cuba. The U.S. complained of damage to its interests, but refused a Cuban offer to discuss the matter.[8] In the spring of 1960, Cuba signed a limited trade agreement with the Soviet Union, receiving Soviet oil and other goods in exchange for sugar. When the U.S.-owned refineries in Cuba refused to refine the Soviet oil, they were promptly nationalized. The U.S. retaliated by terminating Cuba's sugar quota on the U.S. market; whereupon Cuba nationalized the remaining U.S.-owned banks, industrial and agrarian holdings.

While blows were traded at the diplomatic level, the Central Intelligence Agency was already at work on a covert plan for Castro's overthrow. The CIA's quick ouster of Jacobo Arbenz in Guatemala six years earlier was seen as a model, and the Agency began recruiting and training Cuban exiles for an "Operation Guatemala."[9]

The supposedly secret operation was the talk of Miami and Havana. As signs of the preparations mounted, the Cuban population mobilized in defense. At the United Nations Cuba charged that the U.S. was planning to invade the island. The U.S. delegation termed the charges "monstrous distortions and downright falsehoods."[10]

A member of the U.S. diplomatic corps in Havana at the time, Wayne Smith, would later describe the Bay of Pigs invasion as "that rarest of all things—a perfect failure."[11] Cubans met the 1,500 CIA-trained exiles when they landed and turned back the assault in 72 hours. The result was U.S. humiliation and dramatic confirmation of Castro's popular support.

The Shores of Santo Domingo

"No more Cubas" became the rallying cry of U.S. foreign policy in the 1960s. While continuing covert efforts to topple Castro, the U.S. moved to isolate Cuba in the hemisphere. At a meeting of the Organization of American States in 1962, the United States used its dominant position to secure the expulsion of Cuba from the regional body. The proposal passed narrowly, with such important members as Brazil, Mexico and Argentina refusing to support the U.S. measure.

While bringing these diplomatic pressures, the United States also showed itself ready to use covert and overt action against what were seen as "new Cubas in the making." Within four years of the Bay of Pigs, the U.S. carried out two more interventions: in the colony of British Guiana in 1963, and in the Dominican Republic in 1965.

In the first instance, the covert U.S. role in the ouster of the Guyanese government came to light only slowly. It had an impact in the English-speaking Caribbean, but few repercussions beyond.

By contrast, when 23,000 U.S. Marines marched into the Dominican Republic the shock reverberated internationally. The invasion recalled the infamous gunboat diplomacy era, sharpening anti-imperialist feelings in Latin America. Songwriter Phil Ochs' haunting refrain, *The Marines have landed on the shores of Santo Domingo,* symbolized the impact in the United States. Reaction to the invasion prefigured the antiwar movement that would go on to oppose the Vietnam War and later, U.S. involvement in Central America.

Covert Action in Guyana

When Guyanese first went to the polls under universal suffrage in 1953, they elected the People's Progressive Party (PPP), which campaigned on a socialist platform. The PPP was led by Cheddi Jagan, a popular labor leader of East Indian descent, and Forbes Burnham, a British-trained black lawyer. Strongly anti-colonialist, the PPP represented an unprecedented racial unity of Afro-Guyanese and Indo-Guyanese workers and peasants behind a radical program.

With the McCarthy period in full swing, the Eisenhower administration declared a communist threat and pressured the British to act. When Jagan had been in office just 133 days, British troops landed and suspended the colony's Constitution. After the overthrow, Burnham broke from the PPP and formed the People's National Congress (PNC). His move reopened the racial split in the electorate, with most Africans supporting Burnham while Jagan's PPP became mainly Indian. Jagan nonetheless won again in 1957 and again in 1961, each time in free and fair elections.

The Kennedy administration initially was willing to talk with Jagan, given his legitimate electoral victories. But this stance soon gave way to fear of communism and a decision not to let British Guiana become independent under a socialist government, freely elected or not.

In the spring of 1963, the CIA and the American Institute for Free Labor Development sent agents into British Guiana to organize a general strike. Meanwhile, Burnham's PNC and a smaller party, the United Force, attacked PPP supporters in a wave of racial violence. These combined actions fatally weakened the Jagan government. That summer, President Kennedy and British Prime Minister MacMillan met and agreed that Britain would delay the colony's independence until a new government was in office.[1] In an election held the following year under new rules designed by the British, the PNC and United Force combined to win control.

The U.S. role in Jagan's ouster underscored the maturing of the 1950s alliance between the CIA and elements of organized labor in support of Cold War goals. Ironically, Prime Minister Burnham went on to declare "cooperative socialism" in Guyana and bring large portions of the economy under state control. This pseudo-socialism, however, never resembled the serious restructuring taking place in Cuba. Instead, under Burnham's erratic rule Guyana grew steadily more impoverished and repressive.

The Dominican Invasion

While these events unfolded in Guyana, U.S. officials were keeping an eye on developments almost at Cuba's door. The Dominican Republic's history in many ways paralleled that of Cuba. A U.S. Marine occupation from 1916 to 1924 had helped install a dictator, Gen. Rafael Leonidas Trujillo. Like Batista, Trujillo ruled ruthlessly, eliminating opponents through exile, torture, imprisonment and murder. Economically, Trujillo followed the Somoza model by bringing large portions of the Dominican economy under his control.

> It was hardly coincidental that new roads often led to Trujillo's plantations and factories, and new harbors benefited Trujillo's shipping and export enterprises. Ultimately, Trujillo, along with his relatives and friends, owned well over half of the country's economic assets . . . By the time of his death, Trujillo was reckoned to be one of the richest men in the world, with a fortune estimated at from several hundred million to a billion dollars.[2]

His strident anticommunism made Trujillo a favorite of reactionary circles in Washington, and he enjoyed U.S. support for decades. But his exclusion of foreign capital from profitable investments and his fanatical attempts on the lives of prominent opponents (including President Betancourt of Venezuela) ultimately worked against him. After 1959, fears arose that his dictatorship was creating conditions for another Cuba. Trujillo also was an embarrassment at a time when the U.S. was trying to convince Latin countries to take stronger measures against Castro. For all these reasons it was decided that Trujillo had to go. In May 1961 he was executed by a group of his officers using weapons supplied by the CIA.

In the country's first free elections ever, Dominicans gave a landslide victory to Juan Bosch, who promulgated a liberal new Constitution. Bosch was not a socialist, but neither was he willing to persecute the small handful of Dominican leftists to the degree demanded by the U.S. He permitted freedom of speech, and discontinued the U.S. police training program.[3] Land reform was promised to distribute Trujillo's vast holdings to landless peasants.

Forces arrayed against Bosch soon included the Trujillo loyalists, the Dominican military and oligarchy, the conservative Catholic hierarchy and U.S. business. He was overthrown by a right-wing military coup on September 25, 1963, after only seven months in office.

The new military junta discarded the Constitution and reversed Bosch's reforms. Plotting continued, and in April 1965, dissident pro-Bosch officers handed out arms to the people and a popular revolt swept the capital. Virtually the entire population of Santo Domingo poured into the streets to demand the restoration of the Constitution and the legally elected Bosch government.

The military's coup against an elected government had perturbed U.S. officials not at all. By contrast, the uprising to restore democracy was seen as a threat. Leaders of the junta and the U.S. Embassy in Santo Domingo raised the cry that a communist takeover was imminent. On April 28, President Johnson ordered 22,000 U.S. Marines into Santo Domingo. Johnson first asserted that the Marines had landed to protect American lives, but soon shifted to the rationale that the invasion was necessary to prevent "Castro-Communism."

For two months U.S. Marines and the Dominican army battled the "Constitutionalists," resulting in some 3,000 deaths. In May, the United States pressured the OAS to send in an "Inter-American Peace Force" which fought under U.S.

The United States invaded the Dominican Republic under cover of an "Interamerican Peace Force."

command.[4] Washington used their presence to claim its intervention had been a multilateral action under OAS auspices. By September the Constitutionalists had been defeated.

On June 1, 1966, with the country still under U.S. occupation, an election was held in which Bosch ran against Joaquin Balaguer. Balaguer had been titular president under Trujillo and was a direct holdover from the dictatorship. His candidacy was backed by the United States, the Dominican oligarchy and the military. In the months leading up to the election, the Dominican army continued to harass, jail and kill Bosch supporters. Thousands fled to exile in New York; Bosch himself hardly dared leave his house to campaign. Balaguer, by contrast, promised a return to "peace" and "order." In the end, Dominicans had little choice but to bow to the new balance of power. Balaguer won the election and rigged two subsequent ones to remain in power for the next twelve years.[5]

President Balaguer collaborated with the U.S. government to smash what was left of the popular movement. U.S. military and police trainers reorganized the Dominican security forces, and streets became the scene of bloody repression against youth and trade unionists. A paramilitary death squad, La Banda, terrorized poor neighborhoods.

Economic development was to be the other side of the strategy for preventing a resurgence of radicalism. U.S. officials set out to implement a development "miracle" on the basis of U.S. private investment, aid and loans. Large grants from the U.S. Agency for International Development financed the building of an infrastructure for foreign investors. Several "free zones" were established where foreign-owned industries could set up under tax exemptions and non-union conditions. One of Balaguer's first acts was to invite in the U.S. multinational Gulf + Western, which built a sprawling Dominican empire of sugar holdings, beef exports and luxury tourism. President Johnson promised G+W that if another rebellion should occur, Washington would again intervene to protect U.S. interests.

The foreign corporations had virtually free rein to exploit Dominican workers. Gulf + Western, for example, kept wages low for its cane cutters and millhands by crushing the main union in its company town of La Romana. In July 1966, a right-wing Cuban exile named Teobaldo Rosell was put in charge of the La Romana operation. He mounted a vicious union-busting campaign against the Sindicato Unido and its leader, Guido Gil. The union's property and bank account were seized, its meetings broken up, and a spy system was introduced into the mill and fields. In January 1967, Gil disappeared from La Romana; his body has never been found.[6]

Because of high world sugar prices and the influx of U.S. aid, Balaguer's strategy initially produced rapid growth. But the "Dominican miracle" benefited mainly the urban well-to-do and large export producers. It also encouraged rampant corruption, as military and business interests excluded from profit-making during the Trujillo years scrambled for a piece of the action. Dominican peasants and slum-dwellers remained on the sidelines, struggling just to survive. ■

Haiti: Rise of the Duvaliers

As Batista and Trujillo neared the end of their reigns, a new tyrant appeared across the mountainous border dividing the Dominican Republic from Haiti. Coming to power in 1957, François Duvalier founded a regime legendary for corruption and cruelty. Haiti under the Duvaliers became a pariah nation, dependent on foreign handouts and marked by poverty, ignorance and despair.

Papa Doc

In 1804 the slaves of colonial St. Domingue overthrew their French masters in the Caribbean's only successful slave revolt. As an independent black republic, Haiti was surrounded by white-ruled colonies where slavery remained in force. It faced immediate hostility from the United States and France, which viewed the Haitian revolution as a dangerous example to their own slaves. To gain recognition of its sovereignty Haiti paid an indemnity to France of 60 million francs, financed through loans from foreign banks. The resulting debt accentuated the country's poverty until it was finally repaid in 1922.

Haiti thus started out as an isolated "garrison nation," reinforcing the military's dominant role. Officers from Toussaint L'Ouverture's slave army and functionaries of the new government divided up the properties of the French, becoming a new landowning class. This black elite competed with the established mulatto landowners, causing perpetual instability.[1]

The masses of ex-slaves refused to work any longer as plantation laborers and struggled for land of their own. Some rented from the landowners, while others squatted on unoccupied hillside land. But they remained wretchedly poor. As the plantation system crumbled, many landowners moved to the towns where they turned to commerce and to control of the state apparatus as means of personal enrichment.[2]

Rising U.S. involvement in Haitian trade and fear of German influence led the United States to occupy Haiti at the beginning of World War One. It took the Marines four years to crush the peasant resistance led by Charlemagne Péralte, but he was captured and gruesomely executed in 1919. The U.S. occupation lasted 19 years, and created bitter resentment.

Since the mid-19th century, the pattern had been for the mulattos to hold power behind black figurehead presidents.[3] By the 1940s, however, an urban black middle class had grown strong enough to challenge mulatto dominance. A black doctor, Francois Duvalier, was elected president in 1957 with wide black support and the backing of the army. Duvalier portrayed his election as "the victory of our miserable peasant masses" and a black "revolution" against mulatto power.[4] In reality, his rule broke the political but not the economic hold of the mulattos. Although he talked of redistributing wealth, the only redistribution which took place was the siphoning off of state revenues by those newly in power. The peasantry remained marginalized and impoverished.

Duvalier used repression to neutralize rival power bases: the mulatto oligarchy, the press, student organizations, trade unions, the Catholic Church. To counter the army's power and terrorize the population, he created an armed militia, the Tontons Macoutes. With the Macoutes as hit men, "Papa Doc" tortured, imprisoned, exiled and killed thousands, including some of his closest associates. He made himself President-for-Life, with absolute powers, in 1964.

Duvalier combined terror with a mystical and personalist ideology based in part on his reputed voudou powers. He claimed to be the embodiment of past Haitian rulers, saying: "Those who wish to destroy Duvalier wish to destroy the fatherland . . . I am already an immaterial being."[5] There were innumerable plots against him, many by exiles based in Havana or Santo Domingo. All of them were crushed and the perpetrators executed. After one mass killing, according to an often-recounted story, Duvalier had the corpses of his victims propped in chairs along the road to the airport as a warning to his other enemies.

Especially after the Cuban revolution, U.S. officials saw Duvalier as a bulwark against communism and granted him generous aid. There were recurring disputes between Washington and Port-au-Prince over its use, however. This together with Duvalier's notoreity created some ambivalence on the U.S. side.

> Public opinion in the hemisphere counseled against granting him any financial assistance . . . The United States was in a dilemma since not only had Duvalier shown himself for the ruthless dictator that he was, but he had openly refused to comply with even the most elementary requisites in qualifying for assistance.
> Just across the Windward Passage, however, lay Cuba and Fidel Castro . . . [6]

Duvalier knew his main value to the United States was as a barrier to communism. To increase his leverage, he presented himself as anticommunist while slyly suggesting that Haitians might be tempted to stray from the western camp if the U.S. withheld aid. He spoke of Haiti's need to choose between "two great poles of attraction in the world today," i.e. the western and socialist blocs. During Eisenhower's administration, such threats were sufficient to maintain the flow of aid. Under Kennedy, however, Duvalier's repression led to strained relations, and most aid was suspended in 1962. It was resumed midway through President Johnson's term in a new atmosphere of cordiality which set the tone for future relations between Port-au-Prince and Washington.

Jean-Claude Takes Over

François Duvalier died in 1971 after passing on the life presidency to his 19-year-old son Jean-Claude. The choice was ratified by popular referendum with announced results of 2,391,916 to one. U.S. ambassador Clinton Knox stood by at the swearing-in ceremony, signalling Washington's approval.

U.S. officials embraced Jean-Claude's regime as more liberal and modern than his father's. Repression became more

*François and
Jean-Claude Duvalier*

Courtesy of The Resource Center

selective; imprisonment, torture and exile replaced execution as the primary means of dealing with rivals. Whereas Papa Doc had persecuted members of the elite, including Catholic priests, mulatto businessmen and professionals, Jean-Claude concentrated on sectors with a potential for influence at the grassroots. His regime targetted radio journalists, trade unionists, church workers, development workers and would-be political party leaders.

Economic changes provided the principal evidence of modernization. Jean-Claude—soon dubbed "Baby Doc" by the foreign press—opened Haiti's economy to penetration by U.S. capital. Electronics firms like TRW, Motorola, Phillips and Sylvania, garment makers like Levi Strauss, and sporting goods firms like Wilson, Rawlings and Spaulding flocked to Haiti to take advantage of low wages and non-union conditions. Haiti became the world's largest producer of baseballs, handsewn by women factory workers for Haiti's standard wage of $2.64 per day.

These economic trends contributed to new power struggles within the Haitian ruling class. Members of the mulatto oligarchy, whose power Papa Doc had sought to curb, became managers and subcontractors for the foreign firms. Jean-Claude's opening to the mulattos was symbolized by his marriage in 1980 to Michèle Bennett, daughter of a mulatto coffee exporter. The marriage enraged the "old-guard" supporters of François Duvalier, who accused Jean-Claude of letting the mulattos into the palace by the back door.

For the 90% of Haitians who lived in poverty, the Duvaliers and Bennetts alike were symbols of a corrupt minority that excluded the majority from a share in the nation's wealth. A millionaire elite of government officials, army officers and businessmen lived in luxurious Port-au-Prince villas, complete with satellite dishes and swimming pools. The rest of the population was left to scratch a living from the barren mountainsides, or seek refuge in the slums of the capital with their open sewers and sprawling garbage heaps.

While officials diverted state revenues for private gain, aid from the United States and other foreign donors propped up the economy. The United States Agency for International Development (USAID) assumed a powerful role, effectively dictating the government's economic policies. Hundreds of missionary churches and foreign relief agencies such as CARE, Church World Service, and Catholic Relief Services provided most social services. Church-run schools, health clinics and feeding programs filled a critical need in the absence of state initiative. But they also encouraged a culture of dependency, marked by the paternalistic concern of the donors and mixed gratitude, anger and passivity on the part of Haitians.

The Duvalier regime's flagrant corruption and contempt for social welfare prompted some donors, such as Canada, to reduce their aid. But the United States continued large-scale support, at times accompanied by pleas for reform. In the late 1970s, pressures from the Carter administration produced a brief democratic "springtime" in Haiti. Two non-governmental political parties were allowed to form, along with trade unions and an independent press.

The election of U.S. president Ronald Reagan brought this liberalization to an abrupt end. On election day in November 1980, Tontons Macoutes careened through Port-au-Prince streets, firing guns in the air and shouting "Reagan in power; now cowboys rule!" Three weeks later, on November 28, 1980, the Duvalier security forces staged a massive crackdown. Over 200 journalists, trade unionists, development workers and human rights activists were arrested and many sent into exile.

Haiti faced the new decade in the shadow of renewed repression. Hopes for change had risen, yet peaceful paths for achieving it had again been barred. ∎

Failure of the Puerto Rican Model

Starting in 1947, U.S. corporations were invited to open factories in Puerto Rico with promises of a low-wage work force, freedom from U.S. income taxes, and tax-free repatriation of profits. "Operation Bootstrap," as it was called, was to build a modern industrial state on the ruins of Puerto Rico's stagnant sugar economy. Its deeper purpose was to bring the Island into the U.S. economy as an industrial enclave supplying U.S. firms with cheap labor.

Tax exemptions were one reason firms located in Puerto Rico. The other was the Island's special status as a U.S. colony—not stated in so many words, but a reality nonetheless behind the title of "freely associated state." This relationship meant that firms could expect compliant local authorities and a stable political climate, while enjoying low wages typical of the Third World. It also meant U.S. federal subsidies were available to build highways, port facilities and other infrastructure needed by investors.

Operation Bootstrap was touted as an economic miracle, and for a while, it appeared to be. Its results included:
- Average economic growth of 6% in the 1950s, 5% in the 1960s, and 4% in the 1970s.
- U.S. capital investment increasing from $1.4 billion in 1960 to $24 billion in 1979.
- Second highest per capita income in Latin America.
- Literacy and life expectancy approaching that of the United States.
- Highest per capita level of imports from the United States in the world, and 34% of total U.S. direct investment in Latin America.[1]

Behind these glowing figures, however, lay a different reality. Puerto Rico's rapid industrialization was accompanied not by rising employment, but by relentlessly rising *unemployment*. Official unemployment stood at around 12% in the mid-1960s; by 1975 it had risen to 20%, and this was considered an underestimation of true joblessness.[2] Over this same period, and especially after 1970, Puerto Rico became heavily dependent on subsidies from the U.S. federal budget. These subsidies, which stood at $119 million per year in 1950, soared to $3.1 billion per year in 1979.[3]

Contrary to the self-reliance its name implied, the Bootstrap model made Puerto Rico dependent on foreign capital. This capital became increasingly mobile as the transnational corporations extended their operations around the globe. The result was an erosion of investment in Puerto Rico, and mounting dependence on U.S. subsidies.

In the first years of Bootstrap, labor-intensive light industry entered Puerto Rico to take advantage of its low wages. These were mainly firms manufacturing consumer goods like shoes, clothing and glassware from parts or raw materials brought in from the United States. By the mid-sixties, however, the 15-17 year tax exempt period in the initial contracts of these firms began to expire. At the same time, wages in Puerto Rico had risen, due in part to successful labor organizing by U.S.-based unions. Many of the assembly factories closed their Puerto Rico operations and relocated to cheaper wage havens such as Haiti, the Dominican Republic or the Far East.

Petroleum refining and petrochemicals dominated investment from 1965 to 1972. Companies like Sun Oil, Gulf, and Union Carbide were attracted by Puerto Rico's cheap water and land, and by the willingness of federal and local authorities to ignore air quality and other environmental standards. They used huge amounts of land, water and electricity, but created few jobs. After 1973, when world oil prices rose, this sector too went into a slump.

The next wave of investment came from chemical and pharmaceutical firms in the 1970s. Every major drug company built a plant in Puerto Rico, giving the Island the highest concentration of pharmaceutical factories in the world. Like the oil refineries, the pharmaceuticals are heavy polluters, creating volumes of toxic wastes.

Heavy industry in Puerto Rico exacted a grim price in environmental destruction and its health effects. The Island became an industrial dumping ground, where pollution and toxic wastes unacceptable in the United States could be transferred by runaway firms. Industrial communities in Puerto Rico began to register high rates of respiratory problems, cancer, leukemia and other illnesses.[4]

While these waves of industrialization were taking place, jobs were lost in the rural areas due to the virtual abandonment of agriculture. This was part of the Bootstrap plan: Puerto Rico would export industrial products, while importing all the food and consumer goods it needed from the United States. But the labor force displaced from the countryside was too large to be absorbed by the new industries. The result was growing unemployment and dependence on imported food. Today about 90% of what Puerto Ricans eat is imported.[5]

"Yes, in my house we also think that things go better with Coke."

Bootstrap's failure to reduce unemployment was particularly striking in light of two systematic efforts to reduce the size of the work force. One was officially sponsored emigration, resulting in the exodus of some 40% of the Island's population to the United States. The other was a heavily-promoted program of "voluntary" female sterilization which lowered the birth rate from 160 per 1000 women in 1941 to 102 per 1000 in 1970.[6] Without these population control measures, Operation Bootstrap's failure to provide enough jobs would have been even more glaring.

As the factories closed their doors, the U.S. government had increasingly to subsidize the standard of living in its colony. By 1975, 50% of Puerto Rican households were receiving food stamps, while others survived on welfare payments and distribution of surplus U.S. foodstuffs.[7] To relieve unemployment, workers were added to inflated government payrolls underwritten by federal subsidies.

By supporting the Puerto Rican work force at a minimum level, this welfare safety net allowed firms on the Island to pay lower wages. In this sense, federal transfer payments to Puerto Rico became the equivalent of a subsidy by U.S. taxpayers to runaway U.S. firms. The Puerto Rican model, touted as a miracle, became a model for economic dependency and environmental disaster.

The Model in Jamaica and Trinidad

Three North American aluminum companies—Reynolds, Alcan and Kaiser—began exploiting Jamaican bauxite in the 1950s, using U.S. government subsidies under the Marshall Plan. They bought up vast tracts of land in Jamaica, and bauxite soon replaced sugar as the country's major export.

The aluminum companies, however, processed all the bauxite outside Jamaica. The island benefited only from the taxes and royalties paid on the raw ore. The aluminum firms kept these low through a device called "transfer pricing," in which they "sold" the Jamaican ore to their U.S. or Canadian parent companies at an artificially low price, which was used as the basis of taxation. The result was that Jamaica received less than 2% of the world market value of the processed aluminum.

Nor did the bauxite industry have much impact on unemployment. A mechanized industry, bauxite mining provided a small number of relatively well-paid jobs.

Other industries expanded along with bauxite, including construction, transportation, cement and clay production, manufacturing, banking and tourism. All were dominated by North American or British capital, with Jamaican capitalists acting as managers and partners for the foreign firms. This local elite was drawn largely from Jamaica's upper class of 21 white, Chinese and Syrian families, including the Ashenheims, Matalons, Harts, Henriques and others.

The Jamaican economy's swift growth, averaging 6.7% per year from 1950 to 1968, primarily benefited this elite and a growing middle class.[8] Conditions for the black majority only grew worse. Agricultural stagnation displaced many from the rural areas, so that unemployment, after dropping in the 1950s due to emigration, rose again. By 1967, 18% of the work force was unemployed and many more under-employed.[9] Their desperation grew as Jamaica's development "boom" left a majority of the population behind.

In Trinidad and Tobago, Dr. Eric Williams took office in 1956 a firm proponent of industrialization, which had been initiated in Trinidad by the preceding government of Albert Gomes. Under the "Pioneer Status Act," foreign firms were encouraged to set up branch plants to assemble consumer goods such as automobiles, televisions and refrigerators for the local market. Many multinationals established subsidiaries in Trinidad, seeing it as a good regional base in the Eastern Caribbean.

Foreign interests controlled the two dominant sectors in the Trinidad economy, oil refining and sugar. U.S. multinationals, notably Texaco and W.R. Grace, dominated the oil sector, and the sugar industry was owned by Caroni Ltd., a subsidiary of the British firm Tate & Lyle. Strikes against these multinationals in the 1960s caused Williams to reverse his early pro-labor posture in favor of a policy of repressing labor struggles. In 1965, a major strike in the sugar industry threatened to produce an unprecedented unity of African and East Indian workers behind the militant, Butlerite trade unionist George Weekes. Williams declared a state of emergency and passed an Industrial Stabilization Act which outlawed strikes in various industries and replaced union negotiation with arbitration by a government-controlled industrial court.

As in Jamaica, economic growth surged ahead in the early years, with real gross domestic product growing by 8.5% per year from 1951 to 1961. But unemployment also rose, standing at 14% in 1966 with another one-third of the work force under-employed.[10]

By the end of the 1960s, it was clear to many in the region that "industrialization by invitation is really the absentee owner transferred from agriculture to industry."[11] Political power was now in black and brown hands, but foreign interests still dominated Caribbean economies, with the participation of local white, mulatto and other non-black elites. The trickle-down theory of the Puerto Rican model—that growth would automatically improve conditions for everyone—proved false. While the middle class expanded and living standards soared for a privileged few, the majority of farmers, workers and youth were worse off than ever before. ∎

Black Power Protests & Emergence of the Left

In the West Indies, as in many other parts of the world, the sixties were a decade of protest. It brought together two social sectors: radical intellectuals moving to side with the poor, and a new generation of youth, workers and the unemployed, whose anger with the system had reached the breaking point. The mix opened up new possibilities for left politics in the region.

Intellectual Roots of the Movement

Intellectuals began organizing in Guyana in 1962, calling themselves the New World Group. The group acquired branches in Trinidad and Jamaica and began to publish a journal, *New World Quarterly.* Consisting primarily of faculty at the University of Guyana and the three regional campuses of the University of the West Indies (UWI), New World challenged the assumptions of traditional Caribbean social science. The economists of the group, including Maurice Odle and Clive Thomas in Guyana, Lloyd Best in Trinidad, George Beckford and Norman Girvan in Jamaica, compared the economic dependency of the plantation system to that of the Puerto Rican model. Political scientists like James Millette in Trinidad and Trevor Munroe in Jamaica focused on the continuation of the colonial power structure after independence. Historians Walter Rodney, Woodville Marshall and Douglas Hall reinterpreted the region's history from an Afro-Caribbean perspective; while sociologist Orlando Patterson analyzed the effects of colonialism and slavery on the "Caribbean man."[1]

These scholars and others like them were the product of a colonial educational system which sent the highest achievers on to universities in Europe, Canada and the United States. Upon their return home, graduates would move into coveted academic, government and professional posts, ensuring their identification with the system of class privilege. This pattern began to break down with the second generation of graduates when some made the unprecedented choice of siding with the poor. This reflected in part a new understanding of racism gained abroad. Light-complexioned members of the middle class found themselves labeled "black" in Europe and North America, with all the discrimination that entailed.

This new racial awareness was reinforced by their exposure to the Pan-African movement in Paris, London and the United States. The intellectual roots of Pan-Africanism went back to Marcus Garvey, and flowered anew in the 1950s around the struggle to decolonize Africa. A seminal influence in the fifties was the writing of Franz Fanon, a Martiniquan psychiatrist practicing in colonial Algeria. Fanon emphasized the destructive effects of racism on the personality of a colonized people, calling for violent resistance as the only means of achieving liberation. Even more controversial was his criticism of the black intelligensia for failing to lead an active anti-colonial struggle. Fanon thus called into question the whole decolonization process which transferred power grad-ually to a black and brown elite.

In London, West Indian and African intellectuals came together in the International African Service Bureau, founded by Trinidadian George Padmore. Its members included figures who would later lead Africa to independence, among them Kwame Nkrumah, Julius Nyerere and Jomo Kenyatta. The Bureau's journal, *International African Opinion,* was edited by another Trinidadian, C.L.R. James, whose formulation of an independent black Marxism was to strongly influence the English-speaking Caribbean left. James envisioned a direct democracy built on local citizen assemblies.[2] He argued that the worldwide struggle of blacks was independent of, but contributed to, the socialist struggle led by Marxist parties and trade unions.[3]

James and Padmore both spent years in the United States and helped link the civil rights struggle there to the anti-colonial movement. The emerging Black Power movement counted among its leaders Caribbean-Americans such as Stokely Carmichael, born in Trinidad, and Malcolm X, whose mother was Grenadian. The travels of these and other spokespersons helped tie the movement together as it developed in the connected poles of Africa, the West Indies, Europe and the United States.

Frantz Fanon

While these trends developed in relation to the English and French-speaking islands, the Spanish-speaking Caribbean provided the first example of a country to implement radical change. The Cuban revolution's impact on the English-speaking left was mainly symbolic in the sixties, not least because information about Cuba was scarce. But leftwing intellectuals noted with interest the emergence of a development path radically different from the Puerto Rican model, and they admired Cuban daring in severing neocolonial relations with the north. Serious analysis of Cuban socialism would not occur until the next decade, when governments in Jamaica and Grenada used Cuba as a model for some of their reforms.

From its roots in anti-colonialism, the concept of Third World solidarity broadened during the sixties. The positive formulation of this theme came out of Cuban calls for a "Tri-Continental Unity" between the peoples of Asia, Africa and Latin America. The negative side developed fully after the Dominican invasion, leading to a clear anti-imperialist ideology among Caribbean progressives. The war in Vietnam reinforced the image of a United States bent on denying self-determination to Third World peoples.

Walter Rodney

Youth, Students and Rastafari

As these ideological currents took shape, a new Caribbean generation was coming of age. The youth population had expanded at a phenomenal rate: in some territories, 60% of the population was under 25 years old. Secondary education had become generalized in the 1950s, and the mid-60s saw the first wave of educated, unemployed youth hit the streets. They did so just as tourism was assuming a dominant place in Caribbean economies. The sight of black people as waiters, chauffeurs and bellhops for rich tourists seemed to symbolize the foreign domination and racism of the society. Yet widespread unemployment left little choice. A subculture of angry youths emerged in the crowded slums of West Indian capitals, ready to explode.

In this context, Rastafarianism broadened its appeal as a social philosophy proclaiming the dignity of African people. Most numerous in Jamaica, the Rastafari were heavily repressed in the 1950s and 1960s by the Jamaican government. Despite their marginal status, the Rastas' emphasis on Africa and their assertion of black pride shook the color-conscious Caribbean to its foundations.

The late 1960s saw new political groups form on university campuses, drawing cultural inspiration from Rastafarianism and Pan Africanism. Some students and graduates became Rastas, broadening the cult from its base in the urban poor. The groups published newsletters with symbolic names, such as *Abeng* in Jamaica (*abeng* is the Ashanti word for the conch shell blown by slaves as a call to revolt); *Moko* in Trinidad (referring to the Moko-jumbie, an African spirit figure); and *Ratoon* in Guyana (referring to the growth of sugar cane). In the Eastern Caribbean islands of St. Vincent, St. Lucia and Grenada, young intellectuals organized "Forums" to discuss social change. All these groups were the forerunners of left parties which would emerge in the next decade.

1968 Explosions: Jamaica and Antigua

Intellectual leader of the Black Power movement in the Caribbean was Dr. Walter Rodney, a Guyanese historian then teaching at UWI's Jamaica campus. Rodney, a scholar of African history, defined Black Power as follows:

> First, a break with imperialism which is historically white racist. Second, the assumption of power by the Black masses in the islands. Third, the cultural reconstruction of the society in the image of Blacks.[4]

Rodney identified the Rastafarians as "the leading force of this expression of Black consciousness." This message from the respected Rodney, as well as his socialist leanings, threatened the upper class, and in 1968 the Jamaican government banned Rodney from the island. His expulsion triggered rioting which was put down by the Jamaican security forces. Three people died and damages reached one million pounds. Sympathy protests followed in Trinidad, Barbados, Guyana, and among West Indians in New York and Montreal.

That same year, a general strike in Antigua nearly brought down the government of premier Vere C. Bird, one of the original politicians to rise to power through trade unionism. Development during the 1960s had made foreign-owned tourism virtually the only industry in Antigua. Although Bird headed Antigua's largest union, his strategy as head of government was to make concessions to employers in order to keep them in Antigua. When the second-in-command of Bird's union, George Walter, left to form a more militant union, the workers transferred their allegiance overnight.

Bird's refusal to recognize the new union sparked a march of thousands of Antiguans through the streets of St. John's, protesting the exploitation of workers by the foreign owners.

May 30, 1969: Workers at the Shell Oil Refinery in Curaçao prepare to strike.

The leadership of the new union included Tim Hector, a teacher who had studied in Canada. He and Walter organized a general strike, to which the government responded by declaring a state of emergency. Workers and youth battled police in the streets, the British stepped in to mediate, and finally Bird offered to resign.

Influenced by the British, Walter reached an accommodation with Bird, leaving the government in power. This led to a split between Walter and Hector: Walter continued in trade unionism, while Hector entered left politics as leader of the newly-formed Afro-Caribbean Liberation Movement.

Curaçao: The May Movement

From 1917 onward a single multinational, Royal Dutch Shell, dominated the economy of Curaçao. Supplied with crude oil from neighboring Venezuela, the giant Shell refinery initially provided jobs for Curaçaoan workers. But economic power in the Dutch colony remained in the hands of Dutch firms, in partnership with a local elite consisting of whites of Dutch descent, mulattos, Lebanese and Jews. From this group was drawn most of the ruling Democratic Party which controlled the central government of the Netherlands Antilles and stayed in power through economic aid from Holland.

Beginning in the 1950s, automation sharply reduced the number of jobs at the refinery, from 11,000 in 1952 to 4,000 in 1969.[5] Shell also turned over many of its functions to subcontractors who paid lower wages than Shell itself. The government meanwhile imposed a wage freeze in hopes of attracting new industry and tourism. While workers faced joblessness and lower wages, Dutch expatriates and local whites continued to occupy highly-paid positions as bureaucrats, managers and technicians.

As in Antigua, the catalyst was the emergence of new leadership comprising trade unionists (in this case the head of the port workers) and intellectuals. The latter included Curaçaoans who had returned from studies in Holland and were publishing a newspaper in Papiamentu which put forth a class and racial analysis of local labor problems. From mid-1968 on labor unrest spread through the island. The flashpoint came on May 30, 1969 with a wage dispute at WESCAR, one of Shell's Dutch subcontractors. The protest by 400 workers quickly became a riot as 5,000 striking and unemployed workers marched from the refinery into the heart of Willemstad. There their anger exploded in looting, vandalism and arson. Holland rushed in a detachment of 300 Marines who helped local police and Dutch Marines stationed in Curaçao to quell the uprising.

Five days later, threatened with a general strike, the government resigned. A new political party was formed, the "Frente Obrero i Liberacion 30 di Mey 1969" (May 30, 1969 Workers and Liberation Front). Although it was the first worker-led party in Curaçao's history, in elections that September the Frente won only 3 of 12 seats, and the ruling party returned to power. This defeat reflected the spontaneous, unorganized and minority character of the May movement. While most people could identify with the strikers' grievances, they were taken aback by the violence, and the Frente was perceived as having no ideological consensus, organizational base or political plan.[6]

The May movement nonetheless brought pressure for reforms. The government passed a minimum wage law, and wages rose 20-30% in the lower brackets. Shell and its subcontractors replaced many foreign managers and technicians with Curaçaoans, and a similar process took place in the civil service. These nationalistic reforms paved the way for the MAN party which came to power with a social-democratic agenda in 1979.

Trinidad: Black Power Protest

The last of the Black Power protests in the Caribbean broke out in Trinidad. In 1969, a group of Trinidadian and other West Indian students at the Sir George Williams University in Canada were arrested for destroying the university's computers during a protest against the racism of a professor. In Trinidad, students on the University of the West Indies campus organized in support of the arrested students, demanding that the Trinidad government provide legal assistance.

These activities led to the formation of the National Joint Action Committee (NJAC), led by UWI student Geddes Granger. NJAC soon grew beyond its university origins to encompass some two dozen organizations, including the progressive wing of the labor movement. The introduction of the Industrial Stabilization Act in the mid-1960s had split the trade unions into a pro-government and an anti-government camp. A transport strike in open defiance of the ISA strengthened ties between NJAC and union leaders such as George Weekes of the Oilfields Workers Trade Union and Clive Nunez of the Transport and Industrial Workers Union.

As elsewhere, the social backdrop was one of rising unemployment and economic domination by a racial elite. Of the executives and managers of major firms, only 4% were black, while 53% were white and the rest mulatto, Chinese and East Indian.[7] Trinidad differed from other West Indian societies, however, in that the working class was split between blacks—in the oil and industrial sector—and East Indians, in the rural sugar sector.

On February 26, 1970, Geddes Granger and about 200 students began a march through Port-of-Spain to protest the government's handling of the Sir George Williams University affair. To the surprise of even the organizers, the crowd swelled rapidly as thousands of youth and unemployed workers joined its ranks. The marchers turned first on the visible symbols of Canadian imperialism, the Canadian banks in downtown Port-of-Spain. They then moved on to the Chamber of Commerce and the Roman Catholic Cathedral. For 55 days, the city reverberated with the angry chants of the marchers. The Rev. Roy Neehall, then head of the Caribbean Conference of Churches at its Port-of-Spain office, recalls the protest:

> They used the symbols and the language of the Black Power movement, but it was certainly far more than something that had to do with the color of their skin. It grew and grew until they started challenging everything in the society that represented established power and privilege. They challenged the Church too, because the Church seemed to be very much linked up with the government, and to be a place where distinctions were made between those who were privileged and those who were poor.[8]

The march had begun with "Black Power" as its slogan, but the organizers soon had to confront the implications of defining their protest in solely racial terms. In an attempt to manipulate the old African/East Indian division, the Eric Williams government labeled the march "anti-Indian." On March 12, the protesters marched to Caroni, in the heart of the sugar district, to show solidarity with the East Indian sugar workers then locked in struggle with the reactionary head of their union, Bhadase Maraj. The plan was that the sugar workers would march to Port-of-Spain and join black unions in a general strike—the African/Indian unity which the ruling class so feared.

It was at this point that the Williams government broke its long silence and declared a state of emergency, ordering the detention of Granger and other leaders. The same day, a mutiny broke out in Trinidad's 700-man army in support of the demonstrators. Williams called in U.S. and Venezuelan warships which sat offshore while a curfew was imposed, and the protests subsided.

> They probably could have achieved a good deal more if they had been given enough time to unite the urban folk with the rural sugar workers. But because political power had been based on the divisions within the society, including racial divisions, the government realized that any unity between East Indians and people of African descent would be the end of power for them. It was the movement toward the unity of the two groups that led to the declaration of the state of emergency and the structures of oppression against those who were calling for change.[9]

After the Trinidad uprising, governments around the region took measures to curb the spread of Black Power. NJAC leaders were barred from entering Barbados. In Jamaica, officials seized writings by Malcolm X and Eldridge Cleaver. Two members of Belize's United Black Association for Development were tried for "seditious conspiracy" on the basis of an article in their newsletter, *Amandala*. And in Grenada, premier Eric Gairy doubled the size of the police force and created a paramilitary squad, the Mongoose Gang.

Out of the protests of the sixties emerged the leaders and organizations of the contemporary Caribbean left. In the following years, most attempted to move beyond the racial confines of "Black Power." The Afro-Caribbean Liberation Movement, for example, became the Antigua Caribbean Liberation Movement. Most groups initially rejected participation in electoral politics. They styled themselves "movements" or used similar non-party designations, such as the Youlou Liberation Movement in St. Vincent, the Workers' Liberation League in Jamaica, the Working People's Alliance in Guyana, and the New Jewel Movement in Grenada. ■

New Directions: Jamaica and Trinidad

The unrest of the sixties brought pressure on political leaders throughout the West Indies. In the two main centers of protest, Trinidad and Jamaica, governments in the 1970s undertook major experiments in social reform. Of the two, Jamaica's eight-year experiment with democratic socialism was the more serious attempt at social change. Although it failed to break the existing power structure in Jamaica, it had a far-reaching impact on politics throughout the region.

Trinidad's "Third Way"

The 1970 Black Power protest forced a shift in the policies of Eric Williams' government. While responding to the unrest with repressive measures, the government simultaneously released its "Perspectives of the New Society." Tacitly acknowledging that past policies had failed, Williams declared that Trinidad & Tobago would pursue a "Third Way" that was neither Cuban socialism nor the Puerto Rican model. This would be done by bringing the state into the economy as full and part owner of productive enterprise, and by cultivating a new small business class. By 1972, foreign investors in the key economic sectors were required to have local partners.[1]

It was, however, the OPEC countries' increase in the price of oil in 1973 which marked the true turning point. Almost overnight, Trinidad's revenues from oil refining multiplied seven-fold. Williams used the windfall to create a huge state sector. Enterprises which the government acquired in full included Shell's oil refining operations, Tate & Lyle's sugar estates, British West Indian Airways, and the telephone and television companies. New state-owned industries were created in iron and steel production, natural gas and cement.

In other areas, the government entered into joint ventures with private capital. By 1980 the state was the dominant partner in the economy, with assets valued at over $400 million.[2]

These changes were not linked to a socialist vision or even any long-term plan for self-reliance. The economy boomed, but it was a boom due entirely to the price of oil, over which Trinidad had no control. Foreign multinationals, notably Texaco, continued to control the extraction and refining of Trinidadian oil. Most Trinidadians had money to spend in the late 1970s. But beneath the affluent facade, the economy remained vulnerable, setting the stage for trouble when the oil boom ended.

Democratic Socialism in Jamaica

The height of Jamaica's Black Power movement coincided with a transfer of leadership within the People's National Party (PNP). Norman Manley, the party's founder, died in 1969, and his son Michael was elected to replace him. Michael Manley incorporated Black Power and Rastafarian themes into his campaign, and support for him coalesced among youth and the poor. At the same time, members of the elite also were frustrated with the insensitive Jamaica Labour Party government. Supported by a multi-class alliance, Manley won the 1972 election on a platform promising "Power for the People" and "Better Must Come."

The centerpiece of the new government was an array of social programs benefiting the poor, especially women, youth and the unemployed. They included a literacy campaign, free secondary education, a job creation program, the building of public housing, and a program to lease idle lands to small farmers. Rent controls and price controls on basic foods eased the burden on working-class families. The government passed laws to promote women's rights, including maternity leave and equal pay for equal work. A minimum wage law included domestic servants and agricultural laborers, the lowest-paid workers in the society.

This domestic thrust was mirrored by a foreign policy oriented toward the Third World. Manley became a prominent advocate of the New International Economic Order, aimed at gaining fair treatment for raw materials producers. In this context, the government asked the foreign bauxite firms to renegotiate their contracts. When the companies refused, the government imposed a bauxite production levy which tied Jamaica's revenues to the price of the finished aluminum, bypassing transfer pricing. The levy increased Jamaica's income by almost $150 million in the first year.[3]

In 1974 the PNP gave ideological form to these actions by announcing a turn to democratic socialism. It explained the concept largely in terms of values, such as "equality" and "love." Specifics were few, other than that the government would pursue a mixed economy with state, private and cooperative sectors. The government did move to nationalize holdings in key economic sectors. These included the bauxite lands and 51% of the mining operations, as well as the sugar estates, some hotels, the utilities, public transport, and Radio Jamaica.

These nationalizations were a more extensive version of what many other Caribbean governments were doing in the same period. Some of the acquisitions were even forced on the government, as in the case of money-losing hotels and sugar estates. The private sector's overall dominance was never challenged, although the share of state and cooperative ownership rose from 2% to 20% of the total.[4]

Yet by 1975, opinion within the Jamaican upper class and in Washington had turned decisively against the PNP. While its reforms were moderate, the Manley government's socialist rhetoric led Jamaican capitalists to fear that more drastic measures lay ahead. They pointed to the rising influence of the PNP's vocal left wing. At a deeper level, upper and middle-class Jamaicans feared the PNP's efforts to mobilize the poor and black masses as a political force. Elite reaction was spearheaded by the powerful daily newspaper the *Gleaner,* which attacked the government for economic mismanagement and communist leanings.

Against this backdrop, the Manley government's foreign policy and especially its ties with Cuba became symbolic evidence of a lurch to the left. Friendship between Manley and

Fidel Castro led to joint projects between the two countries in agriculture, fishing and education. Cuban volunteers built houses, schools and dams in Jamaica and Cuban doctors worked in the public hospitals.

It was the Cuban connection which received the most attention in the United States. For the Ford administration and Secretary of State Henry Kissinger, a key event may have been Jamaica's diplomatic support for Cuba when Havana sent troops to Angola in 1975. Whatever the precise turning point, relations deteriorated, and U.S. economic aid to Jamaica was cut from $13 million in 1974 to $4 million in 1975.[5]

Official hostility was reflected in a stream of sensational press reports on Jamaica. Prominent publications like the *New York Times* and *Newsweek* warned of growing Cuban influence, citing unnamed U.S. government sources. American tourists, formerly 75% of visitors to Jamaica, stayed away.

Economic Crisis and the IMF

By 1976 the Jamaican economy was in crisis. The government was spending heavily on social programs. Imports from abroad were increasing in cost, led by the huge increase in the price of oil. But while spending soared, revenues had fallen in the key foreign exchange-producing sectors. Bauxite exports, the economic mainstay, were depressed by weak world demand for aluminum and the global restructuring of the bauxite industry. Sugar prices fell sharply, and tourism had all but collapsed. While the bauxite levy provided extra income, it could not make up for the overall losses. The government had financed its spending largely with commercial bank loans, but by 1976 few foreign banks would lend more to Jamaica.

New foreign and domestic investment withered. Jamaican businessmen froze their investments, sent their money abroad and finally emigrated. As the economy deteriorated many middle-class professionals joined them in leaving for Miami and New York.

In 1976 a wave of mysterious violence struck Jamaica, including arson and attacks on firefighters and police. High-powered weapons were entering the country in unprecedented quantities, arming gangs of JLP and PNP partisans in the tough Kingston slums. The PNP leadership believed the rising violence to be part of a CIA plan to destabilize the government. Whether or not the CIA was in direct control, the JLP-*Gleaner* opposition clearly relied on some form of U.S. backing.[6]

Amid these problems the PNP won reelection in 1976 with an even larger margin of support than in 1972. This reflected the party's successful mobilization of ordinary Jamaicans behind the promise of democratic socialism. Yet within the PNP itself, conflict between the party's left and right wings was growing. By 1977, PNP leftwingers who favored deepening the social change process had lost out to those who wanted an accommodation with Jamaican and international capitalists.

This shifting balance of power was reflected in a critical decision Manley made that year. In signing a loan agreement with the International Monetary Fund, Manley signalled to the international community that he desired cooperation, not confrontation. Other western loans hinged on IMF approval, and the new Carter administration was sending signals of its

Michael Manley

Everybody's Magazine

willingness to talk. Manley felt he had no choice. Rejecting a plan favored by the PNP left which called for more radical economic restructuring, he instead placed the failing economy fully in the hands of the IMF.

The austerity imposed by the IMF wrecked the PNP's social programs and brought new hardship to Jamaicans [see Part V, Ch. 2]. By the time the PNP reversed itself and broke with the Fund, its popularity had been destroyed. The government no longer appeared in control of the economy, or the country. This impression was heightened by the PNP's inability to curb the gang warfare which claimed 800 lives in the period leading up to the 1980 election.

Under Edward Seaga's conservative leadership, the JLP had the support of Washington and the international financial community. It could promise access to new loans and investment. It promised also to restore peace to a country torn by political violence, violence instigated in large part by the JLP itself. In October 1980, an exhausted electorate voted the JLP into power by an overwhelming margin. Jamaica's democratic socialist experiment had come to an end. ■

The New Jewel Movement

In 1970, a young Maurice Bishop was returning home to Grenada from England where he had recently qualified as a lawyer. He passed through Trinidad at the moment of the Black Power uprising. Back in Grenada, he and others organized a sympathy demonstration which also attacked the corrupt rule of premier Eric Gairy.

Later that year a group of Grenadian nurses marched peacefully to protest the appalling conditions at the St. George's hospital. They were joined by others, and the march became a larger protest against the government. Gairy's police attacked the march, beating and arresting the nurses. Bishop and another young lawyer, Kenrick Radix, defended the nurses in a trial which attracted regional attention.

Two years later Bishop and Radix formed the Movement for Assembly of the Peoples (MAP). MAP proposed a grassroots democracy based on village assemblies inspired by the Marxian populism of C.L.R. James. Around the same time, a U.S.-educated economist named Unison Whiteman started JEWEL—Joint Endeavor for Welfare, Education and Liberation. In March 1973 the two organizations merged to form the New Jewel Movement.

The NJM resembled other fledgling left groups, but there was a difference: Gairy's repression. Gairy was an eccentric petty tyrant, who held power through patronage, vote fraud and thuggery. Grenadians dubbed his army the "Green Beasts," and his paramilitary Mongoose Gang was made up of convicted criminals. Gairy also profited from a lack of political alternatives. For two decades, the only opposition had come from the Grenada National Party, which was tied to the planter/merchant elite and was unpopular with ordinary Grenadians.

Repression forced the NJM to be a well-organized party with a strategy for building a grassroots base. It organized clandestinely, holding house meetings to discuss an agenda for change. Because Gairy's reputation embarrassed the middle class and his corruption infringed on their interests, the NJM was able to forge a multi-class alliance. In November 1973, the Mongoose Gang attacked six NJM leaders and beat them savagely, shocking public opinion. Soon after that "Bloody Sunday," a coalition of businessmen, clergy and other middle-class leaders joined workers in an island-wide strike that fell just short of toppling Gairy.

The NJM formed a tactical alliance with the Grenada National Party to contest the 1976 election. Gairy won through his usual tactics, but the NJM became the official opposition in Parliament. Gairy rode roughshod over the Parliamentary process. He also moved to strengthen links with Pinochet's Chile, which began supplying weapons to the Grenadian army. It was clear to everyone that Gairy would never allow himself to be voted out.

Gairy's reign ended on March 13, 1979, when 46 armed supporters of the New Jewel Movement stormed the army barracks at True Blue and surprised the sleeping soldiers. From there they captured the radio station and broadcast the

Maurice Bishop

news of liberation. Thousands of jubilant Grenadians poured into the streets and helped capture the remaining members of the army and the Mongoose Gang. By the end of the day, at a cost of three lives, the New Jewel Movement was in control.

The Grenada revolution initially was characterized by populist politics, social reform and broad popular support. It lacked ideological definition, and varying tendencies existed among the members of the NJM inner circle. But as the party was very small, these internal divisions remained hidden from public view. Instead, Grenadians rallied to support the programs of the revolution, which raised the standard of living on the island.

As in Grenada, the left throughout the English-speaking Caribbean was in a process of ideological formation. They had come out of the Black Power movement but sought to move beyond it to define an agenda for social change. The central role of university students infused a strong interest in Marxism and Leninism, but there was no agreement on how these concepts should be applied to the Caribbean. Toward the end of the 1970s, some left groups declared themselves parties and entered the electoral arena. Their weak showing underscored the difficulty of entering into competition with the established parties without having built a strong popular base.

These incipient problems—ideological divisions and elitism—would later spell disaster in Grenada and seriously weaken the left in other countries. But little of this future was visible at the close of the 1970s, when the Grenada revolution stood as a powerful symbol of progressive unity, strength and popular support. ∎

Religious Opening in the 1970s

... and creation of the Caribbean Conference of Churches

After World War Two, the mainline Catholic and Protestant churches in the Caribbean became more broadly middle-class in constituency and attitude. Besides their primary evangelical thrust, they continued their educational and social service activities for the poor. But they remained dominated by expatriate clergy and approached the poor in a paternalistic manner, preaching deference to authority which reinforced the status quo.

The reformist political process of the 1950s and '60s did not profoundly affect the Church. The failed West Indies Federation did not bring regional unity, industrialization did not eliminate unemployment or poverty, and political independence left many of the colonial attitudes in the society untouched. Instead, it was the grassroots protest against these unchanged conditions which shook the Church and forced it to begin dealing internally with the remnants of its colonizing role. The Cuban revolution, the U.S. invasion of the Dominican Republic, and the Black Power movement all were pivotal in forcing the conservative Church to begin to look toward change.

The Cuban revolution galvanized hemispheric awareness of the poverty issue and spurred the search for a "developmentalist" model of change which would avoid the need for revolution. The modern Caribbean ecumenical movement came out of the effort to apply such a developmentalist approach to poverty in the Caribbean. Initially these were small, local initiatives, such as the credit union movement started by a nun in Dominica in the 1950s, or the two Barbadian clergymen who addressed the problem of unemployment in the early sixties. Such projects led to an ecumenical dialogue on social issues, resulting in the formation in 1969 of CADEC, Christian Action for Development in the Eastern Caribbean.

Initially funded by Church World Service, the development and disaster relief arm of the National Council of Churches of the USA, CADEC was to become a huge program spanning the English and Dutch Caribbean, with liaison to the French and Spanish islands. It funded grassroots projects in areas such as agriculture, fisheries, small business, and crafts. Despite the positive impact of these projects at the local level, however, progressive church thinkers increasingly questioned the entire developmentalist approach. Out of this first church response to poverty came a new attitude which sought to wrestle with questions of cause, not merely relief.

The Black Power protest which spun through the region at the close of the sixties ended any illusion that the problem of poverty could be solved without first addressing the racial and class structure of Caribbean society. In response to the upheaval, the churches came together for what was to be a turning point: the Ecumenical Consultation on Development, held in Trinidad in 1971. Out of this meeting came a groundbreaking theological piece by the Rev. Idris Hamid, then principal of St. Andrew's Theological College in Trinidad. Entitled "In Search of New Perspectives," the paper critiqued developmentalism and called for the Church to launch a process of internal change:

> The task of the Church is not merely to provide a few more jobs and promote a few projects, essential as these may be. The Church must undertake the more serious task of deep reflection and searching. Within this endeavor, it must engage in the "de-colonialization" of its theology. "Colonialization" took place on at least four levels: political, economic, cultural, and religious. Political independence is merely the ribbon-cutting stage of "de-colonialization," which has not gone as far as the cultural and religious levels where colonialism has done its dirtiest work.[1]

During the Trinidad consultation, the Rt. Rev. Roque Adames from the Dominican Republic introduced the term *concientizacion* (consciousness-raising), coined by the Brazilian educator Paulo Freire. The Roman Catholic Bishop defined the term in this way: "Concientizacion is not only knowledge . . . it is recognition of oneself and others and at the same time, because of this, it is a choice, decision and commitment. It is the task of being humanized and humanizing others . . . "[2] New voices from other areas of the Caribbean were adding their perspective to the emerging social awareness of the churches.

The context for these developments was a growing international ecumenical movement, led off by the ecumenical and social concerns declarations of Vatican II. This was followed in 1966 by a World Council of Churches conference on church and society, and by a Papal Encyclical on the Development of Peoples in 1967. That year also saw the formation of a joint Vatican/World Council of Churches Committee on Society, Development and Peace (SODEPAX), with a North American Jesuit priest as general secretary and a Trinidadian Presbyterian minister, the Rev. Roy Neehall, as associate general secretary.

Formation of the CCC

In this context, momentum grew toward a Caribbean experiment in ecumenical relations: the joining of forces between the Protestants and Catholics of the region. The mandate for such a body was affirmed at the Trinidad consultation by 260 representatives from 25 denominations spanning 16 territories in the English, Spanish, French and Dutch-speaking Caribbean. Two years later, in 1973, the Caribbean Conference of Churches came into being, with CADEC as its development arm. The CCC called for a regional Christian unity which would transcend the old colonial barriers:

We as Christian people of the Caribbean, separated from each other by barriers of history, language, culture, class and distance, desire, because of our common calling in Christ to join together in a regional fellowship of churches for inspiration, consultation, and cooperative action. We are deeply concerned to promote the human liberation of our people, and are committed to the achievement of social justice and the dignity of man in our society . . . [3]

One sign of the seriousness of this regionalism was that various churches from Cuba were invited to join the CCC. During the 1960s, Cuban Protestant and Catholic leaders had begun to speak out about the biblical and theological lessons of the revolution. By opening itself to this socio-religious process, the CCC reinforced the political opening of the year before, when Jamaica, Barbados, Guyana and Trinidad jointly established diplomatic relations with Cuba.

In the realm of theology, the CCC made an immediate impact through the publication of two anthologies of writings by leading Caribbean theologians, entitled *With Eyes Wide Open* and *Troubling of the Waters*. Edited by Idris Hamid, *Troubling of the Waters* interpreted the Black Power movement as a prophetic call, challenging the Church's complicity with racism and its lack of an incarnational theology. The Rev. Ashley Smith, pastor of the United Church in Jamaica, wrote:

[Falsely preaching] that the Gospel is concerned with man's soul and not with his personality and his rights in the economic and legal situation where he "lives and moves and has his being" . . . has contributed to making the Church a party to the dehumanization of the Black man and also the perpetuation of a situation in which the majority of the people suffer the anaesthetic effects of abject poverty in the midst of growing affluence for a few.[4]

The basic thrust of these writings was to call for the development of a new theology which would be genuinely Caribbean, not an import or imitation. As Idris Hamid argued:

God is really foreign to us. In the religious imagination of our people he is a benign white foreigner—an "expatriate." Even the categories of our religious experience are imports which do not reflect our cultural and native experiences. We experience God as an outsider.[5]

"The foremost task of theology in the Caribbean," wrote the Rev. Hamid, "is to work for the recovery of Caribbean man."[6] This was affirmed by another theologian, Dr. Robert Moore of Guyana, who said:

In order to explore the relationship between God and Caribbean Man, it is necessary that Caribbean Man do more exploration of himself, his environment, and the forces which have given that environment their peculiar structure; in other words, his history.[7]

In keeping with this aim, the CCC complemented its development and theological activities with a monthly newspaper, *Caribbean Contact*. Along with news of the ecumenical movement and reflections by regional religious leaders, *Contact* provided a forum for discussion of social, economic,

political, and cultural developments on a Caribbean-wide basis. It soon became the primary journalistic attempt to tie together the concerns of disparate parts of the region.

Paralleling the CCC's own religious "opening," the 1970s saw the emergence of many small, grassroots church-linked projects dedicated to action for social justice. Sometimes under denominational auspices, these were more often ecumenical or simply the private initiative of activists linked to the Church. The Caribbean Ecumenical Programme, formed in Trinidad in 1976, worked under the direction of Idris Hamid to help people examine their faith in relation to the historical, economic and cultural reality of the Caribbean. In St. Vincent, the Catholic Church set up the Commission for Development of the Peoples to do training and grassroots organizing among Vincentien farmers; while Catholic and Protestant activists independent of the Church organized the Ecumenical Study Group to reflect on social issues in the light of the Gospel message. In the Dominican Republic, the Center for Ecumenical Planning and Action (CEPAE) began in 1969 to work with the Dominican peasantry and base Christian communities on development projects and popular education.

In many cases, these grassroots religious projects overlapped in terms of philosophy and persons with the new political groups emerging during the same era. This was one aspect of a larger process in which activists with religious backgrounds were becoming prominent in regional movements for social change. In Jamaica, for instance, the Jesuit-linked Social Action Centre (SAC, Ltd) helped workers on the sugar estates successfully organize to demand worker-run cooperatives from the Manley government. In the French Antilles, still under colonial rule, Catholic priests and nuns became increasingly involved in the political independence movement. The National Ecumenical Movement of Puerto Rico (PRISA) grew out of an initially modest effort by the Episcopal Church in 1968 to train clergy in a social ministry for the urban San Juan area. It broadened into popular education and organizing among rural communities, workers, youth and Christians, aimed at enabling them to "organize themselves to transform [their] reality and effect their own liberation."[8]

Inevitably, this convergence of religious and secular activism raised hackles in the conservative bastions of the Church. The CCC in the 1970s was not a unified body representing only one religious tendency, nor were all the tendencies within its constituencies equally represented. The CCC leadership basically reflected the thinking of younger, liberal-to-progressive Christians, whereas the Church hierarchies and local Christian Councils were mainly older and more conservative. These two tendencies often found themselves in tension as the decade wore on.

Some of these tensions focused on *Caribbean Contact,* which was steadily gaining recognition as the foremost voice of progressive journalism in the region. *Contact* regularly explored such broad social themes as Caribbean unity, the economic crisis, social change movements, and global issues such as South African apartheid and the north-south dialogue. This made conservative Church leaders highly uneasy to the point of branding *Contact,* privately if not publicly, as "out and out communistic."[9] During the 1970s, these tensions did not erupt into open fights since the Christian Councils in each country tended to go along with the CCC on account of its official status, its large program staff and CADEC's huge financial resources. But there were resentments over the CCC's political positions, theological concepts and bureaucratic privileges (such as staff "junketing" around the Caribbean). These grumblings represented gathering storm clouds which would produce hail and lightning during the 1980s.

The seeds of such divisions were in a sense inherent in the formation of the CCC, with its call not merely to change the social role of the Church, but for the Church itself to change from within. As the CCC's general secretary, the Rev. Roy Neehall, stated at the body's 1973 inaugural assembly:

> In the past the churches have tried to meet the needs of people, but often our efforts have been an inadequate response and have had only a superficial impact. We treated symptoms, yet left the causes untouched. There was an embarrassing gap between the prophetic voice and the practical step. Suggestions for changes in the churches themselves, in approach, method, and priorities, were taken as a threat to their security and privileged status.[10]

Much had changed, but also much had stayed the same. By the end of the decade, concerned Christians were hearing warnings from Dr. Neehall about the gravity of the task before them:

> A massive dose of persuasion will have to be invented in order to have the rich, the powerful and privileged in the churches agree that to support, and even finance, radical social change in the direction of greater justice will be the most Christian and pragmatic way to avoid the violence and alienation that continued resistance to change is sure to create.[11] ■

Dominican campesinos receiving a course on the importance of peasant organizations from CEPAE, the Center for Ecumenical Planning and Action in the Dominican Republic.

CEPAE

67

NOTES TO PART TWO

Revolution in Cuba

1. Eric Williams, *From Columbus to Castro: History of the Caribbean 1492-1969* (New York: Harper & Row, 1970), p. 464.
2. Warren Hinkle and William Turner, *The Fish is Red: The Story of the Secret War Against Castro* (New York: Harper & Row, 1981), p. 290.
3. Eric Williams, *From Columbus to Castro,* pp. 479-480.
4. Sheldon Liss, *Roots of Revolution: Radical Thought in Cuba* (Lincoln: U. of Nebraska Press, 1987), pp. 105-139.
5. Wayne Smith, *The Closest of Enemies: A Personal and Diplomatic History of the Castro Years* (New York: W.W. Norton, 1987), pp. 16-18.
6. Fidel Castro, *History Will Absolve Me* (Havana: Guairas Book Institute, 1967), pp. 69-70.
7. Hinkle and Turner, pp. 282-290.
8. Smith, pp. 55-56.
9. *Ibid.,* pp. 63-64.
10. Lester D. Langley, *The United States and the Caribbean 1900-1970* (Athens: U. of Georgia Press, 1980), p. 219.
11. Smith, p. 70.
12. Langley, p. 225.
13. Hinkle and Turner, p. 13.

The Shores of Santo Domingo

1. David de Caires, "Guyana After Burnham," *Caribbean Affairs,* Jan.-March 1988, p. 190.
2. Jan Knippers Black, *The Dominican Republic: Politics and Development in an Unsovereign State* (Boston: Allen & Unwin, 1986), p. 27.
3. *Ibid.,* p. 33.
4. *Ibid.,* p. 39.
5. Edward S. Herman and Frank Brodhead, *Demonstration Elections: U.S.-Staged Elections in the Dominican Republic, Vietnam and El Salvador* (Boston: South End Press, 1984), pp. 17-53.
6. Alan Howard, "A Report on Gulf & Western in the Dominican Republic," presented at the Dominican Republic 10th Anniversary Seminar, New York, April 1975.

Haiti: Rise of the Duvaliers

1. Latin America Bureau, *Haiti: Family Business* (Latin America Bureau, 1985), p. 18.
2. Alex Dupuy, "Haiti: The Legacy of Colonialism and Slavery," presented at conference on Haiti, Cornell University, Oct. 16-19, 1986.
3. Latin America Bureau, *Haiti: Family Business,* p. 20.
4. Bernard Diederich and Al Burt, *Papa Doc: The Truth About Haiti Today* (Avon Books, 1969), pp. 115-116.
5. *Ibid.,* p. 196.
6. *Ibid.,* p. 138.

Failure of the Puerto Rican Model

1. Ricardo Campos and Frank Bonilla, "Bootstraps and Enterprise Zones: The Underside of Late Capitalism in Puerto Rico and the United States," *Review,* Vol. 4, Spring 1982, p. 559.
2. EPICA, *Puerto Rico: A People Challenging Colonialism* (Washington, DC: EPICA, 1976), p. 59.
3. Dr. Neftali Garcia, "Puerto Rico: Presencia y Efectos de las Companias Trans-nacionales," paper presented in Washington, DC, May 1983.
4. Dr. Neftali Garcia, "Puerto Rico: The Multinational Presence," *Multinational Monitor,* February 1980. Based on the work of Industrial Mission, a church-sponsored environmental group in Puerto Rico.
5. Frank Bonilla and Ricardo Campos, "Up by the Bootstraps: Ideologies of Social Levitation," paper presented at Hunter College, New York, August 1984.
6. *San Juan Star,* January 20, 1975.
7. Testimony by Ramon Garcia Santiago, Secretary of Social Services, Commonwealth of Puerto Rico, before Subcommittee on Agricultural Research and General Legislation of the U.S. Senate, November 17, 1975.
8. Jay R. Mandle, *Patterns of Caribbean Development: An Interpretive Essay on Economic Change* (New York: Gordon & Breach, 1982), p. 60.
9. *Ibid.,* p. 61.
10. *Ibid.,* pp. 60-61.
11. Antigua Caribbean Liberation Movement, *Liberation: From the Old Wreckage to the New Society* (St. John's, Antigua).

Black Power Protests and Emergence of the Left

1. Frank McDonald, "The Commonwealth Caribbean," in Tad Szulc, *The United States and the Caribbean* (New York: Prentice Hall, 1971), p. 147.
2. C.L.R. James, *The Future in the Present* (London: Allison & Busby, 1977), pp. 169-182.
3. *Ibid.,* p. 120.
4. McDonald, p. 153.
5. Adrian M. Moen, "Curacao 1969: Crisis and Change," in Susan Craig, ed., *Contemporary Caribbean: A Sociological Reader* (Trinidad: S. Craig, 1982), Vol. Two, p. 343.
6. EPICA interview with Angel Salsbach, a leader of the May Movement, Willemstad, April 1984.
7. Susan Craig, "Background to the 1970 Confrontation in Trinidad and Tobago," in Craig, ed., p. 402.
8. EPICA interview with Rev. Roy Neehall, Trinidad, August 1982.
9. *Ibid.*

New Directions: Jamaica and Trinidad

1. Raphael Sebastien, "State Sector Development in Trinidad & Tobago 1956-1982," *Tribune* (Trinidad), June 1982, p. 56.
2. *Ibid.,* p. 62.
3. Jamaica Bauxite Institute, "Bauxite: Alumina and Aluminum in 1975," Kingston, 1976, p. 32.
4. Evelyne Huber Stephens and John D. Stephens, *Democratic Socialism in Jamaica* (Princeton: Princeton U. Press, 1986), p. 282.
5. United States Agency for International Development, cited in Stephens and Stephens, p. 397.
6. Stephens and Stephens, p. 236.

Religious Opening in the 1970s

1. Idris Hamid, "In Search of New Perspectives," paper prepared for the Caribbean Ecumenical Consultation for Development, November 1971.
2. *Called to Be—The Official Report of the Caribbean Ecumenical Consultation for Development* (Barbados: CADEC, 1972).
3. Preamble to the Constitution of the Caribbean Conference of Churches.
4. The Rt. Rev. Ashley Smith, "The Religious Significance of Black Power in Caribbean Churches," in Idris Hamid, ed., *Troubling of the Waters* (Trinidad: Idris Hamid, 1973), pp. 87-88.
5. Hamid, "In Search of New Perspectives."
6. Idris Hamid, "Theology and Caribbean Development," in David I. Mitchell, ed., *With Eyes Wide Open* (Barbados: CADEC, 1973), p. 133.
7. Dr. Robert Moore, "The Historical Basis of Theological Reflection," in *Troubling of the Waters,* p. 42.
8. "Inside Puerto Rico 1984: Colonialism and Intervention in the Caribbean and Central America," *PRISA International,* April 1984, p. 19.
9. EPICA interview with Stan Boyd, general secretary of the Dominica Christian Council, August 1982.
10. The Rev. Roy Neehall, "Christian Witness and Mission in Caribbean Development," in *With Eyes Wide Open,* p. 25.
11. *Caribbean Contact,* February 1980.

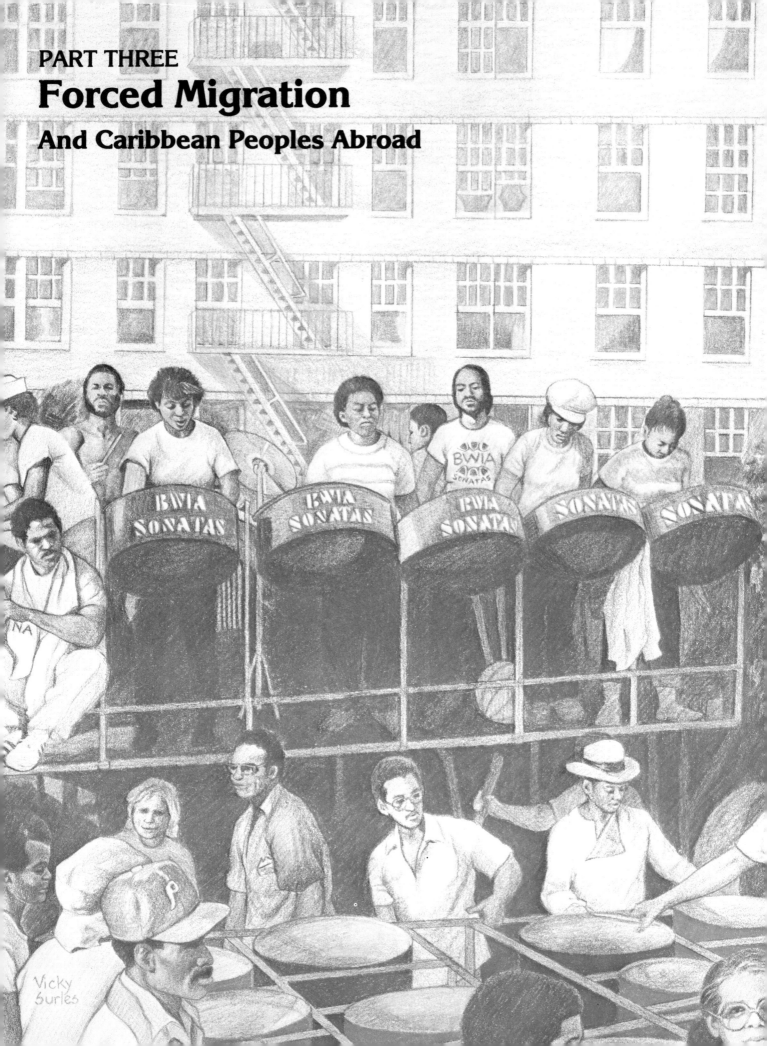

PART THREE
Forced Migration
And Caribbean Peoples Abroad

Vicky
Surles

Migration in Caribbean History

Migration is and always has been an integral part of the Caribbean experience. Modern Caribbean societies were born in the voluntary migration of Europeans to the region and the forced migration of the Africans they enslaved. They were made ethnically complex by immigration from India, China, and other parts of the world. The Caribbean's diversity, its outstanding characteristic, is a diversity founded in migrations.

The history of Caribbean migration since emancipation can be divided into four phases.[1] The first, from 1835 until about 1880, was the movement of the newly freed slaves away from the plantations. They moved to the towns to seek work, to the hills to farm, and where there was no vacant land—as in Barbados—they emigrated, going primarily to Trinidad and Guyana where plantation wages were higher.

This pattern was dramatically altered after 1880 by the flood of U.S. investment into the region. Caribbean migration in its second phase became movement "in search of the Yankee dollar." On the Atlantic coast of Central America, West Indians joined the plantation and railroad workforce for the United Fruit Company's banana operations. U.S. investment also caused a sugar boom in Cuba and the Dominican Republic just as the sugar industry in the British West Indies was dying out. Many West Indian workers, especially from Jamaica, migrated to the Spanish-speaking islands to cut cane.

But it was the building of the gigantic Panama Canal which dominated the migration of the time. Panama became a mecca for the unemployed and underemployed all over the Caribbean. West Indian laborers on the canal lived in disease-ridden slums and did hazardous, debilitating work for discriminatory rates of pay. Nonetheless, their remittances were an unprecedented injection of cash into the stagnant agrarian economies of the islands. For the first time, some peasants and workers were able to buy land, learn a trade, or open a shop. This was especially true in Barbados, where "Panama money" finally permitted the formation of a limited smallholder class through land purchases.[2] The memory of Panama as a source of wealth—as well as memories of hardship and discrimination—endures as part of the West Indian popular consciousness today.

The completion of the Canal in 1914 signaled the end of this boom period of migration. In the years before and during the Great Depression, there were few outlets for the swelling Caribbean work force. The only new destinations in this third phase were the oil fields starting up in Venezuela and the Shell refinery in Curacao, and these did not approach the scale of the Panama operation.

Migration to the Colonial "Mother Countries"

In the 19th and early 20th centuries, migration to England, France and Holland was largely limited to the Caribbean middle and upper classes. It was a common practice for such families to send a son off to the "metropole" to finish his education and qualify for a post in the colonial civil service. This elite pattern continued, but was overshadowed by the

mass popular emigration in search of employment which began during World War Two.

The war ended the Depression and created a labor shortage in the United States and England, leading to the recruitment of West Indians to take up war-time jobs. After the war ended, however, the United States again limited immigration, and the flow turned toward the colonial "mother countries": British West Indians migrated to Britain, French Antilleans to France, Surinamers to Holland, and Puerto Ricans—nominally U.S. citizens—to the United States. France and Britain gave citizenship to their colonial subjects in 1946 and 1948 respectively, which had the effect of allowing free and unselected emigration to the metropoles.

The floodgates opened; the era of mass emigration had begun. People rushed to escape the stifling Caribbean societies with their rigid class distinctions and lack of opportunities for the working class. Between 1946 and 1960, many Caribbean societies saw their natural population increase severely offset by emigration. Most affected were Puerto Rico; Jamaica; and the smaller sugar-producing islands such as Antigua, St. Kitts and Montserrat.[3]

Everybody was leaving—or at least this was the perception in the islands. Hardly a family could be found which did not have some member overseas. Emigrants departed by the boatload, and steel bands would play at the pier as the ship sailed away. Jamaican poet Louise Bennett recalls the epoch in patois:

Wat a joyful news, Miss Mattie,
I feel like me heart gwine burs'
Jamaica people colonizin
Englan in reverse.

By de hundred, by de t'ousan
From country and from town,
By de ship-load, by de plane-load
Jamaica is Englan boun.

Dem a-pour out o' Jamaica,
Everybody future plan
Is fe get a big-time job
An settle in de mother lan.

What a islan! What a people!
Man an woman, old an young
Jusa pack dem bag an baggage
An tun history upside dung![4]

France and Britain had granted citizenship to their colonial subjects in order to reinforce their empires and, in the case of Britain, to avoid a complete break in the near future when the colonies would become independent.[5] The tidal wave of emigrants was an unforeseen result. West Indians, Africans, East Indians and Pakistanis immigrating into England in the 1950s entered a virtually all-white society which reacted to their arrival with racism and hostility. After 1962, the British government responded to the white public's outcry with a series of restrictive immigration laws, reducing the flow of immigrants to a trickle.

At about the same time, however, Canada and the United States opened their doors, as their economies expanded and low-wage jobs needed to be filled. Until 1962, Canada's immigration laws openly discriminated against non-whites. In that year, the law was changed to stress educational and occupational credentials and West Indians began migrating in large numbers to Canada, primarily to Toronto and Montreal. U.S. immigration also was liberalized in 1965, and today Caribbean emigration is primarily to the United States and Canada.

Inter-island migration meanwhile has continued, with the stronger Caribbean economies drawing from nearby weaker ones. Trinidad draws from the Windward Islands, particularly Grenada. Guadeloupe draws from Dominica; Martinique from St. Lucia; while workers from throughout the Leeward Islands go to the Bahamas and the U.S. Virgin Islands to work in the tourist industry. A special, organized migration is the seasonal flow of Haitians to cut sugar cane in the Dominican Republic, which began in the 1920s while both the Dominican Republic and Haiti were under U.S. occupation. Today, Haitians make up 90% of the cane cutting force in the Dominican sugar industry, the backbone of the Dominican economy.

Within the broad context of migration for economic reasons, there have been several major migratory waves which are primarily political in nature. After the Cuban revolution, as is well known, many upper and middle-class Cubans emigrated to the United States, where they formed a militant exile community centered in Miami. Less publicized was the flight of tens of thousands of people from the Dominican Republic after the United States invaded that country in 1965. Today, the Dominican community in New York City numbers some 800,000. Since the beginning of the 1970s, two new groups of political refugees have arrived on the scene: the Haitians and the Guyanese, fleeing the corrupt and repressive regimes of Jean Claude Duvalier and Forbes Burnham.

The Migration Dream

Maurice Bishop of Grenada, criticizing the colonial educational system, referred to the "visa mentality": the obsessive desire to emigrate which is especially prevalent among educated youth and middle-class professionals. The educational system is important because it traditionally has served to impart foreign values and an orientation away from the Caribbean. For many years, West Indian school children learned the history of Europe, but little about their own past. Although Caribbean history and geography now are taught in the region's schools, the educational process still does not emphasize skills needed to build Caribbean societies. The schools prepare one to emigrate.

Reflecting this lack of relevance, unemployment actually is higher among those who have gone part way through high school (secondary school) than it is for those with less than five years of elementary education.[6] Youth with some secondary schooling tend to reject farming and aspire to white-collar or clerical jobs. Yet those few positions are quickly filled by high school graduates, leaving partly educated youth with three options: farming, unemployment, or emigration.

At the upper end of the educational ladder, emigration promises better working conditions, a higher salary, and possibilities for advancement to those in the professions. Certain fields such as teaching and nursing have seen a steady outflow of qualified persons to permanent residence in the developed countries. Another group which emigrates heavily is writers and artists, who often find, to their chagrin, that they must abandon the very societies which give meaning to their work because of greater receptivity and markets abroad.

Most of those who emigrate, however, are ordinary people confronted with the staggering unemployment in their home countries. In a few places—the tiny island of Carriacou is an example—there is so little economic activity that a majority of adult men historically have emigrated.

England Ah Want to Go!

Two years now ah waiting
Ah get ah letter, me voucher coming—
Man ah felt so glad!
Ah send for two grips in Trinidad,
When ah hear the blows—
Me voucher turned in Barbados.

England ah want to go
Send me voucher
Send me passport
Tell me what to do
Ah can't stay no more in Carriacou.

Man ah felt so bad
So very sad,
Everybody leaving
Imagine how ah feeling.
Who going Canada
Also America
But ah can't understand
Why me voucher won't come this time.

— Grenadian calypsonian The Mighty Scraper, 1970

For most Caribbean societies, money sent back by nationals abroad is an important source of foreign exchange. Remittances from family members working overseas have paid for houses, land and schooling in the Caribbean. The recession which began in 1981, however, diminished the flow of remittances because of unemployment in the U.S., Canada and Britain.

Popular mythology in the Caribbean tends to center on the wealth and opportunities abroad, rather than on the unemployment, racial discrimination, and alienation which Caribbean emigrants often suffer. Emigrants often send back artificially glowing reports, lest dissatisfaction be interpreted as a sign that the emigrant is not "making it" in his new milieu. But on a deeper level, the vast divide between the have and have-not nations virtually ensures a steady flow of people to where conditions are better. In that sense, Caribbean people are only following the path of their own resources and the wealth created by their labor: out of the region to the developed world. ∎

Blacks in Britain: A Bitter Trial

In the spring of 1981, the predominantly West Indian neighborhood of Brixton in South London exploded in violent riots which turned the eyes of the world on the bitter, 30-year-old struggle between blacks in Britain and the racist British state. Perhaps more than any other emigrant experience, the saga of British colonial "subjects" in the motherland illustrates the process through which white society creates a black underclass, and the resistance to that pressure which is a continuing part of the Caribbean experience abroad.

Two themes run side by side throughout the history of West Indians in Britain. One is a virulent strain of white racism and neo-fascism which has fueled violence against the black minority. The other is a growing Third World unity across generational and ethnic lines (West Indian, African, and Asian), based on a philosophy which looks beyond the surface of race discrimination to its roots in the system of colonial domination.

British colonial subjects from the Caribbean, Africa, India and Pakistan started coming to the U.K. in large numbers in the 1950s, when Britain was desperate for labor to help with post-war reconstruction. The immigrants filled jobs British workers would not take—the dirtiest, lowest paid, least skilled occupations. But it soon became clear that while their cheap labor was welcome, the immigrants' presence in British society was not. Rampant discrimination in the housing market, particularly in middle-class neighborhoods, forced West Indians to jam together into ghetto apartments. White Britons then pointed to these substandard conditions as evidence of black inferiority, while landlords cited "overcrowding" as a reason not to rent to blacks.

Another form of discrimination was the so-called "color bar," which kept non-whites out of public entertainment spots like pubs, bars and clubs. For the young, working-class men who made up the bulk of the post-war immigrant wave, this was highly provocative and sparked frequent fights between black and white youth.

The presence of a racial minority was a lightning rod for the frustrations and fears of the white working class, at a time when this class could no longer compensate for its own low status by sharing in the illusion of British world supremacy.

> The loss of India and the impending loss of the Caribbean and Africa has spelt the end of empire and the decline of Britain as a great power. All that was left of the colonial enterprise was the ideology of racial superiority; it was something to fall back on . . . [1]

The result was a resurgence of the fascist tendency which had long been an undercurrent of British political life. Societies for "racial preservation" and neo-fascist organizations preaching race hatred began to multiply. Stimulated by racist propaganda put out by these groups and echoed in the press, white youth gangs called "teddy boys" roamed the streets armed with knives and iron pipes, making unprovoked attacks on blacks and Asians. This was called "nigger-hunting" and "Paki-bashing" and was regarded as harmless sport by the police. Finally, in August 1958, an incident in the London district of Nottingham sparked four days of violence in which white mobs ripped through London, attacking blacks and black homes with bricks and gasoline bombs.[2]

The hysteria inflamed by the riots paved the way for the first restrictive immigration legislation, the 1962 Commonwealth Immigration Act. This law sought to "improve" race relations in Britain by limiting the number of non-whites who could enter. Immigration became subject to quotas and controls, institutionalizing racism at the state level.

Polarization in the 1960s

The passage of the Commonwealth Immigration Act deepened the rift between the immigrant community and the larger society. The police became more openly racist and brutal toward blacks. White tenant groups organized to exclude blacks from housing, while black workers found that their demands for fair treatment met with active collaboration between white unions and management. New problems emerged in the area of education, as the first generation of children born in Britain to immigrant parents were entering the schools. Under pressure from white parents, the school system shunted many black children to special schools for the mentally retarded or emotionally disturbed. This threatened to create a generation of miseducated black children who would grow to be adults equipped only for the menial tasks of an underclass.

In the past, immigrants had responded to discrimination by forming their own social institutions: clubs, churches, and mutual associations, such as revolving credit cooperatives

Protesters march past burned-out Ruddock house after fire which killed 13 West Indian schoolchildren. Note banner with portrait of Marcus Garvey, center-left.

Photo: R. MacMillan

based on the Trinidadian *susu*. Barred from the housing market, immigrants pooled their savings to buy property jointly. Afro-Caribbean people (Africans and West Indians) and Asians (primarily Indians and Pakistanis) tended to fight similar battles independently of each other. But as the society became more racist, the quality of resistance began to change.

The fight against the 1962 Commonwealth Immigration Act stimulated a temporary unity between Afro-Caribbean and Asian groups. Now this cooperation was revived and given a political grounding by the rise of the U.S. civil rights movement and the decolonization of various African and Caribbean nations. The visits of prominent black activists to Britain—such as Martin Luther King, Jr. in 1964 and Malcolm X in 1965—spurred the formation of new, militant organizations, notably the Racial Action Adjustment Society (RAAS). RAAS moved quickly to broaden the struggle by supporting an Asian factory workers' strike at the request of the Asian workers.

> RAAS's "nationalism," stemming as it did from the West Indian experience, combined an understanding of how colonialism had divided the Asian and African and Caribbean peoples ("coolie, savage, and slave") with an awareness of how that same colonialism made them one people now: they were all blacks.[3]

A visit by Stokely Carmichael to London in July 1967 helped inspire the formation of the Universal Coloured Peoples' Association (UCPA). UCPA stressed that the struggle for black and Asian rights was fundamentally an anti-capitalist and anti-imperialist struggle, linking racism in Britain to the war in Vietnam, colonialism in Africa, and to the entire system of white domination.

White Britain tried to portray this new consciousness as the machinations of "black power" and communist agitators from abroad. It was, in fact, an indigenous movement with roots in Britain. London in the 1930s and '40s was a major center of the Pan-African movement and the home of intellectuals in the vanguard of the anti-colonial movement: C.L.R. James, George Padmore, Jomo Kenyatta, and Kwame Nkrumah among others.

In 1945, the fifth Pan-African Congress was held in Manchester, England, and vowed to struggle for "the absolute and complete independence of the colonies" and for "the liquidation of colonialism and imperialism." In the same year, Asians, Africans and West Indians in Britain came together for a Subject People's Conference, foreshadowing the multi-ethnic unity reforged twenty years later.

In 1968, the Black People's Alliance was formed as a national coordinating body for over fifty Afro-Caribbean and Asian organizations. Under the BPA's banner, thousands of people marched through the streets to demand the repeal of the Immigration Act. Meanwhile, blacks were organizing at the local level to redress the social deprivation which they and their children had suffered. Militant organizations set up youth centers and schools staffed by black teachers. Black-oriented newspapers, bookstores, counseling centers and other self-help projects proliferated.

Black People's Day of Action, March 1981 in London.

Hansib Publishing Co.

White racist groups reacted by stepping up violence. Hate leaflets circulated, and crosses were burned outside black homes. In 1967, the League of Empire Loyalists, the British National Party, and local groups of the Racial Preservation Society merged into the National Front, a fascist electoral party. Member of Parliament Enoch Powell, a Joseph McCarthy-style demagogue, inflamed public hysteria with warnings of an England overrun by immigrant hordes.

Britain's need for low-wage labor had declined from its postwar high in the fifties, and unemployment was a growing problem. Powell led right-wing calls for repatriating all immigrants now that their labor was no longer in demand. In response to these pressures, new legislation in 1968 and 1971 essentially shut the door on black immigration. The Immigration Act of 1971 restricted entry to "patrials"—persons with a parent or grandparent born in Britain. In practice this excluded most blacks, while whites from Canada, Australia, South Africa and New Zealand could enter freely. The act withdrew residency rights from nonpatrials retroactively, suddenly rendering much of the black population "illegal." Although the retroactive clause was eventually dropped, the Illegal Immigration Intelligence Unit of the police made frequent raids on black homes and workplaces.

> The success of Black Power had brought down on its head the wrath of the system. Its leaders were persecuted, its meetings disrupted, its places of work destroyed. But it had gone on gaining momentum and strength . . . There was hardly a black in the country that did not identify with it, and through it, to all the non-whites of the world, in one way or another. And as for the British-born youth, who had been schooled in white racism, the movement was the cradle of their consciousness.[4]

The 1980s: Youth in Struggle

By the mid-1970s a generation of British-born black youth had come of age. Most had never seen the lands of their parents' birth. Yet because they were black, the society refused to regard them as "British." Their immigrant parents had endured second-class citizenship stoically, but the youth struck back in anger.

Concentrated in inner-city London and Birmingham, they faced discrimination in a shrinking job market. Many had never been employed. In their anger, some turned to petty crime, such as drug selling, mugging and theft. This provided the pretext for harassment of all blacks by the virtually all-white police force (98% of London police are white). Under the notorious "sus laws," police would stop young Afro-Caribbean men on mere "suspicion" that they might be planning a crime. As tensions grew, police and the paramilitary Special Patrol Group placed entire black neighborhoods under virtual siege.

The conflict with the police spurred more unified organization of black communities, a process in which women played a key role. Racism deeply affected them: through low wages, through inferior housing, through their children's troubles in

74

school and with the law. By the late '70s many black women's organizations were active, and women took part in militant factory strikes.

The victory of Margaret Thatcher's Conservative Party in 1979 set the stage for an escalation of racial tension. The new government set out to dismantle much of the British welfare state, slashing spending on social services and aid to the inner cities. Unemployment climbed steadily, reaching 50% for black youth.[5]

The conservative climate of "Thatcherism" encouraged racist attacks and police brutality against blacks, leading eventually to a serious backlash. In 1981 a fire attributed to arson swept a London home, killing thirteen West Indian teenagers. Outraged by the cursory investigation, 10,000 people marched through London in a "Black People's Day of Action." Rioting broke out in Brixton the next month, spreading to over 30 towns and cities across England.

In 1985, police raiding a home in Brixton accidentally shot Cherry Groce, a West Indian mother of six. She was left paralyzed. A week later another West Indian woman collapsed and died while police searched her home. The incidents triggered a virtual insurrection in the Tottenham and Brixton sections of London: rioters fired on the police, killing one, and hundreds of people were wounded and arrested.

The violence of the outbursts stunned white Britain. Conservatives blamed "anarchists and leftists," and police warned that they would meet future outbreaks with tear gas and plastic bullets. But it was clear that race issues could no longer be swept under the carpet.

A Multi-Racial Society

Racial attacks on Afro-Caribbeans and Asians have continued to increase. At the same time, awareness is slowly growing that British society must come to terms with the reality of multi-racialism. Black people account for 4.3% of the population, and 15% of London is black. Moreover, it is no longer simply a question of immigration. More than 40% of the 2.4 million black people living in Britain were born there.[6] It is not immigrants but their British-born daughters and sons who now carry the militant banner of black resistance.

The maturing of the immigrant community has led to increased black participation in mainstream party politics, primarily within the Labour Party. This began with the election of blacks to represent largely black districts on municipal councils. In 1987 four black candidates were elected to the House of Commons, the first non-whites in Parliament in 60 years. Parliamentarians Dianne Abbott and Bernie Grant are of West Indian origin, from Jamaica and Guyana respectively.

People of Caribbean descent make up a quarter of Britain's black population, and have had a marked cultural and political impact. Rastafarianism and reggae are very popular in Britain, forming the major cultural link with the West Indies. At the same time, British-born blacks are making original contributions to the culture of the Caribbean. Some of the best new reggae since the death of Bob Marley has come out of London. Poet Linton Kwesi Johnson, a Jamaican raised and educated in England, helped to pioneer the art form known as dub poetry. Black newspapers, cinema and theater are flourishing as the West Indian diaspora makes its creative imprint on both sides of the Atlantic. ∎

MIGRATION TO THE NETHERLANDS AND FRANCE

Caribbean emigrants to other European countries have fared somewhat better than West Indians in Britain. The Dutch and French governments have been less willing than the British to condone racist violence. But immigrants still face discrimination in securing jobs and housing, social isolation and stereotyping of non-white children in the schools. This has sufficed to turn major segments of the immigrant community into a deprived underclass.

In the years preceding and just after Suriname's 1975 independence from Holland, thousands of Surinamers seized their last opportunity to emigrate. By the time Holland shut its doors to all but dependent kin in 1980, there were some 180,000 Surinamers in the Netherlands.[7] They came from all Suriname's ethnic groups: East Indians, Creoles, "Bush Negroes," Indonesians and Chinese. There are also at least 40,000 persons from the Netherlands Antilles in Holland. This heterogeneous immigrant popu-

lation has had many problems being accepted by white Dutch society. "They told us there was no racism in Holland," says a white Dutchman living in the Caribbean, "until the first Negro appeared."

The experience of French Antilleans in France differs in one major respect: the French government actively promotes emigration as an escape valve for social unrest in the colonies. In addition, the French policy of cultural assimilation favors higher education of Antillean youth in France. Nonetheless, racist attacks on Arab, African and Caribbean immigrants have increased, led by Jean-Marie Le Pen's National Front. The party is the largest of the extreme-right anti-immigrant groups which have sprung up throughout western Europe and which seek to blame problems of unemployment, drugs and crime on immigrants.

Moving North: Caribbean Migration to the United States

As restrictive laws barred immigrants from Britain, doors opened to North America. Canada liberalized entry in 1962. In 1965 new U.S. legislation abolished the system of national quotas, which had favored immigrants from Europe. Instead, migrants were admitted on the basis of the need for their labor, giving preference to those with kin in the U.S. The result was a flood of "new" immigration drawn overwhelmingly from Asia, Latin America and the Caribbean.

Only Cuba and Puerto Rico among Caribbean countries had previously sent large numbers of people to the United States. After 1965, however, immigrants streamed in from nearly every Caribbean country. The Dominican Republic, Jamaica, Haiti and Trinidad jumped near the top of the list of countries sending immigrants to the U.S.[1]

New York, Miami and Toronto became ports of entry for the new arrivals, and the final destination for many. Jamaicans and other English-speaking West Indians clustered in New York and Toronto, while Haitians settled mainly in New York, Miami, Boston and Montreal. Cubans concentrated in Miami and Union City, New Jersey, continuing patterns established before 1965. Puerto Ricans, not officially counted as Caribbean immigrants because of their U.S. citizenship, continued to populate every major east coast city. By contrast, 90% of arriving Dominicans settled in New York.

A second striking feature of the new immigration was the predominance of women. The 1980 census revealed a ratio of 100 women to 83 men among Caribbean-born U.S. residents.[2] One reason is the relative ease with which immigrant women can find work, often as domestics or in garment factories. A typical pattern is for a woman to migrate first, leaving her children and/or husband behind, then to apply for their immigration as kin after she attains permanent resident status.

If the old immigration produced the stereotypes of the Irish cop in Boston or the East European peddler on New York's Lower East Side, the prototype of the "new immigrant" is a woman from the Dominican Republic who migrates directly from her rural village. She leaves her children with her mother and goes to live with a cousin in a Manhattan tenement, earning $130 a week as a sewing machine operator. After she has been in the United States long enough to legalize her status, she sends for her children. The portion of her wages sent home are a major source of support for her extended family in the Dominican Republic.

Caribbean New York

Nostrand Avenue cuts through the Flatbush section of Brooklyn, the heart of New York City's West Indian community. Lilting Jamaican and Grenadian English mingles with Haitian Kreyol on the street. Groceries offer coconuts, plantains, yuca root, mangoes and meat patties. The small businesses which line Nostrand Avenue are West Indian-owned and cater to the immigrant community. Ever Ready Caribbean Shipping will send stateside goods by the box or barrel to families back at home. Alken Group Tours offers

Tobago Crusoe, the 1983 Calypso Monarch of Trinidad, performs in a Brooklyn Carnival tent.

Everybody's Magazine

chartered flights to Trinidad at Carnival time. Dozens of eateries cook up cow foot soup, curry goat and callaloo.

Across the river in Manhattan's Washington Heights section, travel agencies boast cheap fares to Santo Domingo. While Brooklyn is the core district for English-speaking West Indians, Dominicans and Puerto Ricans are concentrated in Manhattan, in the neighborhoods of Spanish Harlem, Washington Heights and the Upper West Side.

New York has become a Caribbean city, the largest in the world. Two million of the city's seven million people now trace their roots to the Caribbean, including Puerto Rico. Of the five countries sending the most legal migrants to New York in 1986, four were Caribbean: the Dominican Republic, Jamaica, Guyana and Haiti. One of every five new legal immigrants was a Dominican; one of every ten a Jamaican.[3] To these arrivals are added those of undocumented immigrants, in large though unknown numbers.

While academics speak of the "Caribbeanization" of New York, ordinary New Yorkers feel the vibrant island presence in the city's street life and culture. Even the *New York Times* took note:

New York seems to be bouncing to a Caribbean beat these days. From the insistent throb of reggae along Brooklyn's Nostrand Avenue . . . to the infectious samba rhythms . . . large sections of the metropolitan area are beginning to look, sound and feel like outposts of the Caribbean.[4]

If outsiders tend to see a unified "Caribbean" influence, the same cannot be said of the immigrants. Language and cultural barriers which divide the Caribbean also divide Caribbean people in New York. A wide gulf separates the Hispanics—Puerto Ricans, Dominicans, Colombians and Cubans—from English-speaking West Indians. Haitians form yet another self-contained group.

Within each broad grouping many divisions persist. Puerto Ricans and Dominicans, while culturally similar, maintain distinct communities. The social life of West Indian Brooklyn is based on island affiliation, at least for the older generation. There are hundreds of social clubs: one can attend a dance sponsored by the Dominica Benevolent Society or a luncheon of the St. Vincent Benefit & Education Fund, fundraising for charities in the islands. While every country has at least one broad-based "national association," there is further elaboration along occupational and other lines. There is the Jamaican Nurses Association, the Jamaican Policemen's Association, and even the St. Andrew's Anglican Secondary School Alumni Association of New York.

Such complexity is made possible by the sheer numbers of Caribbean people living in the city. Some of the smaller islands, such as Nevis or Anguilla, have more nationals in New York than on the island. But it also relates to the close proximity of the Caribbean to the United States, which enables migrants to visit home frequently and to maintain social, cultural and political ties.

Cheap airfares facilitate frequent comings and goings of island peoples and goods . . . On Sundays and holidays, the international telephone circuits are clogged with the relatively inexpensive direct-dial service to and from Area Code 809. That particular "space" in New York City where each Caribbean group first established its center becomes like a distant province of the homeland, part of the same social and, in some cases (where migrants are encouraged to vote in their home country elections) political system.[5]

These continuing ties have encouraged the persistence of national, as opposed to regional, identity. One identifies as a Jamaican, or a Trinidadian, or a Guyanese, even while living in close contact with people from other islands. In England, by contrast, the distance from the Caribbean has reduced the importance of nationality and encouraged a pan-Caribbean identity to emerge.

In addition, most West Indians entering the United States settle in multi-ethnic urban areas, where the presence of other minorities forms a buffer against white society. This has lessened the potential for violence directed specifically against Caribbean people, reducing the need for them to stand together as a group.

What unity exists tends to depend on the same cultural unifiers that bring people together in the Caribbean. Calypso and steelband flourish in Brooklyn; they are popular with the entire West Indian community, not just Trinidadians. Rastafarianism has spread among West Indian youth in the diaspora just as it spread from island to island in the region. The largest Caribbean organization in Brooklyn is a Rastafarian group, the Twelve Tribes of Israel.

But it is Carnival—the two-day "bacchanal" of costumed parades, steelband and calypso—which draws together, however briefly, the whole West Indian community. Held every year on Labor Day (designated "West Indian-American Day" by the New York state legislature) Brooklyn's Carnival draws a

Local steelband performs in Brooklyn.

Trinidadians in Brooklyn pay tribute to Dr. Eric Williams after his death in 1981.

77

crowd of one million for the procession down Eastern Parkway. While dominated by Trinidadian organizers who maintain close touch with Carnival trends in Port-of-Spain, New York's Carnival has nonetheless been, from its inception, "self-consciously pan-West Indian."[6]

The unity symbolized by Carnival has been elusive during the rest of the year. Yet there are signs that a "pan-Caribbean" identity may be slowly emerging among English-speaking West Indians—if not all Caribbean people—in the United States. "New York City nourishes a Caribbean consciousness that has not been actively promoted in the Caribbean," notes a West Indian anthropologist.[7] The Mighty Sparrow expressed the same theme in a 1976 calypso:

You can be from St. Clair, or from John John
In New York, all that done
They haven't to know who is who
New York equalize you
Bajan, Grenadian, Jamaican, "toute moun"
Drinking they rum, beating they bottle and spoon.
And no one who see me can honestly say
They don't like to be in Brooklyn on Labor Day!*

West Indian Success Stories

Whatever shared cultural identity exists has not, as yet, led to the kind of unity which could turn the West Indian community into a political force. While some people see movement in this direction, many doubt that unity can prevail over insularity and personal ambitions. Whether an umbrella Caribbean-American organization could or should be formed is a matter of debate within the community. The Caribbean Action Lobby, headed by Trinidad-born congressman Mervyn Dymally, has attempted to provide such leadership, but its grassroots support remains small.

Ironically, men and women of West Indian descent have long played prominent roles in both New York City and national politics. But they have done so as representatives of the larger black community, not as spokespersons for Caribbean concerns. Between 1900 and 1930 a first wave of West Indians settled in Harlem and Brooklyn, and quickly came to dominate neighborhood politics. Many of New York's black elected officials, judges and civil servants were of Caribbean descent, along with several of the first black politicians to win national office. Former congresswoman Shirley Chisholm, for example, is of Barbadian and Guyanese parentage.

The emergence of Black American institutions and leaders linked to the anti-poverty programs of the 1960s eventually eroded the predominance of the West Indians.[8] At the same time, a new generation of West Indian leaders began

seeking to represent the interests of the Caribbean-American community. These interests, however, have rarely related to participation in U.S. politics. Many West Indian immigrants do not pursue U.S. citizenship which would enable them to vote in U.S. elections. Instead, they remain involved with the politics of their home countries, often supporting home-based political parties.

Politics of any sort remains a secondary concern for most. The dominant ethic is one of personal hard work and material success, a pattern for which West Indian-Americans have become renowned. This is true even though most experience initial downward mobility upon their arrival. Novelist Paule Marshall recalls how her mother and other immigrant women worked as domestics in white homes:

> Looking back on it now it seems to me that those Barbadian women accepted these ill-paying, low status jobs with an astonishing lack of visible resentment. For them they were simply a means to an end: the end being the down payment on a brownstone house, a college education for their children, and the much coveted middle-class status these achievements represented.[9]

Once established, West Indians have moved in large numbers into business, academia and the professions. Various theories have been put forth to explain this mobility, which contrasts to the experience of West Indians in Britain. One factor is the difference in backgrounds: emigrants to Britain in the 1950s were mostly from the working class, while those coming recently to the U.S. tend to have more education before migrating. More important, however, is the differing context of race relations. West Indians entering all-white Britain became a "visible minority" and a target for racism. In the United States they were incorporated within the context of the Black American community, which served as a buffer and vehicle for assimilation.

The latter process has not been without tension. West Indians, conscious of the second-class status of blacks in the U.S., have often chosen to stress their ethnic identity rather than assimilate fully into the Black American community. Strong believers in individual effort, many hold values more conservative than those of U.S. blacks. Yet they recognize their disadvantage as blacks in a white society, leading them to make alliances within the context of black politics.[10]

An aspect of the emerging Caribbean identity has been greater concern with and debate over United States policy toward the region. West Indians in this country have been divided over such controversial issues as the invasion of Grenada. Although they do not speak with a single voice, West Indian-Americans are increasingly making their voices heard on issues which concern them.   ■

---

* St. Clair: a section of Port-of-Spain known for its concentration of old wealth.
John-John: a poor ghetto of Port-of-Spain.
Toute moun: French Creole for "everybody."

The Puerto Rican Experience

Each year, an estimated 250,000 persons crowd the New York-San Juan air corridor that has been called the "aerial bridge" between the United States and Puerto Rico.[1] This restless traffic flows in both directions, from the Island to the U.S. and back again. As U.S. citizens, Puerto Ricans need no visas to make the trip. Says one writer, "Puerto Ricans do not emigrate—they commute."[2]

No Caribbean society has been more deeply affected by migration than Puerto Rico. Most Puerto Ricans migrate at some time in their lives, many leaving and returning repeatedly. The dominant trend has nonetheless been one of movement northward. The U.S. Puerto Rican community grew from 70,000 in 1940 to 1.5 million in 1970 and 2 million in 1980. By 1987 some two and a half million Puerto Ricans lived in the United States, with just over three million in Puerto Rico.[3]

This population shift occurred not by chance, but as a planned aspect of Puerto Rico's incorporation into the U.S. economy. After invading the Island in 1898, the United States made Puerto Rico a colony in all but name. In 1901 the Supreme Court decreed it a "non-incorporated territory which belongs to, but is not part of, the United States."

The first colonial governor, Charles Allen, remarked that it would be preferable for the poor to emigrate since what Puerto Rico needed was "men with capital."[4] American sugar companies moved in and took over lands from coffee estates and peasant farmers. Many of those left landless and unemployed went to cut cane on American-owned sugar plantations in Hawaii, Cuba and the Dominican Republic. In 1917, the Jones Act imposed U.S. citizenship on Puerto Ricans, facilitating migration.

By the Depression years, the Island was an impoverished backwater, with many people near starvation. This suffering fueled a Nationalist movement which attempted to link the question of Puerto Rican independence to socialism. U.S. authorities jailed the movement's leaders, while working with the newly-formed Popular Party on a plan to transform Puerto Rico's economy.

Under Operation Bootstrap, U.S. firms set up factories on the Island to employ the displaced rural workforce. "Surplus" workers migrated to the United States or joined welfare rolls. Touted as a development panacea, Bootstrap's deeper purpose was to provide low-wage labor for the U.S. economy in its postwar period of rapid growth.

The migration strategy was mapped out jointly by Puerto Rican and New York City officials. In 1954 Mayor Wagner of New York traveled to Puerto Rico to advertise the availability of factory jobs in his city. Other U.S. firms, such as steel manufacturers and auto makers, also recruited labor from the Island. Between 1945 and 1965, over half a million Puerto Ricans emigrated.[5]

The Promised Land

Puerto Ricans entered New York and other cities as factory and sweatshop laborers. They were crucial to urban economies; the New York garment industry, in particular, depended on the labor of Puerto Rican women. Two recall:

> We sewed dresses for the Bella Hess Company. I couldn't get ahead because I sewed too slowly, so I would make $20 a week. They were supposed to pay me $30 but they never did. There was no union, all there was was to sew, sew, sew.
>
> I worked in the garment industry for thirty years. Thirty years sitting at a sewing machine is no small feat . . . I worked so I could get to where I am and give my children an education, something I am very proud of.[6]

El Barrio, the part of Manhattan also known as East Harlem, was and remains the heart of the New York Puerto Rican community. Hell's Kitchen, on the west side, and "Loisaida"—the lower east side—were other early areas of settlement. In time, some people were able to move to the outlying boroughs and suburbs, and beyond to New Jersey, Connecticut, Massachusetts, Pennsylvania and Illinois. But

On a "parcela," a resettlement area for landless farm workers. Bayamón, Puerto Rico, 1945.

Photo by L. Rosskam, courtesy of Centro de Estudios Puertorriquenos, City University of New York

79

Street scene in El Barrio: A twin image of poverty and cultural dynamism.

Tony Velez

the greatest concentration remained in the inner cities of the old industrial centers such as New York, Chicago, Philadelphia and Hartford.

By the 1960s industry was abandoning these areas, seeking cheaper non-union labor in the southern states and overseas. The loss of manufacturing jobs hit Puerto Ricans hard, forcing many into minimum-wage service jobs in hospitals, hotels and restaurants. Puerto Ricans remained stuck at the bottom of the occupational ladder, with the lowest median income of any group.[7] Forty percent live below the poverty line, although a small middle class exists.[8]

The Puerto Rican neighborhoods of New York present a picture of entrenched poverty. They include the city's most run-down housing, where red-lining by banks impedes rehabilitation. Although a third of the children in New York public schools are Hispanic, the schools do not serve their needs, and only about half of Puerto Rican youth complete high school.[9] Drug addiction and AIDS are serious problems.

Politically, Puerto Ricans in the U.S. are marginalized and divided. Community leaders emerged from organizations started with anti-poverty funds in the 1960s, but budget cuts during the Reagan years crippled or eliminated many of these programs. Puerto Ricans hold few elected positions, even in New York. There is one Puerto Rican congressman, Rep. Robert García of the Bronx, but no systematic national lobby on behalf of Puerto Ricans.[10]

As a Spanish-speaking and largely non-white community, Puerto Ricans have suffered double discrimination. But they also have lagged behind other Hispanic immigrant groups in education, income and employment. For others, migration is a goal holding promise for the future. Those who gain the opportunity to migrate are a select few. But Puerto Ricans on the Island are already part of the U.S. workforce, incorporated into the U.S. economy as a low-wage, welfare-dependent labor pool. For them, a move from San Juan to New York is less a move to a new society than a mere change of location.

Toward Empowerment

Straddling two societies, Puerto Ricans are a divided people, their culture and language under constant assault from dominant U.S. influences. Yet the community has produced a vibrant cultural response, a witness to the determined survival of the Puerto Rican nation.

More than any other immigrant group, Puerto Ricans have developed the ability to speak two languages and function in two labor markets, two cultures and two competing value systems. They are the most bilingual of U.S. Hispanics, learning English for survival while maintaining Spanish, generation after generation, as an essential part of national identity. The sense of being Puerto Rican remains strong among those born in North America, the so-called Nuyoricans.

The presence of a million Puerto Ricans in New York is a dominant theme in the urban cultural mix. Puerto Rican culture is dynamic and creative, constantly incorporating new elements from the Caribbean and North America.[11] *Salsa,* for example, combines elements of African music, Latin American folk, and rock 'n roll. These fused in New York to form a new music which was then reexported to the Caribbean. In addition, there has been a blossoming of drama, literature and the visual arts by young New York Puerto Ricans, tied to nationalist themes and support for Puerto Rican independence.

This cultural achievement has provided a potential base for political empowerment, as yet only partially realized. Since the mid-eighties many political action groups, some linked to the Democratic Party, have emerged within the Puerto Rican community. They join broader-based organizations such as the National Puerto Rican Coalition and the National Congress for Puerto Rican Rights. Due in part to organizing by such groups, Puerto Ricans have scored recent gains in state and local elections in Chicago, New York and other cities.

One issue which has drawn the community together and forged links with other Hispanics is opposition to the "English-only" movement. Twelve states have passed laws making English their "official" language, threatening bilingual education programs and the rights of language minorities. Puerto Ricans are active in coalitions which have blocked such legislation in other states.[12]

Perhaps the clearest gains have come in the labor arena. A new group of young Puerto Rican trade unionists has come to prominence through involvement in the New York City hotel workers' strike and struggles by farmworkers, garment workers, steelworkers and hospital workers. Many sectors of the Puerto Rican community joined to reject an attempt by the Adolph Coors Co. to buy public support from Latino organizations at a time when Coors was involved in a bitter labor dispute with its largely Chicano work force.[13]

Despite this growing activism, the situation of Puerto Ricans in the diaspora remains bleak. While growing in size, the community continues mired in a poverty exceeded only by that of Puerto Ricans on the Island. In this respect, as in others, the migrants' lives remain linked to the fate of their Caribbean home. ∎

Puerto Rican New Yorkers.

Tony Velez

The Haitian Boat People

In the waters off northern Haiti in June 1984, a U.S. Coast Guard cutter pulled alongside a small wooden sailboat crammed with some 70 Haitian men, women and children. As U.S. agents jumped aboard, the frightened refugees crowded to one side and the boat capsized, drowning twelve people. The tragedy was an "interdiction" under the Haitian Migration Interdiction Operation, aimed at returning would-be refugees to Haiti before they reach U.S. shores.

The first boat people beached on the south Florida coast in 1972. More followed, the weakened survivors of an 800-mile voyage which sent many to their deaths from thirst, hunger and drowning. The sight of bodies washing up on Florida beaches focused world attention on the repression inside Jean-Claude Duvalier's Haiti.

While supporters of the Haitians argued that they were refugees fleeing persecution, and thus eligible for asylum in the United States, the U.S. government insisted that the Haitians were merely "economic migrants" looking for work. Those who fell into the hands of the immigration service were rushed through summary asylum hearings and deported. At the height of the "Haitian program" in 1978, the Miami immigration office was issuing 150 Haitian deportation orders a day.[1]

The 1980 Refugee Act states that the United States must provide political asylum to persons with a "well-founded fear of persecution" in their home country. But it has been applied with a blatant double standard. Persons from Soviet-influenced countries are favored for asylum, while those fleeing right-wing regimes allied to Washington are routinely denied. From 1983 through 1987, applicants from Iran, Romania, Czechoslovakia, Afghanistan, Syria and Poland had the highest approval rates for asylum. Salvadorans, Guatemalans and Haitians had virtually the lowest, despite the gruesome human rights records of their governments. Only 1.7% of Haitians who applied for asylum during this period received it.[2]

Poverty and Persecution

An estimated one million of Haiti's six million people live outside the country. The largest number of exiles, probably half a million, is in the United States. Thousands more live in Canada, the Bahamas, the French Antilles, Europe and Africa. At least 300,000 Haitians live permanently in the Dominican Republic; others migrate there seasonally to cut sugar cane in a trade organized by the two governments.

Although Haitians had migrated as cane cutters from early in the century, the first major wave of political exiles left after François Duvalier's election in 1957. It included rival politicians and their close associates, along with members of the elite such as businessmen, doctors and lawyers. Because this class was historically allied with the United States, the U.S. government welcomed them. As Duvalier consolidated his dictatorship during the 1960s, the exodus broadened to include skilled workers and members of the lower middle class.

Haitian refugee at the Krome Avenue Detention Center, October 1980.

Michael Carlebach

After Jean-Claude Duvalier succeeded his father in 1971, the entry of foreign agribusiness firms began reshaping the rural landscape. Much of the small-scale, semi-feudal farming was swept aside, and displaced peasants began migrating to the towns. Others scraped together cash to pay passage on small boats leaving from Haiti's north coast. This third and largest migrant wave—the boat people—consisted almost entirely of unskilled workers and peasants. By 1981, more than 45,000 Haitians were known to have arrived in the U.S. by boat, along with unknown numbers who entered undetected.[3]

Their reasons for leaving reflected the intertwined terror and impoverishment which characterized the Duvalierist state. Jean-Claude maintained the repressive structures put in place by his father, including some 22,000 Tontons Macoutes who acted as spies and enforcers for the regime. Political parties other than Duvalier's were banned, and many persons suspected of political activity went to prison without ever seeing an arrest warrant, a lawyer or a court. Amnesty International reported in 1984:

> Torture and ill-treatment of detainees in Haiti has been regularly reported to Amnesty International since president for life, Jean-Claude Duvalier took office in 1971.
>
> Methods of torture described in testimonies . . . include beatings on the head or other parts of the body with sticks, obliging detainees to remain standing still for very long periods, and the so-called Parrot's Perch, known in Haiti as the "jack."
>
> Long-term incommunicado detention, unacknowledged by the authorities for months or years, and sometimes never acknowledged, without access to lawyers, relatives or doctors, has become the pattern of political detention in Haiti.[4]

Prison conditions in Haiti ranked among the worst in the world. Most detainees were interrogated in the Port-au-Prince military barracks, the Casernes Dessalines, or in the notorious Fort Dimanche prison.

> Political detainees taken to the Casernes Dessalines are held in damp, dark and dirty cells, either naked or dressed only in their underwear. Detainees leave the cells only once a day, early in the morning, for a shower. There is said to be no furniture at all in the cells, only a dirty mattress and a paint tin which serves as a toilet.
>
> Prisoners are allowed no visits whatsoever and are kept completely isolated. No reading materials or correspondence are permitted and the prisoners do not work. They are not allowed to communicate with each other and if caught doing so are likely to be beaten.[5]

Terror undergirded a system in which a tiny elite systematically drained the country's wealth. The state taxed the peasants heavily, sharing the spoils among the security forces and Duvalier supporters. Ninety percent of Haitians earned less than $180 a year; while a clique of millionaire families, 0.5% of the population, received 46% of the national income.[6] The Duvalier family's own fortune was estimated at between $500 and $900 million.

Unpaid below the officer level, the Tontons Macoutes profited by extorting money and property from their victims. Peasants saw their lands expropriated, risking prison if they protested. Poverty and repression were thus two sides of a coin. Yet U.S. immigration officials, advised by the State Department, insisted that if the Haitians were escaping poverty they could not also be fleeing persecution. Geopolitics underlay this policy, just as geopolitics dictated the policy of U.S. aid to the Duvalier regime. Washington's primary interest was keeping an anticommunist government in Haiti; human rights concerns came afterward, if at all. By shoring up a repressive regime, U.S. policies stimulated the flight of refugees from Haiti. The politics of anticommunism meant they would receive no comfort when they arrived.

No Safe Haven

Events in 1980 dramatically highlighted the double standard in U.S. immigration policy. To the trumpeting of media fanfare, the Carter administration welcomed a "freedom flotilla" of 125,000 Cuban boat people from the port of Mariel. Described by U.S. officials as refugees from communism, most of the Mariels were quickly resettled in the United States with federal funds. The Reagan administration awarded them permanent resident status in 1985, with eligibility for citizenship in half the normal waiting time.

Haitians received very different treatment. In 1981, the immigration service began detaining in federal prison camps all Haitians arriving without entry documents. Undocumented migrants from other countries were routinely paroled until their asylum hearings. But the Haitians were jailed—most in the Krome Detention Center, a converted Nike missile base on the edge of the Everglades. There men were separated from women and children from their parents, in facilities ringed with barbed wire. Some stayed for over a year, their only alternative to return to Haiti.

Under an agreement with the Duvalier government, meanwhile, the U.S. Coast Guard began patrolling Haitian waters and seizing boatloads of refugees. U.S. officials insist that immigration agents interview the Haitians on board the boat and that no one with a valid claim to asylum is sent back. But of the more than 12,000 Haitians interdicted since the program began, only two have been granted asylum. The rest were sent back to Haiti.[7]

This obvious injustice built support for the Haitians among a broad coalition of U.S. religious, civil rights and labor

groups. In 1982, a class action suit brought by the Miami-based Haitian Refugee Center won release on parole for 1,900 Haitians detained in Krome and other federal jails. The suit, *Jean v. Nelson,* eventually reached the Supreme Court, charging the government with discriminating against Haitians. Nearly 100 groups filed supporting briefs, including the National Council of Churches, the Congressional Black Caucus and the AFL-CIO.

Among those pressing for the boat people to gain asylum were Haitian groups in New York and Miami. This activism marked the beginning of a change in the politics of the exile community. The early exiles, centered in New York and Montreal, had continued building their personal political bases in hopes of one day returning. This rivalry hindered the development of a broad anti-Duvalier front, as did fears of retaliation against kin in Haiti. Class divisions also impeded unity, especially the cultural gap between the French-speaking professionals and the uneducated, Kreyol-speaking peasants who arrived after 1972. Eventually, however, class prejudices were put aside as Haitian groups rallied to the boat people's cause.[8]

The campaign formed part of a growing politicization of the exile community, one which stressed a Haitian national identity, use of the Kreyol language, and a political challenge to the Duvalier regime. As the anti-Duvalier movement built during 1985 and early 1986, exiled Haitians were drawn into its momentum. They staged demonstrations in support of the uprisings inside Haiti and met the fall of the regime on February 7, 1986 with rejoicing. Many prominent exiles returned home in the months which followed, some quickly entering the political arena.

The aftermath of Duvalier's fall brought bitter disappointment to those who hoped for rapid change. The military-civilian junta which took over included prominent Duvalierists implicated in past corruption and abuses. Since then, soldiers and former Tontons Macoutes have murdered hundreds of people. In one gruesome incident, the Jean Rabel massacre, Macoutes in the pay of large landowners slaughtered over two hundred peasants who were demanding land reform. Duvalier is gone, but his reign of terror continues.

So too does the flight from the country. In 1986 and 1987, the Coast Guard continued to apprehend boat people at a rate even greater than before Duvalier's fall. The bloodshed surrounding the aborted November 1987 election, when at least 34 people were killed by death squads, shocked the world. Yet, not a single Haitian who applied in 1987 for political asylum in the United States received it.[9]

In the years since Duvalier's fall, Washington has continued to trust the successor regime of Duvalierism without Duvalier. In refugee policy as well, political expediency still takes precedence over justice and compassion. The United States government, which arranged a luxurious exile for Duvalier in France, has no welcome for the victims of his system. ∎

CONTEMPORARY SLAVERY

Each December before the sugar harvest, thousands of Haitian men board trucks for the jolting journey across the border into the Dominican Republic. There they spend six months cutting sugar cane under a contract between the two governments. Their working conditions are so bad and the pay so low that some have called this notorious trade in human beings "contemporary slavery."

Cane cutters work up to 16 hours a day. The pay is 1 peso and 55 centavos per ton of cane cut. A worker might cut two tons a day, making his pay about 3 pesos ($.50). No unions function in the cane fields, so workers have no recourse against injustice such as cheating at the scales.

The Haitians live in camps called *bateyes* adjacent to the cane fields. Here a family of six or more might share a one-room shack, without plumbing or electricity. In addition to the annual laborers, called "congos," some 300,000 Haitians live permanently in the Dominican Republic as an oppressed and scorned minority group. Although many of them have been in the Dominican Republic for two or three generations, they are considered "illegal" and can be forcibly deported at any time.

An elderly Haitian cane cutter.

Lawrence Simon

Cuban Miami: Right-Wing Haven

The story of Miami's transformation from a sleepy Florida resort town into a hub of Latin capitalism, counter-revolution and organized crime is intimately bound to the story of Cuban emigration to the United States.

After 1959, thousands of Cubans fled to Miami when it became clear that Fidel Castro's revolution would be socialist. As part of its anti-Castro strategy, the Kennedy administration encouraged Cubans to emigrate and used federal funds to subsidize their resettlement in Miami. This had the twin purpose of damaging Castro's image and forcing Cuba to remain militarized because of the exile threat so close at hand. The initial migration was drawn largely from the upper class—doctors, lawyers, landowners—and the nearby presence of an affluent exile community exerted a continuing attraction to others. Later, the migration became multi-class, with the most recent wave, from the port of Mariel in 1980, drawn mainly from the working class.

Concentrated in Florida, northern New Jersey, and Puerto Rico, the Cuban exiles became one of the most militantly anticommunist elements in U.S. society. In addition to waging their own terrorist campaigns, they have served the U.S. government in numerous interventions abroad. During the Reagan years, they played a role in U.S. covert warfare in Central America, its full extent still unknown.

The Bay of Pigs operation in 1961 forged the bond between the exile community and the Central Intelligence Agency. After it failed, the Cuban government ransomed the captured exiles back to the U.S. in exchange for $6 million in food and medicine. These Bay of Pigs "veterans" were then incorporated into the U.S. national security apparatus, many of them assigned to counter-insurgency operations in Vietnam, Cambodia, Laos, the Congo and Latin America.[1]

Many others remained on the CIA payroll as agents and informers in the Kennedy administration's "Cuba Project" of ongoing attacks against Castro. The CIA's Miami station, JM-WAVE, became the largest intelligence station in the world. The CIA trained thousands of exiles in paramilitary and sabotage techniques: " . . . bullets that explode on impact, silencer-equipped machine guns, home-made explosives, and self-made napalm . . . We were taught demolition techniques, practicing on late-model cars, railroad trucks, and gas storage tanks . . . "[2] CIA-sponsored commandos launched attacks on Cuban shores, while the CIA and the Mafia cooperated in at least a dozen attempts on Castro's life.

When the Johnson administration wound down the secret war against Cuba, it was too late to dismantle the monster of exile terrorism which had been financed, armed and trained. Beginning in the late 1960s, Bay of Pigs veterans and other militant exiles began bombing targets which included the Cuban Interests Section in Washington and the Soviet and Cuban missions to the United Nations. Much of this activity was coordinated by Omega 7, a shadowy network linked to the Cuban Nationalist Movement based in Miami and Union City, New Jersey. In 1976, exile leaders from various groups gathered in the Dominican Republic and formed CORU, the

"Cuba: To the Martyrs of the Assault Brigade." Monument in Little Havana section of Miami honors fallen members of the Bay of Pigs invasion force.

"Commando of the United Revolutionary Organizations." Four months later, a powerful bomb exploded aboard a Cubana commercial airliner as the plane took off from Barbados, killing all 73 persons aboard. CORU claimed responsibility, and its leader, Orlando Bosch, was jailed in Venezuela.

Cuban exile terrorists linked up with far-flung elements of the international right, including the South Korean secret police, the Mafia, and intelligence services of various Latin American military regimes.[3] In 1976, a conspiracy between the Cuban Nationalist Movement and Pinochet's secret police resulted in the bombing murder of Orlando Letelier, who had served as Chilean ambassador to the United States under Allende. Letelier was blown up on "Embassy Row" in Washington, bringing exile terrorism to the doorstep of the U.S. government.

In 1980, Havana's U.N. attache, Felix García, was machine-gunned to death on the streets of New York, and the Cuban ambassador to the U.N. was targeted in an attempted car-bomb murder. The head of Omega 7 was convicted in 1984 of murder in connection with García's death and conspiracy in a dozen terrorist bombings.

A primary aim of exile terrorism was to intimidate members of the emigré community who do not conform to the anti-Castro model. Among the victims of bombings were firms doing business in Cuba, including those shipping medical supplies. Persons who support dialogue with Cuba, liberal expatriate magazines (*Réplica* and *Areito*) and travel agents organizing trips to Cuba have all been targets. In 1979 Carlos Muñiz Varela, a travel agent handling trips to Cuba, was murdered in San Juan by an offshoot of Omega 7.

Nonetheless, a sizable minority of the emigré community accepts the permanence of Castro's government and favors establishing dialogue and trade ties. The Cuban-American Committee, formed in 1977, gathered 10,000 Cuban-American signatures on a petition calling for normalized relations between Washington and Havana. Others formed the "Committee of 75," which successfully negotiated with Castro for the release of some prisoners and permission for exiles to visit Cuba. The Antonio Maceo Brigade, consisting mainly of young Cuban-Americans, is sympathetic to the revolution. But the climate of intimidation means that such voices are often silenced. In a letter to the *Washington Post,* Manuel Gómez, president of the Cuban-American Committee, wrote:

> At best, to favor a policy of firm dialogue with Cuba is sure to elicit vicious and slanderous attacks in the media; at worst, it can bring death or maiming at the hands of Cuban exile terrorists. I know; the FBI has warned me of threats against my life. Little wonder then that Mr. Evans and Mr. Novak think of Cuban-Americans who favor dialogue with Cuba as a "rare breed." We are not really that rare; it's just that we often have to keep our mouths tightly shut.[4]

Reagan's Miami

The city of Miami bridges two worlds. Located in North America, it is an economic nerve center of Latin America, hub of a sprawling business and crime empire. Wealthy elites from Latin America and the Caribbean stash their capital in Miami banks and invest in Florida real estate. Others fly in for shopping sprees and return laden with Cuisinarts and video recorders. Hundreds of multinational corporations and banks have their Latin American headquarters in Miami; the city hosts the annual conference of Caribbean/Central American Action, which helped design Reagan's Caribbean Basin Initiative. On the illegal side, Miami is the clearinghouse for a voluminous hard drug trade controlled by Cuban exiles and the Mafia, the profits from which are laundered in cooperative Miami banks.[5]

Miami in the '80s is also a center of counterrevolution. It is a refuge for deposed dictators and Central American oligarchs fleeing revolutionary upheaval. To the Cuban community— now 40% of Miami's population—has been added an influx of wealthy Nicaraguans and Salvadorans. As the chance of unseating Castro appears increasingly remote, right-wing Cubans have turned to the anti-Sandinista cause, working closely with the Miami-based contra leaders. The Bay of Pigs veterans' association, Brigade 2506, runs a military training camp in the Everglades which has sent Cuban-Americans to fight with the contras in Nicaragua.[6]

The alliance between the Reagan administration and Miami's Cuban community was cemented early on. An avidly Republican, pro-Reagan voting block, Cuban emigrés enjoyed special favors from the administration, notably the creation of Radio Martí. The rightist Cuban American National Foundation, headed by wealthy Miami businessmen, lobbied Congress for the station, which broadcasts into Cuba programs heavily influenced by the exile community.

At least 50 administration appointments went to Cuban-Americans, many touching on sensitive areas of hemispheric relations. José Sorzano, former president of the Cuban American National Foundation, was added to the National Security Council staff in 1987.[7] Otto Reich headed the State Department's Office of Public Diplomacy from 1983-1986, leading the administration's propaganda campaign in favor of the Nicaraguan contras. Other examples included José Manuel Casanova, U.S. director of the Inter-American Development Bank; Rita Rodríguez, a director of the Export-Import Bank; and Victor Blanco, chairman of the Inter-American Foundation.

The downing of Eugene Hasenfus' plane in October 1986 as it ferried arms to the Nicaraguan rebels provided a glimpse of the role of Cuban exiles in the Reagan administration's covert wars. Two Cubans ran the illegal contra supply operation out of the United States' Ilopango air base in El Salvador: Felix Rodríguez (alias Max Gómez) and Luis Posada (alias Ramón Medina), both members of an elite sabotage team trained by the CIA for anti-Castro warfare. Their ties with Americans in the covert operations network, including Theodore Shackley, Richard Secord and General John Singlaub, date back to the 1960s, when Rodríguez worked under Shackley in CIA operations in Miami, Laos and Vietnam. Posada was a founding member of CORU who was jailed in Venezuela for the bombing of the Cubana airliner. The Cubans' liaison to the White House was Donald Gregg, an aide to vice-president George Bush and former CIA station chief in South Korea.[8]

The reabsorption of many CIA-trained Cubans into covert warfare, along with the emigré elite's political gains, led to a decline in terrorist bombings during the Reagan years. But violent intimidation continued, and was extended to target

Ideological control in Miami: Insignia of the Antonio Maceo Brigade defaced by swastika.

non-Cuban critics of Reagan policies. Threats from Omega 7 forced a North American solidarity group, LACASA, to cancel a demonstration protesting the administration's Central American policies. Cuban thugs broke up a press conference called by LACASA as Miami police looked on. The black city manager of Miami, Howard Gary, received death threats and required police protection after he made a speech criticizing Reagan. At the 1987 Pan American games in Indianapolis, three anti-Castro groups disrupted the games to protest the presence of athletes from Cuba.

Changing of the Guard

Although it is seldom conceded openly, the survival of the Castro government 25 years after the Bay of Pigs invasion has forced a subtle change in attitudes for all but a die-hard minority of exiles. No more sympathetic to the regime than before, they have nonetheless had to accept the failure of efforts to overthrow it. Attacks on the government in Havana now focus less on invasion attempts than on discrediting Cuba through international publicity around human rights issues.

The emergence of new sectors within the exile community has helped dilute ideological unity. The 125,000 Cubans who arrived in 1980 from the port of Mariel, most of them working-class, met with a cold reception from the bourgeois Miami Cubans. Arriving without the education, capital or connections of the early emigrés, many "Marielitos" wound up jobless and indigent. About 7,000 were detained in U.S. prisons on the basis of crimes committed in Cuba or the United States. In 1987, Cuban inmates in federal detention centers in Georgia and Louisiana rioted to protest plans to deport 2,500 of them to Cuba. Like their reasons for leaving Cuba in the first place, however, the Marielitos' primary concerns in exile are economic, not ideological.

But it is the coming of age of a new generation of Cuban-Americans, born in the United States or brought there at a young age, which offers the greatest possibility for eventual change. After a hiatus, the magazine *Areito* reappeared in 1987 offering itself as a forum for debate:

> For many years, intransigent right-wing sectors have hindered free discussion of the events and ideas of greatest importance for our community. Political pluralism is in an embryonic state in Miami, and for many of the intransigents, the very concept is a "communist," diabolical one ... Although we recognize that the Cuban emigré community is in general a conservative one, we also believe that like every other community, ours is subject to evolution and change.[9]

Although many second-generation Cuban-Americans are politically conservative and anticommunist, few share the deep preoccupation with Fidel Castro which marked their parents'

Areito

Carlos Muniz Varela, slain at age 27 by Cuban exile terrorists in Puerto Rico. He was a founding member of the Antonio Maceo Brigade.

generation. That some young Cubans hold more liberal views than their elders was apparent in a poll taken by *Areito,* which found Miami Cubans under age 30 largely critical of the Reagan policy of selling arms to Iran. Cubans over age 50 approved by an 85% majority of using the Iran arms monies to fund the Nicaraguan contras; but two-thirds of those under 24 disapproved.[10] Such results, along with other indications of growing debate, suggest gradual change as the old guard gives way to a new generation. Such evolution could open the way for Cuban-Americans to play a constructive role in shaping new relations between Havana and Washington. Says *Areito:*

> We insist on the necessity of dialogue between ourselves and the people and government of Cuba. Not only because it is our right, but also because it is the only way for us to avoid becoming disconnected from the course and reality of our people.[11] ∎

NOTES TO PART THREE

Migration in Caribbean History

1. Dawn I. Marshall, "The History of Caribbean Migrations: The Case of the West Indies," *Caribbean Review,* Vol. XI, No. 1, Winter 1982, p. 6.
2. Cecilia A. Karch, "The Growth of the Corporate Economy in Barbados: Class/Race Factors 1890-1977," in Susan Craig, ed., *Contemporary Caribbean: A Sociological Reader* (Trinidad: Craig, 1982), Vol. 1, pp. 213-238.
3. Ransford W. Palmer, *Caribbean Dependence on the United States Economy* (New York: Praeger, 1979), chapter 6.
4. Excerpted from "Colonisation in Reverse," in Louise Bennett, *Jamaica Labrish* (Kingston: Sangster's Book Stores, 1966), pp. 179-180.
5. Gary P. Freeman, "Caribbean Migration to Britain and France," *Caribbean Review,* Vol. XI, No. 1, Winter 1982, p. 30.
6. Jack Harewood, "Unemployment and Under-Employment in the Commonwealth Caribbean," in Craig, ed., Vol. 1, pp. 143-166.

Blacks in Britain: A Bitter Trial

1. A. Sivanandan, "From Resistance to Rebellion: Asian and Afro-Caribbean Struggles in Britain," *Race & Class,* XXIII, 2/3 (1981-82), p. 116.
2. Alan Stinton, "From Roots to Riots," in Arif Ali, ed., *Third World Impact* (London: Hansib Publishing Ltd., 1982), pp. 10-11.
3. Sivanandan, pp. 126-127.
4. *Ibid.,* p. 135.
5. Paul Gordon and Anne Newnham, *Different Worlds: Racism and Discrimination in Britain* (London: The Runnymede Trust, 1986), p. 17.
6. *Ibid.,* p. 6.
7. Frank Bovenkerk, "Caribbean Migration to the Netherlands," *Caribbean Review,* Vol. XI, No. 1, p. 37.

Moving North: Caribbean Migration to the U.S.

1. Roy Simon Bryce-Laporte, "New York City and the New Caribbean Immigration," in Constance R. Sutton and Elsa M. Chaney, eds., *Caribbean Life in New York City: Sociocultural Dimensions* (New York: Center for Migration Studies, 1987), p. 57.
2. Statistical Profile of the Foreign-Born Population, 1980 Census of Population.
3. "A Profile of the Newest New Yorkers," *New York Times,* Aug. 9, 1987.
4. "New York Embraces Island Fare," *New York Times,* April 9, 1986.
5. Elsa M. Chaney, "The Context of Caribbean Migration," in Sutton and Chaney, p. 3.
6. Philip Kasinitz and Judith Freidenberg-Herbstein, "The Puerto Rican Parade and West Indian Carnival," in Sutton and Chaney, p. 338.
7. Constance R. Sutton and Susan Makiesky-Barrow, "Migration and West Indian Racial and Ethnic Consciousness," in Sutton and Chaney, p. 105.
8. Jim Sleeper, "The Caribbean Black Challenge," *Washington Post,* Aug. 24, 1986.
9. Paule Marshall, "Black Immigrant Women in *Brown Girl Brownstones,*" in Sutton and Chaney, p. 89.
10. Linda G. Basch, "The Politics of Caribbeanization," in Sutton and Chaney, p. 174.

The Puerto Rican Experience

1. Manuel Maldonado-Denis, "Puerto Rican Emigration: Proposals for Its Study," in *Contemporary Marxism,* No. 5, Summer 1982, p. 24.
2. Gordon K. Lewis, "Migration and Caribbean Consciousness" (Occasional Paper No. 1, Center for Latin American Studies, University of Florida at Gainesville), p. 11.
3. U.S. Census figures, 1940-1980, cited in National Puerto Rican Coalition, *Puerto Ricans in the Mid '80s: An American Challenge* (Arlington, VA, 1985), p. 5. The Census Bureau in 1985 estimated 2.6 million Puerto Ricans in the U.S.; in 1987 it estimated 2.3 million. See U.S. Bureau of the Census, *Persons of Spanish-Speaking Origin in the U.S.,* March 1985; and *The Hispanic Population in the United States, March 1986 and 1987.*
4. First annual report of Gov. Charles Allen, cited in *Sources for the Study of Puerto Rican Migration* (New York: Centro de Estudios Puertorriquenos), pp. 14-15.
5. Maldonado-Denis, "Puerto Rican Emigration: Proposals for Its Study," p. 23.
6. Oral History Task Force, *Stories to Live By: Continuity and Change in Three Generations of Puerto Rican Women* (New York: Centro de Estudios Puertorriquenos, 1987), pp. 59, 56.
7. 1980 Census, cited in *Puerto Ricans in the Mid '80s,* p. 14.
8. U.S. Bureau of the Census, *Persons of Spanish-Speaking Origin in the U.S., March 1985,* p. 5.
9. *Puerto Ricans in the Mid '80s,* p. 15.
10. National Congress for Puerto Rican Rights, *The Status of Puerto Ricans in the United States 1987* (New York: Centro de Estudios Puertorriquenos, 1987), pp. 19-22.
11. Juan Flores, John Attinasi and Pedro Pedraza Jr., "Puerto Rican Language and Culture in New York City," in Sutton and Chaney, pp. 226-229.
12. *The Status of Puerto Ricans in the United States 1987,* pp. 8-13.
13. *Ibid.,* pp. 22-28.

The Haitian Boat People

1. Church World Service Immigration and Refugee Program, "Haitian Refugees Need Asylum: A Briefing Paper," April 9, 1980.
2. Immigration and Naturalization Service, Asylum Cases Filed with INS District Directors Approved and Denied, by Selected Nationalities, June 1983-Sept. 1987. Cited in *Refugee Reports,* Dec. 18, 1987 (American Council for Nationalities Service, Washington, DC).
3. Cuban-Haitian Task Force, *Monthly Entrant Reports,* May 31, 1982. Cited in Josh DeWind and David Kinley, *Aiding Migration: The Impact of International Development Assistance on Haiti* (New York: Center for the Social Sciences, Columbia University, 1986), p. 13.
4. Amnesty International, *Torture in the Eighties* (London: Amnesty International, 1984), pp. 162-163.
5. Amnesty International, "Haiti Briefing," March 1985, p. 12.
6. Michael Hooper, *Haiti: Duvalierism Since Duvalier* (Americas Watch and National Coalition for Haitian Refugees, 1986), pp. 9-10.
7. Bill Frelick, "U.S. Treatment of Haitian Refugees Smacks of Double Standard," United States Committee for Refugees, Washington, DC, 1987.
8. Nina Glock Schiller et al., "All in the Same Boat? Unity and Diversity in Haitian Organizing in New York," in Sutton and Chaney, pp. 182-199.
9. Immigration and Naturalization Service, Asylum Cases Filed with INS District Directors (cf. note 2).

Cuban Miami: Right-Wing Haven

1. Lourdes Arguelles, "Cuban Miami: The Roots, Development and Everyday Life of an Emigre Enclave in the U.S. National Security State," *Contemporary Marxism,* No. 5, Summer 1982, p. 30.
2. Description of training at CIA's demolition training headquarters, where Cubans were trained, by former officer of CIA's Clandestine Services. Cited in Victor Marchetti and J. Marks, *The CIA and the Cult of Intelligence* (New York: Dell, 1974), p. 111.
3. Warren Hinkle and William Turner, *The Fish Is Red: The Story of the Secret War Against Castro* (New York: Harper & Row, 1981), p. 317.
4. *Washington Post,* Aug. 30, 1983.
5. Penny Lernoux, "The Miami Connection," *The Nation,* Feb. 18, 1984.
6. "In the Bushes of Florida, Cuban 'Brigade' Tries to Keep the Flame Alive," *New York Times,* Dec. 26, 1986. In 1984 it was reported that wealthy Miami Cubans were funding a secret base in Costa Rica from which a Cuban team harassed Sandinista targets. Jack Anderson, "Anti-Castro Cubans Aid Contra Rebels," *Washington Post,* Nov. 20, 1984.
7. Jose Sorzano resigned from the NSC in 1988.
8. Numerous press accounts have reported the role of Rodriguez and Posada and their CIA ties. For an overview, see Jonathan Marshall, Peter Dale Scott and Jane Hunter, *The Iran-Contra Connection: Secret Teams and Covert Operations in the Reagan Era* (Boston: South End Press, 1987).
9. Editorial, *Areito,* Vol. 1, No. 1, segunda epoca, Spring 1987, p. 2.
10. "Encuesta sobre el escandalo Iran-Contras," *Areito,* Spring 1987, pp. 12-13.
11. Editorial, *Areito,* Spring 1987, p. 3.

PART FOUR
Alternative Models of Development
Cuba & Grenada

Vicky Surles

Introduction

Revolution in Cuba and Grenada has become an emotional subject for North Americans. We are told that Cuba is a "totalitarian dictatorship," where there are no rights or freedoms. The revolutionary government in Grenada is said to have been a "Cuban-style communist dictatorship," and both are blamed for threatening our security by bringing Soviet influence to the doorstep of the United States.

Barred by U.S. law from visiting Cuba and subjected to a 25-year news blackout punctuated by biased and false reports, most North Americans are abjectly ignorant of the Cuban reality. Behind this shield of ignorance and fear, successive U.S. administrations have elevated the campaign for the downfall of Cuban leader Fidel Castro into a bizarre kind of holy war. The Central Intelligence Agency has tried numerous times to assassinate Castro, and has sponsored attacks by anti-Castro exiles on Cuban shores. CIA-organized mercenaries invaded Cuba in 1961 and were defeated by the Cuban people who defended their country. Cuba has suffered a U.S. trade embargo for twenty years, placing enormous and unnatural strains on its economy—but failing utterly to dislodge the Castro government.

In the case of Grenada, the U.S. campaigned to block the country's access to badly-needed international aid and loans. Hostile propaganda emanating from Washington (such as the untrue story that a Soviet naval base was being built in Grenada) scared U.S. visitors away from the island, cutting deeply into revenues from tourism. Twice—in 1981 and 1982—U.S. armed forces practiced a mock invasion of Grenada, and the constant specter of a U.S. attack helped raise blood pressures on the tiny island. In October 1983, a fatal split in the ruling party opened the door to the real invasion and the Grenada revolution was no more.

The U.S. government campaign against Cuba and Grenada not only has threatened their existence; it has largely hidden from view the real accomplishments and meaning of the two revolutions. Cuba is not a perfect society, nor was revolutionary Grenada. Both encountered many problems and made mistakes in the course of social transformation. But they have won respect in the Caribbean and outside the region for their bold attempts to find solutions to the poverty and inequality which resulted from centuries of domination by outside powers.

Both revolutions put the ordinary people—the poor majority—at the center of their process. In Cuba, the primary task was to rectify the gross social inequalities and foreign domination which marked the society during the dictator Batista's rule. Under the revolution, for the first time, a peasant farmer or sugar worker could get good medical care, eat a nutritious diet, live in a house with running water, and send his or her children to school. And for the first time, ordinary Cubans could see the vast and fertile island as belonging to *them* rather than to colonial powers, a corrupt ruling clique, foreign corporations and wealthy tourists.

Grenada's 1979 revolution borrowed a number of ideas and structures from the Cuban experience, primarily in the areas of health, education and defense, where Cuban technicians assisted the Grenadian government. But there were also significant differences between the two. Grenada, for example, did not attempt to rapidly convert its economy to socialism. The bulk of the Grenadian economy remained in private hands, with the goal for the near future a mixed economy comprising a public sector, a private sector and cooperatives. A more important difference was that Grenada's short-lived experiment never approached the stage of consolidation and maturity achieved by the Cuban revolution after 25 years. While the government of Maurice Bishop instituted many successful programs and raised the standard of living dramatically compared to pre-1979 days, it had only begun the task of creating political institutions which could both provide effective leadership and develop meaningful channels for popular participation.

It is difficult for most North Americans to imagine living all one's life illiterate, malnourished and exploited in a society where everything is controlled by a privileged elite. Because we are distanced from this experience, we fail also to appreciate that education, health care, shelter and employment are *rights* that are fundamental to human freedom and dignity. When we talk about the rights that sometimes are abridged by revolutions—such as the right to publish—we must weigh these against the fulfillment of other rights which have been denied to the majority for many years. It is precisely because these rights are so important that the majority of Cubans support Fidel Castro and the majority of Grenadians supported the Bishop government.

Ruling circles in the United States chose long ago to oppose attempts toward social justice in Latin America, throwing U.S. power instead behind the maintenance of elite privilege and foreign domination. For this reason, both Cuba and Grenada had to defy U.S. dictates in order to be free to transform their societies. In the process, they became vocal adherents of "anti-imperialism," adding to American perceptions of a hostile threat. But as anyone who has visited Cuba or revolutionary Grenada can attest, anti-imperialism does not mean ill-will toward the American *people*. Rather, it is an affirmation of the right to engage in social change and to create a model different from the one imposed by colonial and neocolonial powers. These efforts deserve our understanding and support. Far from threatening the security of the hemisphere, they hold out hope of an alternative path to development for the Caribbean which may succeed where previous attempts have consistently failed. ■

Cuba

In the jubilation which greeted Batista's overthrow, all things seemed possible for the young revolution. To redistribute wealth from the rich to the poor, and from the cities to the rural areas, was one basic goal. Another was to break Cuba's dependence on the United States and reduce reliance on sugar exports. All this was to be done while moving out of underdevelopment to become an economically viable nation.

No blueprint existed for such a transformation. The Cuban revolution sought its own independent path. But it also made use of Soviet models, since the Soviet Union offered the example of the first socialist state. It was also the only nation to offer technical assistance on the scale needed and a military shield against U.S. hostility. The Cuban leaders installed the basic elements of a Soviet-style system, while at the same time pursuing initiatives of their own which did not reflect the Soviet model.

Confronted with the objective reality of underdevelopment and with constant external harassment, the revolution achieved mixed results—and provoked mixed reactions from outsiders. Even many opponents acknowledge that the Cuban revolution has brought impressive advances in such areas as education and health. Even its strongest defenders admit

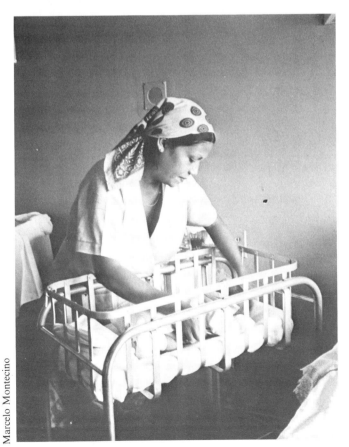

On a Cuban maternity ward.

Marcelo Montecino

mistakes, changes in policies, and unresolved problems. Its survival as an alternative, so close to the United States, continues to provoke admiration, hostility and controversy, and makes its experience a continuing reference point for other countries in the region.

Health and Education: Models of Innovation

In a country where illiteracy was high and malnutrition widespread, education and health became urgent priorities. Cuba's achievements in these areas are the most widely praised and emulated aspects of the revolution.

In 1961 the government closed most of the high schools for a year and sent thousands of students to the countryside, where they lived and worked with the rural population. At night, they taught their campesino hosts to read and write. Illiteracy fell from 25% to about 4%, the lowest in Latin America.[1]

The success of the literacy campaign was highly attractive to other poor countries. New revolutionary states in the 1960s and '70s such as Angola, Mozambique, Nicaragua and Grenada followed the Cuban example, although most opted for a more gradual approach.

Before the revolution, most Cuban high schools were in Havana and the larger towns. The new government built schools throughout rural Cuba, serving the farthest reaches of the countryside. Education became free through the university level. By the mid-1960s most Cubans had attained a third-grade education, and by the mid-1970s a sixth-grade level was the goal. Today the target is that all Cubans complete a ninth-grade education.

Within the span of a generation, Cuba created what is regarded as perhaps the best health care system in the Third World. It did so against formidable odds. In 1959, most doctors and hospitals were concentrated in Havana. Half the country's 6,000 doctors emigrated in the revolution's first two years, and the U.S. embargo cut off essential medicines.

The concept of "social medicine" underlay the new health system.[2] This meant, essentially, that health care was seen not as an isolated service for sale but as an integral part of how the society was organized. The new system was based on a decentralized network of polyclinics, or community health centers, which replaced private physicians as providers of basic care. In 1983 a new program of "family doctors" helped to personalize the system.

A key part of the health strategy was to assure all Cubans a nutritious diet. Basic foods such as rice, beans, milk, meat and sugar are heavily subsidized and sold at prices which have risen only once since 1965. Every family receives a ration book entitling them to buy quantities of these staples at the subsidized prices. Since everyone can afford the foods, rationing ensures equitable distribution. Other foods are sold through non-rationed channels at higher prices.

The San Francisco-based Institute for Food and Development Policy calls eliminating hunger the "single most unassailable achievement of the Cuban revolution."[3] Cuba ranks second in per capita food consumption in Latin America, after Argentina. Childhood malnutrition is virtually unknown.

Cuba's health indicators now resemble those of Western Europe and the United States more than those of other Third World countries. Infant mortality, which was 70 per 1000 in 1960, has dropped to 15 per 1000 in the 1980s. Life expectancy at birth is about 74, just short of the U.S. figure of 75, and contrasting with life expectancy of 62 in the Dominican Republic and 54 in Haiti.[4] Cuba's main health problems are no longer the infectious diseases of poverty, but the "affluent" problems of heart disease, cancer and obesity. There is also a growing problem with teenage pregnancy.

Cuba has become something of a "medical power," with over 3,000 Cuban doctors and health technicians working in 27 Third World countries.[5] Many developing countries have copied aspects of the Cuban system, which has won praise from the World Health Organization and other international bodies.

Evolution of a Socialist Economy

Cuba's achievements in education and health are the result of deliberately setting priorities. Areas deemed less crucial, notably housing, have lagged behind. With limited resources, the country has had to make hard choices. One result is that the channeling of resources into the rural areas has left Havana noticeably delapidated.

Building an economy which can support development has been Cuba's most difficult problem, and a debate over economic policy has continued for three decades. How should Cuba structure its economy in order to ensure social justice, produce enough food and consumer goods and still earn foreign exchange needed for imports?

After coming to power in 1959, Castro's government moved boldly to socialize the economy and redistribute wealth. Basic industries such as sugar mills, oil refineries and factories were nationalized. By the end of the 1960s, nearly the entire economy was in state hands. Only about a third of the agricultural sector, consisting of small farmers, remained private and somewhat outside the revolution.

A radical agrarian reform nationalized land holdings by foreigners and limited private Cuban holdings to 65 hectares. The state took over the largest estates, turning them into state farms. But it also gave over 100,000 tenant farmers title to their plots, along with technical assistance and credit. House rents were reduced by 50%, and rent for new housing fixed at 10% of the household head's income.

Although poor people benefited from these reforms, the early years were hard for the country. The government set out to rapidly industrialize the economy, but this goal proved unrealistic. Neglect of agriculture, the impact of the U.S. embargo and a severe drought combined to send production plummeting in 1962-63. Food shortages developed, and rationing had to be introduced.[6]

By mid-decade the Cuban leaders had accepted that sugar would continue as the economic base, providing foreign exchange to invest in industry. The government set a target of 10 million tons of raw sugar for the 1970 harvest, and the country mobilized for the effort.

Che Guevara, head of the central bank, set the course with his belief in revolutionary fervor as the motor force of production. Supported by Castro, Che argued that as the state provided for more of people's needs, wages would lose their importance. "Moral incentives"—appeals to revolutionary values—would motivate people to work. The experiment was a failure. With all workers in an enterprise paid equally, regardless of their output, production sagged. Store shelves were bare and workplace absenteeism became a nagging problem.

The failure of the 10 million ton harvest in 1970 marked a turning point. Cuba did produce a record 8.5 million tons that year. But the all-out drive diverted investment, labor and resources from other sectors, so that overall production fell sharply in 1971. Cuba's debt to the Soviet Union rose.

Pressured by the Soviets to abandon their unorthodox practices, the Cuban leaders moved away from Che's model during the 1970s. New policies emphasized planning and the introduction of limited market measures. These included the so-called "material incentives," bonuses such as cars and refrigerators for workers who produced the most. The government also permitted a limited amount of private contracting in services such as plumbing and hairdressing.

Small private farmers were encouraged to merge their holdings into cooperatives, in which members own land collectively and divide their earnings. Offered incentives such as pensions and new housing, many farmers joined the collectives, although many others chose not to. The cooperatives soon proved to be more efficient than the large state farms.[7]

In 1980, the government launched a controversial experiment, the free peasant markets. By allowing private farmers to sell their surplus directly to consumers at unregulated prices, the government hoped to curb the black market which had met consumers' demands for a wider variety of foods. The farmers' markets became very popular, supplying hard-to-get foods at premium prices.

Together with Soviet-inspired economic reforms came Cuba's formal integration into the Soviet bloc. Cuba joined the Eastern European Economic Community (COMECON) in 1972, becoming the main supplier of sugar to the group. Although Cuba succeeded in developing industry and new exports such as seafood and citrus, the COMECON agreement ensured that sugar would remain the primary export. But the long-term purchase contracts were on advantageous terms, with the Soviets paying five to six times the world market price. The combination of sugar earnings, industrial growth and more realistic planning led to economic recovery during the decade.

High school students work on a farm as part of a work study program.

A Call to Conciencia

The recovery was to be short-lived. By the late 1970s, malaise was growing. Purchasing power was rising, but the production of goods could not keep pace. Many Cubans looked on enviously as thousands of exiles from Miami, visiting under accords between Havana and the Carter administration, arrived laden with U.S.-made goods. Would-be emigrants were frustrated by the refusal of U.S. authorities to grant visas. Yet Cubans who hijacked small boats to enter Florida illegally were allowed to stay. The situation exploded in 1980 with the exodus of 125,000 Cubans in the Mariel boatlift, shaking the Cuban leadership.[8]

In 1982 the price of sugar collapsed on the world market. Although Cuba was selling 70% of its sugar to the Soviet Union, the remaining sugar sold to Western countries was an important source of hard currency. The sharp fall of petroleum prices was a blow as well. Cuba had been earning about 40% of its export income by reexporting oil donated by the Soviet Union; that income was now halved. Credit from the West was drying up under the pressure of Cuba's $3.5 billion hard-currency debt. A prolonged drought and a hurricane added to the country's woes.

To save on imports, the government launched an austerity campaign. Bus fares doubled from 5 to 10 cents, electricity rates rose and kerosene rations were reduced. Other measures aimed at curbing bureaucratic waste. But wages for the lowest-paid workers were increased, and programs in health and education remained largely untouched.

The government's response went farther, however. At the third Communist Party congress in 1986, Castro delivered a blistering critique of the country's performance. Low productivity and indiscipline, Fidel charged, had eroded the revolutionary work ethic. Corruption, waste and mismanagement were rampant.

The remedy was to be a "rectification" campaign to bring the country back to the correct path. Reminding Cubans that socialism could not be built by becoming "apprentice capitalists," Castro pulled back sharply on private sector activities. He closed the free peasant markets, citing abuse by middlemen who, along with some farmers, had become wealthy selling food at scalpers' prices. For Fidel, the inequality generated by these profits violated the revolution's principles. An experiment in private home sales was also abandoned, and curbs imposed on other free-lance sales.

Castro called instead for a revival of socialist values and spirit, of revolutionary *conciencia*. Its symbol became the minibrigades, the voluntary construction teams which were popular during the '60s but had fallen into disuse. Once again, workers began taking time away from their offices and factories on full pay to build apartments, clinics and schools. The brigades responded to the acute housing problem and, at a deeper level, to what Castro saw as an overgrowth of bureaucracy and planning. In a speech to party members, he set the new tone:

> MICONS [Ministry of Construction] couldn't build a single day-care center, not one! Because simply to ask them to build a day-care center was enough to make them faint. You ran the risk of causing the fellow at the head of the institution to collapse, to have a fainting fit . . . These were the methods we called technocratic, bureaucratic, giving up on the people, giving up on voluntary work.[9]

Courtesy of *Areito*

In Revolution Square, Havana. Portraits show Che Guevara, left, and Camilo Cienfuegos, another hero of Batista's overthrow.

Courtesy of *Areito*

Voluntary labor could repair Havana's crumbling buildings, he suggested, rather than waiting for "a brand-new superorganized overstaffed bureaucratic enterprise with 50 different forms and two million papers" to start the job. In 1987, the revitalized brigades built 6,000 apartments and 54 day-care centers in the capital.

Although not advertised as such, the minibrigades provided a partial solution to another problem as well: unemployment disguised by overstaffing of offices and factories. Although still low, open unemployment has edged upward from its level of 3.4% in 1981. The problem is especially marked among youth. As education levels have risen, many young Cubans aspire to white-collar jobs; some even choose to remain idle rather than work in industry or agriculture.

While moral incentives are back in style, material incentives have not been abandoned. Workers are still paid according to the quantity and quality of their work. Still, Cuba's turn away from the market contrasts to trends in the Soviet Union, China and Eastern European countries, which are loosening some controls in order to stimulate their economies. Whatever the consequences of the Cuban choice, it has reaffirmed the country's revolution as unique and independent of any single model.

Political Reforms and People's Power

Like the country's economy, political structures in Cuba have undergone a process of reform. The direction has been toward more popular participation, although basic policy directions remain firmly in the hands of the party leadership.

The present-day Cuban Communist Party was formed in 1965 to "guide" all aspects of the revolutionary process. Government bureaucracy during the sixties was highly centralized, and channels for popular input limited. Mass organizations such as the Federation of Cuban Women, the Communist Youth Union, and the Committees for Defense of the Revolution mobilized participation in the revolution's programs.

In the 1970s, while reforming the economy, the Cuban leaders moved to anchor the revolution in a set of political institutions. The Communist Party held its first congress in 1975, leading to the promulgation of a new socialist Constitution the following year. The mass organizations were revitalized and given a consultative role in policy-making. For example, the Cuban Workers Confederation helped draft laws giving trade unions more autonomy and introducing material incentives into the workplace.[10]

The Constitution set in place a major new mechanism aimed at making direct representation part of the system. *Poder Popular* (People's Power) began experimentally in Matanzas province in 1974 and was extended to the rest of the country in 1976. The public directly elects delegates to the lowest level of the system, the municipal assemblies. These in turn elect delegates to the provincial assemblies and the National Assembly, which is the state's legislative organ.

While Poder Popular provides an institutional channel from the grassroots to the top, its actual powers are limited. At the municipal and provincial levels it has some authority to address local problems, typically in areas such as health and housing. The National Assembly debates national policies and approves laws. Yet certain areas remain effectively beyond its reach, notably economic, foreign and military policies.

These sensitive areas are the purvue of decision-makers in three elite bodies: the Council of State, the executive committee of the Council of Ministers, and the Communist Party's Political Bureau.[11] They are strongly interlocked in their membership. There is also considerable overlap between the respective lower levels of the party, the government bureaucracy and People's Power. Ranking bureaucrats are generally members of the Communist Party, as are 62% of all Poder Popular delegates and 90% of the National Assembly deputies.[12]

The political directions defined by the Communist Party form the parameters within which Poder Popular and the bureaucracy debate and act. The party is, in effect, the "brains" of the system, reflecting the Leninist concept of a vanguard which leads the people to construct socialism. It is small, comprising about 5% of the population. The Central Committee has 225 full and alternate members and the Political Bureau 24. Fidel Castro is first secretary of the party; his brother Raul is second secretary and designated by the party as Fidel's successor.

While far from the one-man dictatorship that its critics portray, the Cuban system is hierarchical and bureaucratic, with a lot of power concentrated at the top. The mass organizations and People's Power do give ordinary Cubans a means to participate, but at a level which is generally remote from major decision-making. There is lively public debate on many issues, but it seldom challenges basic policy directions defined by the leadership.

An important means of bringing ideas into the system is the elevation of new members to the party's top ranks. At the third Communist Party congress in 1986, a shake-up in the Central Committee and Political Bureau brought in more women, blacks, youth and workers. Although white males still dominate, the percentage of women on the Central Committee rose from 5% in 1975 to 19% in 1986, with one woman in the Political Bureau. Blacks and mulattos make up 28% of the Central Committee.[13] By formally adopting an "affirmative action" strategy, the party broke with assumptions that simply removing discrimination would bring about equality. Applications for party membership from youth, workers and peasants are also receiving preference.

The Challenge of Renewal

In launching his rectification campaign, Castro emphasized that the process of self-criticism is "only open to revolutionaries." That is, the debate concerns methods, not basic goals of the revolution. Within these parameters, however, openness is gradually growing about problems in Cuban society. The state-controlled media has been encouraged to be more informative, lively and critical. In 1987 the youth magazine *Somos Jovenes* carried two exposes, one

Young Cuban dancers practice on outskirts of Havana.

Marcelo Montecino

on prostitution in Havana and the other on cheating in the schools. Such public airing of dirty linen would have been unthinkable a few years before.

One focus of concern is youth, including the emergence of a materialist subculture among some young people. Young Cubans who do not remember the hardships under Batista take for granted that their essential needs are met. Many yearn for more: the designer jeans and video recorders they see on Miami television and in the movies, and which are only obtainable on the black market in Cuba. Another symptom of the problem is the virtual epidemic of teen pregnancies, following the belated arrival of the sexual revolution in Cuba. With half the Cuban population born since 1959, motivating a new generation to adhere to a spirit of disciplined struggle is a critical challenge for the society.

The question of political "space" is another. More than most societies, Cuba guarantees its citizens basic human rights: food, health care, education, employment. The system rests on the idea that the revolution ensures the most good for the most people, therefore individuals have no "right" to work against it.

While most Cubans appear to agree, it is obvious that some freedom of speech (particularly in terms of what is published), along with freedom to organize outside of or against the system, has been sacrificed.

The United States government and other right-wing critics charge that Cuba holds thousands of political prisoners. The Cuban government insists that no dissidents are in prison, but acknowledges holding several hundred persons who have tried to commit sabotage or spy for the CIA. The truth may lie somewhere in between. Many prisoners were in fact involved in counterrevolutionary plots sponsored by the CIA in the 1960s. Others are probably dissidents, such as the three members of the Cuban Committee for Human Rights jailed for eight months in 1986. The question is complicated by an unclear definition of just what constitutes counterrevolution. A Cuban pastor notes: "It is a problem where to draw the line between legitimate criticism of the revolution for the purpose of strengthening it, and something against the revolution."[14]

The Cuban government has recently shown willingness to release many prisoners if the United States will take them. In

1987 the U.S. Catholic Conference working with the Cuban Church won the release of 348 political prisoners. Castro offered in 1988 to release another 385 in response to an appeal by the Roman Catholic Archbishop of New York.

The divergent pictures painted by Cuba's enemies and friends reflect not only their conflicting agendas, but also the contradictions and complexities within Cuba itself. It is a highly creative society, with a vibrant intellectual and cultural life. Yet it is also conformist, with social pressures on people to participate in the revolution and few channels for expressing ideas outside its bounds. Cynicism is widespread, but so is pride. The majority of Cubans clearly support the goals and values of the revolution and feel it has improved their lives.

Fidel Castro's charisma and moral authority has contributed much to this continuing dynamism. "Cubans are very *fidelista*," explains a Baptist pastor. This dynamism must be maintained under new leadership in the next century if the revolution is to thrive. How the revolution can renew itself, can change and adapt while remaining true to its principles, is the central challenge facing Cuba today.

The Revolution and the Church

With his call for a return to *conciencia*, Castro has indirectly acknowledged what others have suggested: renewal requires defining human values, ethics and morality for a post-revolutionary age. In that task, many Cuban clergy feel, and the government cautiously agrees, the Church may have a role to play.

Before the revolution, the churches were very weakly implanted into Cuban society. The Catholic Church had sided with colonial Spain in the independence struggle; virtually all its priests were foreign, mostly pro-Franco Spaniards. The Protestant churches entered the country as a result of U.S. penetration and reflected North American models. Both Catholics and Protestants ministered to an urban elite and had few links to the majority of Cubans who lived in the rural areas and practiced *santería*, an African/Catholic syncretic religion.

Although the Church had sought coexistence with Batista, many clergy welcomed his overthrow. But they were totally unprepared for a socialist revolution. Because of its wealthy class base, the Catholic Church soon allied itself with the counterrevolution. A number of priests and Catholic activists played leading roles in the Bay of Pigs invasion on April 17, 1961.[15] On May 1, the government declared Cuba socialist and nationalized all private schools, including those of the Church. These actions triggered a flight of church leaders, especially Catholics and Methodists, 80% of whose clergy and religious left Cuba.

The next years were hard for those who remained. Church-state relations were rigidly hostile: church leaders saw Marxism as inherently evil, while the government viewed all Christians as counterrevolutionaries. Many clergy were sent to indoctrination camps, although none was physically abused. Most difficult for the Church was the loss of any meaningful role in the society. Its wealthy and middle-class members had emigrated, while poor believers left the Church because of its opposition to the revolution.

As socialism was consolidated, the Church had to adapt or cease to survive as an institution. By the late 1960s internal reflection allowed some clergy to begin coming to terms with the changed social reality. In 1968 fruitful contacts took place between progressive North American and Cuban Protestant clergy. That same year, the Medellín conference gave hierarchical approval to the involvement of Catholics in social change. On April 10, 1969 the Catholic Bishops of Cuba issued a pastoral letter calling for Church cooperation in "national development" and the lifting of the U.S. trade embargo.

For Castro, the main issue was less religious doctrine than the Church's political alliances. The emergence in the 1970s of a Latin American theology of liberation placed this in new perspective. Castro's contacts with Christians for Socialism in Chile and with Catholics active in the Nicaraguan revolution helped persuade the Cuban leader that the Church could stand with the poor.

The symbol of this new opening was a celebrated interview between Castro and a Brazilian priest, Frei Betto, published in 1985 as *Fidel y la Religión*. In it, Castro affirms that "from a political point of view, I believe it is possible for Christians to be Marxists as well, and to work together with Marxist Communists to transform the world."[16] The book sold a million copies in Cuba, equal to one-tenth of the population.

Beginning around 1980, the Cuban government and the Catholic Church moved into a cautious dialogue. The government set up an Office of Religious Affairs within the party's Central Committee, signalling its seriousness about improving relations. A delegation of U.S. Catholic bishops visited Cuba in 1985. The following year, with the government's support, the Cuban Catholic Church held an "encounter" which brought Cuban clergy and laity together with foreign Catholic leaders. The government has provided money to repair some churches, and has allowed Bibles to be imported and foreign priests to come and work in Cuba.

Yet from the churches' perspective many problems remain. Openly religious Cubans are still barred from full social and political participation, although the government has become more responsive to complaints of discrimination. Churchgoers cannot belong to the Communist Party or the Communist Youth Union, effectively excluding them from setting directions for the country. The Church has virtually no access to the state-controlled media, although it may publish materials such as parish bulletins.

There are divisions and ambivalence on both sides. Not all government and party officials share Fidel's openness to talking with the Church. Many church leaders, especially Catholics, affirm the revolution's achievements but strongly reject its ideology as atheist and Marxist. Others reluctantly accept that Marxism is the source of a social transformation in keeping with Christian values. Monsignor Jaime Ortega, Archbishop of Havana, commented in 1985:

Here in Cuba, the word Marxism isn't used much. The term that binds Cubans together is revolution (and socialism). So when we talk about a dialogue, we don't talk about a dialogue between Marxists and Christians . . . [it] has to be between the reality called the socialist revolution and the Church.[17]

Mass at a church in Havana, 1987.

A minority of Protestants, centered in the Cuban Ecumenical Council and the Matanzas Evangelical Seminary, has gone farther in supporting the revolution. They emphasize that the Church must be a servant of the people, contributing to, not just living with, the building of socialism.

In shaping such a role, the Cuban churches have no model to follow. The Church in the Soviet Union is conservative and traditionalist, while the popular church in Latin America is tied to base communities which do not exist in Cuba. Liberation theology cannot apply in the same way to a country which has already had a revolution. But progressive Cuban Christians feel they can help continue the process of liberation in a post-revolutionary age. Castro has said that the Church can help with problems such as divorce, teen pregnancy and abortion, suggesting that the government may in time look to the churches to help provide a moral and spiritual dimension to the "new man." Dr. Adolfo Ham, a former chairman of the ecumenical council, told members of the Caribbean Conference of Churches in 1983:

Pirole, courtesy of Center for Cuban Studies

We are not a martyred or suppressed church but we have lost all the privileges and comforts of churches who were part of the establishment. Some people think it is impossible for the churches to fulfill their mission unless they have a privileged place in society. But we have learned the hard lesson that only when the Church is a servant—when the Church identifies fully with the needs and spirit of the people, is when she can be the Church.[18]

Cuba, the Third World and the United States

Cuba has assumed influence disproportionate to its size as a model of social justice for the poor. But it is a model only in the broad sense. In relations with the Manley government in Jamaica and with the Nicaraguan Sandinistas, Cuban leaders advised against certain policies Cuba itself had followed a decade earlier. Conditions now differ from those of Cuba in the sixties, they are aware, and there is no reason for others to repeat Cuba's mistakes.

Cuba's influence stems also from its power as a symbol of self-determination in the shadow of a superpower. The United States maintains a military base on Cuban soil, at Guantánamo in southeastern Cuba, with some 6,000 U.S. military personnel. South Florida bristles with electronic spy equipment; the U.S. carries out naval maneuvers around Cuba and flies spy planes overhead. "Cuba is not the best place in the world to build socialism," comments one Cuban official.

In this context, Cuba's Soviet alliance has been essential to its survival. But to see Cuban actions as merely an extension of Soviet power, as do many U.S. officials, is a mistake. "It would be a simpler world if Cuba were just a Soviet puppet," asserts Cuba scholar Jorge Domínguez.[19] Moscow defines the limits of Cuban foreign policy, and Cuba supports the Soviets diplomatically. But within these bounds Cuba has its own foreign policy which at times has diverged sharply from Soviet priorities.

Unlike the Soviet Union, Cuba orients its foreign policy toward the Third World. The principle of "internationalism," enshrined in Cuban ideology, reflects the Cubans' belief that it is their duty to help other Third World peoples achieve liberation. During the 1960s, Che Guevara led Cuban attempts to stir up armed insurgencies in Latin America. All failed. Enraged Latin governments joined the United States in isolating Cuba, while the Soviet Union opposed what it saw as reckless adventurism. Che was assassinated by CIA agents in Bolivia in 1967, and the crusade was abandoned.

During the next decade, Cuba attempted to reduce its isolation by building diplomatic and trade ties with Latin America and Europe. Sanctions imposed by the Organization of American States were lifted in 1975. There was also the tentative beginning of a dialogue between Washington and Havana. Under the Carter administration in 1977, the two countries opened interests sections in the respective capitals, exchanging diplomats for the first time in 16 years.

While President Carter's State Department favored detente, hardliners led by national security adviser Zbigniew Brzezinski sought confrontation. They found it in Africa, where Cuba was involved militarily in two countries. In 1975

Cuba responded to the Angolan government's plea for help in repelling a South African invasion supported by the CIA. Cuba subsequently sent troops to defeat a Somali invasion of Ethiopia as well. Both actions received support from African governments, but were condemned by Washington.

At the end of the decade, revolution in Central America and the advent of the Reagan administration coincided to sink U.S.-Cuban detente. The new administration blamed Cuba for everything: the Nicaraguan and Grenadian revolutions and the insurgencies in El Salvador and Guatemala. Cuba had not incited the guerrilla movements, which arose from decades of exploitation. It did attempt to assist them, sending arms to the Salvadoran rebels in 1980 and early 1981. But when the rebels failed to triumph quickly Havana backed off. No proof of further arms shipments was ever found.[20]

Secretary of State Alexander Haig set the tone at the start of Reagan's first term with threats of a direct military attack on Cuba. When these threats failed to intimidate Havana, the White House turned to petty harassment. It tightened the trade embargo, increased restrictions on Cuban diplomats and attempted to crack down on U.S. citizens visiting Cuba. Talks on bilateral issues fell victim to the exchange of snubs. The two countries had signed an agreement in 1984 to regularize migration, in which Cuba was to take back 2,500 Mariel Cubans jailed in the U.S. Before the agreement could be implemented, the Reagan administration launched Radio Martí, and an angry Castro suspended the migration pact.

Relations went into a deep freeze as the United States led an international campaign to discredit Cuba on human rights grounds. The campaign centered on the yearly meetings of the United Nations Human Rights Commission in Geneva, where the U.S. delegation attempted to pressure other countries into condemning Cuba. In 1987 and again in 1988, these efforts failed, largely due to the refusal of Latin American countries to back the U.S. measure.

This outcome signalled Cuba's success in shaping for itself a new role and image in the hemisphere. Fifteen Latin American countries now have normal relations with Havana, and several have called for Cuba to be readmitted to the OAS and other regional bodies. Cuba's leadership on the debt issue has played a significant role. By calling for Latin America's $400 billion foreign debt to be cancelled, Castro has boldly expressed sentiments felt throughout the Latin world, and has strengthened the hand of governments renegotiating their debts with the West.

Underlying this new diplomacy is a more realistic Cuban view of international power relations. "We would certainly like to see Latin America become socialist," says a Communist Party official. "But we also recognize that conditions are not right at this time." For Latin America and the Caribbean, moreover, U.S. military power poses limits from which there is little escape. The Soviet Union, Havana is well aware, is unwilling to take on the economic burden of supporting new client states, and is highly reluctant to challenge the U.S. militarily in the western hemisphere.

Cuban leaders now emphasize that revolution develops internally and cannot be "exported." Cuban involvement in Central America includes aid to the Nicaraguan government, including military advisors, technicians, teachers and health workers. Havana has expressed its willingness to abide by the Contadora proposal, which would require the withdrawal of all foreign military personnel—American and Cuban—from Central America.

Cuban leaders argue that the United States too must come to terms with reality. Relations between Havana and Washington cannot be normal as long as the U.S. government holds Cuba responsible for unrest everywhere in the Third World. Latin American poverty is a time bomb which will explode unless radical changes are made, they say. Americans must accept that such change "not only doesn't challenge America, but is in the interests of America."[21]

The Cuban revolution commands respect even from adversaries on the basis of its sheer survival power. Cuba has ridden out not only its internal development problems, but 30 years of active hostility from its powerful neighbor. The ability of the revolution to survive for a generation while remaining true to its principles has given hope to many others that radical change is possible and can endure.

If Cuba had become such an overwhelming priority in our emotions, it was because we were bearing witness to a miracle that had happened here. This miracle, described simply, was the conquest of fear.

It is my view that a major part of the respect and moral authority which Cuba would later exercise throughout the hemisphere has to do with this triumph. It is also the major source of that extraordinary rage and fury which United States governments experience at the mere sound of the word, "Cuba."

Today, the same furies exist, but the same truth prevails. To say Cuba is to say: "I am not afraid."

— George Lamming ∎

Cuban sugar worker.

Rene Gelpi, courtesy Center for Cuban Studies

99

Grenada

"No examination of the Grenada revolution of 1979-83 should end on a pessimistic note. For there is much to be proud about," writes Caribbean historian Gordon K. Lewis.[1] Grenada's revolution ended in October 1983, and any analysis of its four-and-a-half year lifespan must consider the now-apparent contradictions which led to discord within the ruling party and opened the door to U.S. invasion [see Part V, Chapter 6]. But to focus exclusively on these negatives would be a profound mistake. For the Grenada revolution was, on balance—and at the *popular* level—overwhelmingly positive; and the possibilities it raised have changed the face of the Caribbean forever.

The roster of achievements of the People's Revolutionary Government (PRG) is familiar to many in the Caribbean and throughout the world. Rational and creative economic policies, an egalitarian restructuring of education and health care, and a broad-based spirit of voluntarism were the hallmarks of revolutionary Grenada. To understand what these advances meant for the people of the Caribbean, it is necessary to view them in the context of the entrenched neocolonial social and economic structures in the region. Grenada went farther than any other English-speaking Caribbean society toward identifying these obstacles to development and creating new structures to replace them.

The Economic Program

Judged in conventional economic terms, the revolution was shaping up as a success. The government pursued a mixed economy embracing the traditional private sector plus an expanded public sector and a newly-created cooperative sector. This expanded activity caused unemployment to fall sharply from 49% before the revolution to 14% in 1983, according to Grenadian government figures.

The International Monetary Fund put Grenada's growth over this period at an average of 3% per year.[2] This compared favorably with growth rates in the rest of the Caribbean and Latin America, where many countries were experiencing negative or zero growth. Moreover, it came despite formidable obstacles: low prices for Grenada's export crops, weather disasters, and hostile U.S. propaganda which scared tourists away from the island. The world price of cocoa, Grenada's leading export, fell from $1.90 per pound in 1979 to $1.05 in 1983. The price of nutmeg dropped by almost 50%, while banana exports were severely affected by bad weather and the declining value of the British pound.[3]

In the face of these problems, the PRG's excellent financial management and lack of corruption helped the economy stay afloat. Its policies were praised by the World Bank in a 1982 memorandum which stated:

The government which came to power in 1979 inherited a deteriorating economy, and is now addressing the task of rehabilitation and of laying better foundations for growth

within the framework of a mixed economy . . . Government objectives are centered on the critical development issues and touch on the country's most promising development areas.[4]

Despite the invective heaped upon Grenada for allegedly going "communist," the PRG's economic strategy was distinguished by its gradualism. The New Jewel Movement considered itself a "socialist-oriented" party, meaning that while socialism was the ultimate goal, the government's actual policies were pragmatic and did not envision any sudden transformation. The private sector continued to dominate, accounting for 60% of production.[5] Grenada's private sector, however, consists mainly of peasant farmers and fishermen, who clearly benefitted from the revolution's programs. Whereas in the past they could rarely get credit for lack of collateral, the PRG established two state-owned banks which made loans to small producers, enabling them to expand or diversify their production. A Marketing and National Import Board purchased fruits and vegetables from the farmers and sold them throughout the island. This marketing assistance encouraged the farmers to diversify and helped lessen the country's dependence on imported food. The IMF reported in 1983 that an improvement in domestic food supplies had helped to keep inflation down in Grenada.[6]

Student at the Mirabeau agricultural school.

Bruce Paton

Members of the cabinet (standing, l-r): Prime Minister Maurice Bishop, Deputy Prime Minister Bernard Coard, Minister of Agriculture George Louison, and Minister of Housing Norris Bain.

When the PRG took over in 1979, it nationalized only a few hotels and nightclubs which had been Eric Gairy's personal property and which had become notorious as disguised brothels. Otherwise, the structure of ownership in the country remained much as it had been. In 1981, the government finally implemented a mild land reform law calling for the compulsory lease of unused tracts over 100 acres. Considering the wastage associated with idle land on a small island, this was not an unexpected act and was not openly resisted by landowners.

The major economic change under the PRG was the creation of a state sector which came to encompass about 30% of the economy. Consisting of some 23 enterprises, this sector operated mainly in areas of natural monopolies (i.e. the utilities) and where the private sector had failed to invest. Examples of the latter included an Agro-Industry Plant which made juices and jellies from locally grown fruits, and a Fish Processing Plant which produced dried salted fish (a West Indian dietary staple) from locally caught fish. Other state-owned enterprises included a sugar factory, several hotels, and a number of state farms. Most of these enterprises lost money in the first years of the revolution. They were important, however, because they opened up new areas of production using local resources—a departure from the neocolonial dependency economics of the Caribbean.

The reason for having the state take these initiatives rather than the private sector is that the indigenous business class, in Grenada as in the rest of the Caribbean, generally has been reluctant to invest in production. They are merchants, who buy goods from abroad and resell them at a profit. The PRG placed some curbs on this sector by increasing taxes on imports and by giving the state a monopoly to import certain basic goods such as rice, sugar, flour and fertilizer. Although these measures angered some businessmen, the commercial sector benefitted from the overall growth of the economy, and most realized healthy profits during the revolution.[7]

Despite its innovations, Grenada remained tied to its traditional exports of cocoa, nutmeg, and bananas. This meant that the economy was still vulnerable to declining commodity prices and weather disasters, both of which hit Grenada hard from 1979 to 1983. The PRG's strategy for coping with these problems was also a traditional one: to expand tourism as a source of foreign exchange. To do so required, first and foremost, a modern airport, the *sine qua non* of Caribbean tourism. Every serious analyst of the Grenadian economy, from the IMF to the Caribbean Development Bank to the Grenadian Chamber of Commerce, agreed that the island's rickety old airfield, Pearls, held back the growth of tourism. Only the Reagan administration continued to insist that the new airport was "too big" for Grenada's economic needs and must therefore be intended as a military base.

For Grenadians, the construction of the new airport became a symbol of Grenada's entry into the modern world and its determined bid for self-reliance. Ironically—in light of Washington's attempts to block its construction—the airport was a pet project of the Grenadian business class, which appreciated its potential value to the private sector of merchants and hoteliers. Grenadians of all classes bought "airport bonds" and held neighborhood fundraising events to raise money for the airport's completion.

The People: "Heart and Center"

Maurice Bishop, prime minister of Grenada during the revolution, described the Grenadian people as being "always at the center and heart and focus of all our activities."[8] The revolution's populism was at once its greatest strength and its

Bruce Paton

Primary school children: Education was upgraded under the PRG.

area of deepest contradictions.

There is no question but that the revolution improved life for the majority of the island's people. Among its most successful programs were free education through the high school level; free high-quality medical and dental care; hot school lunches and distribution of milk to mothers and infants; a revolving loan fund to help poor families repair their houses; and a voluntary literacy program which enabled illiterate adults to learn to read and write.

The Bishop government's programs, however, went beyond simple welfarism to attack the elitist social structures in Caribbean society. To take one example, education—fundamental to a people's ability to participate in government—has been treated with pointed neglect by many post-colonial Caribbean leaders. This was certainly true of Gairy, whose educational philosophy could be summed up in a few words: Keep them ignorant to rule them better.

There were two types of education in pre-1979 Grenada. The children of the peasantry received a few years of schooling in deteriorating rural schools, often without bathrooms, desks or even chairs. Teachers were untrained and many had not gone beyond eighth or ninth grade themselves. Since high school enrollment was extremely limited, and most poor families could not afford to pay tuition and purchase books and uniforms, most secondary school pupils came from the small middle and upper classes. Higher education was viewed as leading to one goal: emigration from the Caribbean to "become somebody" in England, Canada or the U.S.

This colonial concept of education was systematically refuted by the Bishop government. Soon after the revolution, the PRG created a Centre for Popular Education which undertook a broad literacy and adult education program. Under the slogan "Each One Teach One," volunteer tutors helped hundreds of mostly rural Grenadians to achieve a functional literacy for the first time in their lives. While up to 1979 the state had built only one high school in Grenada, the PRG opened three in the space of four years and abolished high school entrance fees. Government assistance subsidized school books and uniforms for poor families, further breaking down class barriers to education. A new experiment, the National In-Service Teacher Education Program, upgraded the skills of Grenadian teachers and was viewed as a potential model by other Caribbean educators.

In addition to these major programs, Grenada was abuzz with small discussion groups, skills training seminars, and cultural workshops aimed at developing the talents of the Grenadian people. One observer wrote, "The impression given was that the whole island was one large school constantly engaged in transforming the colonial mentality and the spirit of dependency."[9]

In health, a similarly anti-elitist process took place, drawing on the assistance and experience of the Cubans. Before the revolution, good medical treatment had been a privilege reserved for people who lived in St. George's and could afford to pay private doctors. The poor went to a dirty, understaffed public hospital with inadequate equipment and medicines and sometimes even no bed sheets; while people in the rural areas frequently had no access to health care at all. With help from Cuban health planners, the PRG restructured Grenada's health care system from top to bottom. While preserving the option of private care, the government expanded free health care to the entire country through a network of rural clinics. Cuban volunteer doctors nearly doubled the number of physicians in the country, and seven dental clinics were established (compared to one before 1979). The PRG also sought help from abroad, primarily Europe, to refurbish the main hospital and add specialized new facilities such as an Opthalmic Clinic.

"Perhaps the most celebrated aspect of the Grenadian revolution was the impulse which it gave to the self-organization of the society at large," writes the Latin American Bureau in their post-invasion analysis.[10] After languishing for two decades under Gairy's autocratic rule, Grenadians eagerly embraced the chance to organize at the grassroots level after 1979.

In the first several years, efforts toward creating a "popular democracy" of grassroots decision-making appeared to be making steady progress. Trade union membership reached 80% under a mandatory union recognition law, one of a very few such progressive laws in the Caribbean. Membership swelled in the National Women's Organization (NWO) and the National Youth Organization (NYO), which mobilized their members to take part in the revolution's programs. The unions, the NWO and the NYO elected delegates from among their members to attend national conferences which then made recommendations to the government on policy issues.

In 1982, the decentralization of power went a step further with the formation of zonal councils and parish councils. This fulfilled a part of the New Jewel Movement's original 1973 manifesto, which had called for the creation of "popular assemblies" placing decision-making power directly in people's hands. To a certain extent this goal was realized. At the monthly meetings of the grassroots councils, Grenadians debated local, national, and international issues in a format somewhat like that of a New England town meeting. Most major legislation underwent critique by these councils and by the NWO, the NYO and the trade unions. In this experimental process, the mass organizations would discuss proposed legislation and send back recommendations to the government, which would take their suggestions into account before passing the law in final form. The national budgets for both 1982 and 1983 went through this procedure.

This was an entirely new process in Grenada and in fact one without precedent in the Caribbean. Its relative success was due partly to the fact that Grenada is a micro-society of 110,000 people, making it possible to experiment with new structures which would be impractical in a larger country.

In retrospect, however, it is apparent that the system of popular democracy was in some ways a deception. Not all of the leadership was equally committed to making the system work, and the grassroots organs were only marginally plugged in to the real power structure. While Grenadians turned out in large numbers for the meetings of the parish and zonal councils, these meetings were often top-heavy with speeches by government officials. Debate was lively on a variety of topics, yet actual policy decisions were still being made by the NJM's Central Committee, whose membership was not even known to a majority of Grenadians.

Maurice Bishop is considered by many to have been strongly committed to making popular democracy work. Don Rojas, Bishop's press secretary, reflects:

It was certainly Maurice's hope that this system of councils at the local level, village level, and parish level would

become institutionalized as organs of people's power. It was our hope to have it become part of the ultimate legal framework of the revolution as part of the new people's constitution we were preparing.

Organizationally there were still weaknesses in the organs of popular democracy such as the zonal and parish councils. Weaknesses not so much in terms of the willingness of people to participate in these organs, but more in the way they were structured. For example, in some cases there would be meetings without agendas. In some cases there would be meetings that were not chaired.

The people's reaction was, "Why should we come to this meeting, sit here, and do a lot of rambling? We can identify the problems in our community. Let's look for the solution in a structured way."

Looking at it in hindsight, the process of decentralizing power inside the community was moving faster than the process of decentralizing power inside the party itself.[11]

Yet the final lesson of Grenada is still a positive one. The Grenadian people showed themselves ready to take on the challenge of creating new democratic forms and economic structures to replace dictatorship and stagnation. By the time U.S. pressures and internal conflicts caused the PRG to "implode," enough positive changes had taken place to confirm the potential of Grenada's alternative development model. The impact of this achievement should outlast the tragedy of the revolution's finale and point the way to other Caribbean peoples seeking change.

One Caribbean churchman had this to say:

One can understand why the Grenada revolution upset the dominant classes, the privileged minorities and the leaders of the establishment in the region. Here, for the first time, the poor and powerless masses were being given pride of place. Their needs, problems and aspirations became the raison d'etre, the central focus of policymaking, economic activity and social legislation.

Now, Caribbean governments and centers of power will find it harder to say to the masses that their hopes are but idle dreams . . . [12]

Bruce Paton

NOTES TO PART FOUR

Cuba

1. Marvin Leiner, "Cuba's Schools: 25 Years Later," in Sandor Halebsky and John Kirk, eds., *Cuba: Twenty-Five Years of Revolution 1959-1984* (New York: Praeger, 1985), p. 29.
2. Ross Danielson, "Medicine in the Community," in *ibid.,* pp. 45-61.
3. Medea Benjamin, Joseph Collins and Michael Scott, *No Free Lunch: Food and Revolution in Cuba Today* (San Francisco: Institute for Food and Development Policy, 1984), p. 101.
4. UNICEF, *The State of the World's Children 1984,* pp. 115 and 119; and Cuban government statistics.
5. Government of Cuba, "Health for All: 25 Years of Cuban Experience," (Havana, July 1983), p. 24.
6. Claes Brundenius, *Revolutionary Cuba: The Challenge of Economic Growth with Equity* (Boulder: Westview Press, 1984), pp. 41-53.
7. Benjamin et al., pp. 177-178.
8. Wayne S. Smith, *The Closest of Enemies: A Personal and Diplomatic History of the Castro Years* (New York: W.W. Norton, 1987), chapter 8.
9. Speech by Fidel Castro to City of Havana Provincial Party Meeting, Nov. 29, 1987, *Granma Weekly Review,* Dec. 13, 1987.
10. Marifeli Perez-Stable, "Cuba en los 80," *Areito,* Vol. IX, No. 36, 1984, p. 92.
11. Jorge I. Dominguez, "Revolutionary Politics: The New Demands for Orderliness," in Jorge Dominguez, ed., *Cuba: Internal and International Affairs* (Beverly Hills and London: Sage Publications, 1982), p. 36.
12. *Ibid.,* p. 33. Also, EPICA interview with Poder Popular officials, Havana, June 1987.
13. Nelson Valdes, "The Changing Face of Cuba's Communist Party," *Cuba Update,* Winter/Spring 1986, pp. 1-16.
14. EPICA interview with Dr. Sergio Arce, Havana, June 1987.
15. Margaret E. Crahan, "Cuba: Religion and Revolutionary Institutionalization," *Journal of Latin American Studies,* No. 17, 1985, p. 327.
16. *Fidel and Religion: Castro Talks on Revolution and Religion with Frei Betto* (New York: Simon and Schuster, 1987), p. 276.
17. Interview with Archbishop Jaime Ortega of Havana, Sept. 1985, reprinted in LADOC, XVI, 22, p. 54.
18. *Caribbean Contact,* November 1983.
19. Jorge I. Dominguez, "Cuba in the 1980s," *Foreign Affairs,* Fall 1986, p. 134.
20. Smith, p. 242-243 and 253-256.
21. EPICA interview with a Cuban Communist Party official, Havana, June 1987.

Grenada

1. *Caribbean Contact,* July 1984.
2. International Monetary Fund staff report, EBS/83/164, Aug. 9, 1984, p. 3.
3. [Interim] Government of Grenada and Caribbean Development Bank, "Economic Memorandum on Grenada," Vol. I, 1984, pp. 10-14.
4. World Bank, "Economic Memorandum on Grenada," Report No. 3825-GRD, Aug. 4, 1982, p. i.
5. [Interim] Government of Grenada and Caribbean Development Bank, "Economic Memorandum on Grenada," Vol. I, p. 9.
6. International Monetary Fund staff report, p. 3.
7. Latin America Bureau, *Grenada: Whose Freedom?* (London: Latin America Bureau, 1984), p. 37.
8. Maurice Bishop, speech at Hunter College, New York City, June 5, 1983.
9. Dr. Roy Neehall, "Significance of the Grenada Revolution for the People of the Caribbean," speech at Howard University, Washington, DC, Oct. 25, 1984.
10. Latin America Bureau, p. 37.
11. Interview with Don Rojas, *Intercontinental Press,* Dec. 26, 1983.
12. Dr. Roy Neehall, "Significance of the Grenada Revolution for the People of the Caribbean."

PART FIVE

U.S. in the Caribbean

Strategies of Control 1960-1985

Introduction

The unilateral announcement of American predominance throughout the Western hemisphere was made by the President in the course of his December 1823 annual message to Congress and the country, and it came to be known as the Monroe Doctrine. He bluntly told all European powers that they would not be allowed to reconquer former colonies, transfer them to stronger allies, or establish new outposts of empire. Few contemporaries missed the implication: Hands Off for Europe meant Hands On for the United States.

— William Appleman Williams, *Empire as a Way of Life* (Oxford University Press, 1980)

Politics change, but geography doesn't. This hemisphere is still one-half of the globe—our, the Americas', one-half . . . U.S. global power projection rests upon a cooperative Caribbean and a supportive South America.

— *The Santa Fe Document* (Council for Inter-American Security, 1980).

The concept of American empire shaped at the time of the Monroe Doctrine included an assumption that the Caribbean would be an American lake. Today, the Reagan-linked Santa Fe Committee calls the region "our strategic backyard." While the terminology has changed, the concept of the Caribbean as a U.S. appendage rather than a group of sovereign nations has changed little in 150 years.

Methods of maintaining U.S. control, however, have shifted over time. From 1898 through the 1930s, Marine invasions and occupations of Caribbean countries brought the United States under criticism for "gunboat diplomacy." Subsequent U.S. support for dictators in Nicaragua, Cuba and the Dominican Republic added to resentments.

After World War Two, both the rationale and the methods of intervention shifted. Gunboat diplomacy had as its pretexts instability and debt in neighboring nations. After the war, opposition to communism provided a new rationale, while intervention became less direct and more institutionalized. The Central Intelligence Agency, formed from the wartime Office of Strategic Services in 1947, carried out covert interventions through such sectors as organized labor and the media. In 1953 the American Federation of Labor collaborated with the CIA to oust the Guatemalan government when its land reform threatened the interests of the United Fruit Company. A decade later, the newly-formed American Institute for Free Labor Development helped to overthrow the governments of Brazil and Guyana.

Despite these new strategies, the option of invasion was held in reserve, to be resurrected in Cuba in 1961 and the Dominican Republic in 1965. In both cases the U.S. government sought to disguise its role. The Bay of Pigs was a proxy invasion, carried out by Cuban exiles under CIA control. The Dominican invasion provided a new model, that of the "multilateral" intervention. At U.S. request, token contingents from five Latin American states supported 23,000 U.S. Marines in an "Inter-American Peace Force." The Johnson administration used their presence to claim that the invasion was actually a multilateral action by Latin nations.

From 1965 through the late 1970s the United States kept a low profile in the Caribbean. The Vietnam War preoccupied Washington for a decade, and the domestic political costs of the war restrained military adventurism for several years afterward. But other forms of subversion continued. U.S.

pressures against the Manley government in Jamaica included economic warfare and a hostile press.

President Carter initially made human rights a foreign policy priority. But his administration was divided, and by mid-1979 advocates of a harder line prevailed. They argued successfully for a tough response to the Nicaraguan revolution and other perceived setbacks to U.S. interests. The turning point came in September, when Carter officials suddenly "discovered" a Soviet combat brigade in Cuba. Although it was later forced to admit that the same Soviet advisors had been in Cuba for 17 years, the administration announced aggressive new anti-Cuba measures. These included the creation of a quick-strike "Caribbean Task Force" based in Key West, Florida. The Carter administration also began a steady military build-up in Central America.

In 1980, a paper known as the Santa Fe document summarized the far-right perspective on Latin America which was to dominate the policies of the Reagan administration. Stating bluntly that "Detente is dead," the report declared the United States to be engaged in "World War Three" against the Soviets, with Latin America and the Caribbean as major battlegrounds. It argued for an aggressive strategy of militarism based on the 1948 Rio Treaty, which sanctioned American military interventions in the hemisphere.

Yet the memory of Vietnam and the potential political costs of U.S. casualties still restrained large-scale use of U.S. troops. Only tiny Grenada seemed to promise a quick victory with few losses. As in the Dominican Republic, token troops from regional allies provided the U.S. invasion forces with a multinational image. U.S. helicopters scattered leaflets which read: "People of Grenada: Your Caribbean Neighbors with U.S. Support Have Come to Grenada to Restore Democracy and Insure Your Safety."

The following sections examine some of the methods which the United States has used to maintain its influence in the Caribbean. Through the media, through the labor movement, through loans and aid, U.S. influence has been pervasive. After 1979, Washington used all these methods to polarize the region and court allies for the eventual strike against Grenada. The invasion took many Americans by surprise. In the Caribbean, however, it was an expected confirmation that the United States had not abandoned military intervention in its "backyard." ∎

The American Institute for Free Labor Development

In a region where politics and trade unionism have been closely linked for the last fifty years, it is natural that the labor movement would be a target of U.S. penetration. The primary instrument of this penetration is AIFLD, the American Institute for Free Labor Development. AIFLD, however, must be understood as operating within a regional system of linkages through which the United States has tried—with considerable success—to align the Caribbean labor movement to the U.S. and hinder the growth of progressive unions favoring social change.

The AFL and Business Unionism

Unlike most of the world's trade unions, the American Federation of Labor (AFL) was built on the idea that labor's advance would come through cooperation—not confrontation—with employers. This so-called "business unionism" reflected the AFL leadership's belief that expanded corporate profits would mean higher wages for workers. It led to an unofficial business/labor/government pact in which the AFL supported capitalism and the U.S. government's foreign policy in exchange for gains for organized labor.[1]

As early as 1901, the AFL began organizing in Latin America to oppose "revolutionary unionism," which sought gains for workers through class-based political action. Instead, the AFL sought to build up unions which would cooperate with American corporate expansion abroad.[2] The concept of a business/labor pact, however, was an alien one to most Latin and Caribbean workers. George C. Lodge, Assistant Secretary of Labor for International Affairs from 1958-1960, wrote that because Latin Americans are faced with . . .

the threat of military dictatorship from the right and the continuing exploitative oligarchy of rich landowners and businessmen, the class struggle is very much alive in Latin American society . . . mutuality of interest between management and labor is not an easy concept for the Latin American laborer.[3]

Faced with the popularity of militant, anti-capitalist unions, the AFL resorted to infiltrating and disrupting the Latin labor movement in order to set up parallel or "dual" unions which could be more easily manipulated. In the late 1940s, as the U.S. entered the Cold War, the AFL's activities were stepped up and recast as part of a "world fight against Communism." Under its Latin American representative Serafino Romualdi—a former operative of the wartime Office of Special Services, the precursor of the CIA—the AFL collaborated with the CIA to set up dual unions in various Latin American countries.[4]

A key part of this postwar drive was the splitting of the world trade union movement and the creation of an anticommunist labor network under U.S. control. The World Federation of Trade Unions (WFTU) had been created in 1945, incorporating nearly every major labor union in the world. The AFL, however, refused to join the WFTU because it included Soviet unions; and in 1949, the AFL leadership successfully pressured the Congress of Industrial Organizations (CIO) to expel its progressive unions and withdraw from the WFTU. The AFL, the CIO, and the U.S. State Department then created a parallel body, the International Confederation of Free Trade Unions (ICFTU). Wooed with AFL and Marshall Plan funds, many British and European unions switched their allegiance from the WFTU to the anticommunist ICFTU.

In 1950, Romualdi's Latin American organizing finally bore fruit when the AFL set up a pan-American union confederation called ORIT. Although nominally the Latin American branch of the ICFTU, ORIT was controlled by the AFL through Romualdi. ORIT's impact soon became clear with its role in the overthrow of the elected government of Jacobo Arbenz in Guatemala in 1954. While the coup was planned, financed, and directed by the CIA and the State Department, the AFL led an anti-Arbenz propaganda campaign and supplied the overthrow force with members of a dual union created by Romualdi and ORIT.[5] After the overthrow, the U.S.-backed dictator Castillo Armas dissolved the country's major unions and jailed 5,000-8,000 people, the majority of them trade unionists.[6]

Destruction of Caribbean Labor Unity After World War Two

After the West Indian strikes of the 1930s, the emerging Caribbean labor movement initially took a militant anti-colonial stance. In 1945, the union leaders met in Barbados and founded the Caribbean Labour Congress (CLC), a regional trade union grouping. The years 1945-48 were a period of great enthusiasm within the CLC. Plans were made for a West Indies Federation with a strong central government which could implement economic planning on a regional basis.

The splitting of the world trade union movement soon intruded upon this unity. Caribbean unions, most of which had joined the WFTU, came under pressure from Britain and the United States to defect to the ICFTU. The issue was framed in threatening ideological terms, with the WFTU described as "under totalitarian domination" and the ICFTU as representing "free trade unions." British support for the ICFTU influenced the president of the Caribbean Labour Congress, Sir Grantley Adams, who also headed the Barbados Workers Union. Although Adams supported Caribbean self-government, he was close to the Labour Party which had just come to power in Britain. His Jamaican counterpart, Norman Manley, while more of a serious nationalist, also feared a leftist challenge from within the labor movement.

Adams and Manley became instruments of the ICFTU's takeover of Caribbean labour.[7] From his position as CLC president, Adams pushed for the expulsion of the remaining WFTU-affiliated unions from the CLC. Unable to get majority support for this move, "Adams came to a firm and irrevocable decision. The Caribbean Labour Congress must be dissolved."[8] He engineered the withdrawal of major unions, including his own Barbados Workers Union.

Meanwhile, Norman Manley and the right wing of his People's National Party moved to destroy progressive elements within the Jamaican labor movement. The key figure was Richard Hart, secretary of the CLC. Hart was one of the "four H's"* who were the leading leftists in the PNP and also controlled the Jamaican Trade Union Congress. In March 1952, Manley forced the four H's out of the party and used red-baiting to damage their popularity with workers. Finally, a new union was created to supplant the Trade Union Congress: the National Workers Union, later headed by Norman Manley's son, Michael.[9]

This divisive process spelled the end of the Caribbean Labour Congress. The unions withdrawing from the CLC joined a newly-created Caribbean division of ORIT, called CADORIT. It was headquartered in Barbados and led by Frank Walcott, second-ranking official of the Barbados Workers Union. The real power over CADORIT, however, belonged to Romualdi and the AFL.[10]

The final step in dismantling the radical labor bloc was the ouster of Cheddi Jagan's government in Guyana. Together with Richard Hart, Jagan had led the fight to keep the CLC from being taken over by the ICFTU. ORIT and Romualdi had been active in Guyana since 1951, opposing Jagan's militant union and supporting the union favored by the Bookers sugar company.[11] After Jagan was elected premier in 1953, the British stepped in and deposed his government.

By the end of the 1950s, the Caribbean labor movement had been largely incorporated into an emerging U.S.-controlled labor network. This was formalized in 1960 with the creation of a new regional body to replace the Caribbean Labour Congress. Reflecting the AFL's use of confusing nomenclature for its dual unions, the new organization was

*Richard Hart, Ken Hill, Frank Hill and Arthur Henry.

AIFLD

AIFLD instructor teaching course in Spanish on "Open and Closed Societies."

called the Caribbean Congress of Labour (CCL). It received 50% of its funding from ORIT/ICFTU, and was quickly perceived as "a political organization rather than a workers' organization."[12]

Impact of AIFLD

The success of the Cuban revolution worried U.S. government and business leaders that ORIT was not strong enough to stave off revolution in Latin America. To provide a more reliable vehicle for anticommunist organizing, the American Institute for Free Labor Development was formed in 1961 as an arm of the AFL-CIO's international affairs department. Parallel institutes were later set up for Asia and Africa.

AIFLD's creation gave institutional form to the old tripartite alliance between government, big business and labor. Until 1980, its board of directors was dominated by representatives of U.S. multinationals operating in Latin America, including W.R. Grace, the Rockefeller empire, Anaconda copper, ITT and others. However, 95% of AIFLD's funding came from the U.S. government, initially from the U.S. Agency for International Development as part of the Kennedy administration's Alliance for Progress.

There was, in addition, a silent fourth partner in the venture: the CIA, which ex-agent Philip Agee wrote had put "several years' study and planning" into a new program of anticommunist labor organizing.[13]

The core of AIFLD's program was the training of thousands of Latin American and Caribbean trade unionists in regional extension courses. Some of these students were then invited to the United States for further training at AIFLD's center (originally in Front Royal, Virginia and currently at the George Meany Center outside Washington, DC.) AIFLD preached labor economism—that unions should stay out of politics—yet its courses on collective bargaining and union organizing were imbued with anticommunism. Later, in the

1970s, the curriculum became more overtly political, with courses like "Democratic Theory" and "Totalitarian Ideologies." As one Grenadian unionist remembered his AIFLD training:

> In the opening orientation we saw clearly that these people were very, very anticommunist. The courses were oriented toward getting you to hate communists, to see communists as a group of people trying to create chaos in the world.[14]

From the trainees graduating from the U.S. center, individuals were selected to pursue "internships" under which they returned to their country as organizers on an AIFLD salary. According to labor historian Ronald Radosh, these interns . . .

> function as a corps of salaried anticommunist activists, ready to do the bidding of the Department of State. They work primarily to impose AFL-CIO style unionism upon Latin American workers, and to destroy existing unions outside of the conservative orbit.[15]

By 1966, there were charges within the labor movement that AIFLD was involved with the CIA. Philip Agee later confirmed these charges in his book *Inside the Company,* in which he wrote that the CIA viewed AIFLD's training program as an arena for the "spotting and assessment of potential agents for labor operations." He described Serafino Romualdi, who served as director of AIFLD from 1962 to 1966, as a "long-time agent" of the CIA's international division.[16]

Graduates of AIFLD training were involved in several CIA-linked disruptions in Latin America and the Caribbean during the 1960s. William Doherty Jr., then AIFLD social projects director, boasted of AIFLD's role in the 1964 overthrow of the Goulart regime in Brazil.

AIFLD also played a role in destabilizing Cheddi Jagan's government after his reelection in 1961. Agents, including 11 Guyanese graduates of AIFLD training, entered Guyana as "labor representatives" and worked with the AFL-supported union to organize a general strike. The CIA provided strike funds channeled through the international affairs department of the American Federation of State, County and Municipal Employees.[17] The strike, together with a wave of racial violence, effectively brought down Jagan's government.

In the Dominican Republic, the AFL-CIO entered the country after the election of the popular Juan Bosch government. Although Bosch had strong labor support and gave unprecedented freedom to the country's trade unions, the AFL-CIO went to work against the new government, targeting the newly-formed FOUPSA union. When attempts to control FOUPSA failed, a dual union was created and called Bloque FOUPSA Libre ("Free FOUPSA"). Later known as CONATRAL, the union received funding from AIFLD and ORIT and was run by a group of right-wing Cuban exiles. Alone among Dominican unions, CONATRAL supported the military coup against Bosch, refused to participate in the constitutionalist uprising, and supported the U.S. Marine invasion in 1965. The main AFL-CIO operative in the Dominican Republic was Andrew McLellan, who replaced Romualdi as AIFLD director in 1967.

AIFLD in the Caribbean Today

Since 1962, AIFLD has trained over half a million Latin American and Caribbean trade unionists. As of 1987, 22,985 unionists from the English-speaking Caribbean and 53,976 from the Dominican Republic had attended in-country seminars.[18] These take place mostly at three regional centers: the Barbados Labor College, the Trade Union Education Institute in Jamaica, and the Guyana Industrial Training Center. Advanced training at AIFLD's U.S. center, all expenses paid, is offered to at least 20 Caribbean labor leaders each year.

As a result, AIFLD now has a core of Caribbean unions which are tied to the United States through their leadership. They are grouped in the Caribbean Congress of Labour, which is funded by both AIFLD and the ICFTU. The CCL includes

---

AIFLD'S CARIBBEAN COURSE

The 1983-84 program at AIFLD's George Meany Center in Washington, DC offered one course specifically geared toward the Caribbean. The course description reveals the ideological nature of AIFLD instruction:

The Role of Organized Labor in Developing Democracy (Caribbean)

The course covers the origins and purposes of trade unionism within the framework of a **democratic society.** Particular emphasis will be given to an analysis of **democratic theory,** the **nature of dictatorships,** and the **impact of ideologies** on labor activities, principally in the field of **labor and human rights.** The course will also cover the role of the labor movement in promoting **pluralistic political and economic systems** on the national level, the **difference between democratic labor and other labor forces,** and the role of labor in economic development and other activities being undertaken in the Caribbean. Finally, the course analyzes the current situation of the labor movement in the Caribbean and its institutional role in the **political progress** of the nation.

(Emphasis added.)

unions in 14 countries of the English-speaking Caribbean plus Suriname, Curaçao and St. Maarten. AIFLD also maintains links to unions in the French Antilles and with the FOS labor confederation in Haiti.

Unions whose leaders have been trained by AIFLD are often, although not always, more supportive of conservative governments than are non-AIFLD unions. In Trinidad & Tobago under the Williams government, for instance, unions were divided into the pro-government Labour Congress and the anti-government Council of Progressive Trade Unions. The former had AIFLD ties, while the latter did not.

In addition to training, AIFLD offers material incentives to unions, including a revolving loan fund, and, in the past, new housing for workers. These benefits are—as AIFLD states—only for members of "free democratic trade unions," that is, for unions aligned with AIFLD.[19] In the Caribbean, housing has been built in Barbados, Guyana and the Dominican Republic, reflecting AIFLD's ties with the Barbados Workers Union, the Guyana Trades Union Council, and the National Confederation of Dominican Workers. Recently, AIFLD built or renovated union headquarters for CCL affiliates in five Eastern Caribbean islands. The new "labor community centers" include offices, meeting halls and other facilities, adding to the prestige of AIFLD-linked unions.

While building up its affiliated unions, AIFLD has sought to force out dissenters and to break or bypass left-leaning unions. While the leadership of the Barbados Workers Union (BWU) is prominent in the AIFLD/CCL network, several years ago two minor BWU officials were active in Monali, a small left party. Within a two-month period, the BWU received visits from William Doherty, AIFLD's executive director; Milan Bish, then U.S. ambassador to the Eastern Caribbean; Richard Luce, a British minister; and Hugh Shearer, foreign minister of the Seaga government, all urging the ouster of "Marxist" elements from the union.[20]

In 1982, a leftist lawyer named Bobby Clarke formed a new union in Barbados, the Barbados Industrial and General Workers Union (BIGWU). Its membership grew rapidly, reflecting its activist style as compared to the more bureaucratic Barbados Workers Union. To counter the threat, the BWU hierarchy, the Barbados government, and the U.S. Embassy launched a red-baiting campaign against the union. BIGWU workers on strike at three factories were fired, then rehired with a raise on condition they renounce BIGWU. This effectively broke the union.[21]

AIFLD tried also to undermine the Caribbean Union of Teachers, which came under progressive leadership in 1979. When attempts to co-opt the CUT failed, AIFLD branded its executive "communist" and sought to woo member unions away with the aim of setting up a parallel confederation.[22]

At the time of the 1979 revolution in Grenada, AIFLD had longstanding ties to the Seamen and Waterfront Workers Union (SWWU) and had trained leaders of several other Grenadian unions. Within a few months, these unions began to carry out labor actions aimed at harassing the new government. Officials of the SWWU and the electrical workers union—including one on the AIFLD payroll since 1973—

called strikes on flimsy pretexts, without the support of the rank-and-file. These disruptions failed, and eventually several AIFLD-trained leaders were replaced by rank-and-file vote. But the SWWU, under its general secretary Eric Pierre, remained the one union consistently to oppose the Bishop government. After the U.S. invasion, AIFLD assumed a major role in the campaign to win over Grenadians to anticommunism [see Part V, Ch. 6.]

AIFLD appears to have helped unseat the Bouterse regime in Suriname, although the extent of its role remains unknown. The AIFLD-trained leader of the Moederbond union, Cyriel Daal, publicly called for Bouterse's overthrow, while the union carried out harassment strikes. Daal was among 15 Surinamers killed by the military in December 1982. Afterwards, AIFLD funded activities by exiled Moederbond unionists in Holland.

AIFLD and "Project Democracy"

In the early 1980s a new source of funding for AIFLD coincided with a subtle shift in the organization's focus. The National Endowment for Democracy (NED), created in 1983 as part of President Reagan's "Project Democracy" initiative, was tied into the AFL-CIO through its board of directors [see Part V, Ch. 6.] With an $18 million per year budget funded by Congress, the NED makes grants to organizations for work abroad. The AFL-CIO's Free Trade Union Institute (FTUI) was initially the largest grantee, receiving $11 million in 1984 and $13.8 million in 1985. Much of this funding was passed on to AIFLD.

The result was to reinforce AIFLD's ideological role as it used NED funding to "help Latin American trade unions develop a political-action capacity."[23] Using NED funds, AIFLD and the FTUI have created political education committees within AIFLD-linked unions in the Dominican Republic and Central America. They have funded anticommunist unions (such as the CUS in Nicaragua) and created new unions to supplant others with leftist leadership (such as in St. Lucia). They have also worked to isolate left-leaning unions. In Panama, AIFLD worked through its affiliate, the Workers Confederation of the Republic of Panama, to split labor unity. A NED report noted the success of this venture:

Shortly before the election in May 1984, the CTRP sponsored a May Day rally which offered an alternative to a communist-sponsored rally on the same day. The CTRP rally broke the tradition of "United Front" rallies in which communist and democratic trade unions had previously joined together.[24]

A number of projects funded by the Free Trade Union Institute do not involve labor at all. The FTUI funds Libro Libre, a Costa Rican-based publishing operation which disseminates anticommunist literature in Central America. It gave half a million dollars to an extreme right-wing student group in France, the National Inter-University Union, which was later found to be an offshoot of a banned French paramilitary organization.[25] FTUI also funds the Force Ouvrière, an anticommunist French union which opposes the

Mitterand government. But its most controversial operation was in Panama, where the FTUI allegedly used $20,000 of NED funds to support the election campaign of Nicolás Ardito Barletta in 1984. Congressman Hank Brown of Colorado, a NED critic, commented that "It is ironic when a group given funds to promote democracy ends up interfering in the free elections of other countries."[26]

The direction taken by AIFLD since 1983 has ended any illusion that it is a "non-political" organization. At the same time, greater awareness of its activities among American and foreign trade unionists has led to increasing questions about AIFLD's political role.

Challenges to AIFLD and the CCL

Hard economic times in the Caribbean have brought the contradictions within AIFLD to the fore. These reflect, in part, underlying contradictions within the AFL-CIO itself. While supporting the U.S. government's Cold War foreign policy, the AFL-CIO claims to oppose certain of its economic policies. These include the use of International Monetary Fund programs to keep wages low in Third World countries and the expansion of U.S. multinationals abroad to take advantage of low wages.

The Reagan administration's Caribbean Basin Initiative (CBI) is based on precisely this model. Its emphasis on attracting foreign investors has encouraged Caribbean governments to hold down wages and limit the power of unions. This has placed AIFLD-backed unions in a difficult position. Their ties to the United States and to conservative Caribbean governments create pressure to go along with measures favoring foreign investors. In St. Lucia, AIFLD-trained union leaders cooperated with the Compton government's Tripartite Commission to study wage restraint, even though the plan was unpopular with workers and the largest union in the country opposed it.

At the same time, union leaders must contend with rank-and-file demands to defend wages and workers' protections. This has prompted many to state their reservations about the CBI. Even the Barbados Workers Union—whose general secretary, Frank Walcott, headed the Caribbean Congress of Labor until 1980—has expressed concerns. Criticisms from the BWU and other unions set off a lobbying offensive by U.S. officials, who toured the region attempting to persuade unions to support the CBI.

A similar rank-and-file challenge developed in response to the emergency powers bills introduced by several island governments in the early 1980s. Designed to strengthen government control in case of unrest, the bills contained clauses abrogating the right to strike. Workers strongly opposed the bills, forcing pro-government AIFLD unions to oppose them as well.

St. Vincent's largest union, the Commercial Technical and Allied Workers Union (CTAWU), was formed with AIFLD's help in 1962.[27] It was close to the Milton Cato government; the CTAWU leader, Burns Bonadie, was Cato's nephew and later a parliamentarian for the ruling party. Bonadie was also closely tied to AIFLD and headed the Caribbean Congress of Labor from 1980-1983. Yet when Cato tried to pass an emergency powers bill in 1981, the vehemence of rank-and-file opposition left Bonadie no choice. The CTAWU led a coalition which successfully demonstrated for the bill's repeal.

Caribbean trade unionists are well aware that AIFLD, and by extension the CCL, are funded by the U.S. government and that "he who pays the piper calls the tune." The result has been some alienation from the CCL network, and pressures for it to take a more independent line. An example was the CCL's statement on the Grenada invasion, expressing its "deep concern" and calling for the early withdrawal of U.S. troops. These rank-and-file challenges to the labor establishment mean that AIFLD may see its influence gradually wane as Caribbean unions confront the impact of U.S. policies in the region. ∎

AIFLD

AIFLD director William C. Doherty, Jr., with former Cuban political prisoner Huber Matos.

IMF and the Banks

"When the IMF says they deal only in money and not in politics," remarked Rep. Tom Harkin to Congress on February 22, 1982, "I would suggest that there is nothing in this world more political than money, how it is loaned, and under what conditions it is loaned." In the Caribbean, the multilateral lending agencies and private transnational banks have played an important role in shaping and controlling economic development. This influence takes place in three ways:

- Who gets loans and when: the "political" use of multilateral lending to support or penalize particular governments;
- "Conditionality" on IMF loans which negatively affects the economy of the recipient country;
- Private bank lending, which provides support for international capitalism rather than self-reliant development.

Politicized Lending

Contrary to the image of the multilaterals as not dominated by any one country, the United States actually wields considerable (though not exclusive) influence in their lending decisions. In the Inter-American Development Bank (IDB), the U.S. controls 35% of the voting power and virtually holds free rein.[1] In the International Monetary Fund and the World Bank, where the U.S. holds 19% and 22% of the votes respectively, the United States' influence goes beyond its actual voting share.[2] While it is not always easy for the U.S. to sway other members to its wishes, it frequently manages to do so, often disguising political motives with artfully constructed economic and technical arguments.[3]

Within the U.S. government, power over participation in the multilaterals is closely held by the Executive Branch acting through the Treasury. Thus the banks often end up supporting White House policy objectives. A classic example was the cut-off of World Bank and IDB loans and the denial of an IMF stand-by agreement to the socialist Allende government in Chile, following President Nixon's order to "make the economy scream." Shortly after a U.S.-backed coup replaced Allende with the Pinochet dictatorship, the IMF awarded a $373 million loan to the new government. More recently, the Reagan administration has waged a battle within the IMF, the IDB, and the World Bank to channel huge loans to the governments of El Salvador and Guatemala while freezing aid to Nicaragua. This campaign has been largely successful.[4]

After Edward Seaga defeated the pro-socialist Manley government in the Jamaican election of 1980, President Reagan vowed to make Jamaica a free enterprise model for the Caribbean. Thus no one was surprised when, in addition to generous U.S. bilateral aid, World Bank and IDB loans, Jamaica received a US$650 million aid package from the IMF. Moreover, the IMF was initially lenient when the Seaga administration failed to meet agreed-upon economic targets, adding weight to regional complaints about the "pampering" of Jamaica.[5]

According to a 1983 study which the Congressional Research Service attempted to suppress, the Reagan administration had a "hit list" of five countries which it attempted to prevent from securing multilateral aid. Three of the five were Caribbean Basin countries: Cuba, Nicaragua, and Grenada.[6]

According to an extremely reliable executive branch source, then-Secretary of State Alexander Haig emphatically stated in a meeting of high-ranking State Department officials in 1981 that "not a penny" of indirect, international assistance was to be provided to Grenada. Shortly thereafter, the Treasury provided the U.S. Executive Director to the IMF with objections to the drawing proposed for Grenada . . . objections which focused on the construction of an airport by Grenada as the primary cause of Grenada's economic difficulties.[7]

The result of this pressure was that the IMF reduced its proposal for a three-year loan to Grenada to one year, and one-third of the amount proposed.

While blocking aid to revolutionary governments, the Reagan administration has resisted Congressional attempts to require the U.S. to vote against loans to apartheid South Africa, arguing that this would "politicize" the IMF. Largely on account of U.S. pressure, the IMF approved a $1.1 billion loan to South Africa in November 1982.

IMF as Destabilizer: The Case of Jamaica

The International Monetary Fund was set up by the United States and Britain to help the war-torn countries of Europe cover their balance-of-payments shortfalls. The purpose was to ensure that countries continued to participate in and did not drop out of or hinder the international system of capitalist trade, a goal which continued when the IMF turned to making loans to the Third World. Many Third World economists feel that there is an inherent contradiction between this purpose and the attempt by former colonies to achieve economic independence, since the IMF helps perpetuate the same trade structures which underlay colonialism and underlie neocolonialism today.

The IMF makes loans on condition that the recipient follow a strict program to rectify supposedly faulty economic policies. This "structural adjustment" generally entails a rigid austerity program designed to depress consumption and increase exports and private foreign investment. Typical elements of the IMF prescription include:

- Major cuts in government spending. This means deep cutbacks in social programs, and lay-offs or firings of public sector workers.
- Wage restraint or freeze.
- Currency devaluation to make imports more expensive for the country's people and exports cheaper for foreign buyers.
- Removal of price controls and government subsidies on goods and services.
- Restrictions on government involvement in productive enterprise. Attempts to denationalize parts of the public

Cartoon appearing in the Jamaica Daily News *on May 10, 1978, the day the new agreement with the IMF was announced.*

sector are sometimes included.

The brunt of such a program falls squarely on the backs of the working class. The cost of living rises sharply while wages fail to keep up, and unemployment rises because of public sector layoffs. Public services like hospitals, schools, public transportation and utilities must fire staff and decrease the quality of their services.

The relationship between the IMF and Jamaica in the 1970s is an example of how the economic strings on IMF lending can affect the course of social change in the Caribbean. The Manley government was driven to the IMF after rising oil prices, declining bauxite markets and a "capital strike" by investors and bankers reacting to democratic socialism brought Jamaica's foreign reserves to zero at the end of 1976.[8] Manley initially avoided turning to the Fund, stating that "We are the masters in our house and in our house there shall be no other master but ourselves."[9] But worsening conditions finally forced him to negotiate a loan agreement in July 1977.

This initial agreement came without too many harsh conditions. However, after Jamaica failed the IMF's "performance tests" in December, the agreement was suspended and a new one negotiated in May 1978, bringing with it a severe hardening of the IMF's conditions. The Fund wanted not just the usual austerity measures, but a complete overturn of the Manley government's economic program.[10] Changes imposed by the IMF included a 30% currency devaluation, J$180 million in new taxes, the lifting of price controls to guarantee a 20% profit margin to the private sector, and reduction in real wages of approximately 25%.[11]

These measures were an economic bombshell for Jamaica. Prices skyrocketed 39% in the twelve months following the loan agreement, and social services deteriorated. The falling standard of living sparked strikes and unrest among workers and the middle class, and many people left the country. The government nevertheless carried out the IMF prescription dutifully. It returned to a strategy of export-led growth, yet the economy failed to recover: expected new investments did not materialize, nor did commercial banks resume making loans to Jamaica. In December 1979, Jamaica once again failed the performance tests.

Rising hardship and the government's loss of "moral authority" before the IMF shattered the consensus behind Manley's party, the PNP.[12] By surrendering to the Fund, the Manley government reversed and discredited its own program of social reforms. Democratic socialism had been a promise to improve conditions for the poor, but the IMF austerity delivered the exact opposite. By the time Manley made the belated decision to break with the Fund, the damage had been done, contributing to the crumbling of the PNP's class alliance and its resounding defeat in the 1980 election.

The case of Jamaica is a striking one because the IMF's economic measures conflicted head-on with everything the Manley government stood for, effectively reversing an attempt at social change. But the negative impact of IMF austerity is feared even by governments with more conservative economic policies. Trade unions and popular organizations generally

113

oppose involvement with the Fund, and governments often avoid the IMF for as long as possible because of the political consequences of imposing further "austerity" on an already hard-pressed people. But falling commodity prices and rising interest rates on indebtedness have left many Caribbean countries with little choice but to accept the Fund's conditions.

The Transnational Banks

The private transnational banks originated in the late 19th century and expanded in the 1960s and '70s when many corporations based in the industrialized nations moved abroad.[13] This new global economy required banking services, so U.S., European, Canadian, and Japanese banks acquired overseas branches and subsidiaries to service the transnational corporations. Given their roots in this relationship, it is not surprising that the transnational banks' impact in the Caribbean has been to encourage international capitalism rather than self-reliant development.

Canadian, British, and U.S. banks dominate banking throughout the Caribbean, except in Cuba. The leaders are Barclays (U.K.), Royal Bank of Canada, Chase Manhattan (U.S.), Citibank (U.S.), Canadian Imperial Bank of Commerce, and the Bank of Nova Scotia (Canada).[14] Caribbean countries have relatively few banks of their own, so transnationals provide many local banking services involving deposits, loans, and currency exchange. While they thus take in deposits from the whole population, they tend to lend the money out to a select group of often foreign borrowers. Like all banks, they favor short-term, high interest loans with little risk. This means lending to local branches of multinational corporations; to businessmen involved in the profitable import-export business; and to upper-income consumers buying luxury goods.[15]

On the other hand, the banks hardly ever lend to farmers or fishermen, whose only collateral would be their entire livelihood, i.e., land or a fishing boat. Nor do the banks make many loans for agriculture or local manufacturing, which they perceive as high-risk.

These lending patterns are not politically neutral. They are biased in favor of the old neocolonial habits of import-export dependence. The banks' reluctance to finance indigenous production (for example in agriculture and agro-industry) and their eagerness to loan to foreign enterprise perpetuates the strategy of industrialization by invitation. And by lending local capital to foreign corporations which repatriate their profits, the banks help to channel the Caribbean's wealth out of the region. ∎

Transnational banks line the "Golden Mile" in downtown San Juan, Puerto Rico.

Cathy Sunshine

The Media

Although the U.S. media's reach is worldwide, the Caribbean is especially fertile ground for influence. This is true, first of all, because much of the region speaks English, and until recently was under British control. Britain was the linchpin of the global spread of the U.S. media. Its ascendency as the first media power made English the language of international communications, and collaboration between the U.S. and British media paved the way for U.S. penetration of the Commonwealth market.[1]

Secondly, both the Caribbean and Latin America are subject to special controls aimed at ensuring U.S. hegemony. In media, as in the labor movement, the United States began gaining control during the First World War, and consolidated that control at the end of World War Two.

Today, U.S. media influence in the Caribbean is both direct and indirect. Television programming from satellite and cable, wire service dispatches to newspapers and imported American films bring U.S.-made content directly into the region. Indirect influence takes place through the links between U.S. and Caribbean capitalists, who control the privately-owned media in both societies. The conservative daily newspapers play a role in ideological control, and they have both intentionally and coincidentally supported U.S. efforts to destabilize progressive governments.

Television: The Alien Invasion

Television is the most powerful vehicle of foreign cultural influence in the Caribbean. Some 75% of television programming in the English-speaking Caribbean originates outside the region, primarily in the United States.[2] Stations have large amounts of broadcast time to fill, but little capacity to produce programs locally. The result is a steady diet of "Dallas," "Love Boat," "Miami Vice" and other canned Hollywood fare.

The few programs produced locally generally include news broadcasts and government information programs (most Caribbean television networks are government-owned.) Some countries do not even have this capability, however. In Belize, all programming except for advertisements is beamed by satellite from the United States.

Even local news broadcasts often pick up their international segment from U.S. networks, resulting in an American slant to the interpretation of world events. The U.S.-based Cable News Network produces a "Headline News" broadcast which is widely viewed throughout the region. It highlights events in the United States, with virtually no coverage of the Third World outside of disasters and coups.

New technologies have speeded and intensified this media penetration. Many Caribbean homes are hooked up to cable, which transmits 100% American programming 24 hours per day. In Puerto Rico, cable channels broadcasting in English include the Disney channel and the Playboy channel. Satellite dishes for direct broadcast reception are popular in countries with a large middle class, notably Jamaica, Trinidad and the Bahamas. Video cassette recorders are another middle-class status symbol; Barbados alone has 94 video rental parlors, offering films ranging from comedies to pornography.

Radio typically carries more local programming than television, yet it too has served as a vehicle for foreign influence. Country-and-western music and the "top 40" have nearly crowded Jamaican reggae and Trinidadian calypso off the airwaves. International news comes from the Voice of America, which broadcasts to the Caribbean from a transmitter in Antigua, and from the BBC; the German-owned Radio Antilles broadcasts to the region from Montserrat. Caribbean radio also carries large amounts of fundamentalist religious programming originating in the United States.

Caribbean church leaders, teachers and development workers are among those who are worried about the impact of the media invasion. Although media violence and "sexploitation" are concerns, the real problem is the emphasis on material which is alien and irrelevant to the region's own cultures. Television promotes an unreal picture of American society; the contrast with the daily reality of life in the Caribbean reinforces low self-esteem and a desire to emigrate. Likewise, while Caribbean dance and drama struggle to develop, American pop stars like Michael Jackson captivate Caribbean youth. By displacing and devaluing what is local, the foreign media onslaught has effectively retarded the development of authentic Caribbean cultures.

This process is so powerful that some observers speak of "the very real possibility that unique, autonomous Caribbean

CNN
NEWS REPORT
THE ALL-AMERICAN
VIEW POINT

Outlet

115

Shopping center in San Juan, Puerto Rico.

Cathy Sunshine

cultures will never fully develop." This has worrisome implications for the region's future:

> Because the health of such cultures is vital to true development, this region, perhaps more than others, needs to build and authenticate its identity before it can successfully move to tasks of social and economic change.[3]

The Major Dailies: Voice of the Bourgeoisie

Unlike the electronic media, the major print media in the Caribbean are privately owned. A handful of daily newspapers owned by wealthy families or corporate groups dominate the regional press. While other newspapers can publish, they have difficulty attracting advertising and often do not survive.

The most powerful English-language paper is the Jamaica *Daily Gleaner,* along with its evening edition, *The Star.* It is owned by leading Jamaican capitalists, members of the island's elite "21 families." Heading the company is the Ashenheim family, white Jamaicans with holdings in insurance, real estate, tourism, manufacturing, cement, sugar and steel.

The Trinidad *Guardian* and *Express* belong to Trinidadian commercial conglomerates, the *Guardian* to the McEnearney-Alstons group and the *Express* to the Neal & Massy group. Both papers are strongly pro-business and hostile to labor. McEnearney-Alstons also owns the Barbados *Advocate,*

formerly a part of the U.S.-based Thomson newspaper chain. The Barbados *Nation* is owned by a group of Barbadian companies.

In the Dominican Republic, the prominent *Listin Diario* and *Ultima Hora* are owned by the Pellerano family, members of the Dominican oligarchy. *Hoy* and *El Nacional* belong to a Spanish millionaire businessman whose holdings also include a local television station. *El Nuevo Diario,* at one time progressive, came under nearly fatal pressures from rising costs and loss of advertising, leading to a change in tone.

The press in the colonial territories is dominated, predictably, by metropolitan interests. The only daily newspaper in Guadeloupe and Martinique, *France-Antilles,* is part of a French newspaper chain owned by conservative media tycoon Robert Hersant. The paper views the world from the vantage point of Paris; news of Guadeloupe and Martinique is relegated to pages entitled "In the Department," emphasizing the subordinate link to France.

Likewise, Puerto Rico's major dailies reflect and promote the colonial relationship with the United States. *El Nuevo Día* is owned by the wealthy Ferré family, founders of the New Progressive Party which favors U.S. statehood for Puerto Rico. The English-language *San Juan Star* belongs to the U.S.-based Scripps-Howard newspaper chain. *El Mundo,* which closed in 1988, was for a long time owned by Puerto Rican media magnate Argentina Hills, wife of the former head of the U.S.-based Knight-Ridder newspaper chain.

The major Caribbean dailies are editorially conservative, although dissenting views appear in columns and letters to the editor. They promote capitalism and middle-class consumerism; they are anticommunist and seldom challenge U.S. hegemony in the region. Much of their international news comes directly off the wires (the Associated Press, United Press International and Reuters), leading to an Anglo-American perspective on world events. Most important in shaping their outlook, however, is their ownership by the upper class, whose conservative politics and links abroad make the Caribbean press a natural ally for the U.S. government and major media.

U.S. Influence and the IAPA Connection

As part of the effort to block German influence during World War Two, the United States took over control of most news flowing into Latin America. After the war, this control was institutionalized in the service of Cold War aims.

> The Americans became the senior partners in an Anglo-American governmental media alliance which turned from anti-Nazi to anticommunist propaganda . . . The overt agency was the United States Information Agency. The covert media operations of the United States government were carried on primarily by the Central Intelligence Agency.[4]

The CIA's media assets in Latin America included several wire services (Agencia Orbe Latinoamericana, Forum World Features, and LATIN) and collaborators on key Latin American newspapers. The meeting point for these various strands was the Inter-American Press Association (IAPA), over which the CIA gained substantial influence in 1950.[5] A membership organization of some 1,200 newspapers in the U.S., Latin America and the Caribbean, IAPA is headquartered in Miami, where right-wing Latin exiles play major roles in the organization. The current president of IAPA is Horacio Aguirre, a Nicaraguan exile and founder of the newspaper *Diario de las Américas*.

Reflecting A.J. Liebling's dictum that "freedom of the press belongs to the man who owns one," IAPA is the self-appointed guardian of press freedom. It has used this as a weapon against left-leaning governments, launching its first crusade in the 1950s against the Peron government in Argentina.

In 1975, the Church Committee of the U.S. Senate revealed that the CIA had used IAPA to destabilize the socialist Allende government in Chile. CIA collaborators on the staff of the Chilean newspaper *El Mercurio* had been added to IAPA's board of directors in 1969. From then on, the paper became sensationalist, using manipulative techniques to arouse anti-government feelings. IAPA claimed that the Allende government was against press freedom, and awarded *El Mercurio* its "freedom of the press" award in 1972. These actions helped prepare the way for the 1973 military coup.[6]

According to a consultant to the Church Committee, the Jamaica *Gleaner* underwent a similar change before the election which ousted the Manley government. Oliver Clarke, managing director and chairman of the *Gleaner*, was added to

the IAPA board in 1976. Given the *Gleaner's* upper-class base, the newspaper was by nature hostile to Manley. As the election approached, however, it became sensationalist, focusing on violence and fears of a "Cuban takeover."[7] As in Chile, IAPA cried loudly that press freedom in Jamaica was under attack. The *Gleaner's* campaign played a significant role in Edward Seaga's defeat of Manley in the 1980 election.

The new Seaga government closed down the only other daily newspaper, the government-owned *Daily News,* ensuring the *Gleaner's* complete monopoly. It also purged the state-owned JBC television network of progressive journalists.

It was against this backdrop of media destabilization in Chile and Jamaica that the People's Revolutionary Government (PRG) in Grenada made the controversial decision to close the *Torchlight* newspaper in 1979. It is unlikely that the paper was under direct U.S. influence at this early stage. But it was the voice of the Grenadian business class, and was tied into the regional press establishment through shareholder links with the Trinidad *Express*. Although the *Torchlight* had welcomed Gairy's overthrow, it soon became hostile to the PRG when it turned out the new government was pro-socialist.

By removing the local bourgeois press organ, the *Torchlight* closure forced the regional media to assume the role of press critics of the regime. It also made the PRG's curbs on the media a fact, in contrast to Chile and Jamaica where press freedom was never actually in danger. Regional publishers bristled to see Grenada's privately-owned press replaced with a state-controlled media linked to the Prague-based International Organization of Journalists.

A spiraling confrontation followed between the PRG and the major Caribbean newspapers, organized in the Caribbean Publishers and Broadcasters Association (CPBA). The PRG announced that no new newspapers would be allowed until a media policy could be formulated, and it closed a Catholic paper after just one issue. In December 1980, the *Gleaner, Advocate, Nation, Guardian* and *Express* filed a joint complaint against Grenada with the Organization of American States, focusing on the lack of elections and threats to press freedom.

Several months later, a new newspaper appeared calling itself the *Grenadian Voice*. The PRG closed the paper, citing what it termed convincing evidence that the paper—owned by Grenadian lawyers and businessmen, including the former director of the *Torchlight*—was linked to the CIA. The editor of the *Grenadian Voice* was Leslie Pierre, whose brother Eric Pierre was AIFLD's main operative in Grenada.

Regional press coverage of Grenada was by this time hostile.[8] On September 27, 1981, all the member papers of the CPBA except the Barbados *Nation* ran identical editorials condemning the PRG. The following year, IAPA passed an official resolution condemning the Bishop government.

The PRG was in a no-win situation. If it allowed critical newspapers to publish, they would almost certainly be used to destabilize the government. By closing them down, the PRG marred its international image and damaged relations with the Grenadian middle class. But the greatest cost was to Grenada's own political process, since the tame state-controlled media failed to provide a platform for debate within the revolution.

No hint of the conflicts inside the New Jewel Movement leaked to the public before October 1983, contributing to the explosiveness of the clash when it came.

The U.S. government still views the media as a tool for covert action, despite greater awareness of these linkages at home and abroad. Since 1983, much of this activity has been carried out by the National Endowment for Democracy (NED), which receives all of its funding from the U.S. Information Agency. The Caribbean Publishers and Broadcasters Association received over $100,000 from the NED in 1986 to provide training and advice to Caribbean journalists.[9] The conduit for the grant was a shadowy organization called the Institute for North-South Issues, whose acronym appeared on the flow chart found in the safe of former National Security Council staffer Oliver North. The NED discontinued funding through the Institute in 1987 and began making grants to the CPBA directly.[10]

In 1982, the year the Reagan administration launched its contra war against Nicaragua, IAPA awarded a prize to the Nicaraguan newspaper *La Prensa* for its opposition to "totalitarian regimes." *La Prensa* has received substantial funding from the National Endowment for Democracy as a mouthpiece for critics of the Sandinistas. A controversy erupted when the organization channeling the NED grants to *La Prensa,* known as PRODEMCA, also lobbied for U.S. military aid to the contras, implying a political motive for the grants to the newspaper. Since then, NED grants to *La Prensa* have been channeled through another organization.[11]

The Role of Ruling Parties

While international concern has focused on press curbs by left-leaning governments, restrictions on the media elsewhere in the region have received less attention. In both Haiti and Guyana, authoritarian governments have attempted with varying degrees of success to cripple the independent media. And in some smaller territories, government control of newspapers and radio stations has stifled political debate.

A 1969 law in Haiti provided that anyone who criticized the government could be convicted of being a communist and sentenced to death. It was also a criminal offense for journalists to "offend the chief of state or the first lady." After an independent press began to form in the late 1970s, the Duvalier government cracked down. All independent media were closed down in November 1980, and dozens of journalists jailed or exiled. Only church-owned radio stations survived, operating under continuous harassment.

After the fall of Jean-Claude Duvalier in 1986, the press enjoyed a brief period of liberty during which many new newspapers and magazines started to publish. Within months, however, the ruling junta reintroduced curbs on the media. Violence by the army and former Duvalierists has had a chilling effect on what remains of an independent press.

In Guyana, the Burnham government dismantled the privately-owned media, leaving a single radio station and daily newspaper under state control. Opposition parties were allowed to print bulletins, and the Catholic Church to publish its weekly *Catholic Standard.* But the government's refusal to allow these independent papers to import newsprint reduced them to a few mimeographed sheets. The government also attempted to bankrupt the *Catholic Standard* with libel suits. Politicized courts repeatedly awarded damages to officials of the ruling party, operating on the principle that criticism of government policies constitutes the criminal libel of officials. Burnham's successor, Desmond Hoyte, has continued these practices. To improve its image, however, the Hoyte government has permitted a privately-owned newspaper to open, receiving U.S. funding through the National Endowment for Democracy.

In the smaller Caribbean territories, such as Montserrat, Dominica and St. Lucia, there is a mix of state and private ownership of the media. Government usually owns at least a radio station, reflecting the importance of radio as a means of reaching rural populations. There are usually several small weekly papers, typically owned by or aligned with political parties. In general, opposition parties and other critics have no access to media controlled by the ruling party.

In Antigua, the bimonthly *Nation's Voice* is owned by government, while the *Worker's Voice* is associated with the ruling Antigua Labour Party. The government owns one radio station, and the other is privately owned by the family of Prime Minister Vere Bird. Government owns the television station; the cable TV franchise is held by the prime minister's son, Vere Bird Jr. Swimming against this formidable tide is *Outlet,* weekly paper of the opposition Antigua Caribbean Liberation Movement. The editor of *Outlet* has been arrested, its offices raided and the paper hit with numerous libel suits.

Toward an Alternative Media

"If foreign ownership [of the media] threatens to alienate the Caribbean from itself," argues Jamaican cultural expert Rex Nettleford, "government ownership threatens to imprison an entire people within the platitudes and self-serving propaganda of small groups . . . " The alternative of private monopoly ownership "guarantees power to the well-off and to sections of an articulate intelligensia."[12]

At a series of public seminars sponsored by the University of the West Indies, participants concluded that state ownership had not in itself achieved the type of "social control" of the media which could advance cultural sovereignty. Rather, there is a need for broad-based social sectors such as trade unions, farmers' associations, churches and teachers' associations to help shape a media relevant to the region.[13]

Media independent of foreign and local monopolies do exist, and their number is growing. The Caribbean News Agency (CANA) wire service has become a major source of regional news. *Caribbean Contact,* the monthly organ of the Caribbean Conference of Churches, has for more than a decade been the only paper covering the entire region. It analyzes political, economic and social trends, providing a forum for diverse opinions from within and outside of the churches.

In Jamaica, a number of small, community-oriented publications are challenging the elitist *Gleaner.* The new papers have proved popular, but are struggling against lack of capital and the *Gleaner's* advertising monopoly.

It is radio, however, where popular sectors have made the most inroads and which offers the greatest potential for creative local programming. Unlike the print media, radio can easily be made available to rural, illiterate and Creole-speaking people as a forum for communication. In Haiti, radio broadcasting in Kreyol has been a critical aspect of consciousness-raising. Elsewhere, a variety of educational and cultural programs have opened the airwaves to the community.

Finally, the movement known as "popular theater" is making an important contribution toward the evolution of an alternative media. Pioneered by groups such as Sistren in Jamaica, community-based drama is ideally suited for expressing themes relevant to local realities. Drama also depends less than most forms of public communication on technical know-how and equipment, and it is difficult for governments or private monopolies to control.

Such considerations must underlie the effort to bring Caribbean people into the process of developing a Caribbean cultural identity. Rex Nettleford states . . .

The cultural inventions of the people from below are what invest the society with cultural meaning and purpose. Yet they continue to exist on the margin or as a subculture. It is in the recognition, mobilization and involvement of the creative potential of the mass of the Caribbean population . . . that the region has any future worth contemplating.[14]

CUBA & THE MEDIA: RADIO WHO?

The main exception to the regional media picture is Cuba. Cuba has resisted U.S.-made news and entertainment, orienting its media instead to support of Cuban culture and the revolution. Still, while Cuba may be an island of resistance, it is less cut off from outside influences than many outsiders think.

The Cuban press is state-controlled, with *Granma,* the Communist Party organ, as the main daily newspaper. *Granma* gets news from Cuba's two wire services and from the wire services of other countries such as France, Spain, the Soviet Union, and Third World nations. The Cuban press is self-censoring and reflects official policy. Its reputation as dull and uninformative prompted a government directive in 1984 opening the way for the press to become more critical. This is understood to mean criticism of specific problems, however, not basic principles of the revolution.

Cuban television carries a broad range of news, cultural programs, sports and movies (Cuban-made and foreign, including many American films). Radio stations play primarily Cuban music, from the traditional *trova* (ballads) to the *nueva trova* (new song movement), *son* (an Afro-Cuban music) and *rumba.* Cuban music, drama, dance and film-making are funded by the state through the Instituto Superior de Arte and the Instituto Cubano de Cine.

Despite its emphasis on national culture, Cuba is too close to the United States to escape its influence entirely. Cubans can and do tune into Miami-area radio stations, many of which broadcast in Spanish and reflect the anticommunist politics of the Cuban exile community. American movies have had an impact on Cuban youth, contributing to the desire for U.S.-made consumer goods.

Spanish-language radio broadcasts by the Voice of America and the BBC are heard in Cuba and supplement the news available in the Cuban press. Nonetheless, in 1985 the Reagan administration convinced Congress to fund a special radio station to broadcast to Cuba. Radio Martí operates under the auspices of the Voice of America, with broadcasters drawn from the anti-Castro exile community. Although the Cuban government reacted angrily, the station's impact has proved less than expected. Its soap operas are popular among Cuban listeners. But many consider it merely laughable. "If you ask my opinion, I would say it is right out of the 1950s," one woman told U.S. journalists in Havana. "All these people still have the ideology and outlook of the 1950s. It sounds as if the programs were taped 25 years ago."

What appeared to annoy some Cubans most was the station's name. José Martí, the 19th century Cuban hero, is associated with the struggle for independence from U.S. domination. Exclaimed one elderly Cuban: "They don't have any sense of right and wrong, to use a name like that."

Economic Aid and the Caribbean Basin Initiative

The Reagan administration took office in 1981 stressing the strategic importance of the Caribbean, defined as a key part of the United States' global power base. For Reagan strategists, the traditional modes of influence were insufficient to secure U.S. interests in this vital region. They argued for an aggressive initiative to woo Caribbean nations from "socialism" and into the U.S. camp.

The centerpiece of this effort was to be American aid, tied closely to support for capitalism. Reflecting the president's belief in the private sector as the motor force of development, U.S. aid was largely redirected into support for business. Initially, Jamaica was to be the "showcase" which would demonstrate the effectiveness of these policies. In 1982 the White House launched the Caribbean Basin Initiative (CBI), designed to stimulate Caribbean economies with foreign private investment.

In addition to their ideological thrust, the CBI and other aid programs were intended to convince Caribbean people of the benefits of an alliance with Washington. In 1979-1982— coinciding with the years of the Grenada revolution—these incentives helped pro-U.S. leaders win elections in Jamaica, St. Lucia, Dominica and St. Vincent. These leaders later played important roles in the U.S.-backed invasion of Grenada.

Market Magic

While previous U.S. administrations had promoted capitalism in the Caribbean, the Reagan administration's aid programs were marked by a deep ideological obsession with private enterprise. The "magic of the market"—as President Reagan termed it—was to revitalize ailing Caribbean economies. The primary instrument for this effort was the U.S. Agency for International Development (USAID). Going beyond its traditional function of building infrastructure for industry, USAID's approach during the Reagan presidency became a highly politicized emphasis on "privatization" and private sector support.

In order to carry out these goals, the administration had first to place most economic aid on a government-to-government basis so it could dictate the terms. In the 1970s, most U.S. assistance to the Eastern Caribbean had been channeled through the multilateral Caribbean Development Bank (CDB). In 1981, USAID offered the CDB a $4 million aid package that would have improved roads, water supplies and health facilities throughout the Eastern Caribbean. The offer came with strings attached: Grenada, then under the Bishop government, was to be excluded from benefits. The CDB refused the aid, explaining that it could not be an instrument of U.S. foreign policy.[1]

In retaliation, the Reagan administration shifted most of its aid into bilateral programs, bypassing the regional bank. This allowed the administration to reward client governments, punish those viewed as unfriendly, and direct aid into programs favoring the private sector. In exchange for aid, governments had to agree to divest state-owned enterprises and relax regulation of private business.

U.S. officials' claim that the Caribbean private sector could be a dynamic engine of growth betrayed a lack of knowledge of the region. Aside from peasants, who operate near the subsistence level, the local private sector consists mostly of merchants, who import goods and resell them at a profit. There has never been a real class of venture capitalists who invest in production. The Reagan policy therefore translated into support for *foreign* private investment. Around the region, USAID built factory shells to house foreign manufacturers. It hired the U.S. firm of Coopers & Lybrand to seek out investors, and a corporate-backed body, Caribbean/Central American Action, also promoted investment in the region.

The strategy was based on a specific assumption: that the Caribbean could copy the rapid industrialization achieved by Far Eastern countries during the 1960s. With wages rising in such countries as Taiwan, planners reasoned, there would be an incentive for manufacturers to return to a region just off U.S. shores.

Prime Minister Seaga of Jamaica flanked by President Reagan and Vice-President Bush during a White House visit.

White House photo

120

This argument, however, was seriously flawed. Taiwan's export boom came only after it had achieved self-sufficiency in food, so that low food prices made it possible to hold wages down. Caribbean countries are dependent on expensive, imported food. Secondly, private investment in Taiwan was preceded by huge *public* sector expenditures on infrastructure, much of it financed by U.S. aid. Most Caribbean countries still have very limited infrastructure. Finally, in the Far East unions were very weak and political dissent suppressed.[2]

These facts did not stop the Reagan administration from promoting the "Taiwan model" as the solution for Caribbean countries. Its proving ground was to be Jamaica, where incoming leader Seaga shared Reagan's convictions.

Jamaica: Riding Reagan's Coattails

The alliance between Ronald Reagan and Edward Seaga began well before their respective elections in the fall of 1980. While still in opposition, Seaga's Jamaica Labour Party (JLP) began building ties with right-wing political and business groups in the United States which formed the core of Reagan's support.[3]

The Manley government's disastrous involvement with the International Monetary Fund had caused widespread economic hardship. International bankers and investors showed their displeasure with Manley by shutting off funds, leaving Jamaicans vulnerable to Seaga's promises that he could bring loans and investment into Jamaica again. The U.S. strategy for helping Seaga to power was to convey the impression that his victory would unlock a flood of aid, trade and investment that would restore prosperity.

As early as 1979, Carter administration officials began building ties between Seaga and the international financial establishment. Seaga began negotiating with IMF officials in June 1980, an extraordinary act since he was an opposition party leader, and the Jamaican government had just broken off relations with the Fund.[4] The JLP's manifesto outlined how much aid they expected to receive from the IMF and World Bank and the form in which it would come.

These claims convinced many Jamaicans that the JLP would be able to fulfill its campaign promise to "Make money jingle in your pocket." The pro-JLP *Daily Gleaner* frequently headlined the large sums of money it said would be available to a Seaga administration. In addition, most of the U.S. press was heavily biased against Manley and in favor of Seaga. Seaga's campaign was run by the New York public relations firm of Ann Sabo Associates.

The JLP's victory on October 30, 1980 reflected not only Jamaicans' disillusionment with the Manley government, but also the belief that a government with ties to Washington could get a better deal for Jamaica. The JLP's promises initially came true as both the International Monetary Fund and the World Bank announced large loans to the new government. U.S. bilateral aid flooded the Jamaican treasury, and delegations of USAID consultants arrived to restructure the economy along "free-market" lines.

The Eastern Caribbean: Reversing the "Leftist Tide"

The Grenada revolution in March 1979 opened a period in which people of several Eastern Caribbean states challenged entrenched conservative governments. In May, a popular uprising in Dominica forced the resignation of the corrupt Patrick John government, and its replacement with an interim government headed by O.J. Seraphin. In July, St. Lucians voted out Prime Minister John Compton after 15 years in office; he was replaced by Allan Louisy as prime minister and the liberal, charismatic George Odlum as foreign minister. In St. Vincent and the Grenadines, meanwhile, three opposition parties managed to unite, shaping up as a leftist challenge to the Milton Cato government.

Dominica under Seraphin, St. Lucia under Louisy and Odlum, and Grenada under Bishop then moved to strengthen their ties. A mini-summit in St. George's in the summer of 1979 produced a declaration of cooperation and unity, a move with strong popular support on the three islands. In this context, Grenada and St. Lucia announced that they would not participate in the regional "coast guard" being organized by the Carter administration, because of its militaristic overtones.

U.S. officials saw this series of events as an ominous leftward swing, confirming fears about the model effect of Grenada's revolution. Yet by May 1982—three years later— the trend had been reversed. The liberal governments in Dominica and St. Lucia were out, the Vincentian leftists had been trounced at the polls, and conservative, pro-U.S. regimes were in power in all three islands. *Latin America Regional Reports* wrote of "new confidence by Washington that after months of political work, it has now turned, or at least stemmed, the rising left-wing tide in the sensitive Eastern Caribbean."[5]

The causes were at least twofold. On the one hand, the liberal and progressive politicians were weak, and quickly discredited themselves through internal squabbles and corruption. Equally important, however, was the implied support of the United States for their conservative rivals. Most Caribbean people assume that the candidate preferred by Washington is the one who, if elected, will be able to bring aid and investment into the country.

Such expectations were evident in December 1979 when Cato's St. Vincent Labour Party (SVLP) defeated the left-wing United People's Movement (UPM). Cato ran a very anticommunist campaign: sound trucks patrolled the capital at 4 a.m., booming "Do not let the communists take over in St. Vincent! If you vote UPM, you vote for communism! If you have two sheep, they'll take one! If you have one sheep, they'll cut it in half!" Cato made shrewd use of the aid given to St. Vincent after the eruption of the Soufriere volcano the preceding April. Some of the aid was distributed as electoral bribes, but the larger effect was to suggest that Cato was Washington's candidate:

Cato made much of the international support that his government commanded and of the "special relationship" St. Vincent

121

maintained with its "friends" in the region, particularly Trinidad and Barbados . . . Cato also identified St. Vincent's "special friends" as Canada, the United States and Great Britain. Their relief efforts, which included dramatic airlifts of some refugees and regular visits by ships, were presented as signs of tangible support which the SVLP was able to tap when in need. There was also the threat that less aid would be forthcoming should St. Vincent take the path of Grenada, a revolutionary trajectory with which the UPM was labeled.[6]

In Dominica, meanwhile, the interim government which replaced Patrick John had become enmeshed in scandals of its own. Dominica had been badly hit by Hurricane David in August 1979. In January 1980 the U.S. and British governments used hurricane aid as a lever to pressure Seraphin into expelling two progressive ministers, Atherton Martin and Rosie Douglas, from the cabinet.[7] In contrast to this vacillation, Eugenia Charles' Freedom Party promised strong leadership. Charles emphasized her ideological kinship to the incoming Reagan forces, suggesting it would mean U.S. aid and investment for Dominica. She was elected in a landslide in July 1980.

Finally, the Louisy-Odlum government in St. Lucia tore itself apart in a bitter public split. Louisy had the support of the United States and England, which accurately attributed St. Lucia's earlier accommodation with Grenada to Odlum's influence. Odlum broke off to form the Progressive Labour Party (PLP), and street demonstrations demanded the government's resignation. In a compromise, an interim government was formed under PLP deputy Michael Pilgrim, with the promise of early elections.

Although the PLP had no clear ideology, its liberal tendencies displeased Washington. When President Reagan visited Barbados in the spring of 1982, the White House pointedly did not invite Pilgrim to the meeting between Reagan and the other Eastern Caribbean leaders, citing the upcoming election as the reason. The implication was that a PLP government, if elected, would not have the cooperation of the United States. Washington's choice was clearly Compton, who ran a campaign based on promises of U.S. aid and investment for St. Lucia if he were elected. In May, a tired and disgusted electorate returned Compton's party to power, the same party they had thrown out of office three years earlier over its anti-worker policies.

The Reagan administration trumpeted Compton's election as an important victory for "free enterprise" forces. Immediately after the election, it rushed a special task force to St. Lucia to discuss "economic recovery and development." Yet the promise of a massive rescue effort soon faded as no new economic aid arrived.

The Caribbean Basin Initiative

Soon after Reagan's election, Jamaican prime minister Seaga and Barbadian prime minister Adams had approached the president with their idea for a Caribbean "mini-Marshall Plan," to be patterned on U.S. assistance to Europe after World War Two. In the spring of 1982, the Reagan administration announced it was sending Congress a package of aid, trade and investment incentives called the Caribbean Basin Initiative (CBI).

The White House made clear from the start that the CBI's purpose was counterinsurgency. The very concept of the Caribbean "basin" was a Reagan invention, allowing the administration to annex Central America and its guerrilla insurgencies to the insular Caribbean, and disguise additional funding for the war in El Salvador as "Caribbean aid." In his speech launching the CBI, Reagan passed from a discussion of economic recovery to an anticommunist polemic:

> A new kind of colonialism stalks the world today and threatens our independence. It is brutal and totalitarian. It is not of our hemisphere but it threatens our hemisphere and has established footholds on American soil . . .
> The dark future is foreshadowed by the poverty and repression of Castro's Cuba, the tightening grip of the totalitarian left in Grenada and Nicaragua, and the expansion of Soviet-backed, Cuban-managed support for violent revolution in Central America.
> Nowhere in its whole sordid history have the promises of communism been redeemed . . . [8]

Behind this rhetoric was the troublesome knowledge that in much of the Caribbean and Central America, the promises of *capitalism* had not been redeemed. Reagan officials saw their task as one of making capitalism work for the Caribbean, while working to destroy socialist-oriented governments and movements. In this respect the CBI resembled the Alliance for Progress, launched by the Kennedy administration in the 1960s. The Alliance, however, approached its goals through development aid, while the CBI focused on support to private business.

The CBI's main planks as originally proposed were:
● Duty-free entry to the U.S. market for Caribbean-made products for 12 years, except textiles, footwear, sugar and rum;
● A 10% tax credit for U.S. businesses which invest in the region;
● A supplemental aid appropriation of $350 million in 1982, to be divided among countries of the Reagan administration's choosing.

Announcement of the CBI caused initial excitement in the Caribbean. But as the bill's slow passage through the U.S. Congress allowed time for reflection, its limitations became apparent. The duty-free provisions were of limited import since some 80% of all Caribbean exports already entered the United States duty-free. Nothing in the CBI addressed the problem of low and unstable prices for commodities like sugar, bananas and bauxite—the chief cause of balance-of-payments problems.

Other than its close allies Seaga and Adams, the Reagan administration consulted no Caribbean leaders, technical institutions or popular organizations in designing the CBI. Rather, the plan was developed by Caribbean/Central American Action, a corporate group supported by multinationals such as Alcoa, Gulf + Western, Coca-Cola and United Brands. This helped shape the CBI's emphasis on incentives to foreign business, a recycled version of the Puerto Rican model. Factories set up under the CBI would employ cheap Caribbean labor, but would have no other links to local economies. They would not use local raw materials nor develop local skills.

From the point of view of U.S. labor unions, the CBI threatened to create more runaway shops. Unions and domestic producers fearful of competition from imports pressed for revisions in the CBI bill. Facing Congressional resistance, the Reagan administration dropped the tax credits, while the duty-free provisions languished in Congress for a year.

The only part to be passed immediately, the supplemental aid, was little more than a political gesture. The sum of $350 million hardly registered against the region's $4 billion per year balance-of-payments deficit. The allotments of aid reflected the administration's political agenda, not the realities of need. Initially, over one-third of the total ($128 million) was earmarked for El Salvador. Congress later reduced this to $75 million. Other major recipients were strategic Central American nations—Costa Rica ($70 million), Honduras ($35 million), and Guatemala ($10 million); and U.S. clients in the Caribbean—Jamaica ($50 million), the Dominican Republic ($41 million), and Haiti ($10 million). By contrast, the underdeveloped Eastern Caribbean was to divide a mere $20 million among all of its countries.

The White House reserved the right to decide who would be included in the CBI and who wouldn't. Predictably, Cuba, Grenada and Nicaragua were excluded, as were Suriname and Guyana. All the CARICOM governments except Seaga's objected to this principle of exclusion.

Before long, what had been trumpeted as a Marshall Plan for the region no longer aroused many hopes. The one-time grant of $350 million disappeared into the region's yawning deficit cavern. Although a scaled-down version of the trade incentives was finally passed in 1983, less than 6% of U.S. imports from the Caribbean entered under the CBI's duty-free provisions in the first eight months of 1984.[9] When pressed on the question of Caribbean aid, Reagan continued to talk about exports, private investment and the CBI. But the smaller islands still lacked the infrastructure to attract investors, such as roads and international airports. Instead of economic aid to build infrastructure, Washington began sending military aid in 1982 to the tiny Eastern Caribbean islands.

By the fall of 1983, the popularity of the conservative Eastern Caribbean leaders was ebbing. They could do little to gain more attention from Washington other than echo Reagan's claims about a Cuban and Grenadian threat. Increasingly, Grenada *was* seen as a threat, because its rising prosperity and employment contrasted embarrassingly with conditions in neighboring countries. The threat was that Grenada's revolution would be seen as a model, since more conventional models had failed.

It was not surprising, therefore, that when given the opportunity to join a U.S.-led invasion of Grenada—gaining American gratitude and removing the troublesome Grenadian example—the leaders jumped on board. The invasion was a last chance to solidify the patron-client bond with Washington. As Eugenia Charles bluntly exclaimed, "It is going to mean more aid for us. I think America must recognize that we will require it."[10] The invasion thus capped the process that began in 1979, as U.S. incentives and pressures helped surround Grenada with conservative, U.S.-aligned states. ∎

The Grenada Invasion: Return to the "Big Stick"

The return to a predominantly militaristic strategy in the Caribbean began under the Carter administration in the fall of 1979, after a series of events (revolutions in Iran, Nicaragua and Grenada, and the Soviet invasion of Afghanistan) brought Carter under pressure to discard his human-rights approach to the Third World.[1] This shift in direction helped propel the Reagan administration into office, committed from the start to a foreign policy based on force. The militarization of the Caribbean accelerated swiftly after Reagan took office in January 1981.

With pressure against Cuba, Grenada, and Nicaragua the cornerstone of its policy, the administration systematically laid the basis for military intervention in the region. In December 1981, amid official talk of a naval blockade of Cuba, Reagan upgraded Carter's Caribbean Task Force at Key West to a Caribbean Command. This brought the whole Caribbean "basin" (the Caribbean Sea, the Gulf of Mexico, and portions of the Pacific bordering on Central America) under a unified military command for the first time.[2] It was headed by Rear Admiral Robert P. McKenzie, former commander of the Caribbean Task Force.

An important part of the new militarism was the frequent staging of naval "exercises" or war games in the region. These served two purposes: to intimidate countries considered enemies—Cuba, Nicaragua, and Grenada—and to serve as dress rehearsals for actual intervention.

From August to October 1981, Operation Ocean Venture '81 dramatically foreshadowed the invasion of Grenada which was to take place two years later. The largest peacetime maneuver by Western forces since World War Two, Ocean Venture '81 involved 120,000 troops, 240 warships and 1,000 aircraft from the United States and thirteen western nations. The Caribbean phase of the four-part maneuvers was commanded by Rear Admiral McKenzie and followed a fictional war-game scenario. A hypothetical island in the Eastern Caribbean dubbed "Amber," which has engaged in "anti-democratic revolutionary activities," seizes American hostages. After negotiations with Amber break down, U.S. forces mount an amphibious and air attack on the island to rescue the hostages. Afterwards, according to the scenario, U.S. troops stay on Amber Island until an election can be held and a regime installed which is "favorable to the way of life we espouse."[3]

This hypothetical hostage rescue mission, as the State Department called it, was rehearsed on the U.S.-controlled

U.S. Army Rangers guard captured Grenadians and Cubans on first day of the Grenada invasion.

Department of Defense

124

island of Vieques, part of Puerto Rico. Everyone in the Caribbean understood "Amber" to refer to Grenada, which resembles Vieques in size and terrain. The mock invasion of Vieques matched the later real invasion of Grenada in many details, including a pre-dawn drop of 300 paratroopers, an amphibious landing of Marines, and intervention of an Army contingent. Units of the 75th Ranger Division which later invaded Grenada took part in the Vieques maneuver.

Ocean Venture '81 was the first of what became an almost continuous series of U.S. military maneuvers in the region's waters. The following spring, Ocean Venture '82 again simulated the invasion of a hostile island. This time, Navy families from the U.S. base at Guantanamo were "evacuated" to the aircraft carrier Guam in a further elaboration of the hostage rescue scenario.

A second major aspect of the Reagan strategy was the militarization of various Caribbean countries and their integration into regional alliances under U.S. control. This had three interrelated elements:

- The "Caribbeanization" of Puerto Rico, stressing Puerto Rico's Caribbean identity in order to facilitate its role as a U.S. surrogate in the region;
- The emergence of Jamaica and Barbados as U.S. surrogates in the English-speaking Caribbean;
- Militarization of the small islands of the Eastern Caribbean, culminating in the formation of a five-nation "regional defense force" to surround and isolate Grenada.

Caribbeanization of Puerto Rico. "In the last two years, the government of Puerto Rico has discovered the Caribbean," wrote militarism expert Jorge Rodriguez Beruff in 1982. "The delay in making this discovery should not be too surprising in a country that until a short time ago was geographically located—for advertising purposes—somewhere in the Atlantic Ocean, near the Eastern Seaboard of the United States, and in some cases just off the island of Manhattan."[4]

The official myth that Puerto Rico is part of the U.S., used to attract industry and disguise the island's colonial status, has given way to a rediscovery of Puerto Rico's Caribbean identity. This new emphasis permits Washington to increase its military involvement in the Caribbean without appearing to be an imperial power.

In March 1981, the Puerto Rican governor, Carlos Romero Barcelo, traveled to Panama for a briefing on the political and military situation in the Caribbean from officials of the U.S. Southern Command. He was accompanied by the commander of the Puerto Rican National Guard and the Chief of Civil Defense. Later, Romero met with Secretary of State Alexander Haig to discuss Puerto Rico's "leadership" role in the administration's Caribbean plan.[5]

Long a military bastion for the United States in the Caribbean, Puerto Rico is home to the Roosevelt Roads Naval Station, the largest U.S. naval base in the hemisphere. In preparation for Puerto Rico's expanded military role, the administration undertook a large-scale expansion of Roosevelt Roads. It also reopened the Ramey Air Force Base, closed for over ten years, and reactivated an underground Navy communications network in the nearby town of Aguada. A powerful military communications tower was moved from Panama to Puerto Rico for use in communicating with U.S. nuclear submarines.

Besides its physical location in the Caribbean, Puerto Rico possesses another attribute of interest to the administration—a Spanish-speaking army, the Puerto Rican National Guard (PRNG). Considered one of the most "efficient" of the U.S. national guards, the PRNG has increased in size from 7,000 in the early 1970s to 11,000 in 1980.[6] From 1980-81, federal spending on the PRNG jumped from $3.6 million to $5.4 million, reflecting the Reagan administration's plans to use the Guard for external intervention in the region.[7] The PRNG participated alongside regular U.S. and NATO forces in Ocean Venture '81 and '82, and in January 1983, units of the PRNG were sent to Honduras to take part in the Big Pine military maneuvers on the Nicaraguan border. Puerto Ricans also have increasingly served the U.S. as elite troops and advisors in Central America, and recruitment of Puerto Ricans for the regular U.S. armed forces has risen sharply.[8]

Surrogate role of Barbados and Jamaica. One task of the Puerto Rican National Guard is to train soldiers from other Caribbean countries. Members of the Barbados Defense Force (BDF), the Jamaica Defense Force (JDF), and the army of the Dominican Republic were trained in Puerto Rico in 1980, 1982 and 1983, receiving U.S.-sponsored military training behind a facade of intra-Caribbean cooperation.[9]

Jamaica and Barbados have emerged as U.S. partners in the region for several reasons. The Jamaican security forces have a history of collaboration with the U.S., and the Jamaica Defense Force is the largest army in the Commonwealth Caribbean. Additionally, Jamaica is a leader in setting political trends in the English-speaking Caribbean, and the rise of Seaga made the island available to the Reagan administration for the kingpin role in its regional strategy.

Barbados emerged as the U.S. ally in the Eastern Caribbean partly by inclination—it has a pro-British, pro-American political culture—and partly by default. Washington initially turned to the Tom Adams government after the prime minister of Trinidad, Eric Williams, rebuffed U.S. overtures aimed at enlisting Trinidad's cooperation in the U.S. campaign against Manley in Jamaica.[10] Later, Adams' personal hostility toward the Grenada revolution together with Barbados' proximity to Grenada made Barbados the obvious choice for an active anti-Grenada role.

Since Reagan took office, the United States has been building up and financing both the Jamaican and Barbadian defense forces. U.S. military aid to Jamaica went from zero during the Manley administration to over $4 million in 1984 to train and equip the 5,000-man JDF.[11] Barbados first received U.S. military assistance in 1981, and in 1982 received $2 million in military equipment and training for the BDF. State Department presentations to Congress in that year stated bluntly that Barbados " . . . has supported U.S. global and regional interests," and justified expansion of the Barbados Defense Force "in light of continuing Cuban support for the radical government in Grenada."[12]

Member of U.S. 82nd Airborne instructs Caribbean soldiers who provided token multinational presence in the Grenada invasion. Countries which joined the invasion signed a U.S.-backed regional defense pact in 1982.

Department of Defense

Formation of the Regional Defense Force. Along with U.S. military aid to Barbados and Jamaica came, for the first time, military allocations for the mini-states of the Eastern Caribbean. Initially this meant small sums (about $60,000 per island) for military training. Less important than the quantity of aid, however, was the link being established between the U.S. and the police forces of the small islands, paving the way for their integration into a regional military alliance.

This occurred in the fall of 1982. Since entering office, the Reagan administration had been building ties to conservative leaders in Barbados, St. Vincent, St. Lucia, Dominica and Antigua; and in October 1982, this marriage of convenience took on a military aspect with the formation of a Security and Military Cooperation Pact among the five islands. It was the Caribbean "coast guard" which the U.S. had long sought, presented in terms of its usefulness for controlling smuggling and illegal immigration, search and rescue, and pollution control.[13] The force was headquartered in Barbados and financed through specially allocated U.S. military aid ($3 million in 1984).[14]

The regional leaders' real interest in the "coast guard" was accidentally revealed when Prime Minister Vere Bird of Antigua announced that the force would hinder revolutionaries from taking power in the islands. For the Reagan administration, the regional pact had an additional purpose: to surround Grenada with a U.S.-controlled military alliance of conservative states.

There was a fourth aspect of the Reagan administration's preparations for military action against Grenada, and that was the preparation of U.S. public opinion. The constant talk of hostages was one aspect of this, playing on U.S. fears and anger after the Iranian hostage experience. Another was heightened anti-Cuba propaganda, such as a State Department "White Paper" which made unsubstantiated charges that Cuba was arming and training left-wing parties all over the Caribbean. In March 1983, Reagan delivered his famous "Star Wars" speech in which he declared that Grenada was a threat to U.S. national security. Displaying aerial spy photographs of the airport under construction at Point Salines—which, as Maurice Bishop later pointed out, could just as well have been taken with an instamatic camera at the totally unrestricted site—the President described the new airport as a sophisticated military installation. The allegations came a month after the *Washington Post* published details of a covert destabilization plan which the CIA had prepared against Grenada in the summer of 1981. The plan was said to have been scrapped because of objections from the Senate Intelligence Committee.[15]

Prime Minister Eugenia Charles of Dominica meets with President Reagan, Secretary of State George Shultz and national security advisor Robert McFarlane in the White House on the morning of the invasion. Charles extended the invitation to the U.S. to invade, ostensibly on behalf of the Organization of Eastern Caribbean States.

White House photo

The Grenada Invasion

All these political and military preparations fell into place in the pre-dawn hours of Tuesday, October 25, 1983, after internal developments in Grenada provided the U.S. with its long-sought opportunity to invade. Tragically, it was a split within Grenada's ruling party and the death of Prime Minister Maurice Bishop which caused the revolution to collapse and opened the door to the U.S. attack.

Divisions and tensions had been mounting within the New Jewel Movement since the summer of 1982, although this was unknown to all but a few persons outside the party's inner circle. The context was one of intense pressures on the Grenadian leadership—caused by U.S. hostility, by popular expectations in the face of economic constraints, and by a severe shortage of trained, experienced people to carry out government programs. In this pressure-cooker situation, in which top-level party and government leaders were over-worked and frequently exhausted or ill, both the efficiency of the ruling party and its rapport with the Grenadian people began to suffer. This led to growing friction and arguments over who was to blame, with criticism often framed in ideological rather than personal terms [see Part VII, Ch. 1].

In September 1983, a majority of the New Jewel Movement's Central Committee decided to institute joint leadership of the party between Prime Minister Bishop and Deputy Prime Minister Bernard Coard, a decision subsequently ratified by the NJM's 60-odd full members. This decision was to be kept secret from the Grenadian people because of their attachment to Bishop, who had always been sole party leader. Bishop initially accepted the idea, but subsequently asked for the matter to be reopened. This angered the party's Central Committee, a majority of whose members supported Coard. In the tense days between October 8 and October 15, Bishop was accused of spreading a rumor that Coard planned to kill

him, an accusation Bishop denied. Finally, on October 13, the NJM Central Committee had the prime minister put under house arrest.

Bishop's arrest was the first time ordinary Grenadians knew there were any problems within the party. They reacted with fury: pro-Bishop demonstrations snowballed, and party members met with angry rejection when they tried to convince the people that Bishop was at fault. On Wednesday, October 19, a large crowd moved up to Bishop's house and freed him and education minister Jacqueline Creft. Chanting, "We get we leader," the crowd carried the two to Fort Rupert, an army administrative post, while Coard and his supporters gathered at Fort Frederick on the opposite side of town. Soon afterward, three armored cars and a truckload of soldiers rolled up to Fort Rupert and fired on the crowd. As people fled the scene in panic, soldiers led Bishop, Creft, ministers Unison Whiteman and Norris Bain, and labor leaders Fitzroy Bain and Vincent Noel into the inner courtyard of the fort and shot them.

That night, General Hudson Austin announced the formation of the Revolutionary Military Council (RMC), a sixteen-man governing junta, and imposed a round-the-clock, shoot-on-sight curfew affecting the whole island.

The first conversations regarding possible military action in Grenada to which the U.S. State Department admits took place between Washington officials and Caribbean leaders on October 15, four days before the killings occurred in Grenada. However, unnamed "top Jamaican government officials" later told the *Washington Post* that the Reagan administration had "for several months" been urging Caribbean states to isolate Grenada and to consider military action against the island.[16] The Army Ranger battalion which parachuted into the Grenada airport on October 25 had in fact practiced the maneuver more than a month earlier, from September 23 to

October 2, at a remote municipal airport in eastern Washington state. The manager of the site says the military sought to avoid publicity about the exercise, which resembled the later invasion in many details.[17]

On Friday, October 21, the prime ministers of Antigua & Barbuda, Dominica, St. Lucia, St. Vincent and the Grenadines, St. Kitts-Nevis and Montserrat gathered in Barbados to decide what to do about the Grenada situation. They were joined at their meeting by Prime Minister Adams of Barbados and by a high-ranking U.S. official, Deputy Secretary of State for Inter-American Affairs Charles Gillespie. Out of that meeting came the "urgent invitation" for the United States to intervene militarily in Grenada. The invitation was offered on behalf of the Organization of Eastern Caribbean States (OECS), even though that body's charter called for unanimous decisions and one OECS member—Grenada—was neither present nor consulted. Later, Jamaican prime minister Edward Seaga arrived to take part in the invasion planning.

Five of the inviting countries plus Barbados and Jamaica sent token contingents of troops or policemen to accompany the U.S. invasion force. (Montserrat, a British colony, did not send forces.) The largest contingent consisted of soldiers from the Jamaica Defense Force, followed by a unit from the Barbados Defense Force.

Puerto Rico and Barbados provided the primary bases for launching the invasion. The Ranger battalion which led the assault was transported to Roosevelt Roads naval base in Puerto Rico several days in advance. In the pre-dawn hours of October 25, according to a Navy newsletter, Roosevelt Roads was "swinging into action to support the front line forces" going into Grenada, including the "largest group of C-130's

U.S. Major captures a souvenir.

[troop transport planes] ever brought together at the same time since Danang."[18]

Meanwhile, the Caribbean soldiers and policemen assembled in Barbados, which made its Grantley Adams International Airport available as the staging site for the assault. The U.S. Embassy in Bridgetown served as political command center, overseeing the evacuation of the U.S. medical students from Grenada, coordination between the invading nations, and press relations (which consisted of keeping the press away from Grenada while dispensing the Pentagon and White House version of events).

Perhaps no other political/military event in recent history has been such a masterpiece of deception as the Grenada invasion. By barring the press from the island for the first two days, the White House and the Pentagon achieved total control over information dispensed by the media during the crucial period when public opinion was being formed. Much of this information later turned out to be false, as the *New York Times* detailed in an article entitled "In Wake of Invasion, Much Official Misinformation by U.S. Comes to Light."[19]

Pentagon spokesmen denied up to the last minute that an invasion was underway, saying on the night of October 24 that they knew of no plans for U.S. military action in Grenada.[20] This statement arrived on American breakfast tables the morning of the 25th, as 1,900 Marines and Rangers were bearing down on the island in helicopters and parachutes. Admiral Wesley McDonald, commander of the U.S. Atlantic forces, stated at a news conference that there were at least 1,100 Cubans in Grenada, all "well-trained professional soldiers." Subsequently the State Department admitted that only 784 Cubans—the number given by the Cuban government—were in Grenada, and that the majority were ordinary workers.

The administration insisted that the invasion had not resulted in any known civilian casualties, a position it maintained through October 30. Only after reporters discovered a bombed-out mental hospital strewn with the bodies of patients did the Pentagon admit that a Navy plane had "inadvertently" bombed the hospital on October 25, the first day of the assault.[21]

The official deception went beyond specific falsehoods, however, to embrace the entire rationalization for the invasion and the context in which it was presented to the American people. The administration's first justification for the action was that it was a "rescue mission" to save American students at the St. George's University medical school in Grenada from the threat of being taken hostage. This was a deliberate attempt to play to the strong emotions which even a potential hostage seizure was guaranteed to arouse in the United States. In reality, there was no evident hostage threat and no reason that the students could not have been evacuated peacefully. After the takeover by Coard's military junta, school officials were already in discussion with General Austin regarding protection of the students and arrangements for their departure. On Saturday, October 22, two counselors from the U.S. Embassy in Bridgetown visited Grenada, talked with school officials and with Austin and concluded that there was no immediate danger to the students. Deputy Secretary of State Kenneth

U.S. med students: were they ever in danger?

Department of Defense

Dam later testified to Congress that the State Department had no information that any Americans were either harmed or threatened after the coup took place.[22]

But the White House did not want the students evacuated peacefully; it wanted an invasion. The U.S. ambassador based in Barbados, Milan Bish, telephoned officials of the medical school in New York, seeking a statement of concern for the students and a request for U.S. intervention. The officials declined. While Canada and Britain were arranging charter evacuation flights for their nationals, the U.S. government was making no attempt to evacuate Americans, but was instead deep in planning for the military attack. The White House statement that Grenada's airport was "closed" on Monday, the day before the invasion, was a lie. Four charter planes flew in and departed on that day, carrying out foreign nationals.[23]

While the Reagan administration was talking about the safety of the students, the leaders of Barbados, Jamaica, and the small islands presented the issue in terms of the need to rescue Grenada from the clutches of the Revolutionary Military Council (RMC). The brief reign of the RMC was indeed a bitter experience for Grenadians. After the army's slaughter of Maurice Bishop and five other leaders, the 24-hour, shoot-on-sight curfew angered and frightened the population. Something clearly had to be done, but it is not clear that invasion was the necessary action. The larger community of English-speaking Caribbean nations—CARICOM—had already drawn up plans for a non-violent resolution of the crisis. Meeting in Trinidad on Saturday October 22 and Sunday October 23, the emergency CARICOM summit decided to apply sanctions which would force the RMC to the negotiating table, aimed at an immediate return to civilian government and early elections. These sanctions included Grenada's suspension from CARICOM and all CARICOM trade arrangements. Additionally, no new currency issues would be made to the regime by the East Caribbean Central Bank; and all air and sea links with Grenada would be cut. Foreign nationals would be evacuated peacefully and a CARICOM peace-keeping force deployed on the island.[24]

Only if these sanctions failed to work would the use of force be considered. Prime Minister Chambers of Trinidad asserted in his speech to the Trinidad Parliament that . . .

> . . . force, be it regional or extra regional, should not be the first resort in respect of a sister CARICOM state.[25]

There was every reason to believe that the RMC would have responded to these pressures. The Central Committee members had erred fatally in their takeover, both by assuming that they could strong-arm Grenadians into accepting the change, and by assuming Cuba would support them. Confronting a hostile population, with no external support whatsoever, the RMC was in a quite untenable position by five days after Bishop's death.

The CARICOM plan was never given a chance to work. By Friday, before the U.S. had even lined up its "urgent invitation" from Caribbean allies, the flotilla of U.S. warships had been diverted from Lebanon and was steaming toward Grenada. As Errol Barrow, leader of the Barbadian opposition, later wrote:

> . . . Reagan's mind was made up; like a sheriff whose posse was ready to mount, some of them on donkeys, he rode into town with guns ablaze looking for an enemy.[26]

White House photo

Guns ablaze and looking for an enemy.

Within hours after the attack, doubts were raised about the administration's stories. Officials of the medical school questioned whether the students had been in danger. An examination of the invitation from the OECS revealed it to be a legal fiction. Under pressure to justify sending U.S. troops into combat, President Reagan turned to a new theme in his televised address of October 27. Grenada was "a Soviet-Cuban colony being readied to export terrorism and undermine democracy . . . We got there just in time," intoned the president.

Like the hostage story, this explanation convinced many Americans. But it relied on fantasy—what the *New York Times* called "misleading factual allegations to bolster President Reagan's unproven assertion that the invasion was necessary to prevent a Cuban military takeover."[27] Nothing in any of the documents made public by the White House supported its claim. The weapons later shown to reporters in Grenada consisted of mostly antiquated small arms belonging to the civilian militia.

The real reasons for the invasion were quite different. They reflected above all the Reagan administration's need to win a military victory after a four-year campaign to "roll back communism" which had produced only frustration in its main arena, Central America. Grenada was an easy target, because of its size and because the death of Bishop had destroyed most Grenadians' will to resist. At a deeper level, the U.S. public's support for the invasion reflected the fears of a nation that had not come to terms with the limits of hegemony or with anti-imperialism in the Third World. Grenada came to be seen as a symbol of this Third World defiance, stimulating desires for revenge. As Vice Admiral Joseph Metcalf III proclaimed with satisfaction when it was over, "We blew them away."[28]

Ironically, claims of a brilliant military victory proved to be the biggest deception of all. The U.S. military, assuming little resistance, had planned on less than a day of action. Instead, the fighting raged for three days, during which the Marines lost three helicopters and two Cobra gunships to anti-aircraft fire. The Army lost one Blackhawk troop helicopter and had five more damaged. Nineteen Americans were killed and 115 wounded.

A Marine after-action report, obtained under a Freedom of Information Act request two years later, painted a dismal picture of a military and intelligence fiasco. All four U.S. military services demanded a "piece of the action," resulting in endless confusion. Troops were parachuted into Grenada without accurate intelligence as to the island's defenses, guided in some cases by outdated tourist maps. They did not know where to find the students they were supposed to rescue. At one point, the reported noted, Marines nearly attacked a building they thought might be a Cuban stronghold because it flew an "unknown" flag. It was the Venezuelan Embassy.[29]

At the peak of the occupation, there were over 6,000 U.S. troops in Grenada. This was one for every 18½ Grenadians, or the equivalent of 14 million troops occupying the United States. Most came home in December 1983, leaving behind several hundred U.S. military police and the 400-man Caribbean Peace Force. The troops' withdrawal marked the opening of a new stage in U.S.-Caribbean relations. Temporarily at least, Washington had turned the tide against the regional left and in favor of U.S. control. Afterward, the administration took steps to consolidate that control so that radical change couldn't happen again. ∎

Graffiti in U.S. soldiers' barracks in Grenada.

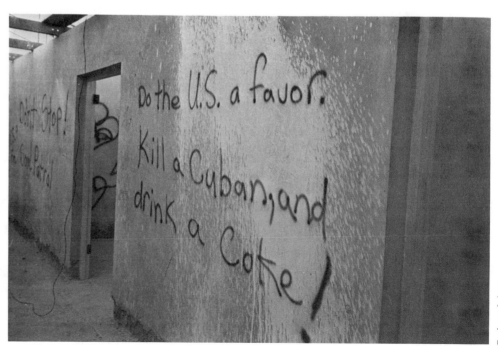

Corinne Johnson

130

Invasion Aftermath: Reagan's New Caribbean Order

The Grenada invasion marked the high point of the Reagan administration's Caribbean strategy. From October 1983 through the end of 1984, everything seemed to be falling into place for the White House in its effort to make the Caribbean an anticommunist bastion of U.S. influence.

The invasion overshadowed the lackluster results of the administration's policies in the region up to then. In particular, it diverted attention from the failure to bring about the promised development miracle in Jamaica. The installation in Grenada of a U.S.-backed regime seemed to offer a fresh opportunity to construct a "showcase" of capitalist development.

Secondly, the participation of six Caribbean governments in the invasion gave the United States an opening to militarize the area. In the following months, U.S. Green Berets trained paramilitary units in the Eastern Caribbean islands. These units were seen as a first line of defense against leftist takeovers in other islands.

Finally, the invasion dealt a blow to the regional left and helped entrench conservative Caribbean leaders in power. Bilateral alliances between these leaders and Washington formed the basis for a new political order, symbolized by the grouping of ten ruling parties into a U.S.-funded "Caribbean Democrat Union."

Grenada: New U.S. Client State

The interim government installed after the invasion thinly veiled direct U.S. control. U.S. and Caribbean troops stayed on the island for over a year, while U.S. diplomatic, aid and intelligence officials transformed Grenada from a Cuban ally to a U.S. client state.

To emphasize Cuba's defeat, the captured Cubans were held for days in outdoor barbed-wire enclosures while CIA officers interrogated them. Administration hard-liners argued against releasing the Cubans, urging that they be made to suffer.[1] But eventually all returned to Havana.

U.S troops rounded up some 1,000 Grenadians suspected of involvement with the Bishop government or the Revolutionary Military Council. During their interrogation by U.S. Army Intelligence, the detainees slept outdoors in wooden packing crates. Gen. Jack Ferris, commander of the U.S. 82nd Airborne forces in Grenada, explained the strategy:

> You develop a human-intelligence network, whereby you have your police and your agents throughout the country and find out who the bad guys are . . . You build a data base on those people, on thousands of them, and bring them all in and question them . . . that's how you stamp out something like that.[2]

U.S. forces detained about 50 Grenadians in prison without charge. Most were eventually released. But many supporters of the revolution lost their jobs as a gradual purge of the civil service took place.

Those who remained in prison included Bernard and Phyllis Coard, Hudson Austin, and the other former members of the Central Committee. Murder charges in connection with Maurice Bishop's death were brought against 19 persons in February 1984. By the end of 1985 their trial had not begun, and Amnesty International expressed concern about reports that they were being mistreated in prison.[3]

"Psychological operations" specialists from Fort Bragg meanwhile mounted a campaign to implant anticommunism among Grenadians. Radio Free Grenada became the U.S.-run Spice Island Radio, broadcasting the propaganda of the psy-ops team. Their message found fertile ground because of the shock and outrage over the Oct. 19 killings. Most although not all Grenadians welcomed the invasion, seeing it as revenge against the Revolutionary Military Council. Emotions of anger and betrayal were easily channeled along broadly anticommunist and pro-American lines.

The American Institute for Free Labor Development held classes for Grenadian workers on "political theories and systems," a thinly disguised process of anticommunist indoctrination. Working through the waterfront workers' union, it red-baited unions which had supported the revolution, calling them "communist-infiltrated" and "pro-Coard." British trade unionists who visited Grenada in December 1983 reported "[attempts] by American-trained and backed Grenadians to remove elected Union officers and take over some unions."[4] But AIFLD failed to gain control of the main labor federation, the Trade Union Congress.

The campaign to purge leftist influence meant the gutting of the revolution's most successful programs. The Center for Popular Education was shut down because U.S. officials objected to the content of its literacy materials. Other programs such as the one to subsidize school books for poor children were condemned as "socialistic." International volunteers who had lent their skills to the revolution were expelled, not only Cubans but also other West Indians such as Jamaicans and Trinidadians. USAID consultants, Peace Corps volunteers and other Americans replaced some of them. With the Cuban doctors gone, USAID contracted the U.S.-based Project Hope to provide health care.

The attempt to erase Cuban influence was especially ironic in the case of the new airport. President Reagan had described the airport as a military threat, and had used it to justify the invasion. Now, however, Grenadian business leaders told U.S. officials that the airport was a necessity.

After kicking out the Cubans who had completed 80% of the construction, the administration contracted U.S. firms to finish the job. On October 29, 1984, as smiling U.S. officials stood by, ribbons were cut on the new Point Salines International Airport in a ceremony to which no Cuban was invited. The dedication speech did not thank or even mention Cuba, and also failed to mention the name of Maurice Bishop, to the annoyance of many Grenadians.

The cost of completing the airport was a major portion of

Comic book titled "Grenada: Rescued from Rape and Slavery" circulated on the island in the weeks preceding the election. Printed in the United States, it was among the propaganda materials which sought to smear the Maurice Bishop government and stir up anti-communist hatred among Grenadians.

the $54 million in U.S. aid to Grenada in 1984 and 1985. Many Grenadians expected that the arrival of the Americans would mean a windfall of aid, jobs and investment. But it soon became clear that ideology and not development was Washington's main concern.

The Grenadian economy was handed over to USAID for restructuring in the free-market mold. Moves toward deregulation included loosening price controls and controls on foreign exchange.[5] Everything owned by the state was to be privatized or shut down; state-owned lands and hotels were put up for sale, while enterprises such as the agro-industry plant were closed. The National Cooperative Development Agency was dismantled and funds for cooperatives frozen.

Fundamental to the strategy was the assumption that once Grenada was "opened" to foreign investment, American firms would locate factories and other export ventures on the island. Grenada was made eligible for the Caribbean Basin Initiative, and USAID built factory shells and hired Coopers and Lybrand to drum up investment. The White House even organized a junket to the island for 21 U.S. business executives.

But by 1985 only two U.S.-owned businesses had started operations, a wooden toy factory and a nutmeg novelty outfit. Despite generous tax breaks and non-union shops, both failed within months. The toymaker, William H. Ingle of Virginia, whom President Reagan praised for his investment, was later convicted of defrauding the U.S. government in the venture.

The investment drive foundered on the fact that Grenada, like the other Windward islands, has little to offer industry. Infrastructure is limited, and power outages are frequent. Yet wages, at around US$4.50 per day for factory workers, are higher than in cheap wage havens such as the Dominican

Republic. What new investment took place in Grenada was almost all in real estate and tourism, and involved mostly local rather than foreign capital.

By a year after the invasion, hopes for a U.S.-funded miracle had faded. The dismantling of the economy set much of the workforce adrift, and unemployment rose. Many Grenadians, especially youth, became bitter and frustrated, and there were incidents of rock-throwing and name-calling against the U.S. and Caribbean soldiers.

By December 1984 Grenada was ready for the final phase of its conversion: the installation of a pro-American government in St. George's. While the U.S. media acclaimed the election as a symbolic "return to democracy," in reality little was left to chance.

For U.S. officials, the main problem was to defeat challenges from Eric Gairy—whose return, it was feared, would provoke another revolution—and from the survivors of Bishop's cabinet, regrouped as the Maurice Bishop Patriotic Movement. But none of the other candidates had a base of support. Washington once again turned to Eastern Caribbean leaders for a solution. In the summer of 1984, they brought together three small Grenadian parties on Union Island in St. Vincent and the Grenadines. Out of that meeting came the New National Party (NNP), a coalition led by a conservative former prime minister, Herbert Blaize.

The U.S. government provided funding to the NNP to build a party structure.[6] The New Right network in the United States sent campaign advisors hired with donations from wealthy conservatives, and the CIA spent $675,000 on the election.[7]

Although much of this assistance remained secret, there was no doubt among Grenadians that the NNP was Washington's choice. U.S. officials made clear that future aid and investment would depend on the election outcome. The party gave away U.S.-made t-shirts, buttons and pens, and even had a plane trail campaign banners across Grenada's skies.

While this outside backing helped the NNP, it probably was not decisive. The party had the active support of the Grenadian middle class, and faced a divided and unpopular opposition. Most Grenadians greatly feared Gairy's return. (True to form, Gairy's campaign platform called for planting "beautiful floral designs" in traffic circles, ensuring a permanent U.S. military presence in Grenada, and reviving horse racing "on a much larger scale than ever before.") And while Grenadians held Maurice Bishop in high esteem, their feelings did not translate into votes for the Maurice Bishop Patriotic Movement.

The NNP thus swept the election with 14 of the 15 parliamentary seats. Prime Minister Blaize promptly confirmed his allegiance to Washington—and his own insecurity—by requesting that the U.S. military remain indefinitely. But the U.S. troops went home in 1985, after the voter registration process had been used to fingerprint and photograph all adult Grenadians. A new police force was trained by the British, and the U.S. trained a paramilitary Special Service Unit.

If the election brought relief from political uncertainty, it did nothing to assuage concern over the stagnating economy. Grenada was again "peaceful," but it was the peace of a moribund colonialism, offering no hope for the future. Instead, with the aging Blaize again at the helm, Grenada took a giant step backward into the past.

Government Boots

With the revolution out of the way, the Reagan administration became preoccupied with preventing "another Grenada." In the spring of 1984, U.S. military trainers arrived in Jamaica, Barbados, Antigua, Dominica, St. Vincent, St. Lucia and Grenada to train Special Service Units. The training was secret, but word got out when island residents spotted weaponry arriving in U.S. military transport planes.

> The smell of cordite hardly had time to dissipate in Grenada when special forces training teams from Fort Bragg, North Carolina began landing on neighboring islands with new weaponry. Although unnoticed by the outside world, the Green Berets did not go unnoticed by opposition political parties on the islands, the first to reveal their presence . . . The six-week training included becoming familiar with new weapons, learning to shoot straight with live ammunition, map reading, and basic military field operations and procedures.[8]

Except in Jamaica and Barbados, which have defense forces, the trainees were members of the island police. U.S. law, however, forbids using U.S. funds to train foreign police. To get around the law, the Reagan administration designated the SSU's as "paramilitaries."

As such, the 80-man units were the first military presence in the smaller islands. Since they clearly were insufficient to deter a foreign attack, people wondered, against whom were they supposed to fight? Police on several islands already had a reputation for brutality. And the deaths of the Grenadian leaders had dramatized the dangers of building up an army. One Vincentian opposition group complained:

U.S.-trained Caribbean soldiers board U.S. helicopter in Grenada.

Department of Defense

133

This army in disguise is likely to be used as an instrument of political oppression of the people. And when this back-door army sees itself as the arbiter of national politics, its more ambitious members will make a bid for direct political power... This army nonsense must stop before it stops us and democracy as we understand it.[9]

Equally worrisome to Caribbean people was the spending of scarce resources on militarization. "We want roads and an international airport for St. Vincent," insisted one party. "We want university scholarships abroad. We want food, technology and cash, not guns please." A Barbadian calypso, "Boots," became a region-wide hit when it criticized expenditures on the Barbados Defense Force:

Left, right, left, right!
The government boots, the government boots!
Is it necessary to have so much soldiers in this small country?
No, no, no, no!
Is it necessary to shine soldiers boots with taxpayers money?
No, no, no, no!
Well don't tell Tommy, he put them in St. Lucy*
Unemployment high and the treasury low
And he buying boots to cover soldiers toe
I see them boots, boots, boots and more boots
On the feet of young trigger-happy recruits
Marching, threatening army troops
Tell Tom I say, that wouldn't do
He's got to see, about me and you
Can we afford to feed an army
When so many children naked and hungry . . . ?

Despite criticism, Prime Minister Adams went ahead to draw up plans with Washington for a 1,500-man standing army involving all the Eastern Caribbean countries. Its purpose, Adams stated, would be to protect against "external aggression and domestic revolution." But by 1985, the idea had been quietly shelved.

The reversal reflected second thoughts regarding militarization and its cost. At a meeting with White House officials in July 1984, Caribbean leaders gently rebuked the administration for paying too much attention to defense and not enough to the economic crisis, the real cause of instability. Prime Minister Compton told the gathering that " . . . Our problems are not military; they are social and economic." Prime Minister Kennedy Simmonds of St. Kitts-Nevis insisted that "Security can't be won with force of arms."[10]

An election in St. Vincent the same month drove the message home. Voters ousted the long-entrenched government of Milton Cato, giving a victory to James Mitchell's New Democratic Party. Although taxes and corruption were the main issues, concern over militarization, including the training of the Special Service Unit, played a role. Mitchell vowed that "not one cent" of his government's money would go to support an army while food, jobs and housing needs were still unmet.

*St. Lucy: former U.S. naval base, now headquarters of the Barbados Defense Force. Tommy: Prime Minister Tom Adams.

The New Political Order

The months following the invasion were a period of right-wing ascendency throughout the Caribbean. The destruction of the Grenada revolution by a faction labeled "ultra-left" opened all the region's left groups and parties to bitter attack. Conservative government, business and church leaders went on a witch hunt against radicals and dissenters. Several ruling parties seized the opportunity to call early elections and renew their mandates, contributing to the entrenchment of conservative regimes.

In Barbados, anticommunism was tinted with xenophobia as the Adams government accused "foreign elements" of subversion. By "foreign elements" Adams meant people from other Caribbean countries living in Barbados. In an act which came to symbolize the attack on dissent, Adams expelled Guyanese journalist Rickey Singh from Barbados for writing articles critical of the invasion. Singh had been editor of the monthly *Caribbean Contact*, published by the Caribbean Conference of Churches at its Bridgetown headquarters.

Adams charged that the church council was full of "foreign elements" and threatened to expel other CCC officials who were non-Barbadians. So heated did the atmosphere become that member of parliament Branford Taitt warned Barbadians, "Do not fall into the trap of believing that you are unpatriotic because you do not agree with the prime minister."[11]

Left-wing party members in a number of islands had their homes and offices raided by police. In St. Vincent, police dug up the earth around the house of activist Renwick Rose in a fruitless search for arms. He was finally charged for possession of several Soviet magazines.

A central propaganda theme was that Cuba had been behind the killing of Bishop and was now working with leftist parties to overthrow other governments. These allegations were an ironic reversal of the truth. Fidel Castro had deep personal links of friendship with Maurice Bishop. After the Central Committee arrested Bishop, Castro sent a message reaffirming Cuba's respect for Bishop and warning that divisions in the party would damage the Grenada revolution. This repudiation came as a blow to Coard supporters. After Bishop was killed, the Cuban leader harshly censured the Revolutionary Military Council, and refused their request for help in defending against the expected invasion.

Nonetheless, Prime Minister Seaga claimed that Havana had given instructions to the Workers Party of Jamaica to "step up action" against his government. He named 25 Jamaicans who he said had traveled to Cuba or the Soviet Union, and he threatened to launch a "shattering offensive" against "saboteurs and traitors." The sensational accusations temporarily diverted attention from Jamaica's economic crisis. Two months after the invasion, Seaga called and won a snap election, gaining a new five-year mandate.

Prime Minister Vere Bird of Antigua denounced the Antigua Caribbean Liberation Movement as "persons with totalitarian aspirations and communist affiliations." Bird called an early election in April 1984. The campaign slogan of

Campaign posters of the Antigua Labour Party promote candidacies of Prime Minister Vere C. Bird's sons, Lester and Vere Jr.

Barbados Nation

his Antigua Labour Party—"It's Safer with Labour"—offered nothing positive, but merely capitalized on the climate of fear. Few issues were raised in the listless campaign. When the ruling party's victory was announced, the streets remained eerily silent, without the usual noisy victory celebrations.

In Dominica, the Eugenia Charles government passed a "treason act" which imposed the death penalty for "forming an intention to overthrow the government." A year later, she won reelection in much the way Bird won in Antigua—through red-baiting of the opposition and by emphasizing her U.S. connection.

At the regional level, the invasion of Grenada signalled the rise of the English-speaking micro-states to the status of important U.S. allies. The new bilateral alliances disrupted the frail regional unity which had been emerging within the framework of CARICOM. In planning the invasion, U.S. officials had colluded with six individual prime ministers. CARICOM, the regional body, was excluded from the decision about how to handle a crisis involving a member-state. CARICOM's four leading members split over the issue, with Trinidad and Guyana opposing the invasion while Jamaica and Barbados played major roles.

The concept of ideological pluralism being debated within CARICOM was abandoned abruptly, as no leader wanted to risk being labeled "communist" by allowing for socialism in the region. Governments joining in U.S.-sponsored militarization ceased talking of a regional "Zone of Peace."

The invasion also symbolized the waning of British influence in the region and Washington's aggressive move into that space. British Prime Minister Margaret Thatcher was not consulted nor even informed of the invasion plans until hours before the action. About to invade a former British colony and present member of the British Commonwealth, U.S. officials were not interested in Britain's opinion.

In January 1986, the launching of the "Caribbean Democrat Union" (CDU) formalized the existence of a pro-American camp. Based in Kingston, the new organization included Seaga's Jamaica Labour Party, Eugenia Charles' Freedom Party, the New National Party in Grenada, and the ruling parties in St. Lucia, St. Vincent, St. Kitts-Nevis, Montserrat and Belize. It soon emerged that this was one of the major Caribbean projects of the National Endowment for Democracy (NED), a new U.S. body set up to promote American interests abroad.

The National Endowment for Democracy

The U.S. Congress created the NED in 1983 as a "private" body which receives all of its funding from the United States government through the U.S. Information Agency. Its official mission is to strengthen democratic institutions abroad. With a budget of some $15 million per year, it channels U.S. taxpayer funds to foreign political parties, trade unions, business associations and other groups.

The NED has thus taken over some of the traditional functions of the Central Intelligence Agency, long involved in covertly funding pro-American and anticommunist groups. A primary motive for the NED's formation was to enable the U.S. government to fund such groups without "tainting" them with a CIA connection.

The NED's chairman is John Richardson, who headed the CIA-funded Radio Free Europe in the 1960s. Other key figures in the NED network include AFL-CIO president Lane Kirkland, conservative labor activist Carl Gershman, right-wing corporate figures J. Peter Grace and Jay Van Andel, and arch-conservative senator Orrin Hatch. NED reflects the same coalition of Republican and Democratic politicians, big business and "big labor" which created AIFLD. Not coincidentally, the AFL-CIO's Free Trade Union Institute is a major conduit for NED funds, passing on grants to AIFLD and to the AFL-CIO institutes in Asia and Africa.

The other major channels for NED grants are the National Republican Institute for International Affairs (NRIIA) and the National Democratic Institute for International Affairs (NDIIA), bodies set up by the respective parties. The NRIIA has been particularly active in the Caribbean, including setting up and financing the Caribbean Democrat Union. The NRIIA—and by extension the U.S. Republican Party—controls the CDU's budget and program and carries out activities to "reinforce the policy positions of member-parties."[12]

In addition, the NRIIA has directly funded the New National Party in Grenada with large grants for "party-building" in 1985 and 1986. Before the election that brought the NNP to power, the NRIIA funded Grenadian business and conservative church leaders to form a Grenada Civic Awareness Organization. This body carried out a program of "voter education" that critics charged favored the NNP. The Free

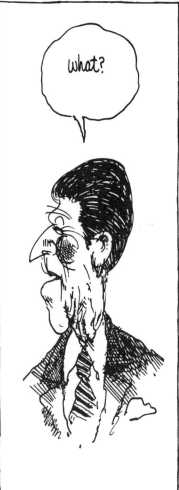

© 1981 *The Miami Herald.* Reprinted by permission.

136

Trade Union Institute also sent $80,000 through AIFLD for a series of political seminars before the vote.[13]

The NED's involvement in Grenada reflects its goal of building up a pro-U.S. leadership in countries experiencing a political transition. A similar process took place in Haiti. Between Duvalier's fall in February 1986 and the Haitian election in November 1987, the NED poured almost $700,000 into Haiti. Most of the funds went to create a "research institute" which provided support to ten center and center-right political candidates.[14]

Another aim of the NED is to promote an anticommunist and pro-capitalist political culture in Third World nations. To do so, it funds various political education programs in the Caribbean, aimed especially at youth. In Dominica, the NED funds the "Committee for Progress in Democracy," controlled by supporters of the Freedom Party. The organization publishes pamphlets and develops radio programs, videotapes and television programs portraying a negative picture of life in socialist countries.[15]

In the Dominican Republic, NED funding has gone through the Center for International Private Enterprise, a project of the U.S. Chamber of Commerce, to lobby Dominican legislators on economic policy. It has also funded an adult education program to provide rural Dominicans with "exposure to free market economics."[16]

Another priority is supporting dissidents inside socialist countries and international publicity against leftist regimes. Since 1984, the NED has funded former Cuban prisoner Armando Valladares to set up committees in Europe and Latin America which publicize human rights violations by Castro's government. Substantial funding has also gone to *La Prensa* and to other internal opponents of the Nicaraguan government. During the leftist military regime of Desi Bouterse in Suriname, the NED funded Henk Chin-a-Sen's Liberation Council in Holland to carry out international agitation against the regime.[17]

Its supporters describe the National Endowment for Democracy as an above-board program which openly supports democratic forces. Nevertheless, some NED-funded projects appear to have direct ties to the covert operations of the Reagan administration, including the creation of a private network to funnel money to the Nicaraguan contras.

One example was the international youth conference held in Jamaica in 1985. The conference, which received $107,000 from the NED and another $1 million from other U.S. agencies, was the brainchild of conservative activists in the United States. The central figure was Roy Godson, a consultant to the National Security Council with close ties to then-CIA director William Casey and NSC staffer Oliver North. Other figures involved in the youth conference had direct ties to North's private contra funding network.[18]

While Godson and officials in the White House, State Department and NSC controlled the planning, a Jamaican secretariat was set up to host the conference. Operating out of what later became the Caribbean Democrat Union office in Kingston, this secretariat was headed by Errol Anderson, a powerful minister in the Seaga government. It continued after the conference under the names International Youth Con-

ference and International Youth Trust. Congressional investigators believed this to be the "Intl. Youth Comm." appearing on Col. North's flow chart with a line leading to the FDN, the main Nicaraguan contra group. Although the probe was inconclusive, some investigators think the Jamaican committee formed part of a CIA operation to raise funds internationally for forces linked to the contras.[19]

By the end of 1985, invasion fever was waning in the Caribbean. Anticommunist hysteria diminished, and more people found the courage to express their doubts or disagreement with the U.S. action.

Although Washington's influence remained strong, conservative leaders found their U.S. alliance little use in solving pressing economic problems. Reagan ally Seaga saw his popularity slip day by day, while Manley's rose. Finally, the death of Tom Adams and the electoral victory of his social-democratic opponent, Errol Barrow, signalled the slowing of the right-wing trend. Photographed as he bid the invading troops farewell, Adams was more closely identified with the invasion than anyone except Ronald Reagan. His sudden death symbolically closed the Grenada episode and encouraged a growing reassessment. ∎

NOTES TO PART FIVE

AIFLD

1. Ronald Radosh, *American Labor and United States Foreign Policy* (New York: Random House, 1969), chapter 1.
2. *Ibid.*, p. 350.
3. *Ibid.*, p. 372.
4. George Morris, *CIA and American Labor: The Subversion of the AFL-CIO's Foreign Policy* (New York: International Publishers, 1967), pp. 63-66.
5. Radosh, p. 388.
6. Morris, p. 83.
7. Richard Hart, "Trade Unionism in the English-speaking Caribbean: The Formative Years and the Caribbean Labour Congress," in Susan Craig, ed., *Contemporary Caribbean* (Trinidad: S. Craig, 1982), vol. 2, pp. 89-91.
8. F.A. Hoyos, *Grantley Adams and the Social Revolution* (London: Macmillan, 1974), p. 178.
9. Hart, pp. 71-84.
10. Serafino Romualdi, *Presidents and Peons: Recollections of a Labor Ambassador in Latin America* (New York: Funk & Wagnalls, 1967), p. 343.
11. Radosh, pp. 393-405.
12. Jamaica *Daily Gleaner*, September 8, 1963, cited in Jeffrey Harrod, *Trade Union Foreign Policy: A Study of British and American Trade Union Activities in Jamaica* (London: Macmillan, 1972), p. 295.
13. Philip Agee, *Inside the Company: CIA Diary* (New York: Stonehill, 1975), p. 243.
14. EPICA interview with former official of the Seamen and Waterfront Workers Union, Grenada, September 1981.
15. Radosh, p. 422.
16. Agee, pp. 244-245.
17. Radosh, pp. 400-404.
18. AIFLD, Annual Progress Report, 1987.
19. *Ibid.*
20. EPICA interview with Monali, Barbados, August 1982.
21. EPICA interview with Ronald Clarke, Caribbean Union of Teachers, Barbados, May 1984.
22. *Ibid.*
23. American Institute for Free Labor Development, *AIFLD: Twenty-Five Years of Solidarity with Latin American Workers*, p. 20.

NOTES TO PART FIVE *(continued from previous page)*

24. National Endowment for Democracy, Annual Report 1984, p. 18.
25. Mark Schapiro and Annette Levy, "NED to the Rescue," *The New Republic,* Dec. 23, 1985, pp. 11-12.
26. Statement by Congressman Hank Brown of Colorado before the Subcommittee on International Operations, House Committee on Foreign Affairs, March 12, 1985.
27. Ralph E. Gonsalves, "The Trade Union Movement in St. Vincent and the Grenadines," (mimeographed paper, April 1983).

IMF and the Banks

1. Center for International Policy, "Central America: The Financial War," (Washington, DC: Center for International Policy, March 1983).
2. *Ibid.,* Also, Lars Schoultz, *Human Rights and United States Policy Toward Latin America* (Princeton: Princeton U. Press, 1981), chapter 7.
3. Caleb Rossiter, "Would an Anti-Apartheid Amendment 'Politicize' the IMF?" (Washington, DC: Center for International Policy, May 4, 1983).
4. Center for International Policy, "Central America: The Financial War."
5. *Latin America Regional Reports—Caribbean,* March 31, 1983.
6. "U.S. Charged with Bias in IMF Votes," *Wall Street Journal,* May 18, 1983. The *Wall Street Journal* obtained the original version of the suppressed study, which was done by Cornell University professor Caleb Rossiter for the Congressional Research Service. The Center for International Policy later released a modified summary of Rossiter's report (cf. note 3).
7. Rossiter, p. 4.
8. Norman Girvan, Richard Bernal and Wesley Hughes, "The IMF and the Third World: The Case of Jamaica 1974-1980," *Development Dialogue,* 1980, p. 113.
9. Prime Minister Michael Manley, speech to the nation, January 5, 1977.
10. Girvan et al., pp. 125-127.
11. *Ibid.,* pp. 125-126.
12. *Ibid.,* p. 154.
13. United Nations Centre on Transnational Corporations, *Transnational Banks: Operations, Strategies, and their Effects on Developing Countries* (New York: United Nations, 1981), pp. 22-23.
14. Maurice Odle, *Multinational Banks and Underdevelopment* (New York: Pergamon Press, 1981), p. 55.
15. Hilbourne Watson, "Transnational Banks and Crisis in the Capitalist World Economy: Impacts on the Caribbean," paper presented at Universidad Nacional Autonomo de Mexico, May 18-20, 1983.

The Media

1. Jeremy Tunstall, *The Media Are American: Anglo-American Media in the World* (New York: Columbia University Press, 1977), chapter 5.
2. Hugh Cholmondeley, "Media's Changing Sights," *Caricom Perspective,* May-June 1984.
3. Stewart M. Hoover, "Report of the Special Study Committee on Emerging Communication Technologies in National Development," report of a joint study by INTERMEDIA and the Caribbean Conference of Churches, 1984.
4. Tunstall, pp. 225-226.
5. Fred Landis, "The CIA and the Media: IAPA and the Jamaica Daily Gleaner," *Covert Action Information Bulletin,* No. 7, Dec. 1979-Jan. 1980, pp. 10-11.
6. Fred Landis, "CIA Media Operations in Chile, Jamaica and Nicaragua," *Covert Action Information Bulletin,* No. 16, Dec. 1981.
7. Fred Landis, "Psychological Warfare in the Media: The Case of Jamaica," (Press Association of Jamaica, 1980).
8. Ramesh Deosaran, "Government vs. the Pen," *Caribbean Contact,* March 1984. A survey of coverage of Grenada in the Trinidad *Express* and *Guardian* between 1979 and 1983 found that 79% of the stories were unfavorable to the PRG.
9. National Endowment for Democracy, Annual Report 1986.
10. National Endowment for Democracy, Annual Report 1987. Also, "Institute Mentioned in Probe Due to Lose Grant Funding," *Washington Post,* March 14, 1987.
11. National Endowment for Democracy, Annual Reports 1985 and 1986. Also, "Grantee of U.S. Endowment Funds Sandinista Opponents," *Washington Post,* March 19, 1986.
12. Rex Nettleford, "Cultivating a Caribbean Sensibility: Media, Education and Culture," *Caribbean Review,* Winter 1987, pp. 6-7.
13. Aggrey Brown and Roderick Santana, *Talking With Whom? A Report on the State of the Media in the Caribbean* (CARIMAC, University of the West Indies, 1987), pp. 11-12.
14. Nettleford, p. 28.

Economic Aid and the CBI

1. U.S. General Accounting Office, "AID Assistance to the Eastern Caribbean: Program Changes and Possible Consequences," July 22, 1983, pp. 12-19.
2. Bernardo Vega, "The CBI Faces Adversity: Lessons from the Asian Export Strategy," *Caribbean Review,* Spring 1985, pp. 18-19.
3. George Beckford and Michael Witter, *Small Garden . . . Bitter Weed: Struggle and Change in Jamaica* (London: Zed Press, 1980), p. 137.
4. Fitzroy Ambursley, "Jamaica: From Michael Manley to Edward Seaga," in Fitzroy Ambursley and Robin Cohen, eds., *Crisis in the Caribbean* (New York: Monthly Review Press, 1983), p. 93.

5. *Latin America Regional Reports—Caribbean,* January 18, 1980.
6. Philip Nanton, "The Changing Patterns of State Control in St. Vincent and the Grenadines," in Ambursley and Cohen, p. 239.
7. *Latin America Regional Reports—Caribbean,* January 18, 1980.
8. President Ronald Reagan, address before the Organization of American States, February 24, 1982.
9. U.S. Commerce Department statistics.
10. *Washington Post,* December 17, 1983.

The Grenada Invasion

1. Jorge Rodriguez Beruff, "Militarization and the Caribbean Basin Initiative," *Puerto Rico Libre,* Vol. VI, No. 4, p. 4.
2. *Washington Post,* November 24, 1981.
3. Rear Admiral Robert P. McKenzie, press conference, August 9, 1981, Vieques, Puerto Rico.
4. Rodriguez Beruff, p. 3.
5. *Ibid.,* p. 3.
6. Governor of Puerto Rico, 1982 budget.
7. *Ibid.*
8. *San Juan Star,* February 8, 1982.
9. *Intercambio* (Caribbean Project for Justice and Peace, Rio Piedras, Puerto Rico), April 1983.
10. EPICA interview with Dr. James Millette, Trinidad, August 1982.
11. U.S. State Department, "Congressional Presentation: Security Assistance," FY 1982.
12. U.S. State Department, "Congressional Presentation: Security Assistance," FY 1984.
13. U.S. State Department, "Congressional Presentation: Security Assistance," FY 1982.
14. U.S. State Department, "Congressional Presentation: Security Assistance," FY 1984.
15. *Washington Post,* February 27, 1983.
16. *Washington Post,* October 27, 1983.
17. Pacific News Service report, *Cleveland Plain Dealer,* November 3, 1983.
18. *El Navegante,* December 1983.
19. *New York Times,* November 6, 1983, p. 20.
20. *Washington Post,* October 25, 1983.
21. *New York Times,* November 6, 1983.
22. Testimony November 2, 1983 to House Foreign Affairs Committee, cited in W. Frick Curry, "Grenada: Force a First Resort" (Washington, DC: Center for International Policy, January 1984).
23. *New York Times,* November 6, 1983.
24. Speech by prime minister George Chambers to Parliament, October 26, 1983.
25. *Ibid.*
26. *Caribbean Review,* Fall 1983, p. 4.
27. *New York Times,* November 6, 1983.
28. *Washington Post,* November 6, 1983.
29. "Flaws Seen in Grenada Invasion," *Washington Post,* March 12, 1985. Also see Edward Luttwak, *The Pentagon and the Art of War: The Question of Military Reform* (New York: Simon and Schuster, 1985).

Invasion Aftermath

1. Bob Woodward, *Veil: The Secret Wars of the CIA 1980-1987* (New York: Simon & Schuster, 1987), p. 294.
2. *Philadelphia Inquirer,* Nov. 7, 1983, p. 14.
3. *Amnesty International Report 1984* (London: Amnesty International, 1984), pp. 153-157.
4. "Grenada: Report of a British Labor-Movement Delegation: December 1983," (4 Grays Inn Bldg., Roseberry Ave., London), p. 23.
5. Agency for International Development, Office of Press Relations, "Summary Highlights of Grenada A.I.D. Program, January 1986," p. 2.
6. National Endowment for Democracy, Annual Reports 1984, 1985, 1986.
7. Woodward, p. 300. Also, "Conservative Unit Raises Funds for Grenada Party," *Washington Post,* Dec. 1, 1984.
8. Bernard Diederich, "The End of West Indian Innocence: Arming the Police," *Caribbean Review,* Spring 1984, p. 11.
9. Movement for National Unity newsletter, Dec. 29, 1983 and May 9, 1984.
10. *Washington Post,* July 19, 1984 and July 26, 1984.
11. *Caribbean Contact,* December 1983.
12. National Republican Institute for International Affairs, 1986 Program Proposal, addendum, April 17, 1986.
13. National Endowment for Democracy, Annual Reports 1985 and 1986. National Republican Institute for International Affairs, Annual Report 1985. Also, "U.S. Groups Helping Get Out the Vote in Grenada," *New York Times,* Dec. 2, 1984.
14. National Endowment for Democracy, Annual Reports 1986 and 1987.
15. EPICA interview with Atherton Martin, Washington, DC, June 18, 1986.
16. National Endowment for Democracy, Annual Reports 1986 and 1987.
17. National Endowment for Democracy, Annual Report 1985.
18. William C. Montague and Corky Johnson, "Jamaica Latest to Enter Contra Puzzle," Gannett News Service, March 23, 1987; Jack Anderson and Joseph Spear, "North Linked to '85 Youth Conference," *Washington Post,* April 9, 1987.
19. EPICA interview with William Montague, Washington, DC, June 1988.

PART SIX
The Caribbean in Crisis

Trials of Independence

For the independent countries of the Caribbean, the 1980s were a difficult decade. With a few exceptions, the region's economies deteriorated, causing widespread hardship and disillusionment. The promises of independent nationhood seemed to recede as Caribbean societies grappled with simply surviving.

The sharp economic decline which began in the mid-1970s stemmed largely from forces beyond the region's control. Most Caribbean countries rely on one or two commodities—typically sugar, bananas, bauxite or petroleum—which they export to the industrialized countries. They use these foreign exchange earnings to import all the food, fuel, manufactured goods and machinery which the region does not produce. Both the prices Caribbean countries receive for their exports and the prices they must pay for imports are determined outside the region.

When a country's import bill exceeds its export earnings, the government must borrow to cover the gap. Interest payments on the debt consume more and more foreign exchange. As a result, the country's people must tighten their belts and consume less. Often a government takes out a new loan to cover the deficit—falling into the "debt trap."

When the price of imported oil quadrupled in 1973, it triggered sharp inflation in the cost of all imports. At the same time, as recession gripped the industrialized countries in the early '80s, prices declined for major Caribbean exports. Sugar fell to 6 cents per pound in 1982, a fraction of the cost of production. Bauxite, banana, coffee and cocoa prices also slumped. The resulting payments imbalance forced a number of governments to seek loans from the International Monetary Fund, bringing layoffs, high food prices and cutbacks in social services.

Even after the recession eased, commodity markets continued stagnant. Their long-term decline was reflected in the withdrawal of major multinationals from the region. Gulf + Western sold out its extensive sugar holdings in the Dominican Republic. Reynolds Aluminum, Alcoa and Kaiser closed bauxite mines in Jamaica and the Dominican Republic. United Brands sold its banana plantations in Costa Rica. Even the oil companies pulled out when petroleum prices fell. The closure of the Exxon and Shell refineries shook the economies of the Netherlands Antilles.

The demise of the sugar industry was the most serious blow, causing hardship throughout the region. It reflected long-term changes in the world market as competition from corn sweeteners reduced demand for cane sugar. To protect domestic producers, the United States cut back sharply on its sugar imports, cutting purchases from the Caribbean in half. Most Caribbean economists now see little future for the cane industry unless a serious effort is made to develop new exports based on sugar byproducts. But this has yet to be done.

The Caribbean Basin Initiative was supposed to stimulate non-traditional exports. Some new investment did arrive, mostly garment manufacturers in the free trade zones of Jamaica, the Dominican Republic and Costa Rica. Such factories provided jobs at low wages, but had little other impact on local economies. They could not make up for lower earnings from sugar, bauxite and petroleum. Largely because of the slump in these commodities, total exports to the United States from countries participating in the CBI actually *declined* by more than 25% between 1983 and 1987. Regional leaders complained of the CBI's meager results, and even the program's U.S. boosters had to admit disappointment.

With traditional exports declining, Caribbean countries turned increasingly to tourism, which became the main growth area in many regional economies. In the long run, however, tourism remains vulnerable—to changes in currency exchange rates, to recession in North America and Europe, and to negative publicity about protests or crime. And the shift from a commodity-producing economy to one which mainly services tourists has many implications.

The crisis in Caribbean economies has had far-reaching social and political consequences. The common sight of youths "liming" on street corners bears witness to the extremely high unemployment rates, from 15% to 50% around the region. Many more persons are under-employed, marginally occupied by part-time work or peddling.

Another negative consequence has been the spreading impact of drugs. While other exports face slack demand, the market for drugs in the United States is virtually limitless. The Caribbean islands sit astride cocaine smuggling routes from South America, and collaboration with the trade allegedly extends to high levels in several territories. A worrisome side effect is the growing use among Caribbean youth of crack, a potent cocaine derivative.

Finally, the economic crisis has created a political crisis of confidence as governments fail to bring about economic recovery. As a result, voters in countries around the region have rejected incumbent governments, only to vote in opposition parties whose ideology and policies differ little. Such election results—in Trinidad and Tobago, Barbados, Belize, St. Vincent, the Dominican Republic and elsewhere—are more an expression of frustration than a response to new ideas. When the new leaders also fail to find solutions, frustration builds anew.

While these broad trends characterized the region in the '80s, each Caribbean society presented a separate reality. The following section profiles ten independent Caribbean nations, focusing on the challenges to each in recent years and the issues emerging for the future. ■

The Bahamas

From his office on the Ministry of Tourism's third floor, tourism director Baltron Bethel can survey the fruits of his labor in the crowds on Bay Street below. Each day half a dozen cruise liners dock at Nassau's Prince George Wharf, disgorging an army of camera-toting Americans toward the Straw Market, the souvenir treasure troves, the discount T-shirt marts and the local Burger King. Nearly three million tourists yearly dwarf the Bahamian population of 250,000 and provide employment for two-thirds of the workforce. "Tourism has been good to the Bahamas," smiles Mr. Bethel. "We see it as our oil, our mineral wealth."[1]

While other Caribbean countries depend on tourism, in none does the industry approach the massive scale, the big-money glitter or the expert organization of the Bahamian trade. Beginning just off south Florida—the closest island, Bimini, is 50 miles from Miami—and stretching 600 miles to the southeast, the Bahamas is for many Americans the perfect offshore playground. It is a perception many Bahamians share, seeing the archipelago not as a Caribbean nation but as some kind of Miami suburb. Distance from the Caribbean and intimate links to the United States have over time shaped a society unique within the region.

Pirates, Bootleggers and Millionaires

A common history of British colonization and slavery links the Bahamas to the Commonwealth Caribbean. Yet Bahamians have long rejected the notion that they are West Indian. Located in the Atlantic, the Bahamas is cut off from the English-speaking West Indies by the large French and Spanish-speaking Greater Antilles. Few Bahamians migrate south, although some West Indians, especially Barbadians, have settled in the Bahamas. Instead, Bahamians move continuously between the islands and Florida.

The Bahamas was never a plantation society on the West Indian model. Its economy was mercantile, based on proximity to shipping lanes and to the U.S. mainland. In the early 1700s the islands were a notorious pirate headquarters. Later, "wrecking"—salvaging from ships wrecked in Bahamian waters—became a mainstay. During the Civil War, the Bahamas provided a base for running guns to the Confederacy, and during Prohibition, for bootlegging rum. These economic booms mainly enriched merchants in Nassau, the capital. People in the neglected "Out Islands" survived on subsistence farming and harvesting of ocean sponges.

In the Bahamas, unlike the West Indies, a large white settler class played an important role. During the American War of Independence thousands of Tory loyalists fled from the southern states to the Bahamas with their slaves. They joined earlier settlers to form a merchant oligarchy, known as the "Bay Street Boys" for their monopoly of business along Nassau's main street. With roots in the segregationist South, this reactionary group controlled the colony for almost 200 years.

In the 1950s and '60s a boom in tourism and real estate laid the basis for the modern economy. The islands' proximity to Florida and their tax-haven status lured millionaire investors, some with links to organized crime. In 1955 financier Wallace Groves, acting on behalf of Meyer Lansky's crime syndicate, bought half the island of Grand Bahama and built Freeport, an industrial and resort enclave including 17 luxury hotels and a casino. A&P supermarket heir Huntington Hartford developed the glittering Paradise Island hotel and casino, which was managed by Lansky men. Revelations that Bahamian government officials were in the pay of the casino interests helped bring about the white politicians' fall from power.[2]

The changes which began in 1938 in the West Indies—the rise of organized labor leading to black majority rule—were twenty years late in coming to the Bahamas. In 1958 black unions staged a major strike protesting Jim Crow segregation and discrimination in hiring. The following years saw the rise of black politicians linked to the unions, culminating in the election of Lynden O. Pindling's Progressive Liberal Party in 1967. Six years later Prime Minister Pindling led the Bahamas to independence.

The Pindling government continued the open door to foreign investors, and it protected the commercial interests of the Bay Street Boys. But it imposed conditions which increased the benefits to the country from these activities. Before 1967, the foreign hotel owners and casino operators had hired mainly white expatriates. Black Bahamians had been confined to menial jobs: they could work as maids or waiters, but not in a bank or at a hotel's front desk. The new government enacted a "Bahamianisation" policy requiring employers to give hiring preference to nationals, and it lowered other social and

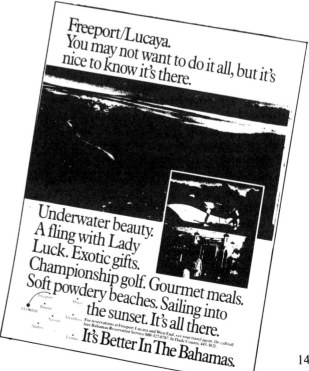

Freeport/Lucaya. You may not want to do it all, but it's nice to know it's there.

Underwater beauty. A fling with Lady Luck. Exotic gifts. Championship golf. Gourmet meals. Soft powdery beaches. Sailing into the sunset. It's all there.

For reservations at Freeport Lucaya and West End, see your travel agent. Or call toll free Bahamas Reservation Service 800-327-0787. In Dade County, 443-3821.

It's Better In The Bahamas.

141

economic barriers to blacks. This opened up new opportunities for all Bahamians, raising living standards and creating a new black middle class.

The government eventually bought out some departing hotel owners, so the tourism sector was no longer wholly foreign-owned. Other pillars of the economy included offshore banking, encouraged by strict bank secrecy laws. Industry at Freeport, including oil refining, chemicals and cement, formed a third, limited sector. The fourth sector by contrast knew no limit in its pervasive impact on the society: drugs.

The Scandal Breaks

The Bahamas includes over 700 islands and cays, all but about 30 uninhabited, spread over 100,000 square miles of water. The same features which had made the islands a base for pirates now turned them into a drug smugglers' haven, beginning with marijuana traders in the 1960s. Cocaine traffickers moved in during the late 1970s, and within a few years some 40% of South American cocaine entering the United States was passing through Bahamian smuggling routes.

On September 5, 1983, the NBC Nightly News reported that Norman's Cay in the Bahamas was the base for a cocaine smuggling ring run by Carlos Lehder Rivas, head of the Colombian Medellin drug cartel. NBC alleged payoffs of $100,000 a month in protection money to top Bahamian officials, including the prime minister. Pindling denied the allegations and appointed a commission to investigate.

The commission's report, released a year later, found no evidence directly connecting the prime minister to drugs. It did say that over seven years Pindling had deposited in his bank account millions of dollars from unexplained sources. The report described a society corrupted from top to bottom by the drug trade: influence-peddling by top officials in the Pindling government; an undermanned police force susceptible to bribes; a legal profession that had grown fat on fees paid by the South American drug lords; and the laundering of millions in drug profits in the country's banks.[3] It stressed that the Bahamas had itself become a market for drugs, with cocaine addiction a growing national problem.

Bahamians watched the drama in fascination, but the scope of the problem was already common knowledge. Many, indeed, did not see it as a problem. Drug money had brought wealth to a poor country, rippling through the economy to reach nearly everyone. Farmers and fishermen in the Out Islands could make many times their yearly income in a few days by assisting the smugglers: providing refueling, lookouts and lighting for night landings; loading drugs from the "mother ships" to speedboats for the dash to south Florida. Additional profits were made by selling portions of the cargo locally. The signs of drug money stood out everywhere: palatial villas next to humble shacks, late-model BMWs and Cadillacs careening down dirt roads.

A rash of resignations from the Pindling cabinet followed, but public reaction was muted. In June 1987, Pindling won reelection to a sixth term. In his election campaign, Pindling angrily accused the United States of interfering in Bahamian

Members of the Bahamas Defense Force offload bales of marijuana from a captured drug-smuggling boat.

affairs. Drugs, he claimed, were an American problem for which the Bahamas was unfairly blamed. But for most Bahamians, the sovereignty issue which Pindling invoked was not of primary importance. The basis of his popularity remained what it had always been: his image as a hero who led the country to black majority rule and independence. If PLP officials were in fact lining their pockets, there were plenty of Bahamians who felt that if given the opportunity, they would probably do the same.

A year later, Carlos Lehder was convicted in a U.S. court of smuggling three tons of cocaine into the United States from Norman's Cay. Three government witnesses testified during the trial that Pindling and other top Bahamian officials had taken cash payoffs from the traffickers. In April 1988 two U.S. federal grand juries opened investigations into the possibility of indicting Pindling.

The threat of an indictment touched off an uproar in the Bahamas. Even opposition politicians warned that such a move would strain ties between the two countries. The U.S. State Department also opposed an indictment of Pindling for several reasons. Although Pindling had been implicated in drug-related corruption, he was, ironically, giving full support to U.S. drug interdiction operations carried out in Bahamian territory. His government had even asked the United States to reinforce its efforts with additional Coast Guard vessels and helicopters. Like Noriega of Panama—with whom nervous U.S. officials increasingly made comparisons—Pindling had been cooperating with the Americans while apparently running his own lucrative sideline.

The other major reason concerned the U.S. bases. The United States maintains a deep-water submarine base, a missile tracking post, and a radar and electronic intercept station in the Bahamas. The Pindling government had already held up renewal of the lease on the bases once, during a dispute over the Bahamas' strict bank secrecy laws which were hindering attempts to investigate the laundering of drug cash. Although the lease was finally signed in 1984, State Department officials argued that the United States should not

The Nassau Guardian

jeopardize Pindling's continued cooperation in order to punish him for "past crimes."[4]

From gun-running to bootlegging to casino gambling, the Bahamas has long provided North Americans with an offshore haven for illicit activities. The U.S. government too has benefited from the islands as an offshore military base. A move against Pindling thus remains unlikely, as few are ready to upset an arrangement that has long been profitable for special interests on both sides.

Problems in Paradise

As a result of these scandals, Pindling has lost favor with the middle class and some trade unions. But many older, working-class Bahamians still support him. For the society as a whole, scandal takes second place to economic issues, where the society's basic prosperity works in Pindling's favor.

The prime minister has promised that within a few years the Bahamas will leave the ranks of its Third World neighbors to become a "First World country." The $16 million spent annually on tourism promotion is paying off: the crowds keep growing, and new high-rise hotels are going up along Nassau's north coast. Paradise Island, which now belongs to New York real estate magnate Donald Trump, is undergoing expansion. The government has opened its $100 million Cable Beach Hotel & Casino, and Carnival Cruise Lines is erecting the equally lavish Crystal Palace Hotel next door.

The Bahamas already has the highest per-capita income in the Caribbean outside of the U.S. Virgin Islands. A worker in a Bahamian hotel or casino can make $150 to $250 a week—more than a Jamaican worker makes in a month or a Haitian in a year.[5] With easy bank credit, due in part to recirculated drug cash, many workers have comfortable houses, new cars and the ubiquitous success symbol, the satellite dish.

It has been women, above all, who have taken advantage of the new opportunities. Often impelled by the need to support children, Bahamian women have taken available jobs and have worked their way up with skill and tenacity. They make up the majority of workers in the tourist industry, and dominate the white-collar workforce in banking, civil service and law.

Prosperity has given rise to an ideology which says that the country is a paradise for Bahamians and tourists alike. But while the affluence is real, it masks problems, including 15% unemployment and a crime wave that is out of control. The uneven distribution of wealth is reflected in the poverty of Nassau's "Over the Hill" section and many of the Out Islands. One woman from the Grant's Town area of Nassau said:

You should see in the ghetto. You see them people houses, them children, it hurt your eye. It's just like any other country: some can make it and some can't. Not everybody is getting a piece of the cake.[6]

The Out Islands, now called the Family Islands, remain underdeveloped. Migration to Nassau has left some virtually depopulated: 65% of the population now lives on 80-square-mile New Providence island. While some of the Family Islands receive income from tourism, the drug trade has become the means of survival for others.

The increase in drug addiction accounts in part for the sharp rise in robberies and other violent crimes. But the roots of the problem go deeper. The high-rolling tourists and the drug dealers have set a standard of consumption that ordinary youth cannot readily match. In this get-rich-quick atmosphere, young men shun the skilled trades, even choosing unemployment over the stigma of manual labor. Some turn to crime as the only way to imitate the lavish lifestyles around them. A Nassau churchman notes:

People here don't produce, they sell services. We have created a playland where instant happiness is the goal. All people see is the tinsel and glitter.[7]

National culture has largely been a casualty of this process. Even the country's most ardent boosters freely admit that "there is nothing left except Junkanoo." The colorful African-influenced parade died out with the rest of Bahamian traditions, but has been revived as a tourist attraction. Another festival, Goombay, is an invention of the tourist board.

Americanization has left little space for a national cultural or intellectual life to develop. Miami television stations provide the main source of entertainment. Long considered educationally backward, the Bahamas had no institution of higher learning until the small College of the Bahamas opened in the 1970s.

Yet while some deplore the vacuousness of what the *Miami Herald* called "a nation for sale," many Bahamians are proud of their living standards. Concludes an Anglican churchman, "I still prefer to deal with the problems of prosperity than those of poverty."[8]

Recent years have seen the beginning of a movement to define and develop a Bahamian identity. Bahamian academics are working hard to improve the College of the Bahamas. A small circle of local writers, playwrights and musicians is nurturing the beginnings of a Bahamian cultural scene. Nassau playwright Winston Saunders' work, *You Can Take a Horse to Water,* portrayed the plight of Bahamian youths from poor homes and enjoyed critical success.

With this cultural exploration has come a tentative new interest in closer Caribbean ties. The Bahamas joined CARICOM in 1983, and hosted the CARICOM heads of government summit in July 1984. These new contacts have been mainly at the official rather than popular level, but that may change in time. "We in the Bahamas have always had a problem with any link to the south," explains the Anglican clergyman. "But Bahamians are slowly becoming more comfortable with being Caribbean."[9]

The dominant tendency is still for intimate ties with the United States. The relationship may be rocky at times: the Bahamas' wealth depends on adroit exploitation of its offshore status, in ways that sometimes upset U.S. officials. Few on either side, however, contemplate a loosening of the economic and cultural bonds between the archipelago nation and its powerful neighbor. ∎

Jamaica

Edward Seaga's Jamaica Labour Party defeated Michael Manley's People's National Party on October 30, 1980, just four days before the election of Seaga's ideological twin Ronald Reagan. For the conservatives arriving in Washington with Reagan, Seaga's victory provided a chance to test "Reaganomics" in the Caribbean and prove that capitalism, not socialism, was the path to prosperity for the Third World. So confident was the administration of success that it spoke of Jamaica as a model for not only the Caribbean, but also Central America. Said President Reagan, "Free-enterprise Jamaica, not Marxist Cuba, should serve as a model for Central America in the struggle to overcome poverty and move towards democracy."[1]

The strategy for rescuing Jamaica from socialism, as the White House framed the issue then, involved an application of free-market economics under the supervision of the international financial establishment—the International Monetary Fund, the World Bank and the U.S. Agency for International Development. These agencies along with the U.S. government "primed the pump" with large infusions of loans and aid. The IMF came through immediately with $698 million for the new government, and the World Bank lent $133 million. U.S. bilateral assistance jumped from $14 million in Manley's last year to over $200 million in Seaga's first two years, making Jamaica second only to Israel in per-capita U.S. economic aid.[2]

The Jamaican economists who had advised the Manley government were sidelined as contingents of American advisors and technicians filled Kingston's posh Pegasus Hotel. Former Chase Manhattan Bank chairman David Rockefeller helped set up a "U.S. Business Committee on Jamaica," including representatives of such corporate giants as Exxon, Alcoa, and Gulf + Western, to advise the Jamaican government on attracting foreign investment.

Edward Seaga.

In return, Seaga became Reagan's primary Caribbean ally and a surrogate for U.S. interests in the region. He severed diplomatic ties with Cuba immediately, and announced that his government would help the United States fight "Marxist adventures" in the region. At home, Seaga ousted radicals, including members of the PNP's left wing and the communist Workers' Party of Jamaica (WPJ), from positions in the civil service, the university and the media. The Jamaican army and police were reinforced with U.S. arms and training.

Reflecting the emphasis on foreign investment, the new government invited corporate takeovers in major economic sectors. It dismantled the worker-run sugar cooperatives formed under the Manley government, and brought back the former multinational owner of the sugar industry, Tate & Lyle, to manage the largest estates. United Brands planted 2,000 acres of land to bananas in a joint venture with the government. Japanese and Israeli investors played major roles in Agro-21, Seaga's showcase program to grow winter vegetables for the U.S. market. The foreign director of Agro-21 received a yearly salary of nearly J$1 million, and other expatriate managers received similar fees.

Impact of the IMF

Most importantly, Seaga took a series of measures demanded by the IMF and the World Bank as conditions for their loans. Prominent among these was devaluation of the Jamaican dollar. By cheapening labor costs for foreign investors, the theory went, Jamaica could attract firms which would produce for export. It was in fact the old Puerto Rican model, although Seaga preferred to make comparisons to countries like South Korea and Singapore.

At the same time, the economy would undergo "structural adjustment," a belt-tightening austerity to save foreign exchange. This involved firing thousands of public sector employees to save on payroll costs. The government slashed spending on social services such as schools, public transportation, health clinics and hospitals.

In keeping with the gospel of deregulation, the government abolished the restrictions on imports which the Manley government had used to conserve scarce foreign exchange. Allowing imports to flood the local market, it was claimed, would force Jamaican manufacturers to produce more efficiently. The move was also intended to pay Seaga's political debt to the Jamaican middle and upper classes. After the privation of the Manley years, imported luxuries would again be available—for those who had money to buy.

Initially the results seemed promising. Buoyed by foreign aid and loans, the economy grew by 2% in 1981 after seven years of zero or negative growth. The government reported 116 new investment projects in 1981 and 1982. There was an atmosphere of jubilation among the well-to-do as imports filled formerly empty store shelves. Late-model Toyotas and Hondas jammed Kingston's gritty streets as affluent Jamaicans

Women's protest march in 1980.

Struggle

launched a buying spree.

By 1983, however, negative signs began appearing. With the exception of Control Data, no large corporations—and none of those on the Rockefeller committee—had invested in Jamaica. Most which did were small firms which expected to raise their financing locally. While the Reagan model called for privatization, few qualified buyers could be found for state holdings in sugar and tourism. Growth remained barely positive in 1982, at one-fifth of 1%. Yet by the end of the year Seaga had borrowed more than $1 billion, an ominously mounting foreign debt.

While new investment was slow to appear, Jamaica's traditional foreign exchange earner—bauxite—was in trouble. After 1980, as world recession depressed demand for aluminum, the United States and Japan began closing the smelters that had refined Jamaica's ore. The aluminum multinationals were moving out of the Caribbean, seeking cheaper bauxite in Brazil and Australia. Jamaica had produced 11.9 million tons of raw bauxite in 1980, but this dropped to 7.7 million tons in 1983.[3]

While export earnings fell, affluent Jamaicans continued to fritter away foreign exchange on imports (dubbed the "Volvo-video syndrome" in reference to two popular items.) The country spent more than US$100 million to import 14,000 new cars in 1982.[4] The result was that Jamaica's trade deficit nearly tripled between 1980 and 1982.

The flood of imports also hurt local producers. Peasant farmers suffered losses from the sudden inflows of cheap foreign onions, potatoes, beans and vegetables. Jamaican manufacturers, such as shoe and clothing makers, had to compete with importers for foreign exchange. One by one the smaller producers closed their doors, laying off workers. The official unemployment rate rose from 26% in 1981 to 29% a year later.

The IMF initially had been lenient with Seaga. But by early 1983, Jamaica could no longer pass the twice-yearly performance tests required to keep the loan installments flowing. After failing the March 1983 test, Seaga requested a waiver. It came with a new set of harsh conditions. The government had to restrict imports, not only of consumer goods but also of raw materials and spare parts needed for production. There were new layoffs of public sector workers. Worst of all for the poor, many basic goods were placed on a "parallel market" which meant they had to be purchased with devalued currency. This sent prices spiraling for such necessities as medicines, soap, bus fares, school books and farm tools. Jamaicans called it "the paralyzed market."

Food prices began a relentless rise, pushing staple foods of the poor—rice, beans, chicken backs, canned corned beef and canned milk—out of reach of working-class families. Dr. Carl Stone, a prominent political analyst, wrote in the *Daily Gleaner:*

The IMF boys, of course, are out to slash the excess consumption of luxuries. But the big spenders and big earners are not the people who are most affected by these drastic reductions in purchasing power. They will continue driving BMW's long after the Jamaican dollar gets down to 20 cents US. But will the working class be able to live and will the bulk of those classified as middle-class survive?

How do these jokers in the IMF expect the country to motivate people to produce when they can't buy food, pay electricity bills, pay their rent, buy clothes and school books for their children, or even afford to drink a few beers?[5]

By late 1983, polls showed public opinion swinging back to Manley and the PNP. The failure of the JLP to restore prosperity, plus its evident disregard for the poor, cast memories of Manley in a more positive light. This was true even though the PNP was keeping a very low profile and offering little active challenge to the Seaga government.

In this context, President Reagan's decision to invade Grenada came as a godsend to Seaga. With Jamaicans swept up in the region-wide hysteria, Seaga seized the moment to call an early election in December 1983. Because Seaga called the election on an outdated electoral list—violating a previous pledge—and because the timing was extremely disadvantageous for the PNP, Manley boycotted the election. The JLP thus not only secured a new five-year term, but won every parliamentary seat.

Seaga had boasted of restoring democracy to Jamaica, but the country now had a *de facto* one-party government. Critics spoke of a constitutional crisis, and people in the streets began grumbling about a "one-party dictatorship." Public disapproval all but neutralized Seaga's gains from his role in the invasion.

"Seaga Has Destroyed Poor People Living"

A mood of desperation prevailed as 1984 drew to a close. A new IMF agreement signed the previous June caused the layoff of some 8,000 public workers. The Jamaican dollar stood at J$4.96 to US$1 and was still falling. While an employed worker might earn J$60 per week, one chicken cost J$12, a liter of cooking oil J$9, and a dozen eggs J$7. As one worker wrote to the WPJ newspaper *Struggle,* "Seaga has destroyed poor people living."

On January 14, 1985, the government raised gasoline prices from J$8.99 to J$10.99 a gallon. It was the dreaded harbinger of a new wave of inflation. In the pre-dawn hours of January 15, people in Kingston and towns around the island barricaded roads with piles of flaming tires and debris. By mid-morning all major roads were blocked, and dark, acrid smoke billowed from the streets. PNP, WPJ and even many JLP supporters took part, and women and youth were prominent among the protesters. Schools and most stores closed, and public transport was paralyzed for two days while the protests raged.

Prime Minister Seaga was informed of the riots while at a breakfast sponsored by the U.S. Information Agency and the Jamaican-American Society, at which an award for "out-standing humanitarianism" was presented to the head of the Coca-Cola Company. The prime minister downplayed the protests, calling them a "letting off of steam." But he knew that the political limits of austerity had been reached.

In the spring of 1986, a team of IMF, USAID and World Bank officials visited Jamaica to take a "fresh look" at the economy. They recommended more of the same—further devaluation, more spending cuts. Rejecting the team's advice, Seaga defied the IMF and presented an expansionary budget which included freezing the Jamaican dollar at J$5.50 to US$1.00. But it was too little and too late.

That summer, the PNP swept municipal elections, winning control of 11 of the island's 13 local government councils. It was a stinging repudiation of Seaga, underscoring public opinion polls which showed the PNP would almost certainly win the next national election due by March 1989. Manley called for an early election, and Jamaicans began looking toward a future beyond Seaga.

Economic and Political Dilemmas

Despite a modest economic upturn in 1988 and an election-year budget of unprecedented social spending, polls continued to predict a PNP win. The question for most Jamaicans was not whether Manley would return to power, but what difference a PNP government could make.

Seaga's failure to turn the economy around has disproved the conservative argument that the PNP's "socialist excesses" were the cause of the country's problems. On the other hand,

Shopper in a Kingston market: Relentlessly rising food prices.

WHAT THE IMF HAS DONE TO PRICES

	BEFORE IMF			IMF YEARS					
	1975	1976	1977	1978	1979	1980	1981	1983	1985
RICE (1 lb.)	29¢	29¢	29¢	41¢	50¢	59¢	75¢	75¢	$1.75
FLOUR (1 lb.)	14¢	16¢	17¢	22¢	30¢	36¢	45¢	45¢	$1.10
CONDENSED MILK (1 tin)	30¢	30¢	30¢	47¢	67¢	77¢	86¢	$1.12	$2.12
CORNED BEEF (1 tin)	78¢	78¢	78¢	$1.00	$1.93	$2.75	$3.00	$4.15	$6.60

Prices in Jamaican currency.

few Jamaicans believe that simply returning to the policies of the 1970s can provide a solution either. The failure of both Manley's liberal reformism and Seaga's dependent capitalism has left Jamaicans disillusioned and desperate. As analyst Carl Stone grimly concludes, the country is fast running out of options.[6]

In eight years of "Reaganomics" in Jamaica, none of the country's underlying problems has been solved, and some have become much worse. The bauxite industry is moribund: Reynolds and Alpart have closed their operations and left the island, leaving only Alcan and Alcoa. Tourism has replaced bauxite as the main foreign exchange earner, but tourism earnings cannot equal the lost bauxite revenues. Agriculture is stagnant. Agro-21, the capital-intensive, high-technology effort to diversify agriculture, proved a failure. Its centerpiece, the Israeli-run Spring Plains vegetable farm, was shut down after incurring large losses. Small farmers, the traditional food producers, have been neglected and have turned increasingly to growing ganja (marijuana) to survive.

The Seaga government takes credit for a rapidly expanding garment manufacturing sector, concentrated in the country's free trade zones. With its devalued currency, Jamaica has become a leading site for the low-wage manufacturers who have also flocked to the Dominican Republic. These new jobs helped reduce official unemployment to 20.8% by the end of 1987. But the average wage of J$90 per week, of which the worker may take home as little as J$50 (US$9) makes jobs in the free zones only marginally better than unemployment. By 1988 women workers in the Kingston Free Zone had begun protesting low wages and non-union conditions.

Jamaica has remained dependent on foreign aid and loans. Bilateral aid from the United States since 1980 has topped $1 billion, and the Seaga government was negotiating its fifth IMF loan in 1988. As a result of this heavy borrowing, Jamaica is now $3.6 billion in debt, with interest on the debt consuming half the country's foreign exchange earnings.[7]

The neglect of social services during the Seaga years has run down the country's human capital. Most of the health clinics set up by the Manley government have been shut down. The hospital of the University of the West Indies, once the premier teaching and research hospital in the Caribbean, is now delapidated. The quality of education has fallen as public schools cannot buy books or pay teachers' salaries. Rebuilding these services will be costly, and will add to the burdens on a new administration.

The strain of economic pressures has accentuated social tensions, and neither Seaga nor Manley appears able to control the violence. Partisan warfare subsided after the bloody 1980 electoral campaign which claimed some 800 lives. But the Kingston ghettos remain polarized into warring PNP and JLP strongholds, and many Jamaicans fear that recent peace agreements between the two leaders will not prevent a resurgence of violence. There has been, in addition, an alarming increase in ordinary crime. The slaying of reggae star Peter Tosh in his home by gunmen was the most publicized of a wave of murders of prominent Jamaicans.

In trying to control the violence, the security forces have added to the problem. Of the 550 Jamaicans who died violently in 1986, 128 were killed by the police. Eleven police officers were themselves slain.[8] The Seaga government's special "Operations Division," dubbed the "eradication squad" by Jamaicans, has been partly responsible for the increased number of killings by the security forces.

Linked to the problem of violence is the growing role of drugs in Jamaican society. Growing ganja is all that is presently keeping many rural Jamaicans from destitution. But profits from the $1 billion trade do not go to peasant farmers but to big traffickers, alleged to include ranking officials of the Seaga government and the police force. Many of the guns coming into Jamaica reportedly enter in a guns-for-ganja exchange

STRUGGLE IN THE FREE TRADE ZONES

The garment industry in Jamaica has expanded rapidly since 1984, when devaluation of the Jamaican dollar reduced wages. Women make up 95% of the garment factory workers, with approximately 20,000 women working in the industry. About half of them are employed in the Kingston Free Zone, where 11 garment firms owned by U.S. and East Asian investors produce clothes for export to the U.S. market.

Jamaican women's organizations, churches and trade unions have documented the conditions in the free zones. A survey of 101 workers in the Kingston Free Zone, carried out by the pastoral team at St. Peter Claver Church in West Kingston, found the average wage to be only J$100 per week (US$18). After subtracting payroll deductions, busfare to work and lunch money, two-thirds of the workers took home less than J$50 per week (US$9). More than 80% of them were supporting children on their wages.

Free zone employers often bring heavy pressure on workers to meet production quotas and work overtime. Conversely, when business is slack, workers are laid off without warning. Workers generally receive vacation and sick leave, but no other fringe benefits. Although workers are supposed to receive maternity leave, it is not uncommon for pregnant workers to be fired.

Work in the garment factories is repetitive, boring and stressful. A worker seldom sews a whole garment, but only a specific part, such as collars. According to a study co-sponsored by Jamaica's Joint Trade Union Research Development Centre and the Canadian development agency CUSO, women in the zones suffer many work-related ailments. These include coughing and sneezing from fabric dust, pain in the back and shoulders, blurred vision, headaches and dizziness.

Only one of the factories in the Kingston Free Zone is unionized. The foreign firms have resisted unionization, and the Jamaican government, anxious to create jobs, has turned a blind eye. Recently, however, workers' protests have focused attention on conditions in the zones.

In March 1988 hundreds of women workers marched through Kingston to protest conditions at East Ocean Textiles, the largest factory in the Kingston Free Zone. Complaints against the Hong Kong-based firm included low wages, forced overtime, repressive labor practices, and violations of the maternity leave law. Pressed to respond, Prime Minister Seaga announced plans to create a joint industrial council. But the companies objected, saying it would lead to unionization of their plants. With the employers threatening to pull out of Jamaica, the Seaga government dropped the plan, announcing instead an inquiry into conditions in the zone.

High unemployment ensures that Jamaica and other Caribbean countries will continue to welcome the multinational garment firms. But greater awareness of conditions in the free trade zones means that controversy over this economic strategy is certain to grow.

Inter-American Development Bank

linked to inter-party warfare. In addition, Jamaicans living in the United States now control much of the distribution of crack to the U.S. market. The drug gangs or "posses" include many ghetto gunmen associated with the two political parties who emigrated after the 1980 election.

The underlying dilemma for Jamaicans is that while Seaga has failed to solve these problems, the PNP has proposed few clear alternatives. Most Jamaicans believe that Manley *wants* to help the poor, and he is sure to restore priority to health, education and other social programs. But a return to the reformist policies of the 1970s, let alone more radical change, is unlikely. The PNP has moved right since 1981, forcing out its left-wing members and cultivating a moderate image. D.K. Duncan, a minister in the Manley government and the leading representative of the party's former left wing, comments:

My view on the PNP's real economic policy is that it's a watered down, more humane version of Seaga's economic policy. [The PNP] has returned to what it was originally, a party of reform and not a party that transforms . . . trying to please every single class. A Social Democratic party capable of mild reforms which definitely cannot meet the aspirations of the people.[9]

Such analysis sidesteps a difficult question facing Manley: how to hold power at all, given the near certainty that the U.S. government and the Jamaican upper class would again hound him from office if he were to attempt a radical course. Manley states that he remains committed to democratic socialism. But he has made clear, in meetings with the U.S. State Department and with Jamaican and American business leaders, that he plans to avoid "quarrels" with the establishment this time. He has promised Jamaican businessmen that he would not restore unpopular measures of the 1970s such as the import licensing system. To Washington, he has tacitly agreed to stay within the bounds imposed by U.S. foreign policy. Although he would reestablish diplomatic relations with Cuba, he says, he would avoid ties "deemed provocative by Washington." A U.S. State Department spokesman confirmed that Manley "understands us better" now.[10]

Even so, major new aid from the United States—or any other source—is unlikely to be available to a Manley government. Washington's interest in Jamaica had already waned by mid-way through the Seaga years. U.S. aid to Jamaica was slashed by over 50% between 1986 and 1988, reflecting region-wide aid reductions. The Reagan administration was interested in Jamaica when it offered the chance to win a round in the Cold War. But when the miracle failed to happen, the country was dropped and forgotten.

The structural crisis of the economy, the need to accommodate to U.S. pressures, and a reduced level of foreign aid will severely limit what a PNP government can accomplish. Still, a Manley comeback would have real and symbolic importance.

Although a return to the Black Power themes of the early seventies is unlikely, the PNP retains nationalistic instincts that the JLP does not share. While Seaga relied heavily on foreign

Jamaican worker at rally demanding an end to IMF program.

advice, a Manley administration would be likely to tap the intellectual and cultural creativity of Jamaicans. In this political opening, progressive Jamaicans may once again be able to influence policy, although less than in Manley's last term. The government will be more sensitive to the impact of its policies on the poor, and grassroots organizations may be able to play a larger role in the search for economic alternatives.

Secondly, Manley's return would symbolize a shift from the right-wing trends that dominated the Caribbean during the Reagan years. Since the United States put so much into backing Seaga, his failure has been seen in the region as a larger failure of the Reagan/IMF economic model. In addition, Seaga's defeat would remove the primary surrogate for the United States within regional institutions and would weaken the Reagan-inspired Caribbean Democrat Union. Such developments could give the region more "space" to define its own political and economic paths.

For whoever wins the Jamaican election, there will be no easy answers or magic solutions this time around. Few Jamaicans still have illusions that a change of leadership will solve the basic problems. Many simply hope for some relief from a government that cares about the poor. The two leaders also have scaled down their expectations, their faith in ideological solutions shaken. This new realism may be Jamaicans' only reason for hope that after more than a decade of hardship, "better must come." ∎

Dominican Republic

On a hill overlooking Avenida de los Mártires in Santo Domingo, high above the heat of the city, sits the mansion of Alejandro Grullón, an owner of the Popular Bank. His is a lifestyle common to the Dominican Republic's wealthiest families—the Pelleranos, owners of the *Listin Diario* newspaper, the Bermúdez rum interests, the Jiménez tobacco oligarchs, the landowning Cabrals and the Viccini sugar barons. Their villas complete with satellite dishes and jacuzzis stare down from hillsides in Santo Domingo, the capital, and Santiago de los Caballeros, second city of the Dominican Republic.

Directly across Avenida de los Mártires, in full view of the mansion, hundreds of cardboard shanties cling precariously to the slope of a ravine. Pigs wallow in the garbage-strewn gullies which serve as paths into the area. *Villa miseria,* Dominicans call such neighborhoods—city of misery. But the young women emerging from the shanties in bright dresses and high heels, their make-up impeccable, betray nothing of the conditions from which they have come. They perch lightly on the backs of motorcycles driven by young men through the mud. The charge is 40 centavos (6 cents) for a ride to the edge of the *barrio* where the grand avenue begins.

In the working-class neighborhoods which ring the city, women tend babies in front of wooden shacks, their doors and windows opened to the dusty streets. Faded party slogans from the 1986 election adorn the walls—purple and yellow for Bosch, red for Balaguer. But no government has paid much attention to life in the barrios, where obtaining food, water, and electricity is a daily battle. The populous sections such as Gualey, Los Guandules, Villa Francisca and Guachupita are known as *barrios calientes,* hot zones. From these areas came the army of the poor who fought for constitutional government in the 1965 "April War." That uprising was echoed almost two decades later, in April 1984, when the barrios again rose up, this time to protest austerity imposed by the International Monetary Fund.

After Balaguer: Popular Forces Reemerge

Following the 1965 rebellion and the U.S. invasion [see Part Two, Ch. 2] Joaquín Balaguer, right-hand man of the assassinated dictator Trujillo, ruled the Dominican Republic in a "semi-dictatorship" that lasted 12 years. The organized left had been smashed, and repression against labor, students and slumdwellers kept popular protests suppressed.

High prices for sugar, the major export, and an influx of foreign loans fueled rapid growth. But the foreign exchange earned from sugar was spent mainly on imported consumer goods for the upper and middle class. Foreign aid paid for large infrastructure projects around Santo Domingo, but the rural areas remained without roads, running water, electricity or schools. As large landowners expanded production for export, many peasants lost their lands. They began an exodus to the cities, swelling the army of the unemployed and underemployed.

While 70% of the population had been rural in 1960, 55% was urban by 1985, with more than a quarter of the population living in the capital.[1] The rural migrants concentrated in the slums along the Ozama River around the city's periphery. These areas also received people evicted from their homes to

Children gaze in a store window on downtown Santo Domingo street. Foreign exchange was spent on imports for the middle class while sugar revenues fell.

Tom Barry

make way for the construction of wide avenues through the city. In part for beautification, these arteries were also to provide access for the security forces in case of future unrest.[2]

Hunger stalked the urban barrios. Whereas in the countryside food could be had from the land, in the city it had to be purchased. In poor families everyone had to work: the men in factories or whatever they could find, the women taking in ironing, the children peddling lottery tickets or shining shoes. *Chiripear*, to hustle odd jobs, became Dominican argot for a common means of survival.

By the mid-1970s rising prices for imported oil began to threaten the economy. Together with continuing human rights abuses, this turned sectors of the establishment against Balaguer's government. In the 1978 election, the Dominican Revolutionary Party (PRD)—originally the party of the Constitutionalist president Juan Bosch—emerged the unexpected winner.

While the PRD retained a populist image from its role in the 1960s, it was no longer the same party. Bosch had left in 1973 to start his own Dominican Liberation Party (PLD). Under landowner Antonio Guzmán and businessman Jacobo Majluta, the PRD moved right to become a "multiclass" party of compromise. When Balaguer attempted to overturn the election results, therefore, the Dominican business class and the Carter administration intervened and demanded that the PRD's victory stand.

Although it no longer really represented the poor, the PRD under President Guzmán brought a political opening which allowed new freedom for organizing. The General Workers Confederation emerged as the largest and most progressive labor federation in the country. In the rural areas, the Independent Peasant Movement (MCI) took shape as a country-wide network, with the associated National Committee of Peasant Women. Under the MCI's leadership, *campesinos* carried out hundreds of land occupations, mostly trying to recover lands from which they had been forcibly displaced. Police met the occupations with mass arrests, and the MCI leadership affirmed that "We will demand our rights to the land even if running the risks entailed should cost us our lives."[3]

Compared to these national structures in the labor and peasant sectors, popular organizing in the urban barrios was spontaneous and locally-based. Many groups formed, including youth clubs, housewives' clubs, and "popular struggle committees." A gradually expanding base Christian community movement supported the demands of slumdwellers and peasants.

The Dominican left also regrouped in the post-1978 period. Left-wing parties forged links to the popular movement, but failed either to develop a strong base or to achieve internal unity. Around 1983 four small parties came together in the Dominican Leftist Front (FID), only to split again over the question of electoral participation.

These positive political developments under the PRD were offset by growing corruption and a deteriorating economy. The cost of oil imports alone equalled the country's income from sugar, and the world price of sugar was falling.[4]

Members of the Independent Peasant Movement (MCI).

CEPAE

Guzmán borrowed more and more money from foreign banks and lending agencies, racking up a $2 billion debt. In 1979 Hurricane David struck the country, causing a billion dollars' worth of damage. The government was blamed for corrupt mishandling of the relief aid, little of which reached victims of the disaster.

Guzmán became so discredited that the PRD took the unusual step of withdrawing support from its own president in office. Under new leaders, lawyer Salvador Jorge Blanco and populist politician Francisco Peña Gómez, the party was able barely to survive the 1982 election. But its electoral win could not rescue the PRD from the economic quagmire. Jorge Blanco concluded secret agreements with the International Monetary Fund in Washington, DC even before assuming the presidency.

Revolt Against the IMF

If you can't swim
And you are pushed to the depths
A sad end awaits you
No one will save you from the bottom [del Fondo].

They speak of tightening the belt
But on someone else's stomach
That is, on our stomachs
In order to keep theirs full.

This crisis they have created
Is not our fault
We are not the ones called upon
To pay for the broken plates.

In this blind alley
There is but one exit
To fight for the poor
Against those above.

— Dominican popular song, 1984

151

After signing a pact with the IMF in January 1983, the government began implementing measures required by the Fund: closing state-run hotels and industries, freezing wages, and removing subsidies on food and fuel. The result was skyrocketing prices and a steady fall in the value of the peso. Business owners felt the pressure as they were unable to get foreign exchange to import products and parts. But the real tragedy took place in the villages and urban barrios, where survival became more difficult each day. As one taxi driver complained:

> The main problem is that bandit IMF. The prices of almost everything have gone up in the past two or three months. Two months ago I bought tires for this car for 100 pesos. Now the same tires cost 330 pesos. I used to be able to pay 40 pesos for a decent pair of shoes. Now it's 90 or even 100. It's a scandal.[5]

In January 1984 it was time for Jorge Blanco to sign the second phase of the IMF accord, bringing with it even harsher measures. By now the IMF was an infamous household word throughout the Dominican Republic. The trade union federations jointly called for a break with the Fund, and street protests increased. Facing domestic pressure to resist the IMF, Jorge Blanco was also under pressure from the international lenders and the Reagan administration to conclude the accord. When the Dominican president confided his fears that further austerity would set off social unrest, President Reagan replied that U.S. aid to the Dominican Republic was contingent on reaching an agreement with the Fund.[6] During an official visit to Washington at the beginning of April, President Jorge Blanco signed the accord.

Almost immediately, prices for essential items like bread, milk, cooking oil, sugar and medicines rose sharply, tripling and quadrupling their previous prices. On April 23, rioting broke out in Santo Domingo and towns around the country. For three days the rebellion raged, as poor people barricaded roads with burning trash, set cars afire, smashed store windows and threw stones at police. Police and soldiers fired into crowds, killing more than 100 persons and wounding hundreds more. More than 4,000 people were arrested.

President Jorge Blanco blamed the opposition parties, but the spontaneous rebellion took all political parties in the country more or less by surprise. It drew in diverse sectors: workers, the unemployed, housewives, students. Because of its disorganized nature, no unified strategy or structure emerged from the uprising. But the protests gave a tremendous push to grassroots organizing, especially what came to be called the *movimiento barrial popular,* the slumdwellers' movement.

The government kept up the repression throughout the year, periodically detaining leftist and labor leaders. In January 1985, new austerity measures drove food and fuel prices up by another 50%. A few days before the announcement, the police and military moved into the poor sections of Santo Domingo to guard against renewed protest. The price increases triggered a series of strikes, resulting in thousands of arrests.

Return of Balaguer

The second "April War," as it came to be called, occurred against a backdrop of flagrant government corruption and incompetence. Jorge Blanco's administration was ridden with patronage and favoritism, and everyone knew government officials and military officers were profiting from corruption. While officials looked after their own interests, the collapse of water, electricity and sanitation services made life miserable for ordinary Dominicans. Garbage mountains accumulated on the streets of graceful middle-class neighborhoods, and blackouts became a nightly occurrence.

In May 1986, the PRD was ousted in an election narrowly won by Joaquín Balaguer's Social Christian Reform Party. To some observers, it seemed strange that the elderly, nearly blind politician, closely associated with the Trujillo dictatorship, could be voted in again. That he was reflected the depths of the country's desperation.

Peasants and workers recalled that food prices were lower during Balaguer's previous term, and many took refuge in the illogical hope that he could return prices to levels of the 1970s. People also believed that Balaguer, by virtue of his authoritarian style, would curb corruption and restore efficiency to the workings of government.

The PRD was discredited not only by its record of thievery, but by severe internal factionalism. This included a violent clash over who would be the presidential candidate, a

Salvador Jorge Blanco.

El Nuevo Diario

Juan Bosch.

El Nuevo Diario

From Sugar to Tourism: End of an Era

Balaguer's "honeymoon" lasted nearly a year, during which the anti-corruption drive riveted the country's attention. By 1987, however, attention refocused on the economy and the dilemma facing the country: the demise of sugar.

Of all Caribbean countries, the Dominican Republic has traditionally depended most heavily on sugar exports, and it has been hardest hit by sugar's decline. Beet sugar and a sugar substitute, high fructose corn syrup, have gradually taken over the world market. While demand for sugar has fallen, European countries and the United States have increased their subsidies to domestic producers. As a result, world sugar prices fell to 4 cents a pound in 1984, about one-quarter the cost of production.

In that year Gulf + Western, transnational giant of Dominican sugar production, sold its 300,000 acres of cane fields and the La Romana sugar mill to the Fanjul family, wealthy Cubans from Palm Beach, Florida. Gulf + Western's departure was a shock to Dominicans, but more shocks lay ahead.

As a form of foreign aid, the United States purchases specific amounts of sugar from some 40 countries at triple the world market price. This U.S. "quota" is set for each country individually; since 1965, the Dominican Republic has had the largest quota of any country.

Beginning in 1981, however, the United States began reducing its sugar imports in order to protect domestic producers. In 1986 it deeply slashed all import quotas, cutting the Dominican Republic's by 47%. In 1986 the United States bought 302,000 tons of Dominican sugar; in 1987 this fell to 160,000 tons, at a loss to the Dominican Republic of $60 million in foreign exchange that year.[7] President Balaguer signed a three-year contract to sell sugar to the Soviet Union; but the end of an era was clearly at hand. The government began closing its 12 sugar mills one by one.

Some cane lands were parcelled out to small and middle-sized farmers, and Balaguer promised a major land reform. But the main thrust was into three areas which the government hoped would replace sugar: tourism, agro-industry, and the expansion of foreign-owned manufacturing in the free zones. Of the three, tourism has shown the most spectacular growth. Lavish hotels, condominiums and casinos are going up in Santo Domingo and along the coasts. Tourists are attracted by cheap prices due to the devaluation of the peso. Prostitution, gambling and drugs also figure prominently in the Dominican tourism scene.

By 1987 the country's foreign exchange earnings from tourism were nearly twice its combined income from sugar, coffee and cocoa.[8] The government also carried out an ambitious urban renewal program involving construction of roads, bridges and buildings in and around Santo Domingo. Due mostly to construction and tourism, economic growth that year was reported at 8%, and the press hailed an economic revival.

For the foreign companies and upper-class Dominicans

struggle finally settled in favor of Jacobo Majluta. Many supporters of Peña Gómez boycotted the poll when he was denied top spot on the ticket.

Although it ran a distant third, Bosch's PLD made an unexpectedly strong showing, doubling its vote from 9% in 1982 to 18% in 1986. It attracted voters from the organized urban sectors, including labor unions and barrio committees. But Bosch was severely damaged by a red-baiting campaign, with Balaguer labeling him "communist" and "atheist."

Balaguer thus emerged as the lesser of evils. A Dominican joke claimed that the electorate had been given a choice between a thief, a blind man and a schizophrenic—the latter a reference to Bosch's notoriously glum demeanor—"and so they chose the blind man."

Soon after taking office President Balaguer launched a high-profile anti-corruption drive. Six ranking military officers who held senior positions in the Jorge Blanco administration were jailed on corruption charges. In April 1987 a court ordered Jorge Blanco's arrest, and the former president fled with his family to the United States. Balaguer also promised a "war on hunger," and said there would be no more concessions to the IMF. Dominicans wondered whether the wily politician had changed, and whether he would work his economic magic once more.

El Nuevo Diario

Protesters in town of Bayaguana set flaming
barricades in street.

who owned and managed the new businesses, things were
looking up. For the poor majority, however, little changed.
Some 70% of the work force remained without stable employment.[9] The new garment and electronics factories made some
jobs available at wages of around 125 pesos per week. But the
peso was devalued again in 1987, making those weekly wages
equivalent to US $20. While devaluation eroded purchasing
power, inflation leapt out of control in the reheated economy.
The continuing impoverishment was reflected in an exodus of
"boat people" to Puerto Rico, which gained publicity when
several boats capsized and the refugees drowned.

To make way for Balaguer's urban renewal program,
thousands of poor Dominicans were evicted from their
homes—mostly from the poorest, most militant neighborhoods in Santo Domingo. Popular organizations predicted
that 100,000 people would eventually be displaced.[10]

Strikes, land occupations and protests picked up tempo in
1987. In early 1988, sharp increases in food prices set off a wave
of rioting over a third of the country. Six people were killed by
the security forces and hundreds arrested. The protests
bypassed the established trade union, political party and
church leaders and focused national attention on the grassroots movement. The government met some of the protesters'
demands, tacitly conceding that the popular movement could
no longer be simply repressed or ignored.

Despite this recognition, however, the Dominican reality
remains grim. No political force in the country has offered a
clear alternative program. The popular movement, while
vibrant, lacks a unified structure, strategy or leadership. It is
basically reactive, without a defined program. The left-wing
parties, which have tried to give leadership to the movement,

*(Right) Woman protests police brutality: A
people destined for more hardship and
repression?*

have largely isolated themselves through sectarianism.

The three major parties are entering a period of uncertainty. The PLD and the Reformist Party revolve around the
personalities of Bosch and Balaguer, both of whom are in their
early eighties. The war within the PRD continues, with
Majluta and Peña Gómez vying for control. All that is certain
is that a new generation of politicians will soon have to
confront the country's problems.

In the Caribbean, the Dominican tragedy is seen as a
warning of the perils of entanglement with the IMF. It is
testimony as well to the dangers of incurring debt in the face of
long-term decline in commodities such as sugar. The *Wall
Street Journal* called the country "a junkheap for failed Third
World debt and development strategies."[11] Dominicans are
well aware that most of those strategies originated in Washington, and anti-imperialist feelings are the strongest here of
any country in the region.

With its $4 billion debt, the Dominican Republic may
soon have to bow once more to the IMF. But poor Dominicans are now highly politicized and determined to resist new
pressures. Under these circumstances, the Dominican Republic
appears to be a society without solutions, where the poor are
destined for still more hardship and repression. ∎

El Nuevo Diario

El Nuevo Diario

*Police arrest protester.
Thousands of poor people,
trade unionists and left
leaders have been arrested
and detained since 1984.*

Haiti

Flying into the Haitian capital of Port-au-Prince, one gazes down on what appears to be a vast waterfront garbage heap through which figures mysteriously move. It is Cité Soleil, "City of the Sun," where the poorest of the poor crowd together amid foraging animals and open sewers. Formerly named for Jean-Claude Duvalier's mother, the shantytown was renamed in 1986 in honor of Radio Soleil, the Catholic Church station which was a voice of hope during the Duvalier years. But although the name has changed, more than two years after Duvalier's February 7, 1986 departure the appalling poverty of Cité Soleil remains unchanged.

The Duvaliers are gone, ensconced in a lavish exile in the south of France. But their legacy lives on, as powerful military men and civilian "Duvalierists" resist Haitians' demands for change. Haiti is still the poorest country in the western hemisphere, its people landless, exploited and hungry. But they are also increasingly organized and aware, reflecting the growth of a popular movement which began in the early 1980s and flowered after Duvalier's fall. Since then, the clash of these two forces—those backing the status quo and those seeking change—has meant continued bloodshed and suffering but, ultimately, new hope.

Opposition to Duvalier Grows

The opposition movement that brought down Jean-Claude Duvalier was in many ways unique. It was not an armed insurgency. Nor was it a movement led by politicians, although the crusades of anti-Duvalier figures such as Sylvio Claude played a role. Rather, the driving energy came from Haitian youth, especially in the provincial towns and rural areas. Their efforts were encouraged by a grassroots religious movement whose principal impetus came from new forces within the Catholic Church, to which some 80% of Haitians nominally belong.

From the late 1970s a number of factors combined to weaken the Duvalier regime. On the one hand was deepening impoverishment, especially in the countryside. Crucial in this regard was the destruction of all Haiti's pigs after African swine fever appeared in 1978. Fearing that the disease might infect U.S. pigs, U.S. and international aid agencies carried out the systematic slaughter of the entire Haitian hog population. The loss of the pigs destroyed many peasants' only cash reserves, forcing many to migrate to the squalid Port-au-Prince slums.

Others set out in small boats to make the 800-mile crossing to Florida. But in 1982 the Haitian government began allowing the U.S. Coast Guard to seize boatloads of refugees. Thousands of "boat people," having sold their meager land or possessions, were sent back to Haiti. A crucial escape valve thus was partially closed off.

Yet the interdiction program only slowed, rather than stopped, the exodus of Haitians to the United States, Canada and elsewhere. Emigration, along with migration from the

Children of Cité Soleil.

Patrick Ahern

rural areas to Port-au-Prince, reduced Haitians' isolation. Radio played a key role in this process, especially Radio Haiti Inter and the Catholic Church's Radio Soleil. Broadcasting in Kreyol, they became critical sources of information for a population which was 80% illiterate.

Radio Soleil's role, which expanded after the government shut down Radio Haiti Inter, reflected a gradual transformation taking place within the Church. The Catholic hierarchy, headed by the Archbishop François Wolf Ligondé, a cousin of Duvalier's wife, had long been supportive of the regime. But in the late 1970s, the belated impact of Vatican Two and the Medellín and Puebla assemblies encouraged a number of priests, religious and lay workers in Haiti to make an "option for the poor." Living and working with peasants and slum-dwellers, grassroots church workers gradually challenged the institutional Church to identify with the people.[1]

One expression of this vision was the growth of base Christian communities, called in Haiti *Ti Legliz* (Little Church). The movement grew rapidly in the early 1980s to encompass over 2,000 base communities. A related movement was that of peasant groups focusing on agricultural cooperation. Both encouraged poor Haitians to analyze and challenge unjust social structures.

The wave of arrests in November 1980 which crushed nascent civic organizations left the Church as the sole institution not under direct government control. The hierarchy's hostility to "political" involvement of the Church gradually lessened under the pressure of repression. In December 1982 the government arrested Gérard Duclerville, a lay Catholic activist who had worked with the Ti Legliz communities. He was imprisoned for 40 days and savagely beaten, while grassroots Christians pressed the hierarchy for a sign of concern. Finally, the Haitian bishops issued a pastoral letter proclaiming that "the Church of Haiti is living now in a situation of challenge." Duclerville was released on Feb. 7, 1983.

A month later, Pope John Paul II visited Haiti and inspired joy with his declaration that "Something must change in this country." He affirmed the activist role of the Haitian Church, citing "... this awakening, this leap, this movement of the Church for the good of the whole country."[2] In the following years the Church emerged as an umbrella for the growing opposition movement. To kick off the U.N.-sponsored International Youth Year in 1985, the Haitian bishops addressed the country's youth: "We count on you and are with you. You can count on us and are with us. Stand up: 1985 is your year! What do you want to make of it?" Tens of thousands of youth marched in processions throughout Haiti, singing and chanting "We would rather die standing up than live on our knees!"[3] They also repeated the slogan which had come to symbolize the new popular identity of the Haitian Church: "We are the Church; the Church is us."

The government reacted harshly to this new church role, even stationing armed Tontons Macoutes inside churches during the celebration of mass. In November 1984, immediately following President Reagan's reelection, church literacy and development workers were rounded up and jailed until widespread protests forced their release.

As opposition grew, cracks in the power structure weakened the regime. These centered on rivalry between the old guard loyal to François Duvalier and the rising class of technocrats and business interests symbolized by Jean-Claude Duvalier's mulatto in-laws, the Bennetts. As infighting escalated, "Baby Doc" was left increasingly isolated in the plush confines of the National Palace, a pawn in the power struggles between his family members and associates.

In May 1984, the first mass uprising in more than two decades directly challenged the regime. Triggered by the police beating of a pregnant woman, the rioting spread from town to town in the impoverished north. Crowds seized food supplies from relief agency warehouses, crying "Down with hunger! Down with misery! Down with Duvalier!" By the time troops had quelled the riots 30 people lay dead.

On the fifth anniversary of the November 1980 crackdown, a demonstration in the provincial capital of Gonaives ended with the army shooting of four schoolchildren. It was the turning point. Rebellion spread through the provinces, finally reaching the capital in early February 1986.

Overthrow and Dechoukaj

Faced with a generalized revolt, the United States belatedly had cut off aid to the Haitian government in January. A decision was made that Duvalier had to go—both to avoid further radicalization of the opposition movement and to ensure U.S. influence over the transition. It was a strategy that U.S. officials would use again within weeks in the Philippines. On February 7, 1986, Jean-Claude Duvalier and his family fled to France aboard a U.S. Air Force jet. Thousands of Haitians took to the streets in joyous celebration.

Afterwards, *Operasyon Dechouké*—Operation Uproot—sought to eradicate all traces of the Duvalierist past. Poor Haitians organized to force out known Duvalier supporters, from high officials down to village-level functionaries. Some members of the Tontons Macoutes were lynched, although most escaped into hiding. Other *dechoukaj* was symbolic, such as the destruction of François Duvalier's mausoleum and the pillaging of mansions belonging to the Bennetts.

But while *dechoukaj* was taking place in the streets, in the National Palace power had been quietly transferred to a National Government Council (CNG) consisting of figures from the old regime. Headed by Gen. Henri Namphy, the army

Maggie Steber

Haitian policeman with Uzi submachine gun.

157

chief of staff, the CNG also included Col. Williams Régala, who had worked closely with the Duvalier secret police. Col. Max Valles commanded the elite Presidential Guard. Alix Cinéas, a civilian, profited from corruption as Duvalier's minister of public works. Only Gérard Gourgue, head of the Haitian Human Rights League, had been a Duvalier opponent.

Of equal importance, the Haitian military continued to operate under the command of officers loyal to Duvalier who were known for brutal repression. Col. Prosper Avril, the powerful inspector-general of the Presidential Guard, became an advisor to the CNG. Other top-ranking officers included Col. Jean-Claude Paul, commander of the Dessalines Battalion, and the commanders of the military police, the Fort Dimanche prison and the Leopard counter-insurgency squad.[4]

While Haitians demanded justice for past abuses, the CNG and its military allies sought to prevent any serious inquiry into the past. Prosecution of anyone risked spinning a web that would ultimately ensnare everyone, given the across-the-board complicity in corruption, torture and murder during the Duvalier years. The junta helped top Duvalier officials slip out of the country, including Madame Max Adolphe, head of the Tontons Macoutes, and Colonel Albert Pierre, a former secret police chief. But when word went out that hated former police chief Luc Desyr was about to flee, thousands of Haitians invaded the airport and blocked the runway, forcing his arrest.

After soldiers shot five civilians dead in March, Gérard Gourgue resigned from the junta. Namphy then removed Cinéas, Valles and Avril and added civilian Jacques François in an attempted balancing act. Régala, in the key post of interior and defense minister, remained the strongman on the junta, while Avril and other powerful officers maneuvered behind the scenes.

Duvalierism Without Duvalier

In the years following Duvalier's fall, Haitians took advantage of a limited political opening to organize a vibrant grassroots movement. Hundreds of groups formed, including peasant associations, neighborhood committees, women's and youth groups, and human rights groups. A project to clean up and paint Port-au-Prince, organized by the neighborhood committees, symbolized the new energies and hopes for immediate change.

There was broad agreement on a basic vision of a new society in which the poor majority would no longer be exploited. Specific demands included land reform, jobs, health services and education. A common strategy, however, was lacking, due in large part to the spontaneous nature of the movement which toppled Duvalier. So identified was Duvalier with the system that many had subconsciously assumed that all would be swept away with the dictator.

Within a short time, renewed repression signalled the limits to change. On April 26, soldiers opened fire on a peaceful march outside Fort Dimanche prison organized by the newly-formed League of Former Political Prisoners. When the carnage was over eight people lay dead. In September, Charlot Jacquelin, a teacher with the Catholic Church literacy program, was rousted from his bed and taken away by soldiers.

Missing since then, he is presumed to have died in prison. Both events marked the return of Duvalier-style repression, and were pivotal in turning Haitians against the junta.

The Tontons Macoutes, who had been officially disbanded but never disarmed, began to reemerge. In October 1986 high-ranking Macoutes and former Duvalier officials formed a neo-Duvalierist party called PREN. It was dissolved after more than 100,000 Haitians marched in outraged protest.

By one year after Duvalier's fall, hopes for rapid change had faded, replaced by disillusionment and anger. Two things were clear. First, the National Government Council was increasingly seen as a front for the old order—for powerful Duvalierists, high-ranking military officers and former Tontons Macoutes who wanted to guard their privileges and escape retribution for the past. Haitians called it "Duvalierism without Duvalier."

Secondly, it was above all support from Washington which allowed the junta to resist pressures for its resignation. Haitians had hoped Washington's role in arranging Duvalier's departure signaled a new attitude after years of supporting dictatorship. These hopes were dashed when the first U.S. aid after February 7 consisted of tear gas, truncheons and rubber bullets for the army. In all, the Reagan administration sent the junta nearly $7 million in "nonlethal" military gear, along with a team of military trainers. In a visit to Haiti, Secretary of State George Shultz declared U.S. support for the junta. Graffiti in Port-au-Prince reflected the widespread anger: "Shultz kriminel."

Haitians correctly perceived the U.S. strategy as contradictory and fatally flawed. The Reagan administration had made an election its primary policy goal in Haiti. Officials

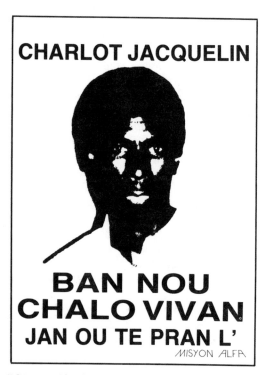

"Give us Charlot alive like when you took him."

sought an election to provide an image of democracy, to install a government with which they could do business, and to forestall the growth of radical popular movements. But while they wanted the *image* of democracy, they feared the *reality,* an open arena in which radical contenders might gain support. Rather than risk this, they armed a murderous and unpopular junta representing the most undemocratic forces in the country.

Haitian popular organizations argued that free elections were not possible as long as Duvalierists remained in power. U.S. officials ignored them, even as swiftly-moving events in the summer and fall of 1987 pointed toward disaster.

November Bloodbath, January Farce

Two themes shaped developments in the critical year of 1987. One was the growing determination of Haitians to see the electoral process through, along with more effective strategizing and coalition-building among grassroots organizations. The other was the steady escalation of violence by the military and Tontons Macoutes, who were equally determined to prevent elections from taking place.

The "First National Congress of Democratic Movements" in January brought together delegates from some 300 grassroots organizations, including peasant associations, trade unions, slumdwellers' committees and human rights groups. The first such event ever held in Haiti, the congress established a model of broad-based discussion, analysis and decision-making. It was followed in March by a national peasant congress in the village of Papaye, which attracted 2,000 members of peasant groups from around the country.

Although disagreements on strategy persisted, a coordinating committee emerging from the first congress swung its weight behind the electoral process. On March 29, Haitians voting by referendum enthusiastically ratified a new Constitution. An independent electoral council was set up under its provisions to oversee a November election. But in June, the CNG abruptly seized control of the electoral machinery, pushing aside the electoral council. A coalition of civic and religious groups, the Committee of 57, led peaceful protests; soldiers fired on protesters, bystanders and journalists, killing at least 59 by summer's end.

As it became clear that the Duvalierists sought to wreck the election, popular support for the voting grew. The Committee of 57 launched the candidacy of Gérard Gourgue, who gained support along with three other candidates. Volunteers helped the electoral council register over 2 million voters.

The prospect of a popular, reformist government enraged key Duvalierists and military men. Mounting violence targetted grassroots organizations and their allies in the Church. The Catholic hierarchy had pulled back from its activist stance after Duvalier's fall, but a progressive minority in the Church continued to speak out. The most radical priest in the country, Fr. Jean-Bertrand Aristide, narrowly escaped assassination when an armed gang attacked his car in full view of soldiers. On July 23, a gang of former Tontons Macoutes and peasants loyal to large landowners massacred over 300 peasants in the

Guardianphoto by Mike Kamber

Man waiting to vote in Port-au-Prince on election day, November 29, 1987.

northern town of Jean-Rabel. Those slain belonged to a group called Tet Ansamn (Heads Together), an outgrowth of the base Christian community movement, which had been demanding land reform.[5]

As the election date neared, death squads armed with submachine guns, bombs and hand grenades terrorized Port-au-Prince, dumping bullet-ridden bodies in the street. Two presidential candidates were killed, one of them as he addressed journalists outside police headquarters. After the electoral council disqualified twelve former Duvalier officials from the race, fire gutted the council's headquarters. Over the next days, homes and party offices of council members and candidates were firebombed and strafed with gunfire. Fire destroyed a company printing ballots, and arsonists burned down a large open-air market in the capital. Armed gangs attacked vehicles transporting ballots to rural areas, while the junta grounded helicopters which had been rented by the electoral council.

By the early morning hours of November 29, election day, a bloodbath was underway. Truckloads of Tontons Macoutes and soldiers sped from one polling station to the next, strafing voters with machine gun fire. At least 15 people were

Guardianphoto by Mike Kamber

*Election day massacre: Scene at the Ecole Argentine Bellegarde, where death squads slaughtered at least 15 voters (above).
A victim of attack on a polling station (below).*

Guardianphoto by Mike Kamber

massacred at one polling place; people who ran to hide were cornered and shot or hacked to death. Shortly after 9 a.m. the election was cancelled. The official death toll stood at 34; eyewitness estimates were much higher.

The United States and other foreign donors immediately cut off aid to the Haitian government. Assistant Secretary of State Elliott Abrams insisted that U.S. support for the junta had nothing to do with the failure of elections. "It looked as if things were very much on track, but the [Haitian] government clearly decided to handle it in a way that turned out to be inadequate. I don't think our policy backfired at all."[6]

The violence achieved its purpose, forcing from the race those candidates likely to pursue reform. Afterwards, restoring foreign aid became an urgent priority for the Namphy government, requiring the "election" of a civilian acceptable to international opinion. Under army supervision, a new election was held on January 17, 1988. The four popular candidates boycotted the poll, and less than 5% of the electorate voted. Many polling stations had ballots for only one candidate, Leslie Manigat, subsequently declared the winner.

A political science professor and conservative Christian Democrat, Manigat had spent most of the Duvalier era in exile, primarily in Venezuela. To international opinion he appeared an acceptable choice. He was also willing to conclude a deal with the military, promising not to investigate past abuses. "There can be no solution to the Haitian problem without the army," he stressed during the campaign.

Race to a Dead End

"With the accession of Leslie F. Manigat to the presidency, there has simply been a change of players on the stage of the National Palace," asserted the popular coordinating committee KONAKOM.[7] Behind the scenes, in the legislature, the judiciary and the military, Duvalierist power remained strong. Observers differed on whether Manigat was a sincere reformer or simply a cynical opportunist. In either case, his installation by the army meant he had no political base or legitimacy from which to challenge the old order.

Manigat's puppet presidency lasted 134 days. The chain of events which led to his June 30 overthrow has yet to be fully explained, but at root was Manigat's attempt to bolster his own power by asserting authority over the military. Such moves were anathema to the army, which was determined to regain its full power and prestige which it saw as weakened by the Duvalier civilian dictatorships.

While carrying out no major reforms, Manigat had taken some steps to curb military involvement in the smuggling of contraband food and goods. The officer corps was known to be involved in rampant corruption, including narcotics trafficking. In March, a U.S. federal grand jury had indicted Colonel Jean-Claude Paul, commander of the Dessalines battalion, on drug-running charges.

On June 14, General Namphy, the army chief of staff, ordered Col. Paul transferred from his post. Siding with Paul, Manigat countermanded the order, and had Namphy placed under house arrest. He also ordered the transfer or retirement of some 30 other officers.

Manigat had overplayed his hand, and the army closed ranks and turned on him. In the early morning hours of June 20 Manigat was arrested and exiled to the Dominican Republic. With Col. Paul at his side—symbolizing the army's unity—General Namphy appeared on Haitian television to announce the suspension of the Constitution and indefinite military rule by decree.

Haiti is now a full-fledged military dictatorship. The new 12-member cabinet contains only one civilian, and the ministries of defense and of the interior have been combined under Gen. Régala, bringing the police force under military control. Gen. Namphy himself may not last as head of the regime; he is in poor health and is seen as having been forced into a figurehead role by other, more ambitious officers who masterminded the coup. Continuing rivalries between factions of the military make further palace coups probable. But military rule in one form or another is likely to last a long time.

It is likely as well that this regime will be more repressive than the interim junta headed by Namphy. A death list with the names of 164 human rights workers, priests, journalists and political party leaders began circulating shortly before the coup. On July 11, three weeks after the military takeover, leading human rights lawyer Lafontant Joseph was found brutally beaten to death, his body stabbed and mutilated.

Haiti has come full circle to the terror of the Duvalier era. But it is mistaken to suggest, as some have, that nothing has changed.

One major change is that Haiti now suffers a crippling international isolation which contrasts to the business-as-usual attitude of foreign governments toward the Duvalier regimes. As of mid-1988, aid donors had not resumed their support, cut off in the wake of the November bloodshed. The coup makes an early resumption unlikely, despite Assistant Secretary of State Abrams' hint that the United States could work with the new regime. The Haitian government is running short of foreign exchange to import critical commodities, and the regime faces bankruptcy.

The second change is in the political consciousness of the Haitian people, both in Haiti and in the diaspora. The coup has, for now, closed the opening for popular organizing, and the mood in Haiti is one of bitter resignation. For the grassroots movement it is a time of reflection and regrouping for a struggle with no end in sight. But while hope for rapid change has died, Haitians have glimpsed freedom. It will be difficult for the country's rulers to repress renewed struggle.

The road ahead is like the roads in Haiti: steep and dangerous, with wrenching twists and boulders in the path. The prospect of popular victories in the months to come is slight, and the chance of more bloodshed still great. But for the people of Haiti there is no going back. They have lost their fear and seen their power. ∎

Dominica

Jagged peaks rise abruptly from the sea, disappearing again into clouds heavy with rain. Sheer cliffs meet the water like a dark green curtain descending. Along the island perimeter skirts a delicate thread of road, linking scattered settlements, at times disappearing into the deep ravines leading down to the sea.

The volcanic terrain of Dominica, St. Lucia, St. Vincent and Grenada has shaped the history of the Windward Island group. During colonization, their wild interiors became strongholds for Carib Indians resisting European incursions. France and Britain initially left Dominica and St. Vincent as Carib "homelands." Today, Dominica is the only island in the region with a surviving Carib population—some 500 pure descendents, plus several thousand of Carib/African descent.

The Caribs were not long left in peace. French settlers gradually took over the land, and the Windwards became spoils in the colonial wars. After changing hands repeatedly, Dominica was ceded to Britain in 1763. But the lengthy French settlement left a cultural legacy, notably the use of Patwa (French Creole) as the island's vernacular. Although Patwa is now spoken less than before, Dominica retains its flavor in hundreds of French place names and family names. French influence was even more pronounced in St. Lucia, where Patwa continues to be spoken widely.

With little flat land, the Windwards were marginal sugar producers and remained the poor relations of Britain's Caribbean empire. Sugar was never important to Dominica; the few estates were small, and the mountains offered refuge to runaway slaves. Major Maroon rebellions took place in Dominica and St. Vincent. After emancipation, the freed slaves abandoned the estates and settled in the hills, forming the independent peasantry which dominates the Windwards today.

The largest of the Windwards, Dominica is also the most sparsely populated and impoverished. Thick forest covers much of the island. Frequent heavy rains send earth slides down the mountains to block the narrow roads. Roseau, the tiny capital, has the rough-and-ready feel of a pioneer town. It is very West Indian, without the pretensions of its French neighbors, Martinique and Guadeloupe. It is also the seat of government of a country of 74,000 people, an extraordinarily small number for viable economic independence.

Growing Bananas

Bananas became the primary Windward crop in the 1950s. They could be grown on small plots, required little capital investment and had a market in England. Colonial officials concerned about social unrest saw bananas as an income-producer for the peasantry. They gave Windward bananas preferential access to the British market and helped a British company, Geest, take over the trade.[1]

The Caribbean Windwards today are the most banana-dependent countries in the world. Bananas provided 64% of Dominica's export earnings in 1986.[2] Half the Dominican population depends on income from bananas, which are grown mainly on family plots of 1 to 5 acres. Farmers also grow coconuts and citrus to sell, along with yams and vegetables for their own consumption.

Under its contract with the Windward Island Banana Growers Association (WINBAN), Geest has the right to buy all export-quality bananas grown in the islands. Geest sets the price it pays by deducting fees for the company's services—freight, handling, and ripening—from the wholesale price of bananas. The local growers' association then makes further deductions. The Dominican farmer ends up receiving about 10% of what the bananas sell for in British grocery stores.[3]

Kathy McAfee

Farmer in Dominica with boxes for bananas to be packed in the field.

162

Geest's monopoly means that Dominica depends not only on a single crop, but on a single buyer. Caribbean governments, let alone the farmers, have little bargaining power in the relationship with Geest. Farmers take all the risks; if disease or bad weather harms the crop, Geest simply makes up the difference with fruit grown elsewhere.

Bananas provide Dominican farmers with a regular, if meager, income. But it is a precarious dependence. In 1978, the year Dominica became independent, leaf-spot disease devastated the banana crop. The next year Hurricane David hit the island, followed by Hurricane Allen in 1980. Much of the country was left under rubble, without electricity, running water or telephones. Storm winds flattened the banana plants, leaving the industry in ruins.

Recovery from the hurricanes took six years. It was complicated by the fall in value of the British pound: while Geest pays for bananas in pounds, growers receive payment in Eastern Caribbean currency pegged to the U.S. dollar. Depreciation of the pound against the dollar means that farmers receive less money for their fruit.

By 1986, the situation was reversed as favorable exchange rates and new packing methods sent prices up to record levels. Dominican farmers seized the opportunity to plant more land with bananas, often at the expense of other crops. This banana "boom," visible in the new pick-up trucks bouncing along Dominican roads, came at a time when the industry's future was more uncertain than ever. In 1992, when the European Unification Act takes effect, Windward bananas could lose their protected British market. Also uncertain is the future role of Geest, which has used its banana profits to become a diversified conglomerate. The company no longer depends on Windward bananas, and could pull out of the region if it chose. But Dominica's economy still depends on Geest.

The Dominican government talks of the need to diversify, but the obstacles are great. Only bananas have a guaranteed market. Other crops are marketed on a small scale by women hucksters who ply their trade between Dominica and neighboring islands. With markets unsure, farmers will not risk planting large amounts of other crops; small supplies in turn make it difficult to develop markets. Only a serious diversification program, giving farmers incentives to plant new crops, holds hope. Until then, Dominica's economy stands in danger of destruction by one severe windstorm.

Charles, the CBI and the CIA

Dominicans celebrated when Eugenia Charles, a conservative lawyer, was elected in 1980 after years of corrupt government. The prime minister promised that her friendship with Washington would mean aid, investment and jobs. The Reagan administration saw Charles as an anticommunist ally, and responded with aid packages for road building and the banana industry.

In 1983 Charles signed a formal request for United States military intervention in Grenada, and stood beside President Reagan as he announced the invasion. Three months later, U.S. officials launched a $9.6 million project to rehabilitate 100 miles of Dominican roads. The badly-needed new roads helped

Charles win reelection in 1985. U.S. support to Charles may have gone even further. In his book *Veil*, journalist Bob Woodward stated that her government received $100,000 from the CIA, a charge Charles denies.[4]

After peaking at the time of the invasion, U.S. interest in the Eastern Caribbean's problems faded once the Grenada "threat" was eliminated. U.S. officials continued to portray the Caribbean Basin Initiative as a major assistance program. But as Charles herself eventually complained, the CBI has done little for Dominica, where lack of basic infrastructure deters investors. New factory shells built with U.S. aid mostly stand empty. One American company which opened a glove factory closed it as soon as a union made demands. It reopened as a non-union shop, paying workers—mostly women—$5.55 per day.

While Charles pressed for more development aid, the Reagan administration instead sent Green Berets to train a paramilitary "Special Service Unit." In May 1987, Dominica became the site of U.S.-led military maneuvers involving the SSU's from seven neighboring islands.

Another major thrust of American assistance was anti-communist "political education" which also served to support Charles' Freedom Party. The Committee for Progress in Democracy, funded through the National Endowment for Democracy, professes no party ties, but its slogan suggests otherwise: "Keep Dominica Free." A similar body, the German-funded Eastern Caribbean Institute for Democracy, is headed by the Freedom Party secretary Alvin Knight.

Despite this outside backing, Charles' domestic political support has been severely eroded. The complaints against her, centering on new taxes she has introduced, mask a deeper malaise. Unemployment is at least 30%, and the population has dwindled through emigration. But if people are disillusioned with Charles, they are not yet flocking to the opposition Labour Party, reorganized after its last term in office. Labour includes some new faces, including several known progressives. But it has focused on criticizing the government rather than presenting its own ideas.

An alternative vision is, however, taking shape among Dominicans working directly with farmers and in small-scale development and community organizing. The Small Projects Assistance Team, known as SPAT, identifies promising local initiatives, then assists them with training and technical advice. Rural Dominica is dotted with small successes: a cooperative bakery in La Plaine, a Village Development Committee in Petite-Savanne, the Southern Women's Organization for Rural Development in Grand Bay. SPAT also supports the Movement for Cultural Awareness, which has formed popular theater groups around the island. The most active is the Karifuna Cultural Group, in which Carib Indian youth explore their cultural traditions.

The vision of groups like SPAT centers on greater self-reliance and local control. A key aspect is the effort to develop new markets for farmers' crops. In 1984, SPAT and the Dominica Farmers Union acquired a cargo ship with Dutch assistance and launched Farm-to-Market. Once each month, the ship loads up with fruits and vegetables and heads north to the Virgin Islands, where the cargo is sold to wholesalers.

Members of the Castle Bruce farm cooperative.

Jethro Pettit

Opening new markets has not been easy, but the organizers press on. "We need to lay the basis for diversification *now,* not in 1991 when the end of the banana industry is at hand," says a member of SPAT.[5]

The Charles government has not encouraged and indeed has actively hindered many such initiatives. Farm-to-Market endured an assault of red tape, including attempts to block funds from Canada for the project. In part, the government's ire stems from the involvement in the project of former leftist activists, including some associated with the now-defunct Dominica Liberation Movement. The Farmers Union, headed by an ex-DLM activist who is now secretary of the Labour Party, has come under constant pressure.

Not unlike its counterparts elsewhere, the Dominican government also fears grassroots organizing for its own sake. Farmers organized in cooperatives are less isolated, and "if things are not going right, you tend to speak out more because you are not alone," explains a coop member. Conservative political and business leaders brand the cooperatives "communist." The largest farm coop in Dominica, Castle Bruce, is battling the government in court to keep its land.

The involvement of activists in such work reflects a maturing of the progressive movement in Dominica. The old Dominica Liberation Movement suffered the weaknesses of much of the Caribbean left, its members perceived as intellectuals with no mass base. The party collapsed in the face of

pressures following the Grenada invasion. Rather than start a new party, Dominican activists have channeled their energies into concrete development work. Their vision calls for greater self-sufficiency in food through poultry-raising, agro-industry and fishing, and less emphasis on wooing foreign investors to exploit cheap labor.

Such a model holds promise but cannot by itself resolve the dilemma of Dominica's survival. The country is too small, too young and too poor: half the population is under 15 years old, and one-third of adults are unemployed. All the costs of government, infrastructure and social services must be borne by a few thousand wage earners. Small size and rugged terrain pose severe constraints on agriculture and industrialization. Even tourism is limited by the absence of sandy beaches.

The question of Caribbean unity takes on new meaning in Dominica, which has close cultural ties to St. Lucia and the other Windwards. This affinity could provide a basis for the merger of the Eastern Caribbean islands into a larger, more viable state. Such attempts have failed in the past. But in 1987, the Eastern Caribbean prime ministers launched a new effort to study the question, promising to bring it to their constituents in a referendum. Progressives in Dominica and other islands emphasize that such an effort must involve the people through their grassroots organizations if it is to succeed this time. For Dominica and the other small islands, this may be the only solution. ∎

Barbados

When British settlers arrived in Barbados almost 400 years ago, they found the flat, uninhabited island "better agreeing with the temper of the English Nacion" than its mountainous, Carib-dominated neighbors.[1] With its gentle terrain, Barbados was ideal for sugar plantations. Britain's claim in 1625 began three and a half centuries of unbroken British rule, making Barbados the only British Caribbean possession never held by another colonial power.

The consummate sugar island, Barbados was a nearly pure plantation economy. A white planter-merchant elite shaped a conservative, Anglophile society that was rigidly stratified by color and class. For the slaves, the endless cane fields meant no escape from the estates, no mountains or forests to shelter runaways. After emancipation, the outlet for many was emigration.

As elsewhere in the West Indies, the labor uprisings of 1937-1939 led to the first major changes in the system. Under Grantley Adams, an Oxford-trained lawyer, the twin movement of the Barbados Workers Union and the Barbados Labour Party emerged to lead reform. Workers won benefits such as paid vacations and workmen's compensation, while progressive taxation and expanded social services raised living standards for the poor. This emphasis on social welfare within the framework of a capitalist economy and the Westminster Parliamentary system came to mark West Indian social democracy.

A split in the movement's leadership in 1955 laid the basis for a two-party system. Under Errol W. Barrow, the newly-formed Democratic Labour Party led Barbados to independence in 1966 and governed for the next decade. Deeply committed to West Indian unity, Barrow helped found CARIFTA, the free trade association which was the forerunner of CARICOM. In 1972, Barrow, together with Michael Manley of Jamaica and the leaders of Guyana and Trinidad, established diplomatic relations with Cuba. This independent opening to Castro's government came at a time when Cuba was still subject to diplomatic sanctions imposed by the Organization of American States at Washington's behest.

Prosperity and Hard Times

In a series marking Barbados' 21st year of independence, journalist Rickey Singh took note of the country's achievements:

> Undoubtedly, Barbados, whatever may be its current social and economic problems, has, over these 21 years of political freedom, distinguished itself among the member states of the Caribbean Community in its management of the national economy; in providing good government, free of the corruption evident elsewhere in the region; and in building up an internationally respected reputation as a parliamentary democracy whose institutions are not being corroded by personality cults and partisan politics.[2]

Literacy in Barbados is nearly universal, and social services, especially health care, are the best in the English-speaking Caribbean. Per capita income was US$4,630 in 1985, placing Barbados in the ranks of middle-income countries.[3] Barbados boasts a strong trade union movement, embodied in the all-encompassing Barbados Workers Union. The BWU has played a vigorous role not only in politics but in education—operating its own Labour College—and in pushing progressive labor legislation.

The island's modern infrastructure includes an excellent road system and an international airport built by the United States during World War Two. Together with an advanced communications network, this has made Barbados the base for scores of regional organizations, among them the Caribbean Development Bank, the Caribbean Conference of Churches, the Caribbean Association of Industry and Commerce, and the Caribbean News Agency.

These advantages of political stability and physical development have made Barbados attractive to tourists and investors. Tourism grew rapidly in the 1960s, trading on the island's special "English" atmosphere and its image of social tranquility. Manufacturing, mainly by foreign-owned electronics firms, also expanded. The strength of these new sectors enabled Barbados to weather economic difficulties better than most countries in the region.

But in the early 1980s, the impact of world recession hit Barbados. North Americans and Europeans could not afford Caribbean vacations, and tourist arrivals fell sharply. Electronics manufacturers, facing a shrinking world market and competition from Japan, closed their Barbados plants, heading for cheaper wage havens. The largest micro-chip manufacturer on the island, Intel, pulled out in 1986, eliminating over 1,000 jobs. These developments sent the Barbadian economy reeling into negative growth.

Tourist and vendor on a Barbados beach.

Barbados *Nation*

Although tourism has recovered, unemployment continues to climb, averaging 18% since 1985. Drug abuse and crime have followed in its wake. While moderate compared to similar problems in some countries, "the twin peril of drugs and joblessness," as the Barbados *Nation* termed it, has Barbadians on edge and the country's leaders at a seeming loss.

The lesson of recent hard times in this prosperous island is that Barbados is vulnerable. Tourism and manufacturing depend on foreign markets and, to a large extent, on foreign investment, tying the Barbadian economy to international economic trends over which it has no control. And while the island's stability attracts investors, an economy based on "guest capital" is not, ultimately, compatible with the Barbadian tradition of high wages and strong trade unions.

Barbados' economic future may lie in attracting high-technology, high-wage industries requiring a skilled labor force. It has already benefited from a new trend in offshore office work, in which firms use satellite technology to transfer tasks such as data entry and word processing overseas. But such an economy would still be vulnerable to changing markets and technologies. Only greater self-sufficiency, including the ability to produce more of its own food, will protect Barbados from future hard times.

Two Leaders

From 1976 to 1986 Errol Barrow's party was out of power. At the helm of the Barbados Labour Party, Grantley Adams' son, Tom Adams, steered Barbados into a close alliance with Washington. Prime Minister Adams took a controversial interventionist stance, seeing Barbados as a kind of policeman of the Eastern Caribbean. In 1979 he sent soldiers from the Barbados Defense Force to help police in St. Vincent and the Grenadines quell a minor rebellion. Barbadian gunboats were dispatched to St. Lucia and St. Vincent during national elections in those countries. Such military posturing on the part of a small nation provoked a sarcastic calypso, "Boots." In 1983, Barbados' Grantley Adams International Airport became the staging point for troops moving into Grenada, and Barbadian soldiers played key roles in the post-invasion occupation force.

Adams' policies were not overtly unpopular. Most Barbadians supported the Grenada invasion, some vociferously. At a deeper level, however, Adams' politics placed him to the right of Barbadian tradition and his own Barbados Labour Party, and his arrogance irritated Barbadians. Respected but not loved, Adams became the butt of a popular calypso, the Mighty Gabby's "Mr. T."

When Adams died suddenly of a heart attack in March 1985, his strong right-wing position went with him. In 1986, the Barbadian electorate returned Errol Barrow's Democratic Labour Party to power in a landslide.

Barrow returned to office a vocal critic of foreign intervention in the region. The Caribbean, he insisted, should not be in the orbit of either superpower. One of the few Caribbean politicians to oppose the Grenada invasion, Barrow referred to President Reagan as "the cowboy in the White House." He was skeptical of Washington's professed concern

Adams bids farewell to Caribbean troops leaving from the Barbados international airport on their way to Grenada in October 1983.

Caribbean Contact

Errol W. Barrow

Government of Barbados

for the Caribbean's problems, saying "The U.S. only worries about the region when it sees a Communist threat looming."[4]

Many members of the Barbadian elite, including some in Barrow's own party, regarded the prime minister's outspokenness with dismay. But Barrow's popularity and his prestige as a senior statesman allowed him considerable license. While Adams' policies had isolated Barbados, under Barrow the country regained its stature as a promoter of Caribbean unity. Barrow's return coincided with rising support for Michael Manley in Jamaica, suggesting a regional swing back to social-democratic politics after the conservative post-invasion mood.

The contrast between the Adams and Barrow eras, however, was as much due to personalities as to any major shifts in policies or public opinion. If Adams' policies did not always reflect broad support, Barrow's positions were also somewhat individualistic, and his rhetoric frequently went farther than his actions. While the prime minister stridently criticized Washington, his foreign minister rushed to assure the public that there would be no significant changes in U.S.-Barbadian relations. Barrow criticized the U.S.-dominated Regional Security System, and refused to sign a treaty to upgrade the pact. But he allowed Barbados to continue as the headquarters of the system and to participate in military exercises organized by the United States.

Domestic issues, not foreign policy, played the main role in Barrow's election. His party promised tax cuts, a major

factor in the outcome. Less tangible but equally important were questions of image and style. Adams was dead, and his successor, Bernard St. John, was not a dynamic leader. Adams' elitist image contrasted to Barrow's profile as a man of the people, dedicated to the working class. Questions persisted about the Adams government's moral credibility, with rumors of corruption and involvement with drugs on the part of certain ministers.

Two weeks before the election, Dr. Don Blackman, a former member of the Adams cabinet, defected to the opposition, accusing the Barbados Labour Party of being overly influenced by white business interests. The suggestion that whites exerted behind-the-scenes influence on a black government set off a sensational debate. Critics of Dr. Blackman's position found his statements, especially his call to curb non-black immigration, racist and extreme. But for many Barbadians they touched a raw nerve.

Underlying the controversy was lingering doubt about the white minority's economic power and its implications for black majority rule. The once all-powerful oligarchy today is symbolized by the row of large department stores they own along Bridgetown's Broad Street. Much of the import and merchandising sector remains in their hands, while foreign multinationals are prominent in tourism, manufacturing and offshore services. Although black Barbadians now own or control many businesses, and the state plays an economic role, the claim of black economic disadvantage struck a responsive chord. Commented *Caribbean Contact,* "Whoever wins will now have to deal with the issue of race and racism in Barbados."[5]

Changing of the Guard

On June 1, 1987 Prime Minister Barrow died of a heart attack, the second Barbadian leader to die in office in just over two years. The loss of the veteran West Indian politician silenced an independent voice, and left Barbadians facing greater uncertainty than ever before.

Barrow's successor, Erskine Sandiford, is a pragmatist who has continued Barrow's policies without the former leader's strong personal image. As in Trinidad after the death of Eric Williams, the passing of the old guard has left a leadership vacuum that the new crop of politicians has as yet been unable to fill.

But neither this fact nor concern over the economy is likely to threaten the stability of this self-assured island nation. With two nearly-identical parties alternating in power, policies will continue in a social-democratic mold. Despite the presence of the tiny Barbados Workers Party, radical politics receive less of a hearing in Barbados than virtually anywhere else in the region. Within these limits, the Barbadian legacy is both Barrow and Adams, both proud promoter of regional sovereignty and conservative U.S. ally. The balance future leaders strike between these roles will make a significant difference for Barbados and the region. ∎

Grenada

Fidel Castro called it "a big revolution in a small country." Today the revolution is gone, and one is constantly reminded of what a tiny island society this is. Farmers trudge along winding roads, cutlass in hand, past youths lounging in the shade of mango and nutmeg trees. Passersby greet each other as they climb the steep streets of the toy-town capital. In the island telephone directory one can find listed Maurice Bishop's mother, former ministers George Louison and Kenrick Radix, opposition politicians Francis Alexis and George Brizan.

Grenada took on magnified dimensions as a symbol for the Reagan presidency and its foreign policy aims. The 1983 U.S. invasion was the only military victory in eight years for an administration that boasted of restoring American might. Afterwards, "liberated" Grenada was supposed to showcase the superiority of free-market capitalism over the socialist path. President Reagan underscored the island's importance with a whirlwind visit in February 1986. The pro-American prime minister, Herbert Blaize, praised the visiting president as "our own hero, our rescuer next to God."

Few Grenadians still speak so effusively. Some four years after the invasion, expectations of massive United States aid have faded, leaving people disillusioned and cynical. Grenada "is still waiting for something to happen," says a development economist in St. George's. For the United States government, it seems, Grenada is a closed case, no longer of concern. "What happened was: the U.S. came in, changed the system, and left," he says. "They didn't want a communist government here and they haven't got one. That's all."

Sleepy Stagnation

The traffic police sport new red and white uniforms, British-colonial style. Yachts dot the harbor, and the cruise ships have returned. Grenada, one reporter noted, "is gradually returning to the sleepy pace that had once made it a favorite with the international yachting set."[1]

The yachting set may be well pleased, but on street corners of St. George's and rural villages, young men restlessly pass the time. Unemployment of around 40% is the most telling evidence of the stagnation which has settled over the island. The revolution's popular social programs in education, health, housing and cooperatives are gone. The Blaize government, advised by the U.S. Agency for International Development (USAID), is dismissing 1,800 civil servants and has imposed a crushing 20% sales tax. It is draining liquidity from state-owned banks and leaning heavily on United States aid to pay its bills. If there has been an economic miracle here, Grenadians do not see it.

The industrial park built in anticipation of a flood of investors stands nearly empty. Eighteen foreign firms have come into Grenada since 1983, seven of them American. Most are small entrepreneurial ventures. Only two are manufacturers providing significant employment: Smith-Kline, which makes frames for eyeglasses, and Johnson & Johnson, manufacturing

rubber gloves.[2]

There are visible improvements, but ironically, many of these are the result of projects started by the People's Revolutionary Government (PRG) before 1983. Tourists arrive by jet at the efficient new Point Salines International Airport, built almost entirely by the Bishop government with Cuban help. Roads around the island have been resurfaced and repaired. Like the airport, most of the road-building projects were begun before the invasion and completed afterwards with U.S. or European funds.

U.S. economic aid to Grenada totaled $80 million in the two years following the invasion. Since then, however, both U.S. assistance and the visible American presence have been sharply reduced. USAID had three separate offices in Grenada in 1984; by 1987 a lone staff person remained. Economic aid is now mostly budgetary support to cover the government's deficits.[3]

This lower profile reflects U.S. officials' confidence that they have accomplished their main objectives in Grenada. The "psy-ops" team that carried out anticommunist propaganda after the invasion has gone home. But there are subtle reminders that this is now, politically and ideologically, American turf. Voice of America is building a radio transmitter on the island which will broadcast to the Eastern Caribbean and Central America. The state-owned Radio Grenada favors American music, especially country and western. Grenada's single television channel has been placed under the control of the U.S.-based Discovery Foundation. Its programs are 90% American, with heavy programming of right-wing televangelists such as Pat Robertson and Jimmy Swaggart.

Private conservative networks also moved into Grenada after the invasion. A "Grenada Institute for Democracy," funded by the Konrad Adenauer Foundation of Germany, distributes tracts by anticommunist fringe fanatic Fred Schwartz from a small office in St. George's. U.S.-based evangelical sects have entered Grenada in large numbers and are recruiting aggressively in this traditionally Catholic country.

It is difficult to say how much lasting impact such activities have had. Many Grenadians seem uninterested, if only because they have retreated from all political involvement. Still, the ideological onslaught has shifted the terms of the debate, giving the word "communist" a place in the national vocabulary it did not have before.

The New National Problem

When U.S.-backed Caribbean leaders midwifed the birth of the New National Party (NNP) on Union Island in 1984, they called 69-year-old Herbert Blaize out of political oblivion to lead it. Anticommunism became his single theme. Grenada under the Bishop government was "a stinking communist hole," he says, an allegation many Grenadians find offensive.

Blaize's government has earned a reputation in the Caribbean as slavishly pro-American. It has sided with the

President Reagan delivers an address during his visit to Grenada in 1986.

J. Rudin

United States on key votes in the United Nations and the Organization of American States, isolating itself from mainstream Caribbean opinion. In 1986 it abstained from a U.N. vote to impose sanctions against South Africa, an almost inconceivable position for a black Caribbean government and one which deeply embarrassed Grenadians.

Along with its foreign policy, the Blaize government's economic policies were designed in Washington. The phasing out of 1,800 government workers comes at a time when unemployment has already reached alarming levels. The layoffs have been used politically, continuing the process of weeding former revolutionary activists from the civil service. The Blaize government also victimized the nearly 200 Grenadians who studied in Cuba to become doctors, dentists, agronomists and engineers. It refused to license the Cuban-trained doctors to practice, despite Grenada's shortage of physicians and the high standards of the Cuban medical school.

The most disliked policy of all is a new sales tax, reportedly forced on the Blaize government by USAID advisors. Replacing a progressive income tax, the new tax has raised prices and hit the poor hardest. A businessman earning $1,500 a month pays the same tax on a pair of shoes as a laborer earning $50 a month. Merchants have complained that the tax reduces sales, and the government has been unable to collect it effectively, resulting in an overall decline in revenues. The tax is one reason why the Grenadian business class, which had backed the NNP in 1984, is now deeply unhappy with the government.

Within a few years of its electoral landslide, the NNP government has achieved historic unpopularity. The Grenadian calypsonian Wizard commented in his popular calypso "The House":

Some builders went up to Union Island
Up there they drew up a construction plan
With a foreign architect
A model house they erect
On a beautiful site called Grenada
But barely two years later
We see signs of disaster
And now the whole population in awe

169

While many middle-class Grenadians still prefer the NNP to the alternatives, nobody really thinks the government is doing a good job. Blaize is laughed at, labeled senile and arrogant. The depth of rejection of Blaize is a measure in retrospect of Maurice Bishop's leadership. One person reflects: "Whether you supported or didn't support the Bishop government, when Maurice spoke, you were proud. But Blaize just hasn't got it. We have moved from a dynamic leader to one who is the total opposite."

The Political Spectrum

The NNP was a creation of the United States and remains dependent on its support. Continued financing for the party has come from the National Republican Institute for International Affairs, funded through the National Endowment for Democracy. But money has not been able to buy legitimacy or popularity for Blaize's beleaguered government.

Originally a three-party coalition, the NNP was ridden with factionalism within months of its election. In early 1987 two key ministers, George Brizan and Francis Alexis, left to form their own party. For Grenadians, the Blaize-Brizan split signaled the beginning of the end for the NNP.

Every day the walls keep cracking
I can see the pillars bending
It's like it didn't have a good foundation
Cause everyday is more erosion
It's rocking to and fro
So if a strong wind blow
Boy the house will be no more

An early member of the New Jewel Movement who quit the party before 1979, Brizan has gained some support as a younger, liberal alternative to Blaize. He has positioned himself as a centrist, claiming to be anticommunist but implying that he would restore some of the PRG's social programs. Alexis is a former exile with a right-wing background and strong U.S. ties. In November 1987 they visited Washington and met with officials at the State Department, suggesting that they would seek an accommodation with the United States in their electoral bid.

With elections due by 1990 and the NNP moribund, U.S. strategists may see Brizan as a potential solution to a difficult problem. There is a specter hanging over the electoral process: Eric Gairy, the right-wing demagogue overthrown in 1979 who made a triumphant post-invasion return to Grenada. Most Grenadians detest Gairy for his brutal and corrupt record. But he has a core of loyal followers among rural, mostly older people who remember his populist crusades of the 1950s. Although his support is unlikely to grow, he won 36% of the vote in the 1984 election, ringing alarm bells in St. George's and Washington.

U.S. officials feared then that if Gairy returned to power, it could provoke another revolution. Now, however, they appear to be hedging their bets by dealing with both Brizan and Gairy, while continuing to support the NNP. Washington's real fear is not Gairy but a future challenge from the left, which

Prime Minister Herbert Blaize.

Government of Grenada

although weakened and divided, is far from destroyed.

With a few exceptions, the top PRG leadership is dead or in prison. But many strong supporters of the revolution, who held posts in the PRG or the mass organizations, are still around. They are divided into two camps, reflecting the split in the party at the time of the revolution's collapse.

On the one hand are Bishop supporters, who blame Bernard Coard and the NJM Central Committee for the October 19 murders and destruction of the revolution. After the invasion, former ministers George Louison and Kenrick Radix formed the Maurice Bishop Patriotic Movement (MBPM). The party proposes to revive the social programs of the Bishop government. It subscribes to the ideals of socialism, but would seek to achieve it "in tune and in time with the people," according to one party leader.[4] Unlike the New Jewel Movement, which had a tightly controlled entry process, the MBPM hopes to be a mass party with a broad membership of ordinary Grenadians.

The MBPM contested the 1984 election but gained only 5% of the vote. With Louison now overseas and Radix in poor health, the party has remained a weak force. In 1988, however, Radix bowed out and 35-year-old Dr. Terry Marryshow was chosen as party leader, a move which may help to revitalize the MBPM.

The other tendency, which has no party structure, holds that Coard and the Central Committee were not solely to blame for the tragedy. They claim that Bishop too was at fault, and suggest a CIA role. Since public opinion in Grenada overwhelmingly favors Bishop, this group has kept a low profile, and has concentrated on defending those accused of Bishop's murder.

On Dec. 4, 1986, convictions were handed down against

17 of the 18 persons on trial for the murder of the PRG leadership. Fourteen were sentenced to death by hanging, including Bernard and Phyllis Coard, former minister Selwyn Strachan, former army chief Hudson Austin, trade unionist John Ventour and a number of soldiers.

The sentences capped an eight-month trial marked by numerous irregularities and an atmosphere of political theater. Pre-trial propaganda included wall posters labeling the defendents "criminals." The case was heard by a judge appointed temporarily by the government; a former member of the prosecution team chose the jury. The trial took place inside the walls of Richmond Hill Prison with U.S. helicopters flying overhead, and was financed by a $5.5 million U.S. grant. There was lengthy legal wrangling over the constitutionality of the court.[5]

Prosecutors offered strong circumstantial evidence but little direct proof that the defendents were responsible for the murders. After dismissing their attorneys in mid-trial, the defendents disrupted the court with stamping and chanting, resulting in their removal for most of the proceedings. In unsworn statements, Coard and other defendents claimed to have been framed by the United States in an effort to wipe out the revolutionary leadership. None addressed the question of who was responsible for the killings. The jury deliberated just three hours before reaching the guilty verdicts.

Doubts about the fairness of the trial, however, did little to moderate public anger at Coard. Many Grenadians expressed satisfaction with the verdicts, although others feared that the execution of 14 people would traumatize the country and harm tourism. The appeal process began in 1988.

While convinced of Coard's guilt, many Grenadians continue to view all former NJM members with distrust. Many youth and former activists who favor the Bishop government's programs have held back from supporting the Maurice Bishop Patriotic Movement, feeling that the events of October 1983 have yet to be fully explained.

Despite this negative image, Coard and Bishop supporters alike have won respect for their creative development work. The Agency for Rural Transformation, one of the few holdovers from the revolution, works with small farmers and cooperatives, channeling international aid into small-scale projects. The Grenada Community Development Agency (GRENCODA) does similar work, assisting cooperatives of women and youth. Both are run by former activists and comprise virtually the only grassroots organizing taking place.

Such work encounters many obstacles, not least of which is Grenadians' fear of joining organizations in the wake of the revolutionary debacle. Individualism has largely replaced the cooperative spirit of revolutionary Grenada. The mood is apathetic, and many people have withdrawn into a protective shell. Comments a Grenadian churchman, "Those who supported the revolution are disappointed and so are those who expected the Americans to work miracles. Nobody has gotten what they wanted."

Grenada faces a fundamental contradiction. Four years of revolution raised expectations that are not now being met. There is a widespread longing for the progressive social programs of the PRG; yet fear of the left lingers, rooted in the feelings of betrayal over the revolution's end. "People are realizing what they lost," says a former activist. "They expect much more than before. They compare the leadership now to then, and say 'we will never find another Maurice Bishop.'" ∎

Roadside sign-painting during the revolution years: Now, an awareness of what was lost.

Trinidad and Tobago

At the southern tip of the island chain, nine miles from Venezuela, lies the twin-island nation of Trinidad and Tobago. Like Jamaica, Trinidad is an economic and political leader in the anglophone Caribbean. It is a place where trends are made and broken—as in 1962, when first Jamaica's and then Trinidad's withdrawal spelled the end of the West Indies Federation. Flush with oil money in the 1970s, Trinidad became the region's wealthiest state, providing economic aid to its neighbors and much of the market for intra-regional trade.

Oil profits helped maintain the popularity of the People's National Movement (PNM), headed by the legendary Dr. Eric Williams. His death in 1981, coinciding with the collapse of oil prices, rendered the ruling party vulnerable for the first time. In 1986, after 30 years in power, the PNM suffered a massive electoral defeat. The election ended the reign of the region's longest-serving government and opened a new political era in Trinidad and Tobago.

A Cultural Crucible

Trinidad's leadership has been not only economic. Much of what outsiders think of as typically "Caribbean"—calypso, Carnival, steelband—originated in Trinidad. These vibrant popular arts have spread around the region and among Caribbean people abroad, contributing to the emergence of a West Indian regional culture.

This creativity reflects in part the unusually diverse cultural influences on Trinidad in its history. Originally a Spanish colony, Trinidad gave haven to French royalists fleeing Guadeloupe, Martinique and Haiti during the French Revolution. By the 1790s Trinidad was "a Spanish colony run by Frenchmen and worked by African slaves."[1] These cultural influences were already well established by the time Britain took over Trinidad in 1814 and annexed Tobago to it in 1889.

Trinidad and Tobago thus escaped the stifling effects of prolonged unbroken British rule.[2] In addition, the division within the ruling class between British Protestants and French Catholics allowed space for a working-class culture to develop. Trinidad became famous for its Carnival, a festival with roots in the French Mardi Gras and the black emancipation celebration called Canboulay.

The emergence of a biracial African/West Indian population set the basic social framework. After emancipation, the planters brought in hundreds of thousands of indentured laborers from India to work on the plantations. They continued after their indentureships as sugar estate workers and small cane farmers. The freed slaves meanwhile moved away from the estates to seek work in the towns.

African and Indian Trinidad developed as two worlds, separate yet interconnected. The racial split largely paralleled the division between urban and rural Trinidad, with East Indians in agriculture and blacks in urban commerce, and later, the oil sector. Tobago, however, remained rural and almost entirely black. Mistrust between the groups pervaded

Eric Williams.

Everybody's Magazine

politics and social relations, with voting along predominantly

Two developments in the twentieth century served to enlarge the Trinidadian working class and infuse North American influences into the already complex cultural scene. First was the arrival of U.S. oil companies in the 1920s to exploit oil discovered in southern Trinidad. A radical trade union movement took root in the oil fields, led by the fiery Tubal Uriah Butler. In 1937 a strike led to rioting which was put down by colonial troops. Out of the uprising came the Oilfields Workers Trade Union, which was to become the most militant union in Trinidad.

The second event was the construction of a U.S. naval base at Chaguaramas and the stationing of thousands of American soldiers at the base during World War Two. The influx of "Yankee dollars" fostered prostitution and a get-rich-quick mentality, as many Trinidadians found high-paying work servicing the base. Calypso, steelband and Carnival absorbed influences from American music, along with a Hollywood gloss.

Calypso came into its own after the war, delighting audiences with catchy tunes, ribald lyrics and flamboyant theatrics. But it had a serious side as well, as the calypsonians used satire to comment on current events from a working-class point of view. In his classic "Jean and Dinah," rising calypso star The Mighty Sparrow commented on the consequences of the war's end:

The PNM stayed in power through Williams' prestige and by appealing to the ethnic loyalties of blacks, who at first outnumbered Indians in the population. Later, when the two groups became numerically equal, the PNM's gerrymandering of electoral boundaries and cooptation of some Indian voters kept the Indian-based opposition parties from winning power. The only serious challenge to the PNM arose after the 1970 Black Power protest, when black oil unions and Indian sugar unions combined to form the United Labour Front. But the ULF split after two years, becoming predominantly Indian and losing its multi-ethnic appeal.

The Boom

In 1973, OPEC quadrupled oil prices and windfall profits surged through the Trinidadian economy. Construction, commerce and real estate boomed as petrodollars financed grandiose projects like the $100 million Caroni racetrack (complete with 700 air-conditioned stables for the horses). Traffic jams choked Port-of-Spain, fast food outlets proliferated, and new office buildings glittered amidst the grunge.

Suddenly it was a sellers' market for labor. Wages rose, and unemployment fell from 17% to 11% in ten years. Working-class families could buy cars, color televisions and video cassette recorders on credit, while middle-class Trinidadians flew to Miami on weekend shopping sprees.

"Money is not the problem," was Prime Minister Williams' famous boast. He never said what the problem was, but his government grew steadily more chaotic and corrupt. Telephones, electricity and running water functioned sporadically, reflecting an infrastructure overwhelmed by the boom and a civil service known as "horrendously inefficient, badly organized, and at top levels . . . backward and incompetent."[4] The use of jobs as patronage inflated public payrolls and caused a relaxation of workplace discipline (some public workers signed off at 10 a.m.!). Charges of corruption were deftly fielded by Williams and shrugged off by a cynical population. One government minister, Johnny O'Halloran, a close confidante of Williams, was implicated in taking a bribe from the McDonnell Douglas corporation in return for a contract to sell aircraft to the national airline. In 1983 he was accused in court of taking a kickback on the Caroni racetrack contract, and fled the country.

Trinidadians enjoyed the consumerism of the boom, which came to be jokingly called the *fete* (party). But while some profited, others suffered in the scramble to keep up with soaring prices and the pressures of a society in rapid flux. As prestige projects bid up the price of land and building materials, housing became scarce, and settlements of squatters appeared. The Mighty Sparrow voiced the anxiety in his calypso "Capitalism Gone Mad":

You have to be a millionaire
Or some kind of petty bourgeoisie
Anytime you living here in this country
You have to be a sculduggery
Making your money illicitly
To live like somebody in this country

own with
litical life
ovement.
orian, the
PNM consisted largely of black intellectuals supported by the black working class. It became a voice for West Indian nationalism by demanding that the United States return Chaguaramas to Trinidad to become the capital site for the West Indies Federation. The base was not returned until 1962, by which time the Federation had collapsed. But this struggle, together with Trinidad's relative wealth due to oil, rendered the PNM leadership resistant to capture by U.S. influence after independence in 1962.

Brilliant, arrogant and eccentric, Dr. Williams totally dominated the politics of Trinidad and Tobago during the 25 years of his rule.

Williams as ideologue, statesman and politician almost singlehandedly ran the whole show, towering over everyone else. He cultivated this situation by weeding out from his party anything and anybody who appeared to be a threat to his supremacy . . .[3]

Everybody's Magazine

The Mighty Sparrow.

It's outrageous and insane
The crazy prices here in Port of Spain . . .
Where you ever hear a television costs seven thousand dollars?
Quarter million dollars for a piece of land
A pair of sneakers two hundred dollars
Eighty to ninety thousand dollars for motor cars
At last here in Trinidad we see capitalism gone mad . . .

The Crash

"The fete is over," announced new PNM prime minister George Chambers, elected after Williams' death, "and the country must go back to work." The oil boom peaked in 1978, and by 1982 the crash was a reality. As oil prices declined, the multinationals—Texaco, Amoco and Tesoro—virtually ceased exploring for Trinidadian crude. The companies cut back on processing in their aging Trinidad refineries, preparing to pull out of the country.

Trinidadians at first refused to accept that the boom was over. Extravagant spending continued even as revenues were shrinking. By 1984, however, few people still had illusions.

> Trinidad & Tobago's standard of living, subsidized for nearly a decade by windfall oil prices, is now seriously threatened. Its foreign reserves have been halved in barely two years. In the same period it moved from a balance of payments surplus to a deficit of over TT$2 billion. The oil industry is struggling to hold production levels at two-thirds of the 1979 figures, and refining has virtually collapsed.[5]

The oil companies and their subcontractors laid off thousands of workers. Employers took advantage of the widespread fear of job loss to demand "higher productivity," wage restraint and give-backs of benefits won by unions. Between 1984 and 1986, according to a trade union group, there were 20 lockouts by major companies, but only six strikes. During the lockouts, employers would sign contracts with individual workers, bypassing the unions.[6]

At the peak of the boom, oil had provided 65% of government revenues. With this income dwindling, the Chambers government raised personal income taxes and removed many subsidies, allowing prices of food, transportation and utilities to rise. The unions argued angrily that the workers were bearing the burden of austerity while the profits of the multinationals and large Trinidadian companies remained untouched. Several companies did, however, fail as a result of the crash.

As Trinidadians tightened their belts, two lessons stood out. First, despite rhetoric about self-reliance, the government had failed to use the windfall to diversify the economy away from dependence on oil. Its major initiative, a new sector of heavy industries including iron and steel, faced depressed world markets and ended up a drain on the treasury. Productivity in other sectors had stagnated, and in agriculture it had declined.

Secondly, the government had failed to deal decisively with the multinationals. Moves to nationalize the oil industry—advocated by the Oilfields Workers Trade Union since 1937—came only after the companies' profits declined and they opted out. The government tried to keep the companies from leaving by lowering taxes and granting other concessions. This lost millions in revenues but in the end made no difference. Texaco completed its withdrawal in 1985 by selling its huge, run-down Point-a-Pierre refinery to the government, which bought it to save 2,500 jobs. A leading economist remarked wryly that it would have been cheaper to put all the workers on the dole.

Vote Dem Out

Ridiculing the Trinidadian public's tolerance for bad government, the Mighty Sparrow had sung sarcastically in 1981, "We like it so." After several years of recession this was no longer true. The drying up of oil money reduced possibilities for patronage, and made the ruling party's corruption and mismanagement stand out. As the 1986 election approached, calypsonian Deple advised:

If their policy is a fallacy
Their bureaucracy a catastrophe
If they cannot cope and you seeing so
Then your only hope is for them to go
If it is fabrications the statements they spout
When you voting—vote dem out, vote dem out.
Before they misuse out, thief out, sell out and digs out
If is you who vote dem in—vote dem out!

The PNM's vulnerability spurred the long-divided opposition finally to unite. Four parties came together to form the National Alliance for Reconstruction, headed by Tobagonian politician A.N.R. Robinson. Drawing support from all ethnic groups, and from both Trinidad and Tobago, the NAR led a crusade of moral outrage against the PNM.

The December 1986 election was a dramatic repudiation of the ruling party. The opposition swept 33 of 36 Parliamentary seats; all but two PNM ministers lost their seats, including the prime minister. As the results came in, thousands of people converged on NAR headquarters, blowing car horns and noisemakers and jamming until dawn to the victory tune, "Vote Dem Out."

The electorate expected nothing short of a miracle. The new government took some popular steps, abolishing income tax in the lowest brackets and moving to build low-cost housing. It introduced integrity legislation and released a report suppressed by the previous government which tied high PNM officials to the drug trade. But the country was nearly bankrupt. More than $3 billion in foreign exchange reserves had been nearly wiped out. Robinson could not long postpone imposing the same sort of austerity that had made the PNM unpopular, cutting civil servants' pay and introducing other belt-tightening measures. Public goodwill turned to impatience, then to disillusionment.

As a coalition of four parties, the NAR had drawn together their disparate constituencies: Africans, Indians and

Oilfields Workers Trade Union leads May Day march through Port-of-Spain. Tubal Uriah Butler, with white beard, waves from truck.

whites; workers and intellectuals; big business and militant unions. Their conflicting interests had been masked by a shared desire to oust the PNM. Now this marriage of convenience began to unravel. Unions, furious about pay cuts, charged the government with being anti-labor. Tensions grew between the party's pro-labor wing, led by former United Labor Front leader Basdeo Panday, and its pro-business wing, led by industry minister Ken Gordon, publisher of the powerful *Trinidad Express*.

The tension soon erupted into a full-blown rift as the NAR fragmented into its constituent parts. Ex-ULF ministers led by Panday charged that Robinson and his inner circle were refusing to share power. They charged that Robinson had failed to dismantle the PNM-dominated bureaucracy, and that figures from the old regime remained in key positions. Most upsetting to many Trinidadians were the racial overtones of the conflict between the black leaders around Robinson and Panday's Indian faction. When Robinson responded by dismissing the four dissident ministers, a stunned nation

questioned openly how long the ruling party would last.

The descent into factionalism came against a backdrop of continued economic decline. Unemployment has reached 20%, and real wages are falling. The government is pursuing an economic strategy similar to that of other countries in the region, emphasizing foreign borrowing, investment and privatization. The prime minister has toured the United States and Canada to solicit investors, and plans to establish Trinidad's first free trade zone. Trinidad has the infrastructure needed by industry, but wages are high compared to elsewhere in the region. And runaway shops seeking docile unions will not find them in Trinidad.

The NAR seems unlikely to last long, at least not in its original configuration. But its election was a turning point for the people of Trinidad and Tobago, symbolizing deep discontent with the old politics of racial division, arrogant authority and moral corruption. That discontent, and hopes for a responsive, genuinely multi-racial government, have set the agenda for the next decade. ■

175

Guyana

Guyana is a country with vast reserves of natural wealth. Larger than the rest of the English-speaking Caribbean put together, it sprawls across 83,000 square miles of the South American coast, rich with bauxite, manganese, diamonds, gold, timber, sugar and rice. Yet this nation of barely 700,000 people is destitute. Under the fraudulent rule of the People's National Congress, Guyana has slipped backward for the last twenty years to become the most impoverished Caribbean country after Haiti.[1]

No roads connect the jungle hinterland to the narrow strip of coast where 90% of the population lives. All travel to the interior is by air or river boat. The Amerindians who live there seldom visit the coast, but cross frequently into border areas of Brazil and Venezuela. They live neglected, prey to malaria and exploitation by the gold diggers and diamond miners who roam the country.

Along the coast, the population clings in a narrow ribbon of settlement along the country's two main roads, one skirting the coast and the other leading to the bauxite mining enclave. African and East Indian villages alternate, contiguous but distinct. Tattered red, pink and white prayer flags on bamboo poles announce the homes of Hindu faithful. The houses are shabby, and many of the rice fields lie fallow. Here and there abandoned dwellings stand as testimony to emigration's toll.

In Georgetown, once-ornate colonial buildings are crumbling, their gingerbread facades faded. Garbage is piled high in the streets. A fetid swampiness hangs over the city, which is built below sea level and drained by canals now choked with weeds and silt. Everything seems in a state of decay. In March 1988, the Demerara Harbor Bridge linking the two sides of the capital collapsed into the river with a shuddering crash. For Guyanese, there could be no more apt symbol of the nation's plight.

The Burnham Dictatorship

After the United States and Britain destabilized Cheddi Jagan's government in the 1960s [see Part II, Ch. 2], they maneuvered Forbes Burnham into power as an Anglo-American client. Burnham's People's National Congress (PNC) initially enjoyed support from Afro-Guyanese who wanted to keep Indo-Guyanese led by Jagan from returning to power. This racial support continued, but on a diminishing basis, prompting Burnham to turn to fraud and intimidation to stay in power.

"The Burnham dictatorship crept up on the Guyanese people like a thief in the night," wrote Guyanese historian Walter Rodney.[2] Guyana maintained the trappings of Westminster democracy: a Constitution, opposition parties, regular elections, a National Assembly. But the ruling PNC subverted and manipulated the entire system. Elections in 1968, 1973 and 1980 were all flagrantly rigged. In 1973, the army seized the ballot boxes when an early count seemed headed against Burnham. Burnham rewrote the Constitution over massive

Guyanese soldiers seizing ballot boxes in 1973 election.

opposition in 1978 to make himself "executive president" with sweeping powers. A team of international observers denounced the 1980 election as "a clumsily managed and blatant fraud."[3]

A doctrine known as "paramountcy of the party" gave ideological form to the dictatorship. The People's National Congress became supreme over all state functions, including the police, the army, the schools and the courts. An office was established with a dual identity: Ministry of National Development and Office of the PNC General Secretary. It became the main executor of the paramountcy doctrine and a conduit for taxpayer monies to flow into party coffers.

The second pillar of PNC rule was control of the economy. Although Burnham had been installed as an alternative to Jagan's socialism, in 1970 he suddenly declared Guyana a "Cooperative Republic" in transition to socialism. He purchased the two foreign bauxite companies, subsidiaries of the Canadian Alcan and the U.S.-based Reynolds. The sugar industry, owned by the British multinational Bookers, was also nationalized. By 1976 Burnham boasted that the state controlled 80% of the economy.

This new thrust was key to the consolidation of the PNC's power. The ruling party treated the nationalized industries as its own property, including all the workers employed in them.

By directly controlling the employment of 80% of the work-force, the PNC could blackmail the population into a show of loyalty.

There was another reason as well for the leftward turn. Alone among the English-speaking Caribbean countries, Guyana had a tradition of mass support for anti-colonial and socialist leadership. This developed in the 1950s under the PPP, the first freely-elected Marxist party in the region.[4] It was reinforced in the 1970s with the emergence of the Working People's Alliance (WPA), a small, multi-racial party built around the leadership of Walter Rodney. Burnham's turn left responded in part to the opposition parties' challenge, allowing him to portray himself as a Third World nationalist and socialist.

Intimidation was the third leg of PNC control. In addition to the police and the army, Burnham created an array of paramilitary and intelligence units, including the People's Militia, the Guyana National Service, and the Young Socialist Movement, or PNC youth arm. A cult known as the House of Israel, headed by black American fugitive Rabbi Washington, functioned as a private army for the regime. Burnham also invited California cult leader Jim Jones to Guyana to set up his "People's Temple" commune, which maintained links with the government through the Ministry of National Development.[5]

Burnham's persecution of his opponents was personalistic and vindictive, and included physical harassment and even assassination. More often, however, victimization was cloaked in a bogus legality made possible by political control of the courts and legislature. WPA and PPP activists were followed and subjected to physical searches at the airport when they entered or left the country. PNC or House of Israel thugs would violently attack party meetings. In 1980, WPA leader Walter Rodney was killed by a bomb concealed in a two-way radio given to him by a member of the Guyana Defense Force. The murder was universally blamed on the Burnham regime, although the government never admitted guilt.

The independent media and the churches were targets as well. The government took control of the only daily paper, the *Chronicle,* and both radio stations. Others, including the WPA and PPP party organs, were curbed by refusing them licenses to import newsprint. The government reserved the harshest treatment for the Catholic Church paper, the *Catholic Standard,* which frequently criticized the regime. Burnham and high PNC officials brought a string of specious libel suits against the paper, claiming that criticism of government policies constituted the criminal libel of officials. In 1979

President Forbes Burnham reviews troops of the Guyana Defense Force.

Guyana Ministry of Information

House of Israel thugs murdered a *Catholic Standard* photographer, Fr. Bernard Darke, as he photographed an opposition demonstration.

The regime in Guyana became the suppressed shame of the Commonwealth Caribbean, a subject few regional leaders wished to pursue in depth. In addition to the electoral facade, Burnham used a progressive foreign policy as a smokescreen for domestic repression. His government supported Nicaragua, opposed the invasion of Grenada, had warm relations with Cuba and spoke out against apartheid. Relations deteriorated with the United States as a result of this posture. But the presence of the pro-Soviet PPP as the principal opposition party provided Burnham with insurance that neither the western powers, nor most Caribbean governments, would ever seriously challenge his rule.

Economic Collapse and Labor's Challenge

Since the mid-1970s the Guyanese economy has been in deep crisis. In 1987 real per capita income was less than it had been in 1970. Production in the three major sectors of sugar, bauxite and rice has declined steadily, despite the availability of markets for Guyana's rice and special high-grade bauxite.[6]

The major reason, according to Guyanese economist Clive Thomas, is corruption and mismanagement in the running of state industries, which have been run for the private benefit of a ruling clique. This pseudo-socialism has brought an array of related problems. Like the harbor bridge, the entire productive system is severely run down, lacking basic maintenance and parts. Large-scale emigration has robbed the country of skilled workers, technicians and managers.[7]

Socialism in Guyana began and ended with nationalizations. Rather than building socialism in a planned fashion, Burnham's economic policies vacillated widely. In 1978 the government laid aside its anti-imperialist rhetoric and turned to the International Monetary Fund for a loan. IMF conditions led to layoffs and reductions in real wages, but Guyana was still unable to meet performance targets. In 1982 Burnham began rejecting the IMF's conditions, and the Fund suspended Guyana's eligibility for loans.

To conserve foreign exchange, the government banned or restricted the import of over 100 items. Incredibly, the bans included many essential foodstuffs, including bread, milk and split peas, all staple foods of the poor. It became a crime to possess bread or any other food made from wheat. Police made armed raids on bakeries, extorting protection money from bakers and seizing "illegal" baked goods.

By 1983 items in shortage or available only on the black market included bread, milk, margarine, salt, onions, cheese, cooking oil, split peas, cooking gas, soap, toilet paper, toothpaste, matches, tires, batteries and light bulbs. A pound of chicken on the black market cost G$15, a sum equal to the daily minimum wage. A 5 lb. tin of powdered milk at G$120 exceeded the weekly earnings of an average worker. White rice became the basic diet for many, leading to widespread malnutrition. In 1983 the Georgetown hospital admitted 141 persons suffering from beri-beri (thiamine deficiency disease) linked to a diet of rice.[8]

This suffering led to the first significant multi-racial resistance to the regime. It was centered in the Trade Union Congress (TUC), long controlled by the PNC through rigged union elections. Within the TUC, the Afro-Guyanese bauxite unions were a PNC stronghold, while the predominantly Indo-Guyanese sugar unions led a minority opposing PNC control.

In 1979 the government had reneged on its agreed minimum wage, breaching its contract with the TUC. The unions took it to court and won a favorable ruling in 1983. But Burnham went to the PNC-dominated National Assembly and railroaded through a "Labour Amendment Bill" which nullified the court decision.

Following this struggle with the government, the bauxite unions joined the independent bloc, creating the first multi-racial worker unity since the 1950s. Bauxite workers striking under the slogan "No Food, No Work" were supported by sugar workers in sympathy strikes. A "Sugar and Bauxite Workers Unity Committee," organized by the WPA, symbolized cooperation between workers from the two racial groups.

At the TUC's annual conference in 1984, delegates voting by secret ballot swept away Burnham operatives from the TUC leadership. The shattering of Burnham's control over the TUC was hailed as the possible harbinger of change. But the government struck back, threatening the life of TUC president George Daniels. Trumped-up charges were brought against members of the rebel unions. In 1986, the TUC executive fell once more under PNC control.

Although the sugar and bauxite unions continued as part of an independent labor bloc, the dynamic multi-racial unity of 1983-84 faded. The division of the working class along racial lines continued as an entrenched obstacle to change. So too, to a lesser extent, did rivalry between the main opposition parties. With its large, well-organized Indo-Guyanese base, the PPP took a dim view of the WPA's organizing in the sugar sector. Conflicting tactics also damaged relations between 1980 and 1985. The WPA advocated an electoral boycott, while the PPP contested elections and participated in a dialogue with the PNC.

Guyana After Burnham

On August 6, 1985, Forbes Burnham died unexpectedly following throat surgery at Georgetown Public Hospital. He was succeeded by Desmond Hoyte as president and Hamilton Greene as prime minister, both hard-line advocates of PNC paramountcy. Burnham's death nonetheless raised hopes for change, focusing on the national election slated for December 1985. In response to pressure, Hoyte cleaned up some aspects of the voting process. But the army was again permitted to "safeguard" the ballot boxes during the time between the closing of the polls and the counting of the ballots. A statement by Guyanese church and civic leaders noted that . . .

. . . the familiar and sordid catalogue of widespread disenfranchisement, multiple voting, ejection of polling agents, threats, intimidation, violence and collusion by police and army personnel characterized the poll.[9]

Karen de Souza

Members of the "Red Thread" women's development project, a multi-racial group.

When the results were finally announced, the PNC had enlarged its majority in the National Assembly to 78% of the seats. But the WPA, running for the first time, was allowed to win one seat, joining the PPP in opposition on the Assembly floor.

The election signalled the continuation of the Burnham system without Burnham. Within this framework, however, Hoyte has pursued policies of his own, including a so-called *glasnost* designed to improve the government's image. This has been a welcome relief to Guyanese. But the change is more of style than substance, and it has been strictly limited so as not to threaten PNC rule.

Guyana since Burnham's death is a more relaxed place. Police violence has decreased, and opposition parties have been permitted to operate relatively freely. The notorious Rabbi Washington has been jailed for murder. But surveillance of opposition parties continues, and small incidents have served as reminders that nothing can be taken for granted. In 1987, police roughly broke up a peaceful gathering marking the end of a fast by WPA parliamentarian Eusi Kwayana. The Guyana Human Rights Association cautioned that the new liberties depended on "moods and circumstances" rather than on the protection of law.[10]

There is more freedom for the media, but here too glasnost has its limits. The PPP and the *Catholic Standard* have been allowed to import printing presses. A new news-paper, the *Stabroek News,* has begun publishing. But persons giving information to the independent media are still vic-timized, and libel suits are being used more than ever. Since Burnham's death, two libel judgments against the *Catholic Standard* have resulted in hundreds of thousands of dollars in fines, and more suits are upcoming.

Hoyte's liberalization is directly linked to his second major policy shift: a rapprochement with the United States and the International Monetary Fund. U.S. officials attended Burnham's funeral and held discussions with Hoyte, who hopes for major aid from Washington and an IMF loan. Such a bailout, Hoyte believes, is the only solution for Guyana. He also sees closer U.S. ties as bolstering his weak position within the ruling party.

Accordingly, the government has announced with much fanfare an open door to foreign investors and tourists. It is speaking of privatization; "socialism" and "imperialism" are no longer mentioned. But while Washington has responded positively, contradictions underlie the new rhetoric. The PNC cannot relinquish state control over the economy without giving up its base of political control. To privatize state industries would remove both the basis for PNC corruption and its source of power over the workers.

In addition, industrialists and tourists are unlikely to tolerate the conditions Guyanese endure. Even a minimum wage equal to barely US$1.00 per day cannot make up for a decaying infrastructure where power outages are constant and water is unfit to drink.

The economic crisis, meanwhile, only gets worse. Hoyte reversed Burnham's most hated policy, the ban on wheat. But while food is in somewhat better supply, it is so expensive that widespread hunger continues. The standard wage in 1988 was G$23.75 per day. But a small can of corned beef cost G$35, a pint of split peas G$14, a pound of margarine G$28, and a pound of chicken G$30. A pair of shoes costs up to G$750.

These prices reflect the fact that most goods are purchased abroad in foreign currencies against which the Guyana dollar is severely devalued. The official exchange rate in 1988 was G$10 = US$1. But in the banks, the U.S. dollar was trading at 21 to 1, and on the flourishing currency black market—known as "Wall Street" in Georgetown—at 30 to 1. The huge black market for both goods and currency is the most vibrant sector of the economy.

For most Guyanese, only gifts of foreign currency from relatives abroad permit a standard of living above the most crude subsistence. This fact has contributed to a staggering emigration rate, reaching 1,500 a month to the U.S. alone, not counting the large flows to Canada and the Caribbean.[11] This exodus of talent and vitality has become perhaps the most serious obstacle of all to economic recovery and political change. Organizing has become very difficult as young Guyanese choose to emigrate rather than stay and fight.

Emigration is one symptom of a general demoralization which has weakened the ability of the opposition parties to mount an effective challenge. This is so despite the presently good relations between the PPP and WPA, which have joined with three other small parties in a "Patriotic Coalition for Democracy." The WPA and PPP support each others' motions in the National Assembly, raising a vocal opposition to the parliamentary charade.

There is common ground between the two parties, both of which come out of a radical social-democratic tradition. But differences remain. In the view of the PPP leadership, "democracy alone is not enough." The opposition must have a definite program for socialist construction, linked to political democracy.[12] The WPA counters that "Guyana is in no position to go forward to socialism" now. Rather, the immediate goal should be to build a multi-racial democracy in which the Guyanese working people can decide what form future development should take.[13]

For both parties and for many Caribbean observers, however, these differing positions do not obscure basic lessons to be drawn from Guyana's experience. The first is that socialism is not merely an economic system, but a political and class concept. Nationalizations do not equal socialism, although they may be a step toward it. Only when state-owned property produces for the benefit of the whole society, rather than for a small clique, can genuine socialism be achieved.

The second lesson is that Guyana's economic problems cannot be solved in the absence of a political transformation. For most Guyanese this must begin with free, fair elections, possibly under international supervision, to install a government with legitimacy. It is possible that no single party can achieve that legitimacy, at least in the short term, and that some form of multi-racial "unity" government could emerge. But such developments must await the decision of the present rulers to step aside and let democracy take its course. ■

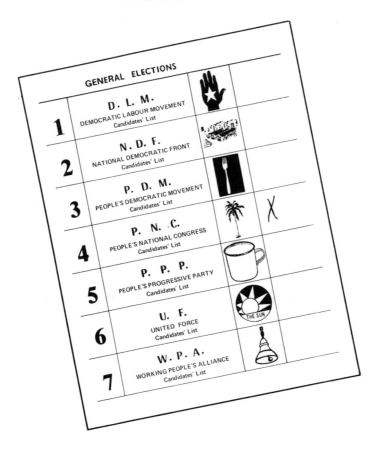

180

Suriname

Until 1980 Suriname was little known within the Caribbean. Tied to the region by its history of sugar and slavery, it is cut off by its location on mainland South America. Yet links to Latin America are even weaker, due in large part to the fact that Suriname speaks Dutch. Suriname's jungle hinterland, blending into the Brazilian rain forest, walls off the coastal enclave from the continent. Their backs to Latin America, Surinamers have always looked outward—across the Atlantic Ocean to Holland.

When junior army officers staged a whirlwind coup in 1980, Suriname was thrust suddenly to prominence. Regional attention to events in Paramaribo paralleled a growing Surinamese orientation toward the Caribbean. Rechristening the coup a "revolution," the Bouterse regime sought to reduce dependency on Holland and build ties to the Caribbean left.

Growing pressures on the regime from inside and outside the country largely ended Suriname's isolation. The powers which conspired to unseat Bouterse included Holland, the United States, and next-door neighbors Brazil and France (the latter through its colony French Guiana). Lacking a strong popular base, and fatally undercut by the loss of Dutch aid, the regime capitulated. The "old politicians" from the pre-coup era are back in power. But the legacy of Suriname's closer integration with the Caribbean is likely to endure.

Dutch Dependency and the "Old Politics"

Suriname before the coup appeared an unlikely candidate for revolution. Ethnically divided, with little nationalist tradition, it experienced no nation-building anti-colonial struggle. Dutch development aid ensured a comfortable living standard, and the affluent colony accepted formal independence reluctantly.

Colonialism produced in Suriname a unique ethnic tapestry. After taking over in 1667, the Dutch set up coastal sugar plantations worked by African slaves. But many slaves escaped to the jungle hinterland to wage war against the Dutch. Isolated in remote villages, these *Bosnegers* or Bush Negroes preserved many aspects of African culture.[1]

After emancipation, the planters brought in thousands of contract laborers from India, Indonesia and China. The population became divided into four major groups. East Indians, called "Hindustani" in Suriname, comprise about 37%. Creoles or urban blacks make up 31%; Indonesians, called "Javanese," 15%; and the Bush Negroes 10%. Smaller minorities include Amerindians, Chinese and Europeans.

Linguistic and religious differences reinforced ethnic separation. In addition to Dutch, the official language, the East Indians and Indonesians speak Hindi and Javanese, while the Creoles speak a language called Sranan Tongo which has become a lingua franca for all the groups. The Asian groups retained their Hindu and Muslim faiths, so Roman Catholic and Moravian missionaries built a following mainly among Creoles.

Sargeant Desi Bouterse

Suriname National Information Service

With the decline of sugar, bauxite mining became the main industry during World War Two. It was controlled by two multinationals, the U.S.-based Alcoa and the Dutch Billiton, a subsidiary of Royal Dutch Shell. The political parties formed in the post-war period reflected this foreign dependence as well as the strength of ethnic rivalries. Their leaders included merchants and managers for the multinationals, who used patronage and ethnic loyalties to mobilize voters. The National Party of Suriname (NPS) drew its support from Creoles, the United Hindu Party (VHP) from East Indians and the Indonesian Peasants' Party (KTPI) from Indonesians.

In the 1950s and '60s, Creole intellectuals led by lawyer Eddy Bruma and poet Robin "Dobru" Ravales promoted a cultural nationalist movement called *Wi Egi Sani* (Our Own Thing). It emphasized the role of Sranan Tongo as a national language. An associated party, the Party for a Nationalist Republic, advocated independence from Holland. But neither made significant inroads into the non-Creole population.[2]

Holland, however, wanted to rid itself of its colonial burden, and in 1975 Suriname became independent. Ethnic tensions rose as many East Indians emigrated, fearing independence under Creole rule. Holland retained a major say in Suriname's development policies through a "golden handshake" of $1.5 billion, to be disbursed over 15 years.

Dissatisfaction grew rapidly in the years following independence. The NPS government led by Henk Arron was corrupt and incompetent, frittering away Dutch aid while social security and pension payments fell years in arrears. Unemployment was high, and a feeling of stagnation overtook the society. Tens of thousands of Surinamers rushed to emigrate to Holland before the scheduled closing of the immigration door in 1980.

The Sargeants' Coup

Although plans for a coup had been afoot for some time, the trigger was the government's refusal to recognize a military union set up by non-commissioned officers in early 1980. Three union leaders were court-martialled. Shortly before their sentencing, on February 25, 1980, Sargeant Desi Bouterse led a coup which overthrew the government.

The coup was enormously popular. Ninety percent of the population rejoiced at the fall of the despised Arron government. With ties to Bruma's nationalists, the young soldiers enjoyed support from trade unions and other popular organizations.

Popularity, however, could not make up for the fact that no political party or other organized structure linked the military to the people. A faction led by sargeants Badrissein Sital and Chas Mijnals had ties to the left-wing People's Party. But their influence was limited, and the military leadership as a whole lacked a political vision. The sargeants, it was later said, "wanted a union and got a country."

The military embarked on a search for effective political structures which was to take the country on an ideological roller coaster ride. Seven civilian cabinets came and went, while the military essentially ruled by decree. Lacking an organized base, the regime became obsessed with threats from counter-coups and destabilization. In defense, it imposed repressive measures including a curfew, press censorship and a ban on political meetings, eroding its initial popularity.

The first swing occurred in August 1980 when Sital and Mijnals, along with five leftist activists, were arrested and charged with conspiring against the regime. Although Bouterse implied that those arrested were too close to Cuba, most people saw the move as an attempt to consolidate his personal power. Whatever the reason, in March 1981 all seven were suddenly released, and Bouterse startled the nation by announcing that Suriname had embarked upon a socialist revolution.

"June 30 Day of Embracement— One Revolution, One People— Unite All Forces."

The Reluctant Revolution

"The military was a blank slate and everyone wanted to write on it," was how one former activist described the role of progressive forces in the Bouterse government. The period 1981-1983 was a time of relatively strong leftist influence, during which the regime carried out its most lasting achievements.

Several small, multi-racial parties had emerged during the 1970s, their members mostly intellectuals returning from studies in Holland. Two of them, the Progressive Union of Workers and Peasants (PALU) and the Revolutionary People's Party (RVP)—a splinter of the People's Party—helped draft programs for the Bouterse government after March 1981. Although somewhat wary of the military, the activists nonetheless saw the potential for a popular revolution. "We hoped the shortcomings could be overcome and that the military would develop politically under the influence of a strong mass movement," one RVP member recalls.

The regime had begun shortly after the coup to enact reforms, including the prompt payment of pensions and other social benefits. It went on to construct a functioning welfare state, in which, for the first time, the needs of the poor were given priority without ethnic favoritism. Measures put in place or upgraded included public assistance to poor families, old-age pensions and medical insurance for civil servants. The government improved drinking water, sanitation and electricity systems and built roads and bridges. It constructed 3,500 low-cost houses in three years, more than had been built in the previous three decades.

A major concern of the progressives was the weaning of the country from excessive dependence on foreign capital and aid. Toward this end, a new agency called INDEX helped local entrepreneurs set up some 150 enterprises in agriculture, fisheries and other sectors.[3] But the government never defined an economic policy clearly. The holdings of the multinationals were never touched, nor were there attempts to socialize other parts of the economy.

While the reforms followed no single model, many resembled aspects of the revolutionary process in Cuba and, especially, Grenada. Under the influence of the Surinamese

left, relations were upgraded with both countries while those with Holland deteriorated. In May 1981 the 12-man Dutch military mission was expelled, and shortly afterward Cuba was invited to open a diplomatic mission in Paramaribo. In July of that year Surinamese leaders attended a regional meeting of the Socialist International in Grenada, and Grenadian foreign minister Unison Whiteman visited Suriname in August. Planning began for a visit by Grenadian prime minister Maurice Bishop.

Bouterse clearly was influenced by the example of Grenada and by his friendship with Bishop. Above all, he yearned for the kind of popularity Bishop enjoyed. Surinamese leftists, especially the RVP, urged the military to create structures of mass participation that could lead to the formation of a popular base. But it never really worked. Some 150 "people's committees" were set up throughout the country and initially spurred participation. But they remained cut off from real decision-making, and came to be seen as tools of the regime. An attempt to form a civilian "revolutionary front" at the end of 1981 was short-lived. Later, in 1984, the military tried once more to construct a mass base for its rule. Called the February 25 Movement, it became the equivalent of a political party supporting the military. By then, however, it was too late: the regime had alienated most of the population, and the potential for revolution was lost.

Counter-Revolution and Collapse

Had there been no destabilization, it is possible that efforts at mobilization might in time have born fruit. As it was, the emergence of organized internal and external opposition during 1982 drew the regime into a repressive rule that sealed its unpopularity. In February the final split took place between Bouterse and the civilian president, Dr. Henk Chin-a-Sen, who made his way to Holland and emerged as a principal opponent of the regime. In March the government crushed a coup attempt by renegade officers and executed a ringleader, Sgt. Wilfred Hawker.

Chin-a-Sen's resignation and the execution of Hawker were pivotal in turning middle-class Surinamers, already nervous about the swing to the left, against the regime. The Committee of Christian Churches, business groups and other sectors increasingly protested the failure to return to civilian rule. While this movement gained its own momentum, events also suggested external involvement. The main actor was the Moederbond labor federation, whose leader, Cyriel Daal, had been trained by the American Institute for Free Labor Development and was considered close to the U.S. Embassy. Daal chose the occasion of an October visit by Prime Minister Bishop of Grenada to mount his challenge. The Moederbond called a strike of air traffic controllers which nearly prevented Bishop's plane from landing. Daal was arrested, and other strikes followed:

Owing to a strike at the electrical company, Bouterse suffered the humiliation of having to receive his friend Bishop by candlelight, precisely at the time he had hoped to show his counterpart the achievements of Suriname's revolution . . . The

strike[s] would be rounded off with a mass meeting on Sunday, October 30, precisely at the moment when Bouterse and Bishop were to hold a joint rally at another location in Paramaribo. On that day, 15,000 demonstrators rallied to Daal's side, while no more than 1,500 people attended Bouterse's and Bishop's rally. One could scarcely imagine a more forceful challenge for Bouterse.[4]

The next month all four labor federations, backed by religious, professional and industry groups, presented Bouterse with a 4-step democratization plan. The government rejected the proposal.

On Dec. 8, 1982, fifteen opposition leaders were rousted from their beds, taken to military headquarters and executed. The victims included Moederbond leader Daal, five prominent lawyers, among them the president of the bar association, a university professor, several journalists and a former cabinet minister.

The killings stunned the nation. The government argued heatedly that its action had prevented a counter-coup by "agents of imperialism." Several months later the U.S. press revealed that President Reagan had approved a plan to topple the Bouterse government, but that it had been shelved. But the military's explanation did little to counter the growing panic among Surinamers. Many members of the elite fled to Holland, where they began working with the Dutch media to discredit the regime.

Holland suspended its $100 million a year development aid, which had contributed more than 10% of the gross national product. Together with falling bauxite revenues, the aid cut-off plunged the country into economic crisis. Shortages developed, prices increased five and six-fold, and many necessities became available only on the black market. The Dutch government made clear that its aid would only be resumed when Bouterse left office.

Brazil, meanwhile, acting at the United States' urging, told Bouterse that it would no longer tolerate Cuban influence in Suriname.[5] A Brazilian general visited Paramaribo to offer arms sales in exchange for expelling the Cubans, and the U.S. Embassy in Paramaribo reinforced the message. On October 25, 1983, the day the United States invaded Grenada, the Bouterse government summarily expelled the Cubans.

This abrupt reversal marked the first of many as Bouterse began a desperate bid for survival. After a rash of wildcat strikes in December 1983, he dismissed the cabinet, ending the period of left-wing influence. Bouterse now turned to the only forces who could help him. He invited representatives of industry and labor to join the military in a new cabinet. In 1985, the government signed a pact with leaders of the "old" political parties, providing for a return to constitutional rule.

Opponents of the regime were taking no chances, however. In July 1986 a guerrilla war broke out in eastern Suriname. Led by former soldier Ronnie Brunswyke, a Bosneger, the insurgency was partly fueled by the traditional grievances of the Bush Negroes and by Brunswyke's personal grudge. But Brunswyke's open alliance with Chin-a-Sen left no doubt that exile groups were backing the rebels, with the probable complicity of the Dutch government. France, for its part, allowed the rebels to use neighboring French Guiana as a base of operations. The rebels attacked key bauxite installations, shutting down the Alcoa mine and smelter and causing production to plummet.

The rest of the population did not support the insurgency, which the government denounced as the "Dutch dirty war." But as the army pursued the rebels in the bush, alleged atrocities further tarnished the regime's image. Reports circulated of massacres by the army in Bush Negro villages, prompting investigations by international agencies. Some 10,000 refugees, mostly Bush Negroes, fled across the border to French Guiana.

The Civilians Try Again

Under a new Constitution approved by referendum, an election for a National Assembly was held in Suriname on November 25, 1987. The "Front," a coalition of the three old parties, decisively defeated the military, which formed its own party to run. Businessman Ramsewak Shankar was inaugurated as president in early 1988.

International observer teams unanimously praised the election as free and fair. Caribbean observers, reeling from the shock of Haiti's bloody election, noted with amazement that the Surinamese army had organized free elections and allowed itself to lose.[6] Amid the atmosphere of relief in Paramaribo, however, many questions remained. An urgent one was the future of the bush war. The rebels have presumably lost the support of the Dutch and French governments, but the intentions of the exile groups remained unclear as negotiations

began for a ceasefire.

The larger unknown concerns the new government. With the pre-coup leaders back in power—Henk Arron is now vice-president—the risk exists that the government will fall back into the old patterns of corruption and ethnic polarization. Surinamers are counting on the Front to end the economic crisis, and the expected resumption of Dutch aid should bring some relief. But the low price of bauxite and economic damage from the war mean that Suriname cannot return soon, if at all, to the affluent consumption levels of the past. If recovery lags, disillusionment could be rapid.

A final question concerns the military's role. Few observers expect Bouterse to give up power completely. The new Surinamese Constitution allows the army a political role through participation in a State Council and Security Council. What this will mean in practice is still unclear.

While few visible traces of Suriname's "revolution" remain, it is still unlikely that the country can revert fully to the pre-1980 status quo. "In eight years of revolution, although it was not as you would have wanted, still people have undergone development you cannot erase," commented one Surinamer. Despite popular rejection of the Bouterse regime, its progressive initiatives fostered an awareness of Suriname's need to develop a self-reliant economy. Holland's heavy-handed interference aroused new anti-colonial sentiments, even among many people who opposed the military. Although ties to Holland remain, Surinamers now realize that their country must find its own way within a Caribbean and Third World context. ∎

President Ramsewak Shankar speaking to the National Assembly in March 1988. On his right is vice-president Henk Arron and on his left minister Willy Soemita, leaders of the "Front" coalition.

Suriname National Information Service

The Last Colonies' Dilemma

While most of the region struggles with a neocolonial independence, the problem for several territories is more basic. They are colonies, aberrations in an age when most of the Caribbean has achieved political independence. Their continuing ties to Europe and the United States keep the last colonies isolated economically, culturally and politically from the rest of the Caribbean.

For the people of these territories, the question of whether to push for independence is a complex dilemma. The economic crisis affecting the region is a major deterrent: colonial subsidies buffer the impact of the crisis and keep living standards artificially high. Opponents of independence argue that the loss of these subsidies would leave the colonies "as poor as the rest of the Caribbean."

Independence advocates argue that it is precisely this dependence which stands in the way of economic development. Without the subsidies, they say, life will be harder for a while, but the country will have a chance to develop its own potential. And severing the colonial link is essential if a people is to achieve nationhood and preserve its culture.

Four western powers maintain colonies in the region: Britain, France, Holland and the United States. The British dependencies include Bermuda, historically linked to the Caribbean although located in the Atlantic; Montserrat; the British Virgin Islands; the Cayman Islands; the Turks & Caicos; and Anguilla. All are extremely small, and independence has scarcely been an issue during most of their history. But Britain would like to rid itself of its lingering colonial burden, and for Bermuda and Montserrat at least, a break may be inevitable.

France, by contrast, is determined to keep its Caribbean possessions. The French Antilles consist of Guadeloupe and Martinique, along with Guadeloupe's small dependencies: St. Barthelemy, Marie-Galant, Desirade, Ile des Saintes, and St. Martin (half of an island shared with Holland). French Guiana, sometimes called Cayenne, is a much larger territory on the South American mainland. Technically they are not colonies but overseas provinces of France, equal in status to the 95 departments of continental France.

Holland's Caribbean possessions consist of six islands. Aruba, Bonaire and Curacao are located off the coast of Venezuela. The smaller islands of St. Eustatius, Saba and St. Maarten (the Dutch half) are part of the Leeward Island chain. But they are known as the Dutch Windwards since they lie to the east or windward side of the other three. The Netherlands Antilles was a six-island federation until 1986; in that year, Aruba seceded from the group and established a separate colonial link to Holland.

Officially, Puerto Rico is a "state in free association" with the United States, an arrangement known as Commonwealth. But the reality is inescapably colonial. The Island is part of the United States in terms of its defense, legal and judicial system, immigration, customs, currency and mails. Puerto Ricans are U.S. citizens, and vote in U.S. presidential primaries. But they cannot vote in presidential elections, and the Island's representative to the U.S. Congress votes only in committee.

Since the American takeover in 1898, Puerto Rican politics have revolved around the question of the Island's relationship to the United States. The major political parties on the Island are distinguished by the political "status" they favor: independence, statehood or continued Commonwealth status. All agree, however, that the Island's present situation is colonial. The Decolonization Committee of the United Nations has called repeatedly for Puerto Rican self-determination.

Finally, the U.S. Virgin Islands are an "unincorporated territory" of the United States, like Guam and American Samoa. Consisting of St. Thomas, St. Croix and St. John, they are internally self-governing but subject to most U.S. laws. Like Puerto Ricans, Virgin Islanders are citizens but have only non-voting representation in the U.S. Congress. ■

Guadeloupe

Arriving in Pointe-à-Pitre from the English-speaking Caribbean, one has the sensation of entering a different world. Store shelves overflow with French clothing and housewares. Newspapers inform on the latest news and weather in Paris. Although Guadeloupe is a Caribbean island, places like Trinidad and Jamaica seem alien and remote. The center of the Guadeloupean universe is France.

The superimposition of French consumer culture on a West Indian island has produced ironic contrasts. Daily flights bring in fresh fruits and vegetables from Europe while fertile lands lie idle. Magazines like *Belle Maison* (House Beautiful) and *La Voiture Individuelle* (The Personal Automobile) mock the reality of unemployment. Guadeloupeans—who are mostly of African descent—speak not of France but of *la métropole.* It is easier to telephone across the Atlantic Ocean to *la métropole* than to call Dominica, 30 miles away.

Yet Guadeloupe and its sister island, Martinique, are linked to their Caribbean neighbors by a common history. The same African peoples provided the labor force for sugar plantations on the French and British islands. Today, Guadeloupeans and Martiniquans speak a French Creole that is nearly identical to that spoken in St. Lucia and Dominica, and differs only slightly from Haitian *Kreyol.* Indigenous drum music called *gwoka* recalls a hidden African past.

The paths of the French and British islands diverged in the 20th century. While Britain's colonies moved toward independence, France "decolonized" its empire in the opposite manner, by making the colonies part of France. In 1946 Guadeloupe, Martinique, French Guiana, and the island of Réunion in the Indian Ocean became French "overseas departments" or provinces. People born in the overseas departments hold French citizenship, vote in French elections and elect representatives to the National Assembly in Paris.

Departmentalization, as it was called, deepened France's political, economic and cultural hold over the Antilles. French culture became *la culture officielle,* and everything indigenous was devalued.

Living on Welfare

Guadeloupe's economy, like that of Martinique and French Guiana, functions on the basis of French subsidies for the purchase of French goods. Income from bananas and sugar, Guadeloupe's main exports, pays for only about 15% of its imports from France.[1] To support the standard of living, France pays out an array of social security benefits, such as unemployment compensation, public assistance and old age pensions. Civil servants in the overseas departments receive a lucrative bonus of 40% over equivalent salaries in France as overseas hardship pay.

To ease unemployment, a special office called BUMIDOM promoted emigration through incentives such as free air tickets. The movement of mostly young Guadeloupeans to fill low-wage jobs in France became a huge transfer of some 3,000 persons per year. At the same time, many *métropolitains*—people from continental France—moved to Guadeloupe, Martinique and French Guiana to take highly-paid civil service jobs.

When France joined the European Economic Community in 1958, Antillean sugar, produced on antiquated, labor-intensive plantations, came into competition with cheaper European beet sugar. France began systematically cutting

"Young person don't leave your country. No to BUMIDOM!"

production in its Caribbean departments, eventually closing all but three of Guadeloupe's 28 sugar factories. The white plantocracy, known as *békés* in Martinique and *blanc-pays* in Guadeloupe, transferred much of its capital from sugar into commerce, tourism and real estate. French multinationals, such as the Compagnie Fruitière, also moved in to plant pineapples and bananas on former cane lands.

Some sugar factory workers, cane cutters and small cane farmers became wage laborers on the fruit plantations. But many were idled. Unemployment climbed to its present level of 30%, and the economy grew steadily more dependent on welfare subsidies.

Although their agricultural production is no longer wanted, the Antilles remain valuable to France. They are a "window" on the Americas, a base for French influence in the western hemisphere. Guadeloupe's primary role is commercial: warehouses in Pointe-à-Pitre are filled with French merchandise awaiting reexport to Latin American markets. Its Caribbean territories also provide France with a political and military foothold in the region, through the French aerospace base in French Guiana and the thousands of French police, army and national guard units based in the Antilles. Although their role is mainly for internal control, French troops based in Guadeloupe were sent to neighboring Dominica after a coup attempt there in 1981.

Finally, as vestiges of the former French empire in Africa, the Pacific and the Caribbean, the Antilles retain a purely symbolic value as well. Subsidies are a price Paris willingly pays to hold onto its last colonies and ensure that pro-independence sentiments never take root beyond a minority of the population.

The Independence Movement

General Charles de Gaulle, the father of modern French imperialism, condescendingly referred to the French Antilles as "mere specks of dust on the map." Antilleans, he said, had no national traditions of their own: "You are French, you have always been French, and you will remain French."

Today the French justification for colonialism still invokes the Gaullist myth that Antilleans are "black Frenchmen," loyal to the "mother country," France. This view is shared by the white béké class, and by some blacks and mulattos as well. An editorial in the rightist magazine *Guadeloupe 2000* states:

What we must constantly emphasize is that we are French, for reasons of language, culture and history, for better or for worse . . . One doesn't choose his country, the land of his forefathers, any more than one chooses his father and mother. One is born French by an accident of birth.[2]

A majority of Antilleans say they favor continued ties to France. But the reasons for most have little to do with any sentimental attachment to French culture. Trapped in a welfare-dependent economy, most Guadeloupeans, Martiniquans and Guyanais fear their standard of living would plummet if subsidies were withdrawn. The right wing capitalizes on these fears by threatening that an independent Guadeloupe or Martinique would become "like Haiti" or "like Dominica"—poor independent countries which were once French colonies.

The independence question is, nonetheless, more complex than the seemingly clear-cut case to be made for economic interests. If the benefits of colonialism are obvious and material, its drawbacks are largely intangible: idleness, alienation, and a depressing welfare mentality that affects youth most of all. A Roman Catholic priest who works with youth sums up:

The Guadeloupean is not his own person. Under the present system we don't really exist; we exist only in relation to France.

At the economic level French control has been a failure. Our economy is based exclusively on the needs of France. All the real potential of our country, especially in agriculture, has been ignored. Importing French social laws and economic structures doesn't work for us. For example, when France raises the minimum wage at home, it goes up here too, which we can't afford to do. The result is layoffs and worse unemployment.

Independence would undoubtedly create hardship, but it's hard already, especially for the young people. They run after unattainable material success. As a society, we are torn by internal conflict and alienated by what is our own.

We haven't yet explored our own possibilities. We assume someone else will solve our problems. Haitians and Dominicans are poor, but they are creators. We create nothing.[3]

The independence movement originated among Antillean students in France in the late 1950s. Paris was a center of anti-colonial ferment, and two Antilleans had a major intellectual impact on the movement. Aimé Césaire of Martinique had originated the concept of negritude. Frantz Fanon, also a Martiniquan, became a spokesman for national liberation movements through his writings in *The Wretched of the Earth* and *Black Skin, White Masks.*

The wars against French colonial control in Algeria and Tunisia provided a powerful example of anti-colonial struggle. Some young Antilleans were drafted into the French army and sent to fight against the liberation movements. This experience, as well as the racism they encountered in France, convinced many that France was not the benevolent "motherland" but a racist colonial power. In 1963 an association of Guadeloupean nationals in France, GONG, began promoting the idea of an Antillean independence struggle. DeGaulle's government smashed the group by arresting key members and sympathizers.

Independence activists saw that the movement needed a mass base. They began organizing among sugar cane cutters and cane farmers in Guadeloupe, resulting in the formation of the Union of Agricultural Workers (UTA) in 1970. The UTA was the first union in Guadeloupe not affiliated to a French union. It won a battle for recognition that pitted the peasants against the combined forces of the French-based unions, the landowners and the French government.

In the following years growing peasant militancy led to numerous strikes in the sugar sector. The UTA linked economic and political demands, arguing that colonialism underlay the exploitation of the workers. It became the model for a set of new unions grouped in a pro-independence federation, the General Union of Guadeloupean Workers (UGTG).

The movement also contained a strong middle-class and grassroots Christian element. Students, teachers and church people cut cane with the peasants to show their solidarity. During a prolonged strike in the cane fields in 1975, a Catholic priest, Chérubin Céleste, staged a hunger strike to protest the use of Haitian immigrants as scab labor. Groups supporting his action included Working-Class Christian Youth and the Rural Movement of Christian Youth, both within the Catholic Church but frowned upon by the hierarchy for being "too political."

Another group, Christians for the Liberation of the Guadeloupean People, supported the movement from outside the institutional Church. In the early 1980s it joined with unions and student groups in a coalition headed by a political organization, the Popular Union for the Liberation of Guadeloupe (UPLG).

In its call for a new society, the independence movement emphasizes three themes. One is pride in a national culture, especially the Kreyol language. Kreyol seems to express the heart of the Antillean identity which is separate from that of France. It has become a nationalist symbol, as has gwoka music.

Secondly, the movement stresses the Caribbean identity of Guadeloupe, Martinique and French Guiana. Colonial status and the French language have isolated the Antilles from other countries in the region. "We know everything that happens in France, and close ourselves to what happens in the rest of the Caribbean," insists one activist.

Thirdly, and most importantly, independence advocates call for the Antilles to develop their own production rather than rely on French subsidies. "We have economic possibilities that haven't been tapped," asserts a young teacher active in a Christian independence group. The UPLG's platform calls for Guadeloupe to produce more of its own food through farming, fisheries, and stock-raising. It recommends developing new industries based on sugar cane byproducts and agro-industry.[4]

Few would argue the need to strengthen the islands' productive base, but questions remain. Independence activists identify French political control as the obstacle to self-reliance. But economic dependency, to a greater or lesser degree, has persisted in nearly all the politically *independent* countries of the Caribbean. The UPLG's development plan is similar to that offered by other progressive Caribbean groups. For the rest of the region, political independence has not led to economic independence; would it be different for the French Antilles?

The question is complicated by differences in goals and tactics among those calling for change. One division is over the use of violence. The majority wing of the Antillean independence movement, including the UPLG and associated groups, rejects the use of violence. But a smaller faction, known under various names over the years, has carried out highly-publicized bombings against symbols of the French state. This group claims to be engaged in armed struggle in the Algerian tradition, arguing that violence is necessary to keep the colonial issue visible. While defending their right to use any tactics necessary, most independence activists believe violence alienates the public and hinders the movement's growth.

There are divisions as well over what political form independence should take. A few tiny groups (mainly Trotskyists) advocate both independence and socialism, but most of the movement is ideologically vague. The Socialist and Communist parties in the Antilles, influenced by their French counterparts, traditionally have not advocated independence, but have called for departmental status with "autonomy." The Guadeloupean Communist Party adopted a pro-independence position in 1988, but tensions persist with the pro-independence camp. These are reflected in rivalry between the two main labor federations, the pro-independence UGTG and the Communist-controlled CGTG.

Lastly, there is fragmentation along territorial lines. Guadeloupeans have traditionally resented what they perceive as French favoritism toward Martinique. While the two societies share a basic culture, there are subtle differences. Martinique, the seat of the colonial administration, has a tradition of assimilation, reinforced by the presence of a large beke class. Martiniquans speak mostly French, and national identity is subsumed into that of France. Aimé Césaire, now mayor of Fort-de-France and the island's leading political figure, favors autonomy rather than independence.

In Guadeloupe, on the other hand, Kreyol dominates, and nationalist sentiments run deep. While there are a few pro-independence groups in Martinique and French Guiana, the movement is strongest in Guadeloupe. Most activists there envision independence for Guadeloupe alone. An independent federated Antilles, which might be more economically viable, is rarely a topic of discussion.

The Rhythm of Resistance

The late 1970s and early '80s were a period of intense popular mobilization in Guadeloupe. One reason was the deepening economic malaise. As the planters transferred their capital from sugar into commerce, lands were turned over to non-agricultural uses such as hotels and shopping centers. Groups of displaced farmers, underpaid laborers and unemployed people began taking over lands for collective farming, in some cases simply resisting eviction when land they had worked for years was sold. In one case, people lay down in front of bulldozers sent to clear their huts from land being sold to the Compagnie Fruitière.

Political developments contributed as well to the mood of unrest. The socialist Mitterand government which came to power in France in 1981 tried to soft-pedal the colonial question, promising "decentralization" to give elected officials in the overseas departments more power. It withdrew some riot police from the Antilles and freed a dozen jailed independence militants. And in 1984, the outbreak of an active anti-colonial rebellion in New Caledonia, a French territory in the Pacific, seemed to put France on the defensive.

The New Caledonia uprising had its echo in Guadeloupe. Strikes and protests multiplied, urged on by the UPLG. "It is everywhere, this 'patriotic camp'!" exclaimed the French daily *Le Monde*. "At strikes, in the sugar cane fields, in the

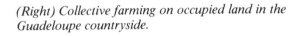

"Negroes back to Africa—Long live the French in Guadeloupe." Racist graffiti on Point-à-Pitre walls expresses right-wing sentiment.

(Right) Collective farming on occupied land in the Guadeloupe countryside.

streets..."[5] The protests culminated in six days of insurrection in July 1985, triggered by the jailing in France of a Guadeloupean activist, Georges Faisans. Faisans had assaulted a white Frenchman who was said to have kicked and insulted a Guadeloupean; to Antilleans, his jailing was dramatic proof of French racism. Thousands of people poured into the streets of Pointe-à-Pitre; stores were looted and all major routes into the capital blocked. France rushed in military reinforcements and the protest subsided. But Faisans was freed, and to some it seemed that the days of French colonialism might be numbered.

The feeling was short-lived. The impact of New Caledonia, half a world away, eventually faded. In Guadeloupe the dismantling of the sugar industry weakened the agricultural unions which had provided the movement's base. Few small peasants remained on the land: most became wage laborers or joined welfare rolls, reluctant in either case to press demands. The large quantity of land occupied by squatters proved too great for the level of organization, and little by little it was abandoned.

The conservative takeover of the French Parliament in 1986 dealt a further blow. Prime Minister Jacques Chirac, head of a neo-Gaullist party, engineered a return to an openly colonial ideology and hard-line tactics. A beefed-up state security apparatus cracked down on strikes and protests. Leaders of the armed groups were imprisoned in France.

The current picture is one of deepening economic dependency and a subdued political mood. Unemployment continues to grow, and social security payments from France account for an ever-greater share of consumption. Although BUMIDOM no longer functions, emigration remains high, about 2,600 persons a year.[6]

Despite the promise of decentralization, the departments are more politically powerless than ever. Local elected officials were not even consulted when the French government passed the *Loi Programme,* a new set of policies for the overseas departments. The law anticipates changes in 1992, when the European Unification Act will make France—together with its overseas departments—part of a newly integrated Europe. Aimed at strengthening Europe's economic competitiveness, the Act will permit the free circulation of goods and capital among member states. Its impact on the Antilles is still unclear, but many people fear further loss of autonomy.

The coalition centered around the UPLG has weakened as the various organizations pursue their own concerns. The unions are preoccupied with economic survival and reluctant to take on political battles. The UPLG, in a tactical shift, has adopted an electoral strategy, running candidates for local elections in 1988. Both reflect a tacit admission that public support is lacking at present for protests in the streets.

Grassroots Christian groups have assumed a lower profile, while continuing to favor independence. Christians for the Liberation of the Guadeloupean People has withdrawn from the unity coalition, feeling sidelined by the dominance of the UPLG. Progressive Christians, always a minority in the Church, have come under heavy criticism for their engagement in social issues. But a small circle of Roman Catholic clergy, religious and lay people have continued a grassroots ministry aimed at "integrated development of the person, inspired by a liberating gospel, with an option for the poor." Their educational work with youth, women, peasants and workers has contributed to a slowly growing understanding of the Guadeloupean reality.

189

While organized social protest is at a low ebb, there has been, paradoxically, a quiet rise in the sense of national identity and pride. Anti-colonial Guadeloupean writers such as Maryse Conde and Simone Schwartz-Bart are enjoying unprecedented popularity. After the death of a popular gwoka musician, thousands of people paid him homage in a spirited Kreyol service affirming the music as a symbol of nationhood. Conservatives denounced the celebration as a "political meeting of extremists."[7]

From time to time, the surface calm is broken by an incident which, like the Faisans affair, reveals the continuing deep-seated resentments against French rule. In 1987 Jean-Marie Le Pen, leader of the racist National Front in France, attempted to visit the Antilles. Upon his arrival in Fort-de-France, Martiniquans invaded the airport runway by the thousands, preventing the plane from landing. He proceeded to Guadeloupe, where crowds of protesters prevented Le Pen from leaving his plane. He was forced to turn around and fly back to France.

For most Guadeloupeans, economic uncertainties and strong French political control rule out independence as an immediate option. Yet few are happy with the present relationship to France. The reality of nationhood and the desire for control over the island's destiny ensure the repeated emergence of new forms of struggle. ∎

GUIANA: FRENCH FOOTHOLD IN LATIN AMERICA

One writer called it "the forgotten colony"—"under-populated, underexploited . . . [but] never abandoned." French Guiana, known in French as Guyane, is the last remaining colony on the South American mainland and the largest Caribbean territory still under colonial control.

Actually French Guiana has never been forgotten, at least not by the French. It has always served a specific purpose, although that purpose has changed over time. After France lost its North American colonies in the 1700s, it opened French Guiana to settlement in order to establish a new foothold in the Americas. Thousands of Frenchmen died in the ill-conceived attempt to settle the dense jungle, giving the colony the nickname of the "Green Hell." In 1852 a prison was constructed at Devil's Island, and French Guiana became a notorious graveyard for French prisoners.

Today the French interest focuses on the Guyane Space Center, the European equivalent of Cape Canaveral, located at Kourou on the coast. The European Space Agency launched the Ariane rocket from Kourou in 1979 and has since fired 18 shots. The tenth shot in 1984 launched two telecommunications satellites, representing the European consortium's bid to become a major player in the commercial space race.

The space center is a European enclave, guarded by the French Foreign Legion. Its airconditioned boutiques and restaurants provide the European engineers, technicians and other employees with the amenities of home. The space center has few economic links with the rest of French Guiana, which is sustained through subsidies. The territory has natural resources—seafood and timber, among others—but none is fully exploited. With the population a sparse 87,000, France clearly feels that keeping the space center is worth the price of subsidizing the colony.

For these reasons, independence is a remote prospect for French Guiana. Small pro-independence groups have formed, and there have been scattered bombings coordinated with those in Guadeloupe and Martinique. But the problem of economic dependence is even more acute here than in the French Antilles. This is compounded by the territory's geographic isolation and by ethnic diversity. Instead of a largely black population which can look to a common African heritage, French Guiana is home to Creoles (blacks), six Amerindian groups, and many smaller immigrant groups including Chinese, Indonesians, Brazilians, Haitians, Hmong people from Laos and Bosnegers from Suriname. None of these latter groups are likely to be enthusiastic about an independence movement dominated politically by the Creoles.

Curaçao

A crossroads of Africa, Europe and Latin America, the Netherlands Antilles are a microcosm of the Caribbean's diversity.

The islands are divided in two groups: the Dutch Windwards, comprising St. Maarten, Saba and St. Eustatius (Statia); and the "ABC islands" of Aruba, Bonaire and Curaçao. Despite their differences, the islands share several basic traits. They were never plantation societies, but were used mainly as bases for commerce and trade. As Dutch colonies, they enjoy a comparatively high standard of living. Yet Dutch cultural influence has remained weak, creating space for diverse cultures to evolve.

The arid, cactus-dotted landscape of the ABC islands is more reminiscent of Arizona than of the Caribbean. The early Spanish colonizers called them *Islas inútiles,* useless islands, and put up only token resistence when Holland seized them in the early 17th century. Curaçao, the largest, became a Dutch slaving station and the base of Holland's commercial empire in the region. Its population is mainly of African descent, with minorities of Dutch, Portuguese Jewish, Lebanese and Surinamese origin.[1]

Proximity to Latin America strongly influenced the three islands. Arawak Indians traveled continuously between the islands and the coast, and Aruba's population is largely of Venezuelan/Arawak descent. Until this century, poor roads in Venezuela meant that east-west travelers in that country often went by boat, usually with a stopover of several days in Curaçao. During the independence wars in Venezuela and Colombia, the islands harbored independence advocates (Simon Bolivar visited Curaçao twice), and many Curaçaoans and Arubans joined the liberation armies.[2] Thousands of Venezuelan refugees settled in Curaçao and Aruba after the wars. The Creole language of the three islands, Papiamentu, includes many words drawn from Portuguese and Spanish.

Separated from the ABC islands by 600 miles of water, the Dutch Windwards seem part of another world. They are rainy, steep and lush. They are also among the smallest populated islands in the Caribbean. St. Eustatius, with eight square miles, and Saba, with five, have little more than 1,000 inhabitants each. St. Maarten, with 16 square miles, is the dominant partner in the triad.

The Windwards' historical orientation is toward Britain and North America. Frequent periods of British rule left their mark in English place and family names, and in the English Creole spoken on the three islands. St. Eustatius in the 1700s was a base for the booming illicit trade between the Caribbean and the North American colonies. Today, the fortunes of the three islands are tied to the U.S. tourist trade.

Migration between the six islands led to some contact and cultural exchange. But racial, cultural and language differences hindered the emergence of an "Antillean" identity. An additional factor was resentment of Curaçao's dominant role, especially on the part of Arubans. When the Netherlands Antilles joined the Kingdom of the Netherlands in 1954, the six islands became self-governing, with a shared central government as the liaison to Holland. Due to its larger population and more developed economy, Curaçao became the seat of the central government and held majority representation. This led to an image of Curaçao as an agent of Dutch colonialism and the major beneficiary of Dutch aid.

Paradoxically, the tendency of the Dutch colonists to remain socially aloof limited the spread of the Dutch language

"Independence? And how?" The Curaçao Federation of Workers, the largest labor federation on the island, held a conference in 1979 to discuss concerns about independence.

Amigoe

191

and allowed Papiamentu to develop. It became the language of universal use in Curaçao, Aruba and Bonaire, achieving an unusually strong position for a Creole language. The first written text in Papiamentu dates to 1775, and journalism in the language began in 1870.[3]

Dutch, however, remained the official language and the only one permitted in government, courts of law, and the schools. Children were punished for speaking Papiamentu in school, even though their parents spoke it at home. Dutch was essential for higher education in Holland, the key to social and economic advancement. So while Papiamentu was a cultural unifier, its official status remained low.

Impact of 1969: The Cultural Nationalist Movement

The start of multinational oil refining sharpened class and cultural conflicts in Curaçao and Aruba. Royal Dutch Shell opened its Curaçao refinery in 1918, and Standard Oil (Exxon) began refining in Aruba in 1930. Curaçaoans and Arubans became workers in the refineries, along with many immigrants from the West Indies. But the higher-level positions were all filled by expatriates, mostly from Holland, the United States and Suriname. This two-tier system was reflected in language: the workers spoke Papiamentu, the managers and technicians Dutch or English.

After 1958, automation at the refineries led to widespread layoffs. The oil companies also increasingly subcontracted their work to firms which paid lower wages. These grievances fueled a protest movement led by trade unionists and radical intellectuals [see Part I, Ch. 5]. In May 1969, tensions exploded as striking Shell workers burned down parts of Willemstad in a violent, spontaneous riot.

The "May Movement" was a turning point for Curaçao. It led during the 1970s to a new class consciousness and to gains for workers, including wage increases and social security programs. Black Curaçaoans entered the upper ranks of the oil sector and the civil service, and blacks entered politics in important roles for the first time.

These social changes were accompanied by a cultural nationalist movement which raised the status and acceptance of Papiamentu. During the 1969 unrest, Papiamentu had become a political symbol, used in union meetings and even by some radical teachers in their classrooms. Afterwards, politicians, advertisers and the press turned increasingly to Papiamentu for public communication. More controversial was the question of whether to introduce Papiamentu into the schools. Intellectuals argued the benefits of teaching young children in their mother tongue, but many people still felt Dutch to be necessary for educational advancement. Not until 1986 was Papiamentu finally allowed into the curriculum, and then for only a half-hour per day.

The cultural movement included groups influenced by the Black Power movement and stressing an appreciation of Curaçao's African heritage. Groups such as Grupo Trinchera and Kaska di Pinda used popular theater and traditional music and dance to raise consciousness. The traditional drum-dance

known as *tambu,* long suppressed as an allegedly "vulgar" expression of primitive culture, was revived as a symbol of this new pride.

Accompanying the cultural thrust was the tentative beginning of a movement favoring independence from Holland, based among black intellectuals. Radical teachers and students formed groups such as Hubentut 70 (Youth '70) to educate and organize Curaçaoan youth. Progressive groups rallied behind the Movement for a New Antilles (MAN), a party which emerged from a split in the leadership of the May Movement and was linked to radical trade unions.

The MAN, led by Don Martina, initially favored independence. But after winning power in 1979, the party and its allied union leaders pulled back from their more radical positions. They moved toward an accommodation with Holland and the local business sector, which denounced the nationalist movement as "racist" and "communist." Deprived of leadership, the movement lost momentum. By the mid-1980s few cultural groups survived, and independence fell from fashion among Curaçaoan youth.

Aruba's "Status Aparte"

The impact of the 1969 riots reverberated throughout Holland's colonial empire. The Dutch government, stung by criticism of its behavior in sending troops to Curaçao, told the Antilles they could have independence the next day "by air mail." Aruba reacted with alarm, fearing independence within a federation dominated by Curaçao. Aruban politician Betico Croes split off from the ruling party to press separatist demands.

Until then, Aruban separatism had been essentially an upper-class concern, based among politicians and businessmen who felt that Aruba's dependence on Curaçao hurt their economic interests. They used racism to build support, claiming that light-skinned Arubans should not be ruled by blacks. In the 1970s the charismatic Croes led a vocal drive for secession that attracted mass support.

Holland finally agreed to Aruba's demand for *status aparte,* or separate status. In 1986, Aruba left the Netherlands Antilles and became a separate colony with its own link to Holland. As a condition, however, Holland required Aruba to accept full independence in 1996.

Aruba's departure left the "Antilles of the Five" unstable and unsure. It was a catalyst for long-felt discontent, threatening to trigger the eventual dissolution of the federation. St. Maarten, riding the crest of a tourism boom, also asked for *status aparte.* But Holland, which prefers the federation to stay together, rejected the proposal.

Although it is believed to want to rid itself of the Antilles, Holland's signals regarding independence have been ambiguous. Subsidies to the colonies are a burden, but the islands also serve Dutch economic interests. Curaçao is the base for Dutch capitalism in Latin America, where multinationals such as Phillips, Unilever and KLM have extensive investments. In addition, both the United States and Venezuela are believed to oppose Antillean independence.

There is little ambiguity on the Antillean side, where large majorities favor continuing links to Holland. Aruba, having achieved the desired break with Curaçao, is trying to back out of its agreement to become fully independent. In a recent poll of Curaçaoans, 95% of those surveyed said they preferred to stay with Holland. Reluctantly facing an eventual change in status, however, many Antilleans are looking to the creation of some form of Dutch Commonwealth linking Holland's former colonies.

Also likely, although not widely desired, is a larger role for Venezuela. Venezuelan investment in the Antilles has expanded rapidly, and Dutch and Venezuelan officials have held quiet talks on the possible shift of some economic responsibilities. Should the Antilles become independent, Holland could well turn to Venezuela to take on aspects of an informal colonial role.

The Multinationals Pull Out

Hanging over the discussion is a larger unknown: the economic future of the Netherlands Antilles. The decline in the oil industry has undercut the prosperity of Curaçao and Aruba, long among the most affluent colonies in the region.

Shell began scaling down its Curaçao operation in the early '80s, demanding concessions in return for a promise to keep the refinery open. After bitter negotiations with the company, refinery workers voted in 1984 to accept a large pay cut. Although the island establishment feared a repetition of the 1969 unrest, there was neither protest nor a strike—because Shell held the trump card:

> Mr. Wilson, Shell's manager, declared that his orders from London were quite clear. Either the union agrees to the proposed pay cuts and other economizing measures, in which case Shell will continue its construction plans for the next five years, or the Shell Company will leave the island within three or four years.[4]

Despite the union's compliance, Shell pulled out of Curaçao in October 1985. Its departure followed the closure of the Exxon refinery in Auba eight months earlier.

The departure of the multinationals left Antilleans in shock. In Aruba, where the refinery shut down permanently, thousands of workers emigrated with their families to Holland. The Curaçao refinery did not close, but there was a period of uncertainty during which many Curaçaoans also emigrated. Relief was widespread when Venezuela finally agreed to lease the refinery through its state corporation, Isla. But the refinery now employs only half as many workers as in 1981, and only one-fifth the number employed during the 1970s.[5] Wages are lower, and Venezuela pays no taxes to Curaçao.

Both Curaçao and Aruba are aggressively promoting tourism as a future economic base. In addition, business and political leaders hope to make the islands into regional financial centers, serving as a gateway to Latin America for U.S. and European capital. They are modernizing telecommunications and other facilities, and a large international trade center is under construction in Curaçao.

In the long term, Curaçao may prosper as an international service and tourist economy. In the short term, the decline of the oil sector has meant an economic squeeze and greater dependence on Holland. As a condition for budget support, the Dutch government has required layoffs of thousands of public sector workers. Official unemployment already stands at 28%, and is higher among youth. Curaçao's economic problems are masked by a comprehensive social welfare system that meets basic food, housing and medical needs. But although the crisis is hidden, it is real, and any cutbacks in welfare programs could have serious consequences. This has left Antilleans even more nervous than before about the prospect of independence.

However the status question is resolved, basic questions remain concerning the Antilles' relationship to each other and the wider Caribbean. The struggle to build an identity within each island is making progress, and there is a slowly growing awareness of Caribbean links. But few see hope for the development of an "Antillean" nationhood that would provide a solid base for the federation's survival. Throughout Caribbean history, divisions between the colonial domains have separated peoples who share cultural roots. The case of the Netherlands Antilles reveals an inverse process: how colonialism forced distinct peoples into artificial groupings, and left them with the task of forging a nation in the post-colonial era. ∎

Mario Cornelia, a traditional seu *drummer of Curaçao.*

Grupo Rais

Puerto Rico

On September 23, 1868, the Puerto Rican patriot Ramón Emeterio Betances led the *Grito de Lares* rebellion, which ended by proclaiming the First Republic of Puerto Rico. Although it was quickly crushed by the Spanish militia, the Lares revolt seemed to signal that Puerto Rican independence was not far off.

This was not to be. Instead, the United States replaced Spain as the occupying power, making Puerto Rico a colony in all but name. The impact of American colonialism and the search for alternatives became the central focus of Puerto Rican politics in the twentieth century.

From Conquest to Commonwealth

In 1898, at the end of the Spanish-American War, the United States claimed Puerto Rico as "compensation" for wartime losses. Military rule lasted for 21 months. Afterwards, the Foraker Act set up a civilian administration headed by an American governor and a U.S.-appointed executive council. The United States kept complete power over Puerto Rican laws, currency, customs, immigration, defense and trade. In 1917, the Jones Act imposed U.S. citizenship on Puerto Ricans, making them eligible for military conscription a month before the United States entered World War One.

American sugar companies took over large tracts of land, leaving many peasants landless and jobless. The schools, churches and media became instruments of Americanization. English was imposed as the language of school instruction, even though the students and indeed most of the teachers could not speak it. U.S.-based Protestant mission churches arrived to evangelize and promote an Americanized way of life.

José de Diego, president of the elected Chamber of Deputies, spearheaded Puerto Rican opposition to the U.S. takeover. For de Diego, and for other early Puerto Rican leaders, colonialism would eventually have to give way to one of two solutions: "Puerto Rico, State of the Union; [or] Puerto Rico, Independent State."[1]

The extreme poverty of the Depression years led to an upsurge of anti-colonial sentiment. The pro-independence Liberal Party represented nearly half the electorate, while the smaller Nationalist Party carried out violent protests against U.S. control. U.S. authorities harshly repressed the Nationalists, imprisoning their leader Pedro Albizu Campos. In 1937 police opened fire on an unarmed Nationalist march in the city of Ponce, killing 18 protesters in what came to be known as the Ponce Massacre.

Albizu's imprisonment weakened the Nationalist Party and opened the way for new forces to coopt the independence movement. In 1938, splits within the Liberal Party produced the Popular Democratic Party (*los Populares*), led by Luis Muñoz Marín. He promised economic reform under the slogan *pan, tierra y libertad*—bread, land and liberty. Elected governor in 1948, Muñoz cooperated with U.S. officials to launch Operation Bootstrap, an industrialization program which was to transform the Puerto Rican economy.

A former independence advocate, Muñoz now believed that his economic program could only work if the status question were settled so as to both end the image of colonialism and ensure a permanent connection to the United States. His solution was for Puerto Rico to enter a "free association" with the United States, an arrangement dubbed "Commonwealth." The Island would gain internal self-government, although the U.S. Congress could still veto laws passed by the Puerto Rican legislature. Puerto Rico would have its own Constitution and could fly its flag alongside the American flag.

The Nationalists feared this compromise spelled the end of hopes for independence. In October 1950 the Nationalist Insurrection broke out across Puerto Rico, while in Washington, two Nationalists attacked the residence of President Truman. The military and police suppressed the uprisings and jailed thousands of independence sympathizers.

The implementation of Commonwealth in 1952 changed the terms of the debate, providing an apparent third option

Schoolchild reads from an English-language primer in a Puerto Rican classroom around 1950.

Courtesy of Pedro Rivera

between independence and statehood. In reality, it institutionalized the Island's colonial status. The limited political autonomy was overshadowed by closer integration with the United States economy under Operation Bootstrap. Wooed by tax-free repatriation of profits, U.S. firms set up factories on the Island, and thousands of Puerto Ricans emigrated to the United States. The economy grew rapidly during Bootstrap's early years, reducing support for independence and entrenching the rule of the Popular Party.

The Model Breaks Down

From the mid-1960s onward, the Bootstrap model began to falter as light industry left the Island [see Part II, Ch. 4]. Most new investment was by petrochemical and pharmaceutical companies, capital-intensive heavy industries which polluted the environment but provided few jobs. Unemployment rose, and Puerto Rico became dependent on some $3 billion per year in federal subsidies, leading to the derogatory label "Welfare Island."

Operation Bootstrap contributed to the growth of a middle-class, urbanized culture in and around metropolitan San Juan. The Los Angeles-style freeways around the capital and the giant shopping mall called *Plaza de las Américas* symbolized this Americanized consumer lifestyle. But beneath the affluent veneer, many people still lived in poverty. Federal transfer payments, including welfare, food stamps, social security and unemployment compensation came to account for 30% of all personal income.[2]

In the early 1980s, recession in the United States brought new problems to Puerto Rico. A slump in the petrochemical and electronics industries led to a wave of plant closures, and unemployment peaked at 23% in 1983. Policymakers in Washington seemed insensitive to Puerto Rico's predicament. Federal budget cuts reduced funds for many social service programs such as food stamps and employment training. The Caribbean Basin Initiative threatened to cancel out Puerto Rico's advantages over the other islands in attracting investment. Congress even tried to abolish the tax exemption for U.S. companies operating in Puerto Rico; vigorous lobbying saved the program.

In an effort to keep industry from deserting the Island, Puerto Rican officials pushed what became known as the "twin plant program." Under this scheme, companies could manufacture products partially in Puerto Rico and then ship them to lower-wage Caribbean countries for the most labor-intensive steps. Twelve twin-plant projects were set up in 1986, ten of them paired with factories in the Dominican Republic's free trade zones. But these new projects created only about 1,400 new jobs, less than 30% of the layoffs in the electronics industry alone that year.[3]

Politically, the breakdown of the Bootstrap model led to growing discontent with the Commonwealth arrangement. In the 1960s the independence movement took on new life, becoming a non-violent movement based among radical intellectuals. The Puerto Rican Independence Party (PIP) and the Puerto Rican Socialist Party (PSP) led electoral campaigns for independence. *Independentistas* in student groups and

trade unions opposed Puerto Rican involvement with the United States military, especially the drafting of Puerto Ricans during the Vietnam War.

At the other end of the political spectrum, wealthy Puerto Ricans with ties to the U.S. Republican Party stepped up their campaign for statehood, inspired by Alaska's and Hawaii's incorporation into the union. Led by the millionaire Ferré family, statehooders formed the New Progressive Party (NPP) in 1967. Due to splits in the Popular Party, the NPP candidate, Luis Ferré, was elected in 1968, ending the two-decade monopoly of the Populares.

The election of a statehood candidate did not mean that Puerto Rico became a state. That decision remained controversial, and could only be made in Washington in any case. NPP governor Carlos Romero Barceló, elected in 1976, did promote a policy of cultural assimilation. He pushed for English programs in the schools (Spanish having been reinstated as the language of instruction in 1938) and attempted to close down the Puerto Rican Cultural Institute. His administration also stepped up surveillance and harassment of pro-independence groups.

Scandal and corruption in Romero's administration helped bring the Populares back to power in 1984. Gov. Rafael Hernández Colón continued Romero's basic policies, including close collaboration with the Reagan administration's Caribbean strategy. Within the Popular Party, however, an *autonomista* wing pushed for greater distance from the United States. Pressure from these legislators, together with public protests, forced Hernández Colón to resist certain American demands.

Since 1968, electoral politics in Puerto Rico have settled largely into the American mold. Two similar parties alternate in power, neither actively challenging the status quo of Commonwealth. Elections are fought less on the status question than on economic issues and corruption. But the struggle for change continues, largely through grassroots organizing rather than through the ballot box.

Pollution and Militarism: Issues of the '80s

While the Island's political status remains the underlying issue, grassroots politics have focused on two more immediate problems: pollution and militarism. Community organizing around these concerns has crossed party lines and raised awareness of the hidden costs of Puerto Rico's United States connection.

In order to encourage investment, U.S. and Puerto Rican authorities closed their eyes to federal environmental regulations. Oil refineries, power plants and petrochemical factories have polluted the air, while toxic wastes from chemical and pharmaceutical plants have contaminated drinking water and killed fish along the shore. In 1982 the U.S. Geological Survey tested 19 wells on the Island and shut down ten as dangerously contaminated. Among the substances found were carbon tetrachloride, trichloroethylene, tetrachloroethylene, mercury, benzene, dieldrin and phenols.[4]

Assisted by the church-supported organization Industrial Mission, numerous Puerto Rican communities have organized

Air pollution from a south coast oil refinery.

Claridad

to fight environmental contamination and its health effects. In the town of Yabucoa, where a Union Carbide plant polluted the air with heavy soot, residents fought a long battle to prove that the town's high rate of respiratory disease and throat cancer were due to the plant's emissions. In Mayaguez, toxic gases released from an industrial complex forced 700 people to be hospitalized for nausea, breathing difficulties and loss of consciousness. Mayaguez residents formed a "Committee to Save Our Health" which successfully pressured the government to investigate. But although the inquiry confirmed that the escaping gases contained neurotoxic poisons, the leaks continued.[5]

Twelve percent of all illegal toxic waste dumps in the United States are located in Puerto Rico, an island less than half the size of Massachusetts.[6] Industries dump toxic wastes in the ocean, in rivers, and in municipal dumps, as well as in legal but loosely-operated toxic waste sites. Three hundred families had to be relocated from the community of Ciudad Cristiana de Humacao when it was discovered that the houses had been built on landfill containing toxic wastes. Two-thirds of the residents showed some degree of mercury poisoning when their blood was tested.[7]

A number of communities in Puerto Rico show abnormal rates of respiratory disease, cancer and birth defects. But federal and Puerto Rican authorities have strongly resisted communities' attempts to prove that the problems are pollution-related. For the authorities, pollution is the price Puerto Ricans must pay for industrial investment.

The other issue which has mobilized Puerto Ricans, in this case challenging Washington directly, is opposition to the U.S. military's use of the Island. Puerto Rico houses a vast complex of U.S. air, naval and communications facilities, including the huge Roosevelt Roads Naval Station, the Ramey Air Force Base, the Salinas National Guard Camp, and the Caribbean Police School. The U.S. Navy has long used the small offshore island of Vieques for bombing target practice.

Puerto Rico's military role expanded during the Reagan presidency [see Part V, Ch. 5]. The annual "Ocean Venture" naval exercises brought thousands of U.S. and Caribbean troops to Puerto Rico for mock assaults on Vieques. Fifty thousand Puerto Ricans marched in 1984 to protest Ocean Venture and the participation of the Puerto Rican National Guard in the maneuvers. Even more controversial was the Guard's growing role in Central America. Units of the PRNG were sent to Honduras to take part in the "Big Pine" and "Solid Shield" military maneuvers, involving simulated assaults on Nicaragua and the building of roads and airstrips for the U.S. military. The PRNG also took part in maneuvers in Belize and at the Southern Command in Panama.

These mobilizations suggested that Puerto Ricans might one day find themselves fighting for the United States against other Spanish-speaking people. Puerto Ricans are "a Caribbean and Latin American people," insisted legislator Severo Colberg, urging Hernandez Colon to resist involvement in Central America. The president of the Island Senate, Miguel Hernández Agosto, warned that Puerto Ricans would not willingly fight for the United States in Nicaragua. "The U.S. government," he said, "must understand that Puerto Rico is united to Latin America by what we call blood ties."[8]

In 1986 the Reagan administration announced plans to use Puerto Rico's El Yunque forest reserve to train 1,000 troops, widely assumed to be Nicaraguan contras, in "jungle warfare." The outcry was so strong that Hernández Colón refused permission for the training, saying "Puerto Rican public opinion is 99% against it."

Equally controversial was the revelation that Washington had secret plans to deploy nuclear weapons in Puerto Rico. The Puerto Rican Bar Association first charged that the Roosevelt Roads base was prepared to "function as a center for command and control operations for nuclear weapons." Several months later, the *New York Times* reported that leaked documents confirmed U.S. contingency plans to deploy nuclear weapons in Puerto Rico, Canada, Bermuda and Iceland.[9]

The revelations caused an uproar. It was pointed out that such deployment would violate the Tlatelolco treaty which makes Latin America a nuclear-free zone, and which the United States signed on Puerto Rico's behalf. The fact that Washington could violate the treaty and make Puerto Rico a target in case of war—and that Puerto Rico could do nothing to prevent this—dramatically illustrated the Island's lack of sovereignty.

The Status Debate

Environmental contamination, welfare dependency and militarism are the most visible ills in a system which many Puerto Ricans feel just isn't working. Although the Popular Party has broad support, most Puerto Ricans no longer see Commonwealth status as a solution to their problems. Yet there is no strong movement in favor of either of the alternatives, statehood or independence.

Statehood is supported by powerful social sectors, including affluent Puerto Ricans, North Americans living on the Island and the large community of right-wing Cuban emigres. They argue that Puerto Rico would have more bargaining power with Washington if it became a state. Some working-class and middle-class Puerto Ricans also favor statehood in the belief that closer links to the United States would mean higher living standards. But the prospect of having to pay federal income taxes, from which Puerto Ricans are presently exempted, is a major deterrent.

At a deeper level, many Puerto Ricans fear that statehood would mean total assimilation into North American society and the loss of their identity. The pro-statehood NPP calls for a *jíbaro* statehood that would allow Puerto Rico to retain its culture and the Spanish language. But few believe this would be possible.

If there is ambivalence about statehood, visible support for independence is even more limited. No more than 6-7% of the electorate votes for the Puerto Rican Independence Party or the Puerto Rican Socialist Party. But the question of Puerto Rican independence is a complex and subtle one.

Economic insecurity, ideological control and repression all contribute to making independence seem a radical or simply impossible goal to many Puerto Ricans. The main barrier is the reality of a colonial, dependent economy. If the U.S. connection were severed, it is said, the loss of subsidies would mean great hardship. Puerto Ricans may resent dependence on emigration, welfare and food stamps, but many still fear the future without them.

The mass media and the educational system constantly reinforce the message that Puerto Rico benefits from its association with the United States. The Puerto Rican media is linked to the U.S. media, with many North Americans and right-wing Cuban emigres in high-level positions. The schools downplay Puerto Rican history, emphasizing instead the history of the United States. Puerto Rican schoolchildren sing both the U.S. and Puerto Rican national anthems and salute both flags. The schools actively facilitate recruitment by the U.S. military.

The establishment labels all independence advocates "terrorists," despite the commitment of both the PIP and PSP to non-violence. The PSP's pro-Cuban socialism and the PIP's vaguer democratic socialism have also led to red-baiting of both parties. They remain based among middle-class intellectuals, and have been unable to build strong ties to the

Fish killed by chemical wastes discharged into a lagoon outside San Juan.

Claridad

197

mainstream.

The existence of splinter groups which use violence—notably the Macheteros—has provided government agencies with a pretext for repression of the entire independence movement. The Federal Bureau of Investigation has used wiretappings, infiltration of agents and the fabrication of criminal cases to harass activist groups. Dozens of Puerto Rican activists are serving time in federal prisons, many of them for refusing to testify before grand juries.

On July 25, 1978, an undercover police agent lured two young independence activists to a remote mountain site called Cerro Maravilla, or Mountain of Wonder. At the mountain top, heavily armed police encircled and shot Carlos Soto Arriví, 18, and Arnaldo Darío Rosado, 24. For five years the Romero administration covered up the truth, claiming that the youths had been going to blow up a communications tower and that the police had fired in self-defense. In 1983, the Puerto Rican Senate opened televised public hearings. Puerto Ricans watched in shocked fascination as three policemen testified to the planned murders.

In August 1985, 200 FBI agents armed with machine guns swooped down on 37 homes and offices in Puerto Rico in a pre-dawn paramilitary-style raid. Eleven people were arrested, most of them prominent pro-independence writers and artists, including two board members of the magazine *Pensamiento Crítico*. They were shipped to Hartford, Connecticut and taken to court in chains, charged with plotting a 1983 armed robbery carried out by the Macheteros. Despite 18 months of wiretapping and other surveillance before the raid, the indictment detailed no specific connections between the defendants and the robbery. By the summer of 1988, the trial had not begun.[10]

Many Puerto Ricans who say that independence is not presently *possible* or *practical* still believe deeply in the ideal of an independent Puerto Rico. This romantic nationalism may not translate any time soon into a political movement for independence. But as awareness grows of colonialism's costs, the search for alternatives will continue. ∎

Juan Ibañez - *Claridad*

U.S. VIRGIN ISLANDS: TOURISM AND TENSION

If Puerto Rico is an industrial enclave of the United States economy, the U.S. Virgin Islands are its tourist playground. At least ten cruise liners dock daily at the duty-free port of Charlotte Amalie, St. Thomas, and Virgin Islanders must elbow their way through throngs of American tourists on downtown streets. Many North Americans also live in the Virgin Islands, where they own land, businesses, luxury condominiums and retirement villas facing onto private beaches. The best-known luxury resort is the Caneel Bay Plantation on St. John, built and operated by the Rockefeller family empire.

The Virgin Islands' economy is thoroughly controlled by U.S. corporations. The U.S.-based Amerada Hess Oil Co. is the largest private employer, operating the western world's largest oil refinery on St. Croix. The relationship between Hess and the Virgin Islands administration has been tense, with Hess threatening to leave in response to demands for greater benefits for the islands. Other U.S. companies include Martin Marietta, an aerospace giant which produces aluminum on St. Croix, and plants assembling items like watches. Most small businesses are owned by non-blacks, including North Americans, Syrians and Lebanese. The working class consists of native Virgin Islanders and West Indian immigrants from the "down islands," as the Leewards and Windwards are called. However, small business owners not infrequently hire transient white job seekers from the United States in preference to local blacks.

Not surprisingly, the island air is often laden with tension. The continuous tourist invasion, the economic dominance of foreigners and the extreme congestion of the islands has fueled a suppressed hostility which occasionally breaks to the surface, as in 1972 when nine tourists were murdered in St. Croix. There is also some tension between native Virgin Islanders and the down-island immigrants because of competition over scarce jobs. This has been exacerbated by the decline of the industrial sector, most recently with the closing of a Martin Marietta plant and cutbacks at the Hess Oil refinery in St. Croix.

As in other heavily touristed countries, however, most resentment is suppressed because everyone is acutely aware of the economy's dependence on tourism. The island government periodically launches "courtesy campaigns" to encourage more welcoming behavior toward tourists. In the

Struggling to define a Caribbean identity in an American tourist playground.

case of the Virgin Islands, however, there is an additional dependence on U.S. federal subsidies. For these reasons, there is little talk of independence, nor have the Virgin Islands traditionally had a well-defined sense of Caribbean identity. This is changing somewhat with the impact of the down-islanders who have helped to spread an interest in reggae and Rastafarianism among Virgin Island youth.

199

New Directions for the Atlantic Coast

The people who migrated from the West Indies to the Atlantic rim of Central America formed the human link uniting the Caribbean and Central America in history. Today, their descendents retain few direct ties to the Caribbean islands. At the same time, these Atlantic coast peoples, or *costeños,* have been isolated from the Central American mainstream by geography, by racial and language differences, and by economic marginalization. No longer directly connected to the Caribbean, but only weakly integrated into Central American societies, the coastal enclaves have been shaped by their traditional cultures and by foreign influences, especially that of the United States.

One result is a history of cultural and economic links along the coast itself. Black, English-speaking people in Belize, Honduras, Nicaragua, Costa Rica and Panama share a common past as workers for British, and later, North American companies. They also share a largely common culture with Caribbean roots. Esmeralda Browne, a Panamanian of West Indian descent, emphasizes this unity:

> There is a close connection between people of West Indian descent all along the Atlantic coast. For instance, you would find Panamanian blacks having relatives on the Atlantic coast of Costa Rica or Nicaragua.
>
> Because of the historic racism in our countries and the way West Indians have been marginalized, they haven't related closely to the national societies. Costa Rica is a good example: Limón has been totally isolated from the reality of San José. The people of Limón had a closer relationship with us in Colón [Panama] than with their own capital of San José. There's a kind of solidarity. If someone from Limón or from Bluefields [Nicaragua] comes to Panama, you feel like they're one of yours. When I go to the Atlantic coast of Nicaragua or Costa Rica, people feel we speak the same language even though they identify my accent as Panamanian.
>
> I think there's been an attempt to keep us separate from the Caribbean. The dominant culture places more emphasis on being close to the United States and to "La Madre Patria," Spain.

Since 1980, the coast has become less isolated as the Central American wars thrust the region into new prominence. In Nicaragua, the United States was able to manipulate the coastal ethnic groups' demands for self-determination into part of the strategy for overthrowing the Sandinistas. This goal also led to the militarization of Honduras and to a lesser extent Costa Rica—a military build-up taking place primarily in the Atlantic coast areas and adding a new chapter to their history of foreign domination.

Central American governments have historically done little to reach out to their Atlantic coast regions, but in recent years several have made new efforts. The Torrijos government in Panama made ethnic integration a goal of its nationalist "revolution," breaking down barriers between Latino Panamanians and those of West Indian descent. More recently, the Nicaraguan government has reached out to the coastal groups through development programs and, since 1985, by offering them local autonomy within the revolution. Thus the potential for change is in the air even as the growing U.S. military presence along the coast draws the once-forgotten area deeper into the vortex of war. ■

Belize

Alone among the Central American countries, Belize faces the Caribbean. Its sparse population of about 170,000 clings to the Caribbean coast, with one-third of the total in the old colonial port of Belize City. A former British colony, Belize defines itself as "a Caribbean and Central American country." But this identity is an ambiguous one, shaped by ties to both subregions but also by a peculiar isolation from both. One local publication notes:

> The truth is that Belize, for historical, geographic, institutional and cultural reasons, is both a Caribbean and a Central American state. But it has existed historically as a stagnant backwater of the anglophone Caribbean and an alienated nation of Central America . . . [1]

Belize's Caribbean identity is the result of its colonial past. Originally a frontier settlement of English logwood cutters, "British Honduras" was administered as a dependency of Jamaica until 1884. Renamed Belize, the colony inherited British political, legal and educational institutions, along with English as its official language. Its government and party system is patterned on the Westminster model, with parliamentary elections and a prime minister.

On the other hand, neglect by Britain, combined with Belize's physical distance from the islands, meant there was little popular consciousness of belonging to the Caribbean. Geographically, Belize is part of Central America. Daily flights link Belize to the Central American capitals, while there is no direct air link at all with the Caribbean. In the multi-ethnic population, the relatively equal weight of two dominant groups—English-speaking "Creoles" and Spanish-speaking "Mestizos"—fosters a dual cultural identity.

These factors contributed historically to split loyalties on the part of Belizean politicians. In the 1950s George Price, nationalist leader and founder of the first political party, tilted toward Central America and the United States as a way of rejecting British colonialism. He rejected Belizean membership in the West Indies Federation, seeing the country's destiny as linked instead to the more economically powerful Central American countries.[2]

Standing in the way of such a vision, however, was the dispute with neighboring Guatemala, which cast a shadow over Belize's internal politics and international relations. Guatemala claims to have inherited sovereignty over Belizean territory from Spain, although the Spanish never actually occupied Belize. Under the slogan *Belice es Nuestra*—Belize is Ours—the Guatemalan military and oligarchy have used the territorial claim to rally nationalist fervor.

After Belize obtained self-governing status from Britain in 1964, the Guatemalan claim held up independence for 17 years. Initially all the Latin American countries except Cuba sided

Belize City in the 1920s shows British and American influences.

Belize Government Information Service

with Guatemala in international forums. The first to break ranks, in 1976, was Omar Torrijos of Panama. Other Latin countries followed, and in 1979 Nicaragua became the first Central American state to support Belizean independence.

But it was the English-speaking Caribbean countries which became Belize's staunchest allies, supporting Belizean sovereignty at the United Nations, within the British Commonwealth and at the Organization of American States. Influenced by its English-speaking members, the OAS gave its endorsement in 1981, clearing the way for Belizean independence that year. When the British left, a 1,600-man British garrison remained behind to guard against a Guatemalan invasion.

As a result of this struggle, Belize strengthened its institutional ties to the Commonwealth Caribbean. Excluded from joining the Central American Common Market, Belize became a founding member of the Caribbean Free Trade Association (CARIFTA) in 1973. It is a member of CARICOM and participates in other Caribbean regional institutions such as the Caribbean Development Bank and the University of the West Indies.

The dispute with Guatemala perpetuated animosities on the part of many Belizeans toward all Central Americans. Still, government-to-government relations with all the Central American states except Guatemala have improved since independence. In addition, some Belize business leaders question whether their economic interests are served within the Caribbean common market. Belize thus remains awkwardly with a foot in both camps, both Central American and Caribbean yet fully committed to neither.

H. Spruyt, courtesy of NACLA

Since Belizean independence, the CARICOM states have helped persuade the OAS to amend its charter to permit Belize to join while the dispute with Guatemala is still pending. Officially Guatemala continues to claim all of Belizean territory, but an invasion is no longer considered likely. In 1986, Guatemala's new civilian president, Vinicio Cerezo, indicated he would seek settlement of the dispute. But real power remained with the right-wing military and oligarchy, which oppose dropping the Belizean claim. In 1987, to the dismay of Belizeans, Guatemala returned to its hardline position of demanding land cession.

Ethnic Arithmetic

The question of regional loyalties is related to another ongoing debate: how to preserve the "ethnic balance" in Belizean society which is perceived as the basis for social harmony and nation-building.

Successive waves of immigration produced in Belize one of the most diverse populations in the region. British settlers arriving in the late 17th century drove most of the indigenous Maya back into the interior jungles, and brought in African slaves to work in the timber camps. The mingling of Africans and Europeans produced the Creoles, who currently comprise an estimated 40% of the population. Today Creoles are the most heterogeneous of all the ethnic groups, but also the most culturally West Indian.

Next to arrive were the Garífuna, or Black Caribs, who settled along the Atlantic coast of Central America after being expelled from St. Vincent by the British. Distinguished from the Creoles by language and culture, they now make up 8% of the population. During the lengthy Caste War in the Yucatan in the mid-1800s, Mayan and Mestizo refugees streamed over the border into Belize, nearly doubling the population of the colony. Mestizos now represent about 33% of the population. Mopan and Ketchi Maya also immigrated from Guatemala, bringing the Amerindian population to about 10%. Smaller minorities include East Indians, Chinese, Arabs, Europeans and North Americans, along with a small but economically powerful group of "local whites." To this mix has been added, since 1980, an influx of an estimated 15,000 to 20,000 Central American refugees.[3]

The ethnic groups tend to cluster geographically, with Mestizos in the north and west, Creoles in Belize City, Garífuna around Dangriga, and Maya in the south and west. They speak different languages, although many Belizeans are bilingual or multilingual, generally speaking some English in addition to their own language. Geographic separation, cultural differences and competition for scarce jobs have combined to encourage ethnic prejudice. The primary antagonism is between the two largest groups: Mestizos often portray Creoles as "lazy," while Creoles, concerned about the economic advances of the lighter-skinned Mestizos, increasingly claim to be the "only true Belizeans." But the official myth remains one of ethnic harmony and balance.

Harmony, in fact, has largely prevailed at the level of national politics. Belize differs from such countries as Guyana and Trinidad in that politics are not racially based. Both major political parties draw support from all ethnic groups, and no single group has controlled the state for its own benefit.

Instead, party politics for years centered around the personalistic leadership of George Price, whose People's United Party (PUP) won every general election between 1954 and 1979. Strongly nationalist, the PUP rallied Belizeans around the drive for independence. The opposition Honduran Independence Party—later to become the United Democratic Party (UDP)—opposed independence under Price, in part because they mistrusted his intentions regarding Guatemala.

From the 1950s onward, the nationalist movement led by Price helped break down ethnic segregation. Broader primary schooling and the expansion of communications by road, radio and telephone also encouraged interaction. In the last few years, however, this integrative trend has given way to a resurgence of ethnic consciousness. Ethnic councils and associations are proliferating, leading some observers to fear that rising tensions between the groups may imperil the fragile nationalist alliance.[4]

It is in this context that the immigration of thousands of Salvadoran and Guatemalan refugees has become a source of controversy. Reflecting the prejudice against Central Americans, the newcomers have been blamed for everything from rising crime to a malaria epidemic. Underlying the debate is the belief that the influx of Spanish-speakers, combined with heavy emigration of Creoles to the United States, is threatening Creole dominance. The emergence of such issues in the 1984 campaign, when the UDP accused Price of encouraging the refugee flow in order to "latinize" the country, provided ominous indications that ethnic rivalries are coming to play a more important role in Belizean politics.

Young men in Belize City: Unemployment has increased.

H. Spruyt, courtesy of NACLA

Preserving Dependence

The basic problems facing Belize, however, are not caused by race relations or refugees, despite public concern with these issues. Anthropologist O. Nigel Bolland argues that . . .

the basic problems are caused by the nature of the country's economy, which is open, dependent, and largely foreign-controlled; by the continuing threat of Guatemala's claim; and by the increasingly pervasive influence of the United States. These problems may give rise to social tensions that could all too easily be translated into inter-ethnic rivalry and competition.[5]

More than any Caribbean nation except Guyana, Belize is endowed with immense economic potential. It has large areas of forest, fertile farmlands, and the longest barrier reef in the western hemisphere. With a population density of only about 18 per square mile, the country has the potential to be self-sufficient in food. But this potential has never been realized, in part due to the small domestic market. Instead, foreign interests have controlled much of the land for resource extraction and monocrop production. By the end of the colonial period, the British-based Belize Estate and Produce Company owned over a million acres—one-fifth of the country—for timber cutting. After World War Two sugar replaced timber as the main export, coming under control of the British multinational Tate & Lyle.

During its three decades in office, the Price government took steps to minimize foreign ownership and make Belize more self-reliant. Under a tough land-alienation law it gradually bought up lands left idle by foreign owners, making tracts available to Belizeans under generous terms. Local fishermen and citrus growers were helped to form cooperatives. But despite some gains, the economy remained dependent on sugar. At independence in 1981, only 15% of arable land was under cultivation, while food imports continued to cost the country heavily. More than 80% of privately-owned lands remained in the hands of foreigners.[6]

Belizean independence unfortunately coincided with the recession of the early 1980s. Falling sugar prices and the devaluation of the Mexican peso buffeted the economy, forcing Price to deepen the very foreign dependence he had hoped to combat. In 1983, the government signed an agreement with the U.S. Agency for International Development (USAID), and the following year turned to the International Monetary Fund for a $7.5 million loan. Two transnationals, Nestle and Hershey, were invited into Belize to grow citrus and cocoa. But unemployment increased, spending on social services had to be cut back, and in 1984 Tate & Lyle announced it would close its two sugar factories. Many farmers began growing marijuana as the most profitable crop.

203

Presiding over an economic decline, Price's PUP also suffered from an image of corruption—although Price himself was considered honest—and splits in the party leadership. In the December 1984 election, Manuel Esquivel's United Democratic Party defeated the PUP in a landslide.

The new government positioned itself to the right of the PUP in economic policy, announcing a new emphasis on privatization and incentives to foreign investors. The centerpiece of the new policy was the "Coca-Cola land deal," the sale of almost 700,000 acres—roughly 12% of Belize's land area—to a consortium made up of Coca-Cola Foods, two Houston businessmen and the original owner, a rich Belizean. Coca-Cola was to plant 25,000 acres in citrus to provide juice concentrate for its Minute Maid subsidiary, but shelved the plans under pressure from local citrus growers and international environmental groups. Anxious to cut its public relations losses, Coke gave some 40,000 acres to the Belize government for a forest reserve. The fate of the rest of the land remains uncertain.

Coca-Cola's foray into Belizean real estate was just one aspect of the growing U.S. economic role in the country. Small and large investors and speculators, many from Texas, have arrived to assess the opportunities. There remains the danger that Belize will merely shift from one export crop to another, and from one foreign investor to another, in the search for an economic solution. The goal of self-reliance has been abandoned, but development is more remote than ever.

Into the U.S. Orbit

The United States has long exerted a strong economic, cultural and political attraction to Belizean politicians of both parties. Heavy emigration of Belizeans to the United States and the impact of the U.S. media, particularly television, have shaped Belizean culture in a pro-American mold. Within this context, however, the shift from the Price to the Esquivel government opened the door to greatly increased U.S. influence.

Several factors coincided in the early 1980s to focus U.S. attention on Belize. Belize became independent at a time when official Washington was alarmed over leftist gains in the region, leading to a U.S. rush to fill the "vacuum" left by Britain's departure. As a neighbor of Honduras, Guatemala and El Salvador, moreover, Belize appeared particularly strategic in the widening Central American wars. The Price government was increasingly obliged to bow to U.S. wishes. Although Nicaragua had supported Belizean independence, Price refrained from establishing diplomatic relations with Managua after Washington warned against it. Price also permitted the Voice of America to build a tower in southern Belize for broadcasting to all of Central America.

After the election, however, U.S. involvement escalated rapidly. Although the Esquivel government established diplomatic ties with Nicaragua, it also pursued an explicitly pro-U.S. foreign policy, becoming a founding member of the Reagan-inspired Caribbean Democrat Union. The number of diplomats attached to the U.S. embassy increased sharply

from 7 to 47. A Peace Corps contingent of approximately 140 volunteers in 1986 was the largest in the world in relation to local population, with volunteers assigned to nearly every government ministry.[7]

Loans and grants from USAID jumped from $7.8 million in 1983-84 to $26.5 million in 1985-86.[8] Under a 1985 loan agreement, USAID gained wide sway over Belize's economic policies, requiring the government to pursue deregulation, privatization and investment promotion.

The presence of the British garrison and its role in training the Belize Defense Force had long been a symbolic barrier to U.S. military involvement. In 1986, however, U.S. military aid of $1 million signalled Washington's interest. Officers of the Belize Defense Force have trained at the U.S. Southern Command in Panama. U.S. observers have witnessed joint British/Belizean maneuvers, and in 1986 an American "sports team" from the Southern Command visited the British base. That year also, 120 soldiers from the U.S. Army Corps of Engineers spent three months in Belize building a bridge. Other cooperation has come in the area of drug control, where Belizean police and the British soldiers have helped the U.S. Drug Enforcement Agency destroy marijuana fields.

Most Belizeans, conditioned by years of the Guatemalan threat, accept and even welcome the presence of either British or American forces. But others view the growing U.S. presence with concern. The Society for the Promotion of Education and Research (SPEAR), headed by a former government minister and staffed by disaffected people from both parties, warns:

> That's the way to infiltrate forces into a country—just a "sports team," then construction workers . . . Pretty soon people get used to the idea of having U.S. forces on our soil. They become a virtually permanent presence, and we become another Honduras, although on a smaller scale.[9]

In February 1987, the PUP party newspaper *The Belize Times* reported that customs agents had been prevented from inspecting the cargo of a C-130 transport plane which landed at the Belize international airport. The plane belonged to Southern Air Transport, a company associated with the CIA and used in supply operations to the Nicaraguan contras. The full extent of Belizean cooperation with the operation is unknown.[10]

Despite its foreign dependence, Belizeans are proud of their country's stable democratic institutions and social peace. New pressures since independence, however, threaten to put these achievements to a severe test. Belizeans face the difficult task of economic development and nation-building amid an encroaching regional war. Sovereignty and development are possible for Belize, but achieving them will not be easy in the years to come. ∎

Nicaragua

The Atlantic coast region of Nicaragua includes nearly half the country's territory, but less than 10% of its population. Cut off from the rest of Nicaragua, this vast, sparsely populated land has a history of foreign ties, first to British and later to North American economic interests.

Ethnic differences between the coastal people and other Nicaraguans compound this isolation. Although Spanish-speaking mestizos are now the largest group in the region, the traditionally dominant groups on the coast were the Miskitu Amerindians and the Afro-Caribbean Creoles. The Miskitu population today is estimated at 75,000, concentrated in the north along the Honduran border. The English-speaking Creoles number some 26,000 and live in and around the town of Bluefields. Smaller minorities include Sumu (9,000), Garífuna (1,750), and Rama (850).

Concerned above all with their rights as ethnic minorities, these groups have remained in an uneasy and sometimes hostile relationship to the Sandinista government. But the autonomy process launched in 1984 has begun to heal old wounds, laying the foundation for a national unity which includes the right of minority groups to preserve their cultures, languages and self-government within the revolution.

A History of Foreign Influence

From the 1500s through the mid-19th century, Britain controlled the Atlantic coast region through trade and indirect rule. The Miskitu were the dominant group in the north, their *Moskitia* domain extending into Honduras. The British used the Miskitu as a proxy army to hold back the line of Spanish colonization to the west. Three centuries later, Miskitu collaboration with the U.S. war against the Sandinistas would recall this historic British/Miskitu military alliance.[1]

Along the southern part of the coast, British settlers at Bluefields, Pearl Lagoon and Corn Island brought in African slaves to work on plantations and in the timber camps. The Africans mixed with the Indians and with the British settlers to produce a black group known as the Creoles. They gradually displaced the Miskitu economically and politically, coming to dominate the coast by the early 19th century.

Both the Creoles and the Amerindians viewed as outsiders the mestizo Nicaraguans from the Pacific region, whom they referred to as "Spaniards." The Atlantic coast's physical remoteness reinforced this alienation. The only way to reach the Pacific was to travel by boat up the Escondido River to Rama, with a rough overland connection between Rama and Managua. Indeed, it was easier to reach Bluefields from New Orleans than from Managua.[2] The coastal people thus developed a perspective which was both inward-looking (focusing on their indigenous cultures) and outward-looking (across the ocean to Britain and America), but did not relate closely to the rest of Nicaragua.

In 1894, the Atlantic coast region was formally reincorporated into Nicaragua by President Zelaya and renamed

Creole children in the town of Pearl Lagoon.

Rick Reinhard

Zelaya province in his honor. This political change, however, did nothing to diminish foreign economic control along the coast. Instead, influence shifted from the British to the Americans as U.S. firms moved into the area. They included companies mining silver and gold, such as the Rockefeller-owned Rosario Mining Co., which also had mines in Honduras. Other American firms exported timber and bananas. By the 1890s U.S. interests controlled 90% of the capital investment in the region.[3]

To service this growing business, the Americans brought in two new groups of workers: one group from the Caribbean islands, primarily Jamaica, and the other black Americans from New Orleans. Both eventually blended into the Creole population, reinforcing its Caribbean cultural links.

Along with this shift to U.S. economic control came the rise of the American mission churches, led by the Moravians, as the dominant social institution along the coast. German Moravians established a mission in 1849, working mainly among the Creoles. They turned over their work in 1916 to the American Moravians based in Bethlehem, Pennsylvania. The Anglican Church, whose presence was smaller, turned over its mission to the American Episcopal Church; while the American Capuchins expanded the limited Catholic presence. The mission churches provided almost all the social services in the area, with the Moravian high school the center of higher learning for all of Zelaya.

Their knowledge of English and American Protestant education caused the Creoles to be favored for jobs with the U.S. companies. Yet they also suffered racist discrimination on the part of both the white company managers from the United States and the Spanish-speaking government officials sent from Managua. One result was that many Creoles joined Marcus Garvey's Universal Negro Improvement Association, which established a strong presence in Bluefields around 1920. The superintendent of the Moravian mission described the impact of the Garvey movement, saying, "I do not think that anything during my stay here in Bluefields has taken the people so quickly as this new movement. The majority of our male church members and a goodly number of the female as well are active members of the Black Star Line," the steamship company that was one of Garvey's projects.[4]

But the primary loyalties of the coastal people remained oriented toward the American companies and the mission churches. They purchased their food, clothing and housewares in company commissaries, developing a taste for imported American goods. After the 1930s, when a banana plague hit the area and the forests were overharvested, the American firms pulled out. Although they had reinvested almost nothing in the local economy, many costeños recall the Americans as bene-factors and the turn-of-the-century economic boom as the area's "golden years."[5]

During the 1960s the U.S. government's Alliance for Progress channeled development aid and relief funds into the area, continuing the pattern of U.S. dependence. Except for a few individuals, the coastal groups were not involved in the struggle to overthrow Somoza. They largely escaped the repression which Somoza inflicted on the western part of the country, and greeted the triumph of the revolution with indifference.

The Atlantic Coast and the Revolution

Although the Sandinistas carried out almost no organiz-ing on the Atlantic coast before 1979, the Sandinista National Liberation Front declared when it took power that it would end the age-old isolation and underdevelopment of the region.

Four months after the victory, the new Sandinista government, together with the Indian organization ALPRO-MISU, created MISURASATA (Miskitu, Sumus, Ramas and Sandinistas All Together). It was to serve as the mass organization of the Indian peoples, and as its name implied, officially aligned itself with the revolution. A charismatic Miskitu leader, Steadman Fagoth, was elected coordinator of MISURASATA and was given a seat on the Council of State, the national legislative body.

The Sandinistas hoped that this indigenous organization would mobilize Indian participation in the revolution and produce benefits for the impoverished Zelaya region. Literacy programs in English, Miskitu and Sumu were carried out, along with the development of cooperatives, housing and

water systems, and the beginning of some small industries.

These early initiatives, motivated by idealism, were marred by the Sandinistas' failure to understand or take seriously the differences between the Pacific and Atlantic regions. When young Sandinista cadre from Managua were sent to Zelaya, they showed little sensitivity to local cultures, to say nothing of being unable to communicate in the coastal languages. More than any one transgression of the Sandinistas, however, the costenos resented the arrogance of a revolu-tionary movement in which they had not been involved but which now sought to come into their communities to "improve" their way of life. This paternalistic attitude was illustrated by government billboards in Managua which displayed a brilliant sun rising out of the darkness with the slogan *La Costa Atlántica: Un gigante que despierta* (The Atlantic Coast: A Giant that Awakens). Many costeños felt it was the people of the Pacific side of the country who had been asleep.

Sandinista-Miskitu relations deteriorated sharply in 1981. Steadman Fagoth emerged as a power-seeking demagogue, promising the Miskitu that one day *they* would control Zelaya. He and another Miskitu leader, Brooklyn Rivera, claimed credit for the benefits brought by the revolutionary programs, while condemning the Sandinistas' errors. In early 1981, it was learned that MISURASATA planned to demand control of three-quarters of Zelaya department, equal to one-third of all Nicaraguan territory.

The Reagan administration, meanwhile, was laying the foundations of its war to overthrow the Sandinistas. Former National Guardsmen loyal to Somoza, who had fled to Honduras, were organized by the Central Intelligence Agency into an armed insurgency, the Nicaraguan Democratic Force (FDN). The Sandinistas reacted with alarm to Fagoth's territorial claim, which threatened to give the Somocistas a base inside Nicaragua. The government arrested Fagoth along with other Miskitu leaders, and published evidence showing him to have been an informer for Somoza in the 1970s.

After he was released in response to Indian protests, Fagoth fled to the contra camps in Honduras, where he used the Somocistas' radio station to broadcast charges of Sandi-nista "atrocities." He urged others to join him, and several thousand Miskitu crossed over into Honduras. In late 1981, Fagoth's followers launched a series of attacks from Honduras in coordination with the CIA and the FDN, an operation code-named "Red Christmas."

The Nicaraguan government responded by relocating some 8,500 Miskitu from their border villages along the Río Coco to camps at Tasba Pri, some 35 miles inland. Another 15,000 fled into Honduras to escape relocation.[6] The move to Tasba Pri, and the Sandinistas' burning of the evacuated villages left behind, marked the low point of Sandinista-Miskitu relations. Over the next three years fighting took place in much of the region, involving both the FDN contras and armed Miskitu factions.

Many Creoles also resented Sandinista rule. Accustomed to a privileged position as the dominant coastal group, they felt sidelined by Sandinistas who took over important political posts in the area. The ideological influence of the Moravian Church and the Creoles' pro-American sympathies fostered suspicion of Sandinista "communism." As the U.S. embargo weakened the national economy, many Creoles bitterly blamed the Sandinistas for the lack of consumer goods.[7]

Despite anti-Sandinista protests in Bluefields in 1980, the Creole population did not join the armed struggle. Their basic attitude to the revolution remained one of passive indifference, in contrast to the deeply-felt ethnic nationalism of the Miskitu. The Miskitu also antagonized some Creole communities which were told that when MISURASATA controlled the region, they would have to "go find an island somewhere."[8]

Gradually, however, many Miskitu became disaffected from the contras as it became apparent that neither the Somoza guardsmen nor the CIA really cared about the Indians' ethnic rights. MISURASATA had split in 1981, and Brooklyn Rivera's faction, after three years of fighting, sought to distance itself from the CIA. In late 1984 Rivera returned from exile in Costa Rica to begin negotiations with the government. The first cease-fire agreements were reached with Miskitu fighters in the field in mid-1985. Under the terms, the Indians could keep their weapons to defend their communities against contra attack.

Although the talks with Rivera broke down after several sessions, they were only the beginning of a longer dialogue between the Sandinistas and the coastal groups. It focused on the Indians' and Creoles' desire for self-government, and for recognition of their economic and cultural rights. After initially seeing such demands as a threat, the Sandinistas gradually came to view them as fair and reasonable—and as a path to peace.[9]

Elected local and regional "autonomy commissions" spent two and a half years in discussion with the public before drafting an autonomy statute. The draft was refined by a Multiethnic Assembly of local delegates on the coast, and became law in September 1987. Under its provisions, North and South Zelaya became autonomous regions, each with its own locally-elected regional council. Among other things, the law gives the coastal groups the right to their own forms of land ownership and transfer. It affirms their right to bilingual education and to their cultural traditions. While Spanish remains Nicaragua's official language, the coastal languages now are also official within those regions.

The autonomy law has not erased all distrust of the Sandinistas, nor has it eliminated divisions among the coastal groups. Different sides still have different expectations of what autonomy will mean. The most difficult question may be that of the coastal peoples' claim to economic benefits derived from the land and resources in their traditional areas. The new law affirms their right to a fair share of these benefits, but what constitutes a fair share has yet to be defined.

Still, the autonomy process has defused tensions and tempered skepticism with hope. Thousands of Miskitu have returned to Nicaragua since 1986, repopulating the Río Coco villages. Despite continuing U.S. attempts to unify the Miskitu fighters and bring them into line with U.S. strategies, the process of reconciliation appears likely to continue. Overcoming historical legacies will not be easy. But by recognizing the problem and beginning a genuine dialogue, the government has taken the essential first step. ∎

Rick Reinhard

A community cultural program sponsored by the Sandinista army in El Bluff, near Bluefields.

Costa Rica

Much like the Zelaya department of Nicaragua, Costa Rica's Limón province is a culturally distinct region which has been under the dominance of foreign companies for the last 100 years. As in the Bluefields area of Nicaragua, the arrival of English-speaking West Indian laborers shaped the cultural history of Limón. But Limón and the Zelaya are dissimilar in other ways. Unlike Nicaragua, Costa Rica depends on banana revenues, making its Atlantic coast region an integral part of the national economy. Moreover, it is linked to the rest of Costa Rica by a railroad. So while Limón is a banana company enclave, its social history including aggressive labor organizing has played an important role in modern Costa Rica.

The Costa Rican railroad, completed in 1890, was built and owned by Minor Keith, the North American banana magnate. The Costa Rican government granted Keith generous rights to land along the rail line in exchange for his investment. Keith developed banana plantations on the lands, merging his interests with the Boston Fruit Company in 1899 to form the United Fruit Company.[1]

Since the coastal region was sparsely settled by Amerindians, a foreign labor force was imported to build the railroad. The first to arrive were 600 Jamaicans, 400 Chinese and 500 workers from the Cape Verde islands off the coast of Africa. Another 1,500 came in the second wave, including Barbadians, Italians, East Indians and Chinese.[2]

Working conditions were harsh, due to the hot climate and danger from malaria and yellow fever. The Italians staged a major strike in 1888—the first organized labor protest in the country's history—but left the coast afterwards, many returning to Italy. The Chinese could not withstand the impact of malaria and many died, although some went to set up small businesses in Puerto Limón. Only the Afro-Caribbean peoples survived and remained, turning Limón into a black, English-speaking enclave.

After the completion of the railroad, almost all the Afro-Caribbean workers (often called "Jamaicans") worked for the United Fruit Company in one way or another: on the banana plantations, on the railroad, or loading bananas at the port. They were controlled by the company's rules and dependent on its wages, buying their supplies in company commissaries. As an imported foreign labor force, they were not recognized as citizens by the Costa Rican government, and most of the country was off-limits to them because of an unwritten color bar.

Their culture and loyalties remained strongly West Indian, as the Pan-Africanist Marcus Garvey discovered when he visited Costa Rica in 1910. Garvey's Universal Negro Improvement Association (UNIA) had an active branch in Puerto Limón and several other coastal towns, and old Jamaicans are proud of their participation in Garvey's movement. As one recalled:

You had men come in from Limón, and afterwards they formed a branch [of the UNIA] with president from right here, and secretary, treasurer and all. Practically all the families around was in it. They was trying to unite the people, get all the Negroes together, say they was fighting to go to Africa, to go home back, for they claim that Africa was the home of the Negroes. They didn't succeed in that part. But you had about two men come from Africa here visit all the UNIA branches.[3]

Obstacles to Development

During the 1930s major changes took place in Limón. Because of a banana disease, United Fruit began pulling out of the area, shifting its operations to the Pacific coast around Golfito. Costa Rican peasants took over some of the company's lands to grow bananas or cocoa. By 1935 only one-quarter of the bananas produced in Limón came from United Fruit's plantations, although most independent growers still sold their fruit to the company.[4]

Many banana workers were left unemployed. They could not even travel to Golfito to work, due to racist attitudes and laws. Indeed, trains from Limón regularly stopped at Turrialba, the half-way point, to change crews—from black to white—before continuing on to San José.

Nonetheless, linkages were developing between the Afro-Caribbean workers and the national labor movement, then led by the Costa Rican Communist Party (PCCR). In 1934, the PCCR organized a successful strike among the banana workers through the Confederation of Workers of Costa Rica. The strike mobilized large sectors of the Afro-Caribbean population, gaining support even from black workers who were not members of the labor confederation.

The 1940 election brought to power the head of the Social Christian party, Rafael Calderón Guardia. The Communist Party's Workers and Peasant Bloc (BOC) received 11% of the vote, reflecting its strong trade union support. This led to a marriage of convenience between the two as Calderón, whose popularity soon ebbed, turned to the Communists to shore up his failing popular base. The Catholic Church, motivated by the spirit of the liberal Papal Encyclical called the *Rerum Novarum,* supported the government. With the start of the Cold War, however, this "triple alliance" broke down. Street clashes erupted in San Jose between the Calderón/Communist forces on the one hand and an organized mass resistance on the other. In 1948, the clashes escalated into a 40-day civil war.

The victor was José Figueres, whose Liberation Movement took control of Cartago in the highlands and Limón on the coast, thus controlling the railroad. "Don Pepe," as Figueres was often called, won the affection of the Afro-Caribbean population through his genuine concern about the poverty and discrimination they suffered. His government allowed blacks to travel and settle anywhere in Costa Rica. In

1954, the government signed new contracts with the United Fruit Company, obliging the company to build schools and hospitals, control malaria and provide social security benefits for workers.

Despite this, Figueres' government did not challenge United Fruit's monopolistic control. The company owned 500,000 acres of land in Limón and Golfito, 75% of which lay fallow.[5] From 1940 to 1960, United Fruit's inactivity on the Atlantic coast opened space for tentative efforts at nationally-based development. Banana workers moved in on idle company lands to grow bananas and cocoa independently. Some even took out loans from the government to start cooperatives.[6] The most successful was the "Cooperative of Cocoa Producers of the Atlantic Zone," which had its best year in 1954 due to high cocoa prices. But eventually it failed, deeply in debt.

The government began trying to develop Limón province under the supervision of the Administrative Board for the Development of the Atlantic Strip. A few small nationally-owned industries were started, producing such items as soap, soft drinks and coconut oil. Alliance for Progress funds underwrote infrastructural projects such as roads, making possible the start of a small tourist industry. But by the end of the decade, United Fruit had returned to Limón, while Standard Fruit moved into the Estrella Valley. Together the companies doubled banana production between 1965 and 1970. The development projects of the sixties thus failed to break the hold of foreign control, as the banana companies continued to monopolize production at the expense of national producers and small farmers.

In the 1970s changes in the banana industry and the national economy deepened poverty on the Atlantic coast. As the result of a strike in 1973, United Fruit agreed to sell the run-down railroad to the government for $1.00. This left the government with the burden of maintaining a rail line that would continue to serve the banana companies and coffee exporters at no cost to them. In addition, the banana companies automated their cargo handling system, relegating the stevedores to more menial jobs. As a result, many *costeños,* particularly blacks, moved to San José or migrated to Panama or the United States, looking for work.

Rising prices for imported oil combined with falling prices for banana and coffee exports plunged the Costa Rican economy into deep distress. The government borrowed heavily to finance imports, but interest payments and capital flight due to the growing regional turmoil caused foreign exchange reserves to run out in 1980. As a result, the national currency had to be devalued, dropping from 9 to 60 *colones* per US$1 in 1980 alone. Because of the inflation, the Central Workers Confederation and Unitary Workers Confederation (CUT) demanded pay hikes, leading to a series of strikes in the banana zone.

The pending collapse of the economy forced President Monge to turn to the International Monetary Fund in 1982. When the IMF conditions were imposed, they caused wide-spread suffering. Although Monge appealed to Costa Ricans to "tighten their belts" and "return to the land," he ignored demands for a much-needed agrarian reform. Many peasants and banana workers began occupying fallow lands either privately owned or held by the fruit companies.

In September 1982, the communist-backed CUT labor federation led a strike for a 17% wage increase at BANDECO, a Del Monte subsidiary based in Limón. Anti-labor advertising by BANDECO labelled the strikers Soviet-led terrorists, while President Monge threatened to declare the Communist Party illegal.[7] After 63 days, with the support of the banana workers on the Pacific coast, the CUT won its principal demands.

The banana companies used the threat of their withdrawal to force the government to control labor unrest. Both Standard Fruit and United Fruit (now United Brands) have also pressured the Costa Rican government to reduce its nominal taxation. For both companies, mobility is easy because of their extensive holdings throughout Central America. In 1984, United Brands laid off its workers in Golfito and moved its equipment across the border into Panama. Fearing riots by unemployed workers, the Costa Rican government bought out the company's Pacific coast plantations, paying $1.24 million for 4,200 acres of the country's own land. One Costa Rican popular organization bitterly sums up the attitude of the banana companies: "If you serve me, I rob you; if not, I leave."[8]

In Limón province today, the Afro-Caribbean population is dying out, moving away and intermarrying with mestizo Costa Ricans who have moved into the area. While West Indian language and customs are still common, the future of this Caribbean link is uncertain. The remaining "Jamaicans" look at the past nostalgically and at the future with a sense of resignation:

> Limón will always be different from the rest of Costa Rica. As a matter of culture I think we should stick to our English language. I think in Limón they should give classes in English to people who want it, of course not forgetting Spanish as the language of *our* country. But we need to continue the English as a matter of culture and of international communication. Costa Rica should be proud that they have a group of Costa Ricans that speak English. But as a matter of time I think the Protestant churches will go. The grandchildren will drop away from it, and at the end I think it will be all Catholic, as a matter of convenience, not conviction.[9] ∎

Panama

After conquering Panama in the 16th century, the Spanish used the narrow isthmus as the principal passageway for shipping gold from Peru back to Spain. The indigenous Amerindians could not survive forced labor, so the Spanish brought in Africans to transport the gold and work on small farms. The importance of slave labor was reflected in a 1583 letter to the Spanish Crown stating that "in this Kingdom there is no other service but that of the blacks and without them no one can live in this land."[1]

Many of the slaves escaped and formed rebel communities of *cimarrones* (Maroons) in the mountains, where they were led by the "Black King" Bayano. Other slaves were freed through manumission. Over the next 300 years, intermixing between Africans, Spaniards and Amerindians produced a predominantly black and mestizo population which identified itself as Panamanian. But it was a society ridden with racial and class animosities, in which Indians were at the bottom of the social ladder while descendents of the Spanish settlers formed a ruling elite.

West Indian-Panamanian Links

A new era of Panamanian history began in the mid-19th century as the United States moved into the country, importing its own foreign labor force. Three thousand Chinese and 4,000 other foreign laborers arrived around 1850 to build the Panama railroad.[2] Between 1881, when France began digging a canal, and 1914, when the United States completed the project, some 83,000 laborers came to Panama, the majority from the Caribbean islands [see Part I, Ch. 4].

Thousands of the canal construction workers died, victims of accidents and disease. Others returned home or migrated to the United States when the canal work was completed. About 5,000 were transferred to the United Fruit Company's banana plantations in Bocas del Toro, and later, Chiriquí province. These became a secondary U.S. enclave, also using mainly West Indian labor.[3]

Most of the West Indians, however, settled permanently in Panama City and Colón, the terminal points of the canal. In Colón, people were called "Jamaicans"—meaning they came from the English-speaking islands—or "French," referring to those from Haiti, Martinique and Guadeloupe. They ate Caribbean food such as rice with red beans and coconut, a dish of Jamaican origins. Their music was calypso and their language English or French Creole. One Panamanian recalls her childhood in Colón:

> My great-grandmother came from Martinique, and my great-grandfather from Guadeloupe. They came for the building of the Panama railroad. My maternal grandparents came from Jamaica for the building of the canal. They lived in the Canal Zone during the construction, and afterwards went to live in Colón.
>
> The culture in Colón was very rich, very Caribbean. There was what they called the "French" community, and in fact French Creole was the first language I was taught. Although

the people were poor, they had a Caribbean tradition of hospitality and would welcome you into their houses and offer food. The mestizo Panamanians even adopted some of our West Indian culture, such as the food and the calypso.

> But the Caribbean community was also marginalized from the larger Panamanian reality. My great-grandparents, for instance, never spoke Spanish, although they lived in Panama for years and years and had their children there.
>
> The Caribbean people always talked about going back to their countries, but most of them never were able to. Many did keep in contact with their relatives at home, for forty or fifty years in some cases.[4]

To preserve their culture, the West Indians set up special schools for their children with instruction in English. This cultural separatism, along with the West Indians' position as workers for the North Americans, created tensions with the native black Panamanians. The native blacks—called *negros coloniales,* to distinguish them from the *negros antillanos* who came from the West Indies—tended to view the newcomers as pawns of the Americans who had facilitated the U.S. takeover of the country. Thus the West Indians were resented for their special "privileges," such as being welcome in the U.S.-run Canal Zone while native Panamanians were not.

This was true even though the West Indians were second-class citizens in the Zone compared to the white Americans or "Zonians." The alliance between the North Americans and Panamanian landowners and businessmen reinforced the exclusion of all blacks from political and economic power. The oligarchy controlled both the government and the Panama National Guard for decades, in a racist society where blacks were denigrated as "chombos" and "cholos" while the upper class bragged of its Spanish blood.

Flag Riots and the Torrijos Revolution

The Canal Zone was a U.S.-controlled strip, five miles wide on either side of the canal, which effectively cut Panama in two. U.S. laws held sway in the Zone, which had its own schools, postal system, police and courts, all run by North Americans. During the Second World War, the United States installed 14 military bases and 130 air and intelligence facilities in the Zone, supposedly to defend the canal. This military build-up led to a permanent U.S. military enclave known as the U.S. Southern Command.

After the war, a growing nationalist movement centered in the student population challenged U.S. domination of the Canal Zone. Frequent protests culminated in the "Flag Riots" of 1964, which began when Panamanian students tried to fly the Panamanian flag beside the U.S. flag at Balboa High School in the Zone. North American Zone residents attacked the demonstrators, leading to intervention by the U.S. military and more than 20 deaths.

Coming to power in a 1968 military coup, General Omar Torrijos made sovereignty over the canal a central demand of his nationalist "revolution." After lengthy negotiations, the

Panamanians celebrate Carnival.

Marcelo Montecino

U.S. Senate ratified the Torrijos-Carter treaties in 1978, agreeing to transfer control of the canal to Panama and end the U.S. military presence in the Zone in the year 2000. The leading opponent of the treaty was presidential aspirant Ronald Reagan, who denounced it as a "surrender" of vital U.S. interests.

A pragmatic populist with an ideology neither right nor left, Torrijos effectively broke the political power of the oligarchy. He promoted blacks within the government, the civil service and the Panama National Guard. New laws under Torrijos included a progressive labor code and an agrarian reform. Spending increased on education, health and housing, and the government invested in banana and sugar production and promoted agricultural cooperatives.

As a result of these reforms, poor and black Panamanians were for the first time fully integrated into the national society. The government encouraged the assimilation of West Indian Panamanians, abolishing the special English schools and promoting a unified Panamanian culture. Today, younger Panamanians of West Indian descent speak more Spanish than English, and few still see themselves as a distinct group or identify with American interests. The term "antillano" has fallen gradually into disuse.

Torrijos' progressive reforms, however, were offset by the negative impact of Panama's new role as an offshore financial center. The Banking Law of 1970 turned Panama into the "Little Switzerland" of Latin America, with some 87 offshore banks and 150,000 "paper companies" paying no taxes and exempt from scrutiny by U.S. agencies. Panama became a haven for the laundering of money by transnational banks and corporations, and soon, international narcotics and arms dealers. These developments favored the economic interests of the oligarchy, but also encouraged growing corruption within the military.

The United States and General Noriega

When Torrijos died in a small plane crash in 1981—under suspicious circumstances—both his social programs and the tentative national unity he fostered fell apart. He was followed over the next three years by three different presidents and three heads of the military, who vainly attempted to hold onto Torrijos' support while abandoning his progressive policies.

With United States assistance and training, the Panama National Guard more than doubled its size between 1968 and 1983.[5] Leading Panamanian officers were trained at the School of the Americas, the U.S.-run military academy then located in the Canal Zone. Among them was General Manuel Antonio Noriega, head of Panamanian "G-2" military intelligence, who had been providing information to the CIA since 1967. In 1984, Noriega became commander of the renamed Panama Defense Forces and *de facto* head of the government.

Key U.S. officials had known since the 1970s that the Panamanian military, and Noriega in particular, were heavily involved in corrupt business dealings including drugs and arms smuggling. They chose to overlook this because of the

Panamanian military's cooperation with the United States its readiness to conclude a canal treaty, and later, its willingness to allow the U.S. to maintain a huge military enclave in the Canal Zone, going beyond the limits laid out in the 1978 treaty.[6] Ambler Moss, former U.S. ambassador to Panama, noted:

> Under the treaty, the bases are there for only one purpose: to defend the canal. But you don't need a four-star general and 10,000 troops and airplanes coming and going when the canal isn't being attacked by anyone. So there was a great deal of permissiveness on the part of the Panamanians.[7]

Beginning in the early 1980s, the Southern Command redoubled its importance as a base for intervention in Central America. The National Security Agency monitored the whole region from its Panama installations, and the CIA used the Southern Command as a base for intelligence-gathering and for sending agents into Nicaragua.[8] In addition, cash to fund the contras, some originating from arms sales to Iran, apparently was routed through dummy companies based in Panama.[9] Although Noriega was known to be cooperating with Cuban as well as U.S. intelligence, he was providing Washington with valuable assistance in the contra war.

At an unknown point, and for still-mysterious reasons, the unwritten pact between Noriega and the United States broke down. White House, State Department and intelligence officials began leaking information in 1986 to the U.S. press that Noriega was involved in illicit activities. In June 1987 Noriega's second-in-command, Col. Roberto Díaz Herrera, charged publicly that Noriega had murdered a political opponent, Dr. Hugo Spadafora. He claimed also that Noriega had rigged the 1984 Panamanian election and that Torrijos' death was the result of an assassination conspiracy between Noriega and the CIA.

The Reagan administration responded by launching a high-profile campaign to force out the Panamanian leader. All U.S. economic and military aid to Panama was cut off in July 1987, and wide-ranging economic sanctions imposed later that year. The United States backed an opposition coalition, the National Civic Crusade, made up of business and professional groups. In early 1988, two federal grand juries in Florida indicted Noriega on drug-running charges.

Since Díaz Herrera's allegations merely repeated what was already widely known or suspected about Noriega, the Reagan administration's precise reasons for moving against the general remained unclear. The most likely explanation involves a combination of factors, adding up to U.S. disenchantment with an increasingly nationalist, headstrong and uncontrollable client.

One area of conflict may well have been Central American policy. Although Noriega collaborated with the contra war, at the level of public diplomacy Panama was an initiator of the Contadora peace plan, which the United States strongly opposed. It is possible that in demanding greater and greater cooperation on Central America, Washington may finally have pushed Noriega farther than he was willing to go.

The second conflict involves the canal. In making allegations against Noriega, many U.S. officials hinted their concern about turning over the canal to an "unreliable" government. The explanation advanced by Panamanian nationalists, including Noriega himself, was that Washington planned to keep control of the canal with its associated military bases, and saw the nationalist Panamanian military as standing in the way. Panamanian journalist Luis Restrepo, arguing that the United States had already violated numerous provisions of the canal treaty, stated:

> The United States never intended to hand over the Canal and that is why it has kept a militarization policy in the Panama Canal administration . . . The United States is exerting pressure on the Panamanian government so it will accept the renegotiation of the permanence of the Southern Command in Panama beyond the year 2000.[10]

This explanation tied into another aspect of the situation, one connected to racial and class conflicts in Panamanian society. Although Noriega had lost much of Torrijos' popular base, many poor and black Panamanians still saw the military as defending their rights against the oligarchy. It was the oligarchy which was behind the Civic Crusade, spearheading domestic opposition to Noriega. In an attempt to install a more compliant government, the argument went, the United States was now backing the upper class in its bid to regain power.[11]

There was yet another explanation, one which surfaced with increasing insistence in the Central American press. It concerned Japan. Japan had quietly been moving into the Panamanian economy for more than a decade to become, by the late 1980s, a major player in the $1 billion per year offshore finance sector. Noriega apparently encouraged these inroads, which both threatened to break the stranglehold of U.S. finance in Panama and to give Japan an economic foothold in Latin America.

If the motives for the move against Noriega remained confused, its impact was clear and dramatic. International attention focused on the spectacle of the powerful United States unable to remove a military client. In the space of a year, economic sanctions devastated the Panamanian economy, causing tremendous hardship and turning many people against Noriega. But as the suffering continued with no resolution in sight, anti-Noriega sentiment gradually gave way to growing anger against the United States. Some Panamanians, especially those from the upper class, blamed Washington for failing to finish what it had started. But many others felt that however bad Noriega might be, his refusal to be overthrown made him a symbol of Panamanian nationalism and resistance to U.S. pressures.

It was this ironic symbolism which dominated international reaction as well. As the stalemate continued into 1988, Latin American and Caribbean governments on the left and right called for an end to foreign intervention in Panama. For right-wing regimes, the U.S. vendetta against Panama was a disquieting reminder of their own vulnerability. For the regional left, it was a classic case of imperialist intervention. That U.S. attacks could transform a corrupt CIA client into a symbol of Latin American nationalism dramatically revealed the depths of anti-imperialist sentiment in the region. ∎

NOTES TO PART SIX

The Bahamas

1. EPICA interview, Nassau, Oct. 1987.
2. Michael Craton, *A History of the Bahamas* (Waterloo, Ontario: San Salvador Press, 1986), p. 276.
3. "Inquiry Exposes Bahamas' Corruption," by Nicki Kelly, *Financial Times*, July 3, 1984.
4. "U.S. Weighs Pindling Indictment," *Washington Post*, June 25, 1988.
5. EPICA interview with Thomas Bastian, president, Bahamas Hotel Catering and Allied Workers Union, Nassau, Oct. 1987.
6. EPICA interview, Nassau, Oct. 1987.
7. EPICA interview, Nassau, Oct. 1987.
8. EPICA interview with Canon William Thompson, Nassau, Oct. 1987.
9. Ibid.

Jamaica

1. *Daily Gleaner*, August 16, 1983.
2. Carl Stone, "Continuing Crisis of Jamaica's Economy," *Caribbean Contact*, December 1984.
3. Jamaica Bauxite Institute figures.
4. EPICA interview with a Jamaican economist, September 1983.
5. *Daily Gleaner*, May 7, 1984.
6. Carl Stone, "Running Out of Options in Jamaica," *Caribbean Review*, Winter 1987, p. 32.
7. *Caribbean Insight*, June 1988.
8. *Caribbean Contact*, September 1987.
9. *Sunday Gleaner*, May 5, 1985.
10. *New York Times*, September 21, 1987.

Dominican Republic

1. Bernardo Matias, *El Poder Barrial: Accion Liberadora* (Santo Domingo: Ediciones CEDEE, 1986), pp. 30-31.
2. *Ibid.*, p. 24.
3. *La Noticia*, Jan. 31, 1980.
4. Speech by vice-president Majluta to Miami Conference on the Caribbean, Nov. 1979.
5. *Miami Herald*, April 5, 1984.
6. Letter from President Ronald Reagan to President Jorge Blanco, March 23, 1984.
7. *Latinamerica Press*, May 28, 1987.
8. Joseph Treaster, "Dominican Republic Tourism Booms," *New York Times*, April 11, 1988.
9. "Mas Alla del Primer Ano: Gobierno, Desalojos y Desarraigo," (Santo Domingo: Ediciones CEDEE, 1987), p. 13.
10. *Ibid.*, p. 6.
11. "Debt Crisis is Inflicting a Heavy Human Toll in Dominican Republic," *Wall Street Journal*, Aug. 20, 1987.

Haiti

1. For a detailed account of the role of the Haitian Church in the anti-Duvalier movement, see *Report of the Mission of Pax Christi International to Haiti* (Erie, PA: Pax Christi International, 1986.)
2. *Washington Post*, March 10, 1983.
3. *Report of the Mission of Pax Christi International to Haiti*, pp. 82-83.
4. *Haiti: Duvalierism Since Duvalier* (National Coalition for Haitian Refugees and the Americas Watch Committee, 1986), pp. 15-16.
5. *Haiti: Terror and the 1987 Elections* (National Coalition for Haitian Refugees and the Americas Watch Committee, 1987), pp. 49-53.
6. *Washington Post*, Dec. 4, 1988.
7. National Committee of the Democratic Movements Congress (KONAKOM), "The Impossibility of Any Democratic Changes Under the Presidency of Leslie F. Manigat," March 29, 1988.

Dominica

1. Robert Thompson, *Green Gold: Bananas and Dependency in the Eastern Caribbean* (London: Latin America Bureau, 1987), pp. 4-5 and 27-31.
2. Prime Minister Eugenia Charles, budget address, July 1987.
3. Thompson, p. 45.
4. Bob Woodward, *Veil: The Secret Wars of the CIA 1981-1987* (New York: Simon and Schuster, 1987), p. 290.
5. EPICA interview with Noreen John, Roseau, Nov. 1987.

Barbados

1. "A Briefe Discription of the Ilande of Barbados," in Vincent T. Harlow, ed., *Colonising Expeditions to the West Indies and Guiana, 1623-1667* (London: Hakluyt Society, 1925), pp. 42-43.
2. Rickey Singh, "Barbados at 21: Celebration of Progress," *Caribbean Contact*, Dec. 1987.
3. Dr. Courtney Blackman, former Central Bank governor, "The Economy in Review," Barbados *Nation*, Dec. 2, 1987.
4. *Latinamerica Press*, May 28, 1987.
5. Colin Hope and Michael Richards, "Barbados' Tight Elections," *Caribbean Contact*, June 1986.

Grenada

1. Joseph Treaster, "To Ordeals in Grenada Add a Trial," *New York Times*, July 28, 1986.
2. Grenada Industrial Development Corporation, correspondence, Dec. 22, 1987.
3. In 1987 U.S. economic aid to Grenada was $6.3 million for capital expenditures, accounting for 21% of the capital budget, and $8.3 million for budgetary support to cover the deficit.
4. EPICA interview with Einstein Louison, MBPM, Dec. 1987.
5. After the invasion the 1974 constitution was restored, but the court system established by the PRG was retained for the trial. The effect was to deny the option of appeal to the Privy Council in England.

Trinidad and Tobago

1. Eric Williams, *History of the People of Trinidad & Tobago* (London: Andre Deutch, 1964), p. 40.
2. Gordon K. Lewis, *The Growth of the Modern West Indies* (New York: Monthly Review Press, 1968), p. 69.
3. Raphael Sebastien, "State-Sector Development in Trinidad and Tobago, 1956-1982," *Contemporary Marxism*, No. 10 (1985), p. 110.
4. Dr. Trevor Farrell, "Mr. Chambers' First Year," *Caribbean Contact*, November 1982.
5. *Caribbean Contact*, August 1984.
6. Concerned Group of Trade Unions, "Statement from the Trade Union Movement to the Working People, Farmers, Housewives, Youths, Unemployeds of Trinidad and Tobago on the Economic Crisis," (Port-of-Spain, 1986).

Guyana

1. The official population figure used by the Guyana government was 793,000 in 1986. However, reliable estimates are closer to 700,000. The 1987 annual report of the World Bank cites Guyana's per capita GNP as lowest in the Caribbean except for Haiti.
2. Walter Rodney, "People's Power, No Dictator" (Working People's Alliance, 1979).
3. "Report of the International Team of Observers at the December 1980 Elections" (the Avebury Report). Cited in *Caribbean Contact*, Jan. 1981.
4. Clive Y. Thomas, *The Poor and the Powerless: Economic Policy and Change in the Caribbean* (New York: Monthly Review Press, 1988), p. 252.
5. EPICA interview with Eusi Kwayana, Guyana, March 1988.
6. Clive Y. Thomas, *The Poor and the Powerless*, pp. 255-257.
7. *Ibid.*, pp. 258-260.
8. Guyana Human Rights Association, *Guyana Human Rights Report 1984*, p. 34.
9. "Civic Bodies Record Profound Disappointment Over Elections," mimeographed statement issued Dec. 10, 1985 and signed by the Anglican and Catholic bishops, and officials of four trade unions, the Guyana Bar Association and the Guyana Human Rights Association.
10. Guyana Human Rights Association, *Guyana Human Rights Report 1987*, p. 11.
11. EPICA interview with Bishop Randolph George, Guyana, March 1988.
12. EPICA interview with Dr. Cheddi Jagan, PPP, Guyana, March 1988. Also, "Report of the Central Committee to the 22nd Congress of the People's Progressive Party," August 3-5, 1985, pp. 76-87.
13. EPICA interview with Eusi Kwayana, WPA, Guyana, March 1988. Also, "Socialist Guyana—The Way Forward and Upward: Some Key Issues," presentation by Eusi Kwayana at Critchlow Labour College, Guyana, March 1985.

Suriname

1. "The Bush Negroes of Suriname," *Caricom Perspective*, Sept./Oct. 1984, p. 20.
2. Henk E. Chin and Hans Buddingh', *Surinam: Politics, Economics and Society* (London: Francis Pinter Ltd., 1987), pp. 26-27.
3. EPICA interview with Rob Leter, director of INDEX, Suriname, March 1988.
4. Chin and Buddingh', p. 53.
5. *Ibid.*, p. 60.
6. EPICA interview with Neville Duncan, representative of Caribbean Rights, December 1987.

NOTES TO PART SIX, *continued*

Guadeloupe

1. *New York Times,* July 26, 1985.
2. *Guadeloupe 2000,* July/August 1982, p. 2.
3. EPICA interview with Fr. Serge Plocoste, Working-Class Christian Youth, Guadeloupe, August 1982.
4. UPLG, "Pou Nou Vanse au Chimen a Lendepandans," June 1981.
5. *Le Monde,* March 2, 1985.
6. Institut National de la Statistique et des Etudes Economiques, Service Interregional Antilles-Guyane, *Bilan Annuel de la Guadeloupe 1986,* pp. 31-36.
7. Letter from Edouard Boulogne, president of Association Guadeloupe 2000, disseminated in leaflet form.

Curacao

1. J. Hartog, *Curacao: Short History* (Aruba: De Wit Stores, 1979), p. 53.
2. "First Conclusion of Antillean-Venezuelan Project," *Antillen Review,* Dec. 1983/Jan. 1984, pp. 43-45.
3. EPICA interview with Henry Habibe, Antillean Linguistic Institute, Curacao, March 1988.
4. *Antillen Review,* Dec. 1983/Jan. 1984, p. 7.
5. EPICA interview with Raymond Rojer, Curacao, March 1988.

Puerto Rico

1. Raymond Carr, *Puerto Rico: A Colonial Experiment* (New York: Vintage Books, 1984), pp. 49-50.
2. Jose Villamil, "Economia y Status Politico," *El Reportero,* April 12, 1983.
3. *Caribbean Insight,* April 1987.
4. "Island Tests of 19 Wells Found All But 1 Contaminated," *San Juan Star,* March 1, 1983.
5. Industrial Mission of Puerto Rico, 1985 Annual Report; "Mayaguez: Esta es la Verdad," *Noti Ambiente,* No. 4, 1986.
6. Industrial Mission of Puerto Rico, 1985 Annual Report.
7. "The Poisoning of Christian City," *Washington Post,* June 30, 1986.
8. *The Militant,* January 11, 1985.
9. *New York Times,* February 13, 1985.
10. "FBI Conduct an Issue in Robbery Case," *Washington Post,* February 17, 1988.

Belize

1. *Spearhead,* March/April 1988.
2. Alma H. Young and Dennis H. Young, "The Impact of the Anglo-Guatemalan Dispute on the Internal Politics of Belize," *Latin American Perspectives,* Vol. 15, No. 2, Spring 1988, pp. 12-18.
3. Population figures (rounded) from 1985 Belizean census, cited in Harriot W. Topsey, "The Ethnic War in Belize," paper presented at the First Annual Studies on Belize conference, Belize City, May 1987.
4. *Ibid.*
5. O. Nigel Bolland, "Race, Ethnicity and National Integration in Belize," paper presented at First Annual Studies on Belize conference.
6. Assad Shoman, "Profile of Belize," paper prepared for Oxfam America, 1986, pp. 10-11.
7. The Peace Corps has since reduced the number of volunteers to around 117, and has pulled many out of government agencies, in response to criticism. *Central America Report,* Feb. 12, 1988.
8. *Spearhead,* March/April 1988, based on interview with then head of USAID mission in Belize.
9. *Spearhead,* April/May 1987.
10. *Caribbean Insight,* March 1987.

Nicaragua

1. Philippe Bourgois, "The Miskitu of Nicaragua: Politicized Ethnicity," *Anthropology Today* Vol. 2, No. 2, 1986, p. 5.
2. *Ibid.,* p. 6.
3. Katharine Yih, "Autonomy & the Revolution: Nicaragua's Atlantic Coast Dialogue," *Against the Current,* Nov.-Dec. 1987, p. 41.
4. G. Grossman, "Bluefields Station Report 1920," at Moravian Church archives, Bethlehem, Pennsylvania, cited in V. Wunderich, "Seguidores de Marcus Garvey in Bluefields 1920," *WANI,* No. 4, July-Sept. 1986, p. 35.
5. Centro de Investigaciones y Documentacion de la Costa Atlantica (CIDCA), *Trabil Nani: Historical Background and Current Situation of the Atlantic Coast* (Managua: CIDCA, 1984), pp. 11-12.
6. Yih, p. 42.
7. Edmundo T. Gordon, "History, Identity, Consciousness and Revolution: Afro-Nicaraguans and the Nicaraguan Revolution," in *Ethnic Groups and the Nation State: The Case of the Atlantic Coast of Nicaragua* (edited by CIDCA and the Development Study Unit, Department of Social Anthropology, University of Stockholm, 1987), pp. 156-159.
8. *Trabil Nani,* p. 23.
9. Yih, p. 43.

Costa Rica

1. Jeffrey Casey Gaspar, *Limon 1880-1940: Un Estudio de la Industria Bananera en Costa Rica* (San Jose: Editorial Costa Rica, 1979), p. 23.
2. Rodrigo Quesada Monge, "Ferrocarriles y Crecimiento Economica: El Caso de la Costa Rica Railroad Company," *Annuario de Estudios Centroamericanos* (Instituto de Investigaciones Sociales, Universidad de Costa Rica), Vol. 8, 1983, p. 98.
3. Paula Palmer, *"What Happen": A Folk History of Costa Rica's Talamanca Coast* (San Jose Ecodesarrollos, 1977), p. 200.
4. Casey Gaspar, p. 91.
5. Carlos Araya Pochet, *Historia Economica de Costa Rica 1950-1970* (San Jose: Editorial Fernandez Ara, 1975), p. 41.
6. EPICA interview with cooperative leader, Siquirres, Costa Rica, July 1985.
7. Marc Edelman and Jayne Hutchcroft, "Costa Rica: Resisting Austerity," *NACLA Report on the Americas,* January/February 1984, p. 39.
8. COPAN, *Revista Teorica,* August 6-12, 1984, p. 6.
9. Palmer, p. 324.

Panama

1. Juan Materno Vasquez, *El Pais por Conquistar* (Panama: J.M. Vasquez, 1974), p. 36.
2. Luis A. Diez Castillo, *Los Cimarrones y los Negros Antillanos en Panama* (Panama: L. Diez Castillo, 1981), p. 63. Also, Xavier Gorostiaga, "La Zona del Canal y su Impacto en el Movimiento Obrero Panameno," *Tareas* (Panama), #32, July/August 1975, pp. 34-35.
3. Jorge Arosemena, "Los Panamenos Negros Descendientes de Antillanos? Un Caso de Marginalidad Social?" *Tareas,* #32, July/August 1975, p. 57.
4. EPICA interview with Esmeralda Brown, Washington, DC, May 1985.
5. Larry Rohter, "America's Blind Eye," *New York Times Magazine,* May 29, 1988, p. 29.
6. *Ibid.* Also, Seymour M. Hersh, "Panama Strongman Said to Trade in Drugs, Arms and Illicit Money," *New York Times,* June 12, 1986.
7. Rohter, p. 34.
8. Hersh, p. 14.
9. "Panama Offers Haven for Shadowy Concerns," *Washington Post,* December 21, 1986, p. 20.
10. Luis Restrepo, "50 U.S. Violations of the Carter-Torrijos Treaties," *Frontera News,* Feb.-March 1988.
11. Tony Best, "Race and Class in Panama's Crisis," *Caribbean Contact,* April 1988.

PART SEVEN
Winds of Change
Building Alternatives for the Future

Vicky Surles

Introduction

While the problems facing the Caribbean are the subject of much discussion, the search for solutions has barely begun. Caribbean governments have played a role in this effort, but the real creativity has come from non-governmental sectors. Organizations of women, youth and farmers, trade unions, community development groups, religious leaders and grass-roots Christians, intellectuals and left activists all have offered ideas for alternatives. Their proposals vary, but certain common themes have shaped a progressive vision of change.

A central point of agreement is the need to redirect resources toward the poor majority, placing priority on education, health care, housing, nutrition and employment programs. This contrasts to the International Monetary Fund's structural adjustment model, with its sharp cuts in social services and consumption by the poor. While there is agreement on this general goal, however, there is no consensus on how to achieve it. Some progressive groups favor socialism, in the long if not the short term. Most favor a mixed economy, or simply a redirection of priorities within the framework of social democracy.

Linked to this is the question of greater economic self-reliance. If Caribbean countries produced more of what they consume, they could reduce their dependence on unstable commodity exports. Due in part to the limitations of small markets, the Caribbean will always need to import many items, and thus a strong export base will remain important. But the potential for diversifying production, especially of food, has hardly been tapped. Such an effort implies giving priority to agriculture, with development of food crops, fisheries, poultry and stockraising. It would require technical and financial support to small farmers, many of them women, who are the region's primary food producers. With creative planning on a regional basis, Caribbean countries could lead the way in developing political economies appropriate to small states.

Creativity likewise is needed to solve the region's funda-mental political problem: working out a constructive relationship with the United States. Progressives have made respect for Caribbean sovereignty and non-alignment a basic demand. At the same time, many acknowledge that U.S. hegemony is a reality that cannot simply be wished away; the challenge is to find a way to deal with it. This implies diversifying political alliances and trade relations to include a range of partners, including other regional powers such as Mexico which can help to buffer hemispheric relationships.

All agree that the Caribbean must resist further U.S. militarization. The Caribbean Conference of Churches introduced the concept of the Zone of Peace, a non-militarized, non-aligned region which would be protected from involvement in superpower conflicts. Endorsed by the CCC's member churches, the Zone of Peace proposal also received strong support from grassroots organizations and left activists, and from the Bishop government in Grenada.

Finally, the concept of Caribbean unity is an integral part of the progressive vision. Caribbean economists long have argued that greater regional cooperation would permit more efficient use of resources and diversified production. Politically, greater unity between Caribbean states is essential to the effort to strengthen the region's position vis-a-vis the major powers.

The long-dormant regional integration movement was revived in 1982 as the CARICOM heads of government met twice within one year. The invasion of Grenada a year later disrupted the fragile unity process. But in 1987, the leaders of the small Eastern Caribbean states began discussing a possible unity plan. Their move reflects the continuing desire to find solutions to the problems of "small sovereignty."

While official progress toward integration remains slow, people's organizations in various terrorities have been forging their own links. This gradual strengthening of unity at the grassroots level may in time provide a more solid basis for regional integration and progressive change. ∎

Barbadian group protests presence of U.S. nuclear-powered aircraft carrier Dwight D. Eisenhower in Caribbean waters.

The Left Debate

The year 1984 was a crucible for the Caribbean progressive movement. Whirled in controversy, under pressure from the establishment, and burning with mutual recriminations, the left began dealing with the trauma of Grenada. All agreed that the destruction of the revolution set back the movement, probably by years. The process of recovery has barely begun. But that process holds out hope: hope that through questioning and defining basic principles, and opening them to public debate, the left will emerge with a new clarity and a stronger popular base.

Two factors produced the crisis. One was the split within the New Jewel Movement, culminating in the executions of Maurice Bishop and the other leaders. The other was the invasion. Both were important, but it can be argued that the significance of the first factor outweighed that of the second. If the U.S. invasion had occurred without the executions, it most likely would have strengthened the left and hurt the right by underscoring the truth of allegations about U.S. imperialism in the region.

As it was, the New Jewel Movement's apparent self-destruction confused the situation. For many people, the execution of Bishop destroyed the revolution from within and made the invasion an inevitable, even justifiable, consequence. In the Dominican Republic, where the largest protests against the U.S. action took place—due to the island's own history of U.S. invasion—one progressive leader wrote:

> Solidarity with Grenada could have been 100 times more powerful if the events there had not been so difficult to understand, owing to the murder of Bishop and his comrades. Had that situation not arisen, the imperialists would have encountered not only much greater resistance from the Grenadian people, but also far more serious mass protests in all the countries of the region.[1]

Paradoxically, one effect of the invasion was to partially restore the revolution's positive image after it had been tarnished by the killings. The superpower attack once again cast Grenada in the role of innocent victim. In the process, many people were prompted to reflect on what the Grenada revolution stood for and why it had been important. As Fidel Castro stated:

> The United States wanted to kill the symbol of the Grenadian revolution, but the symbol was already dead. The Grenadian revolutionaries themselves destroyed it with their spirit and their colossal errors. We believe that, after the death of Bishop and his closest comrades, after the army fired on the people and after the [New Jewel Movement] and the government divorced themselves from the world, the Grenadian revolutionary process could not survive.
>
> In its efforts to destroy a symbol, the United States killed a corpse and brought the symbol back to life at the same time.[2]

The Party and the People

How and why the Grenada revolution fell apart will be the subject of debate for years to come. Some of the internal process has come to light through interviews with surviving members of the New Jewel Movement, especially former government ministers Kenrick Radix and George Louison. Further information may eventually become available if Bernard Coard and his supporters tell their story.

The conflict which developed within the New Jewel Movement apparently hinged on both personal rivalries and political disputes. Some observers say that Coard, who was minister of finance and deputy prime minister in the government headed by Maurice Bishop, envied Bishop's power and popularity. However, larger issues were also involved. All of the leadership, including Bishop and Coard, saw the New Jewel movement as a vanguard party structured along Leninist lines, with decision-making by majority vote within the party's Central Committee. For Bishop, however, it was the Grenadian people, not the party, who ultimately were key to the revolutionary process. He favored building organs of "popular democracy," village and parish councils where the people could have a direct voice. The tendency led by Coard showed less interest in these structures and favored tight party control through a disciplined and "ideologically advanced" Central Committee.

Coard's faction grew out of a Marxist study group called OREL which he led in the 1970s, bringing a number of young Grenadians under his influence at a time when the New Jewel Movement was in formation. Although OREL joined the NJM in 1973, some of its members formed a clique around Coard within the party, concentrated in the NJM's youth arm.[3]

By the end of 1982, two identifiable factions had emerged, although it appears that Bishop was not aware of the split or at least not convinced of its seriousness. According to Radix and Louison, Coard used his influence to stack the Central Committee with former OREL members, some of whom were also officers in the People's Revolutionary Army. The perception of a military threat from the United States contributed to this tendency toward enlarging the army and bringing its officers into important party positions. Most of the original founders of the NJM, meanwhile, remained loyal to Bishop, including foreign minister Unison Whiteman, education minister Jacqueline Creft, Radix, Louison and a number of others.

The issues at stake did not primarily concern the programs or goals of the revolution. Both Bishop and Coard saw the revolution's ultimate goal as building socialism in Grenada. Both also favored a mixed economy in the near term, with public, private and cooperative sectors. Economists and bankers in the region praised Coard for his competence as a financial manager and his harmonious dealings with inter-

Bernard Coard, left, and Maurice Bishop in happier times.

Barbados *Nation*

national lending agencies such as the International Monetary Fund, the Caribbean Development Bank and the World Bank. Both Bishop and Coard also wanted normal relations with the United States and other capitalist countries, although not at the price of giving up the revolution's principles. It is erroneous to suggest, as some have, that Coard wanted "instant socialism" while Bishop favored a reconciliation with the capitalist world.

Rather, the conflict was over the nature and leadership of the party and its relationship to the people. By mid-1983, there was a perception in the party that popular enthusiasm for the revolution was flagging and that many government programs were disorganized. While the latter at least was probably true, the Central Committee's reaction seems to have been out of proportion to the actual problems. While everyone agreed there was a crisis, the party split over how to deal with it. Bishop argued for strengthening the party's "weak links" with

the masses and for greater accountability. Coard supporters, on the other hand, blamed Bishop himself, accusing him of weak leadership and attacking him and his supporters as "petty bourgeois" and "right opportunist." The heavy ideological tone of these accusations contributed to the later theory of an "ultra-left" group within the party, but it does not appear that any substantive ideological debate took place.

Since Bishop remained extremely popular with a majority of Grenadians, the move against him marked the party's alienation from mainstream sentiment in the country. As the crisis deepened, the Central Committee's disdain for popular wishes seemed almost vengeful. Bishop's decision to question the Central Committee order to share leadership with Coard may have violated the norms of a Leninist party, as some argue.[4] But the more important reality was that Bishop's stature as a leader in Grenada and internationally, and the affection Grenadians held for him, enabled the revolution to go forward. For the Central Committee members to strip such a figure of his leadership, to say nothing of backing up their decision with murder, was to blindly cast away the only basis for the revolution's survival—its popular support.

Debate Within the Movement

Events in Grenada produced a new pressure on Caribbean left groups to define where they stood in terms of basic ideology and models. This caught some groups unprepared as they had never really dealt clearly with these issues, despite having specific platforms of economic and social reforms. No longer could parties claim to be simply "popular movements" advocating progressive change. Especially in the case of the stronger opposition parties, people demanded to know what they believed, how they operated, and how they would govern.

In Jamaica and Guyana, the search for alternatives to Seaga and Burnham made the character of opposition parties a matter of pressing concern. The Workers Party of Jamaica published a letter from a reader in its newspaper, Struggle, which read in part:

> . . . Now many people are looking for your Party's activity in youth and community development here in southern Trelawney. The JLP [Seaga's party] showing themselves as very strong but they do not do much work toward the poor only the rich. So your party supporters are asking you to contest the next General Elections in Southern Trelawney.
> . . . I know your Party's policy is very strong towards our economy. But I don't think many Jamaicans fully understand the intention of the Party because they think you would take away their freedom and democracy from them and also hold no elections. So I am asking you to hold meetings and give the people the fullest idea of your party so they cooperate with it.[5]

Similarly, a columnist in the Guyanese weekly the Catholic Standard wanted to know:

> What is the position of the WPA [Working People's Alliance] on the Grenadian debacle?
> Did it support the Bishop faction or the Coard faction? Has that issue provoked debate within the party?
> Arising out of this, is the WPA a Marxist-Leninist party and what does that mean in practice?[6]

In part, such questions were stimulated by the anticommunist histrionics of conservative leaders. But they also reflected concern about the real differences existing among left groups—differences which had developed over a period of time and emerged publicly in response to events in Grenada.

In analyzing the debate, it is important to recognize that broad points of agreement continued to characterize the left. No progressive party or group in the region supported the U.S. invasion of Grenada. All opposed it in the strongest terms, no matter what their position on internal events in Grenada. In addition, all recognized that while there was a crisis in Grenada after the death of Bishop, it merely presented the Reagan administration with an opportunity to implement intervention plans. For example, the Oilfields Workers Trade Union (OWTU) in Trinidad wrote:

> The Reagan administration has always wished to see an end to the process of new democracy in Grenada. They wanted to put an end to the efforts of the Grenadian people who were building a free country that was an inspiration to the entire working people of the Caribbean. Indeed the records will show that over the past four years the Reagan administration secretly decided on a military rather than a political solution and therefore had developed sophisticated plans for the military's invasion of Grenada.[7]

Like many others, however, the OWTU also bitterly condemned the Coard faction for Bishop's death and blamed their actions for opening the door to invasion:

> Freedom was first highjacked by the Butchers of St. George's and this laid the foundation for the invasion of foreign troops.[8]

On the other hand, several groups in the region argued that the regional condemnation and isolation of the Revolutionary Military Council (RMC) had encouraged the United States to invade. These groups sent solidarity messages to be read on Grenadian radio during the period the RMC was in control. They blamed Bishop for disobeying the decision of the Central Committee on joint leadership, and saw this as provoking the violence. A few even questioned whether the killings at Fort Rupert had really been executions:

> . . . If [Bishop] was executed and if he was assassinated, then we cannot agree with such a thing, we are against it and we condemn it.[9]

Those perceived as supporting the RMC and Coard quickly found their position unpopular. The Caribbean public was distraught over Bishop's murder and uninterested in arguments about party prerogatives. As a result, several parties which had initially sided with the Central Committee eventually backed away from this position.

The perception remained, however, of a split within the left over reaction to Grenada. These divisions concerned fundamental issues such as the role of the party versus that of the people; the nature and pace of social change in the Caribbean; and the role of democratic institutions in a revolutionary process.

Coard's tendency within the NJM stressed the principle of democratic centralism, or decision-making by majority vote in which lower levels of the party are bound by decisions of higher organs. This in turn is linked to the Leninist concept of the vanguard party, the elite group which uses its theoretical understanding of social forces to lead the masses to socialism.

After the death of Bishop, left-wing parties around the region began taking a closer look at these concepts. Democratic centralism had been used by the Coard faction to justify the removal of Bishop, on the basis of a party majority but in direct defiance of the masses. This betrayed a serious misunderstanding of the Grenadian revolutionary process by some of its own leaders, for, as Barbadian novelist George

Lamming put it, Bishop "existed in the popular consciousness of the Grenada people as their most organic link to the revolution."

> Even those who had remained doubtful about the revolutionary process had found in Maurice Bishop a symbol of national pride with which they could identify. In the context of that political culture, the question we ask is this:
> "How do you put such a leader under house arrest without arresting the revolution itself? By what failure of the imagination could such an act be separated from its consequences?"[10]

The question of vanguardism was pertinent because the New Jewel Movement was a very small party, with less than 300 members, of whom only about 65 were full members. The Central Committee numbered 17. Since the People's Revolutionary Government enjoyed mass support, the narrow composition of the decision-making organs attracted little attention until the crisis hit. Clive Thomas, a Guyanese political economist associated with the Working People's Alliance, commented:

> One of the issues which comes out of these events is the failure of the [New Jewel Movement] to recognize that the very development of the idea of vanguardism during the period of its control was leading in effect to a *depoliticization* of the people and the rise of authoritarianism—whatever might have been their well-meaning intentions to the contrary.
> When one reads the [Central Committee] record, one sees for example such ridiculous statements as "the position of the Central Committee and of the masses of workers do not always coincide, because in many instances we have the advantage of science." It shows how divorced a small vanguard group had become from the very people they were seeking to represent.[11]

The realization of the NJM's isolation raised new questions as to whether the Grenadian people and the party had seen the revolutionary process in the same way. One Grenadian trade union leader later reflected:

> The socialist aims of the revolution were a long way off. In the short term, the PRG was bringing immediate benefits to the workers, especially the right to organize. That's why they supported the revolution.
> Socialism was being discussed by a broad cross section of the working class, but they weren't convinced yet. We needed time, a lot more time.[12]

The roots of the Grenada revolution were not socialist but democratic and anti-dictatorial. The leadership agreed that the revolution in its initial stages was merely "oriented" toward socialism. In his 1982 "Line of March for the Party," Bishop argued that Grenada could not build socialism quickly, due to the small size of the Grenadian working class (as opposed to the peasantry) and the country's underdevelopment.

While there is little evidence that Coard's supporters thought they could speed up the transition to socialism, the perception that they sought to do so was a factor in the regional debate. Since the Grenada tragedy, progressive parties have moved to define more precisely their position on the transition to socialism. Tim Hector of the Antigua Caribbean Liberation Movement writes:

> At this juncture, ACLM proposes not a socialist economy in Antigua, but a national economy, based on three pillars: the public sector, 2) the private sector, and 3) the cooperative sector. For the question at this time is not overcoming capitalism, but first, overcoming the root cause of our historical woe, absentee ownership or foreign domination.[13]

Even for those parties which identify themselves as Marxist-Leninist, a guarded tone has entered the debate. The Bloque Socialista in the Dominican Republic states:

> The Socialist Bloc defines itself as a Marxist-Leninist revolutionary organization . . . Its program of revolutionary transformations has a socialist perspective, although it is not fully committed to the immediate construction of socialism.[14]

Perhaps the deepest soul-searching took place within the Workers' Party of Jamaica, a self-proclaimed Communist party which faced a serious erosion of its support after the Grenada invasion. After a ten-month absence, the WPJ newspaper *Struggle* returned to anounce that the party was seeking to broaden its base and "come out of our little corner." WPJ leader Trevor Monroe wrote:

> My own concept is that we have not sufficiently understood and applied a basic principle of marxists—that principle is that Marxism is not a dogma; it is a guide. This needs to be more deeply understood and applied, and in applying it, our Party needs to ensure that it is linked more into the concrete conditions of Jamaica and the Jamaican people.[15]

A final area of debate concerns the role of elections, the multi-party system, and constitutionality in the process of social change. The New Jewel Movement had rejected these structures, at least in the short term, as incapable of bringing about true democracy. Since Gairy had used fraudulent elections to maintain his dictatorship, few progressives in the region criticized the NJM for deferring elections and attempting to build a new system. But when that effort fell apart, the left reopened debate on the problem.

The discussion is not about whether left parties should contest elections while in opposition, since most already do so. The question is whether the structures of "Westminster democracy"—multiple parties, a Parliament, a Constitution, periodic elections—should be the model progressive parties retain once in power.

One response has come from the opposition parties in Guyana. Like Gairy, Guyanese president Forbes Burnham held regular, fraudulent elections to mask dictatorial rule. Rather than dispense with elections entirely, both the People's Progressive Party and the Working People's Alliance have called for genuine electoral democracy to replace the present fraud. The WPA, which boycotted the 1980 election, shifted its strategy after the Grenada disaster, saying:

The WPA believes in free and fair elections, fully elected representative bodies and legislature at all levels of the state, the freedom of special interests to campaign for due process and the constitutional behavior of all who exercise authority . . . The WPA in respect of Guyana does not support a one-party state, formal or informal.[16]

Despite the electoral model's vulnerability to abuse, it has retained a strong legitimacy and importance in Caribbean popular culture. For many Caribbean people, universal suffrage, like the right to organize trade unions, is an important victory won only a few decades ago. It is linked symbolically with emancipation and political independence. On the left, therefore, there is a growing conviction that some form of the electoral process must be a part of progressive politics in the region.

This does not mean that elections are seen as a panacea which automatically ensures democracy, nor as protection against external pressures. People recall that the United States and Britain twice overthrew Cheddi Jagan's democratically elected government. For this reason, few believe that the Bishop government could have avoided destabilization simply by holding elections. Gordon K. Lewis writes:

Even if the PRG regime had held elections after 1979—which might at least have been a prudent move—that in itself could not have guaranteed safety, for [Guyana] showed that imperialism will destabilize a leftwing regime even though it has been constitutionally elected.[17]

Rather, the new reflections on democracy deal primarily with strengthening the social change process. Events in Grenada suggested that while the old structures had been eliminated, those which replaced them had not created adequate channels for popular input into the governmental process. The question of institutionalizing a successful revolution has thus become a crucial one. Tim Hector reflects:

We have to begin to review the role of the party: not in an anti-Leninist way, but we are in a dynamic changing situation and there is a need for changing theory. We need to look at the *concept* of the vanguard party. The transformation of party leaders into a ruling elite can and must be avoided.

Party building must be based in productive activity—cooperatives, agriculture, education. We need to understand the problems of organizing the masses. In Grenada, the people responded enthusiastically to the parish and village councils, but the whole state machinery worked to negate it.[18]

Themes of Hope

Out of the painful reassessment which followed the invasion, some hope for the future has emerged.

First, there is now a more sober and realistic understanding of the constraints that a progressive government in the Caribbean will face. The economic crisis, hostility from Washington, physical underdevelopment and the shortage of skilled persons all place limits on what a revolutionary government can accomplish in its first years. Yet popular expectations of immediate benefits place the new leadership under tremendous pressure to "deliver." The Grenada experience showed how devastating these pressures could be, and the level of political and personal maturity needed to survive them.

Secondly, there is a new emphasis on the need for honesty. Most left parties in the region did not know of the divisions within the New Jewel Movement, just as most Grenadians did not know, and many share the Grenadian people's sense of betrayal. The NJM's secrecy stemmed in part from the siege mentality which developed in response to external pressures. In retrospect, it is evident that this secrecy allowed internal differences to build up to the point of explosion. Concludes one party: "The tragic events of October 19 raise a question that all serious parties will have to face: whether or not differences which develop inside the party should be put out for public discussion before they get out of hand."

Linked to this is a heightened respect for the role of the people in social change. While strong leadership is necessary, there is danger in allowing the role of the party to overshadow the opinions, desires and creativity of the masses. It is this popular creativity, many now realize, that was at the heart of the Grenada revolution's success.

Finally, the Grenada revolution is by no means discredited in the Caribbean. Rather, it has been personified in the memory of Bishop, who has become even larger in death than in life. Many who were skeptical or undecided while the NJM was in power now characterize Bishop as the force for "good" behind the revolution. While this polarized view of Bishop-good/Coard-evil may be an unfair judgement, it has helped some see that the revolution had positive elements. Bishop is seen as representing a Caribbean progressive tradition which includes such figures as George Padmore, C.L.R. James, Marcus Garvey, and Walter Rodney. All based their political philosophy on empowering the masses of people through direct involvement in governing themselves. This positive message is one final lesson of Grenada. ∎

Religious Challenge and Conformity in the 1980's

Ecumenism in the Wake of the Grenada Invasion

Religion in the Caribbean traditionally has both shaped and mirrored the values and class structure of the society. This meant that the churches were at once deeply affected by the Grenada invasion and agents in furthering the social divisiveness caused by the event. This was all the more true because of the latent tensions between the conservative religious tradition and the liberal perspective of the ecumenical movement, embodied in the Caribbean Conference of Churches. This division within the Church between the roles of guardian and changer of the social order came dramatically to the surface in response to the events of 1983.

Developments during the 1970s had seemed to justify and reinforce the ideals behind the founding of the Caribbean Conference of Churches. While the protests of the 1960s challenged the neocolonial order, the seventies saw a growing search for and experimentation with alternatives. The formation of CARICOM in 1973 symbolized a new official commitment to regionalism which paralleled the ecumenical unity of the churches. The Manley experiment with democratic socialism in Jamaica, the opening of diplomatic relations between four English-speaking states and Cuba, and the choice in favor of non-alignment by Guyana signaled an openness to ideological pluralism in the region. The Grenadian and Nicaraguan revolutions, coming at the climax of the decade, reinforced the impact of these changes.

Furthermore, a decade of innovative thinking had begun gradually to affect the perspective of the traditional Church. The untimely death of Trinidadian theologian Idris Hamid in August 1981 left deep sorrow but not a vacuum. Others, such as Leo Erskine of Jamaica, Roy Neehall of Trinidad, Leslie Lett of Antigua, Sergio Arce of Cuba, and Francisco Reus Froylan of Puerto Rico—to mention only a few—continued to work toward a decolonizing of Caribbean theology.[1] Pastors and laypersons were becoming more familiar with this new thinking, which was frequently explored in the pages of the CCC's widely-read newspaper *Caribbean Contact*.

At the same time, the seventies had shown that resistance to change was still deep-seated within the churches. In the fall of 1981, the Rev. Ashley Smith of Jamaica asserted that "ecumenism must succeed" as part of the larger task of freeing the Caribbean from its colonial past. But he added:

> There is covert mistrust of the regional ecumenical body by rank and file Christians of the respective churches, a situation created largely out of the disparity in the use of language between those in the pew and the ecumenical bureaucrats who often speak on behalf of the churches . . .[2]

This mistrust sometimes took the form of tensions between the CCC and the local Christian Councils, which were especially conservative in the small Eastern Caribbean islands. There were also occasional differences between agencies and levels of the CCC, with the board of directors of CADEC—the

CCC's development arm—often taking a more traditional developmentalist perspective. Thus when the Dominica Christian Council objected to the hiring of two local activists as CADEC field staff in that island, the CADEC hierarchy in Bridgetown backed up their objections. Together with other factors, this led to the collapse of the CADEC program in Dominica, with the progressive staffers leaving to found their own grassroots development group (the Small Projects Assistance Team). Around the region, clergy and lay Christians working toward self-organization of the poor or speaking out on social issues encountered opposition both from some church hierarchies and from governments. This led to instances of progressive priests and pastors being removed from their congregations or transferred from one island to another when their activities were deemed controversial.

So while the CCC had succeeded in bringing about various forms of interdenominational cooperation since 1973, many of the local churches remained tied to old colonial patterns and middle-class conservatism. As the CCC General Secretary, Dr. Roy Neehall, admitted shortly before his retirement:

> Ecumenism has not led to any basic transformation within the heart of the churches themselves . . . There is a limit to how far you can push an institution like the Church.[3]

"Politics Dividing the Church"

This tenuous unity around the ecumenical project of the seventies was soon to come under seige from opposing political forces at the start of the 1980s. The daring experimentation of the Grenada and Nicaragua revolutions on the one hand, and the reactionary militancy of the newly-elected Reagan administration on the other produced a growing polarization in the region. This disunity deeply affected the churches, leading Dr. Neehall to warn that "politics and ideology are dividing the Church."[4]

In its reaction to the Grenada revolution of March 1979, *Caribbean Contact* hailed the removal of the Gairy regime—as did many in Grenada and in the region—and pointed out that the "blind eye" which Caribbean governments had turned to Gairy's abuses had contributed to closing off non-violent avenues for change. By November of that year, however, *Contact* voiced editorial criticism of the Bishop government for closing the *Torchlight* newspaper and for failing to hold elections. It found the latter especially perplexing In view of the fact that the Bishop government could "easily have won" an election on the basis of its popularity in the country.

During the years of the revolution, *Contact* gave basic support to the Bishop government while expressing strong reservations and sometimes criticism regarding certain of its actions. But even this balanced approach exacerbated tensions with conservative church leaders. This was all the more true

Pentecostal church service in Barbados.

Barbados *Nation*

because the Conference of Churches of Grenada soon hardened its opposition to the People's Revolutionary Government, citing the lack of elections, censorship of the press and political detainees. *Contact* continued to comment on these negative issues, but also highlighted the positive accomplishments of the revolution in bringing about social and economic change.

By 1981, the Reagan administration's growing military involvement in Central America and its militaristic posturing in the Caribbean were alarming many Caribbean Christians. While the Ocean Venture '81 naval maneuvers were underway, the CCC convened a "Working Conference on Peace" at a Catholic retreat center in Trinidad, where representatives from churches in the English, Spanish, French and Dutch-speaking Caribbean hammered out proposals to be submitted to the CCC's Third General Assembly the following month. This "Zone of Peace" initiative was finally ratified by the CCC's General Assembly in October 1982, calling for:

- The CCC to request the United Nations to declare the Caribbean a Zone of Peace
- The CCC to request governments of the Caribbean to commit themselves to:
  - non-participation in the development of nuclear weapons and their emplacement in the Caribbean and Latin America

- pursuance of a genuine policy of non-alignment
- work for the elimination of all foreign military bases in the region and for an end to foreign military maneuvers in the area
- a policy of military non-intervention among Caribbean territories and from outside the region.[5]

Along with the issue of militarism, the divide-and-rule tactics of the Reagan White House troubled Caribbean Christians who saw the goal of ecumenism as linked to the overall strengthening of unity between the people and countries of the region. The Caribbean Basin Initiative, announced in the spring of 1982, favored U.S. client states like Jamaica and El Salvador while excluding Cuba, Nicaragua, and Grenada. Soon after the announcement of the CBI, President Reagan made an Easter vacation visit to Barbados where he met with selected "friendly" Caribbean leaders and invited them to join him in a verbal attack on Grenada and Cuba which he launched from Barbadian soil. Reflecting on this bid to turn Caribbean countries against each other, *Contact* wrote:

> The Reagan administration has indeed offered a great challenge to CARICOM's resolve . . . a serious testing of the region's governments' determination to make of their people not "fellow Americans," as the President feels, but citizens of One Caribbean.[6]

As U.S. attacks on Nicaragua and Grenada escalated during Reagan's first term, *Contact* outspokenly urged Caribbean peoples and governments to reject the U.S. approach. The newspaper dismissed as hypocrisy Reagan's professed concern about freedom in Grenada, noting that "the Reagan White House can live with Burnham's brand of 'cooperative socialism,' Duvalier's Haiti, or South Africa's apartheid system; but not, apparently, with Bishop's PRG."[7] After President Reagan's "Star Wars" speech of March 1983, in which he called Grenada a threat to the U.S., *Contact* said:

> When a head of state of one of the superpowers vilifies, as President Reagan has done, a tiny and vulnerable tourist island of the Caribbean as being a threat to the 'national security' of the USA, without offering a shred of evidence, then, irrespective of ideological differences and chosen paths of development, member governments and organizations of the Caribbean Community should, as a matter of principle, express publicly their concern—if not support for Grenada.[8]

The CCC's defense of Grenada, Cuba and Nicaragua along with its other progressive positions brought the ecumenical body up against powerful forces gathering on the right of the religious spectrum. The wave of conservatism accompanying Reagan's election saw "moral majority" types gain influence in various U.S., European and Caribbean churches, affecting both the CCC and its funding partners overseas. By mid-1982, there was pressure within some sectors of the CCC to remove Rickey Singh as editor of *Contact*. There were also attacks on the CCC from the U.S. right wing, such as a Heritage Foundation report which called CADEC "anti-U.S. and Marxist." Potentially the most far-reaching threat, however, came from the growth of the conservative evangelical sects—the so-called "television evangelists"—which were rapidly expanding from their U.S. bases into ambitious activities throughout the Caribbean and Central America.

Rise of the Right-Wing Sects

Several factors came together in the mid-1970s to produce an explosion of right-wing evangelical religion in the Caribbean, influencing political culture and posing a direct challenge to the mainline churches. One factor was the intrinsic appeal of fundamentalist religion to many Caribbean people. After World War II, Pentecostal churches had filled the gap between the historic churches (such as Catholic, Anglican and Methodist) and the traditional African and Revivalist religions. Whereas the mainline churches tended to be reserved and "proper" in their style of worship, the Pentecostals appealed to the fervent religiosity of the Caribbean masses with an emphasis on singing, collective emotion and "closeness" to God. These same qualities also drew people to the new North American sects* which resembled the Pentecostals in their fundamentalist style but were distinguished from them by their right-wing politics and tight organizational control from the top.

*Called "evangelicals" in the English-speaking Caribbean.

The second factor was a reaction against the emerging social consciousness of the historic churches marked by the formation of the CCC in 1973. Some people who had difficulty accepting this concept of social action ministry and who found the mainline churches becoming "too secular" were drawn to the sects, which stressed personal piety, individual salvation, and future hope rather than concrete action in the present.

Thirdly, the expansion of the ultra-conservative sects was linked to the ascendence of right-wing forces leading up to the election of Reagan. Based mostly in the southern United States, they expanded throughout the U.S. in the 1960s and early '70s, and by the latter part of the seventies were sending numerous missions into Central America and the Caribbean. There they bought land and established churches with local or sometimes North American pastors. With their U.S. backing, the sects had virtually limitless funds and purchased enormous amounts of radio and television time for religious programming patterned after the Christian Broadcasting Network's "700 Club."

In the deepest sense, the explosive growth of the new sects reflects a profound popular discontent with the status quo. But the remedy they propose for this discontent is a fundamentally passive one, which precludes any action to challenge social injustice. The sects assert that mankind is basically evil, that the present world is beyond redemption, and that the only hope lies in the reward of salvation in the hereafter. The faithful are exhorted not to think about their worldly problems because involvement in "politics" equals sin. This message reaches the poorest and most remote corners of the Caribbean through ubiquitous radio programs with names like "Gospel Hall" and "Streams of Power," permeating political and religious attitudes at the grassroots.

Despite this formal renunciation of politics, the sects have not hesitated to translate their popular following into political leverage. In Puerto Rico, for example, where the sects have grown much more rapidly in the last decade than the historic Protestant or Catholic churches, their pastors increasingly serve as intermediaries between the government and the people. Led by the "four evangelists" of Puerto Rico, they warn elected officials that they are monitoring their performance and will force a reckoning at election time.

The close ties of the conservative sects to the Reagan administration and the New Right network in the United States has had a definite impact on politics in the region. Right-wing religious leaders like Jerry Falwell and Billy Graham formed the link between the Reagan White House and General Efraín Ríos Montt in Guatemala, whose "born-again" government slaughtered thousands of peasants in the Guatemalan countryside in 1982. In Jamaica, the rise of the right-wing sects helped prepare the political climate for the election of Edward Seaga in 1980:

> The evangelicals definitely played a role in helping to remove Manley. They came into Jamaica in large numbers from about the end of 1979 and into 1980. You could see their tents mushrooming around the city and along the main highways, and in the countryside.
>
> The message they carried was anti-socialist, anti-communist. They included the Manley government, in some cases

quite openly, under the label communist, which was by no means an objectively correct classification at all.

Seaga has attempted to split the churches between the mainstream denominations and the evangelicals, lining up the evangelicals behind him. He has tried to isolate the Jamaica Council of Churches, the older established churches which were mostly supportive of the Manley government.[10]

The sects operate entirely outside the structure of mainline ecumenism and the CCC, whose social action concerns they brand as "communist." They have rejected invitations to engage in dialogue with the mainline denominations or join local Christian Councils. On the other hand there is a high degree of cooperation among the different evangelical sects, and ongoing contact between the Caribbean missions and their U.S. sponsors.

Despite these divisions, many Caribbean people have retained their membership in one of the historic churches while simultaneously participating in some activities of the North American sects. Partly in response to the fundamentalist challenge, the Catholic Church (and to a lesser extent, the Anglican Church) has developed within its structure a "charismatic" movement with an exuberant, fundamentalist style which has helped keep people within the Church. Nonetheless, the growth of the sects continues, fueled by economic suffering which causes people to seek relief in an emotional faith. Given the already existing divisions between liberal and conservative influence within the mainline denominations, these religious trends combined to place a majority of church-goers somewhere on the right of the political/religious spectrum at the time of the invasion of Grenada.

Impact of the Invasion

When it became known that Grenada was suffering an internal political crisis in October 1983, the CCC offered to mediate between the Bishop and Coard sides of the dispute. Before that could happen, however, the October 19 killings occurred and the CCC immediately cut off all relations with the military junta of Coard and his supporters. At the same time, the CCC called for the crisis to be resolved without external military intervention into Grenada.[11]

On October 25, 1983, as U.S. forces were overrunning Grenada, the CCC declared:

The Caribbean Conference of Churches, reaffirming its principled stance against military intervention in the Caribbean by forces external to the region, strongly deplores the events of the past few hours leading to this morning's invasion of Grenada. The fact of a Caribbean presence among the invading forces by no means alters the principle . . . [12]

In addition to invoking its previous commitment to the Zone of Peace resolution, the CCC justified its position by pointing to CARICOM's own endorsement of the principle of non-intervention reached at the Ocho Rios summit in November 1982. It also noted the breach of the "unanimity" requirement in the charter of the Organization of Eastern Caribbean States, contradicting the U.S. claim to have been legally invited to invade by the OECS.

The statement by CCC General Secretary Allan Kirton came as the Caribbean churches were being swept up in the regional controversy over the U.S. action. In the Eastern Caribbean islands (St. Vincent, Barbados, St. Lucia, Dominica, and Antigua) the local Christian Councils strongly supported the invasion to which their governments had lent troops and political support. In Trinidad, conversely, both the government and the churches opposed the invasion, and an ecumenical service for Maurice Bishop and the other slain leaders was held in Trinity Cathedral in Port-of-Spain. The main exception to the pattern of church/government parallelism was Jamaica, where the Jamaica Council of Churches opposed the invasion despite the Seaga government's involvement. Support for the CCC position also came from the churches in Curaçao, Cuba, the Dominican Republic, and Haiti.

There was more than deference to political authority behind the pro-invasion enthusiasm of the Eastern Caribbean churches. Many conservative church leaders had long opposed the Grenada revolution, but had refrained from attacking it openly for fear of antagonizing relations between the PRG and the Grenadian churches. Other factors contributing to their restraint were the relationship with the CCC which supported the Grenadian process; and finally, guilt about not having spoken out against Gairy before the revolution. Once the revolution had been overthrown, however, these clergy welcomed the opportunity to vigorously condemn the entire Grenadian experiment.

This brought to light the churches' underlying ambivalence toward a social change process which had delivered obvious benefits to the people but which also undercut the privileges and status of the middle and upper class—and by extension, of the churches rooted in these classes. Nowhere was this more evident than in Grenada itself. Ironically, the Grenadian churches were among the most conservative in the region, remaining (with a few exceptions) largely unaffected by the social upheavals of the 1960s and '70s. In 1979, the Grenadian Catholic Church broke its ties to its one progressive project, the Pope Paul Ecumenical Center. During the revolution, the churches did not respond beyond their traditional activities in education, and they were sometimes critical of projects the CCC sponsored in Grenada (through the local CADEC committee) for following too closely the development policies of the government. Relations between the PRG and the Conference of Churches of Grenada became increasingly suspicious and finally hostile. Church leaders expressed their disapproval in terms of concern about press freedom, detainees and elections, while the government accused the churches of working to turn Grenadians against the revolution.

After the invasion, therefore, the Grenada churches expressed gratitude to "the American and Caribbean forces who responded to the call for help," and called for a return to "respect for law, persons and property as enshrined in the Constitution."[13] Under the direction of the Anglican Archdeacon Hoskins Huggins, the churches distributed toys and candy sent from the U.S. to the "poor children" of Grenada. The Catholic Church handed over the site of the Pope Paul

225

Rickey Singh, editor of Caribbean Contact *from 1974-1983.*

center to the conservative Catholic organization SERVOL to offer employment training. Such initiatives represented support for the post-invasion rebuilding that had not been offered after the fall of Gairy.

The Grenadian church statement offered "thanks to God" that the country could look forward to peace and freedom. Others in the region also thanked God for the invasion, including the Barbadian churches, which held a "Thank You" mass at which it was claimed that the invasion was "in full accordance with the principles of Christianity." This suggestion of divine inspiration for a U.S. military action dismayed progressive Christians. The Roman Catholic Archbishop of Port-of-Spain, Reverend Anthony Pantin, warned against allowing any Caribbean country to become a "toy" in superpower conflicts. The Rev. Leslie Lett, an Anglican from Antigua, commented on what he called the "parachute incarnation" theology:

> From the colonial perspective, the story of the Incarnation was and continues to be distorted to mean that the "inherent inferiority" of black people always requires a miraculous Rescuer, Invader, Big Brother, to parachute down in our midst to sort things out and save us from ourselves . . . [14]

The Grenadian churches' support for the invasion placed the CCC in a difficult position. So did the extreme proinvasion stance of the Barbadian government and churches, which launched verbal attacks on the CCC's Bridgetown headquarters. Finally, the Adams government expelled from Barbados the outspoken editor of *Caribbean Contact,* Rickey Singh, after he wrote articles critical of the invasion. Singh's expulsion was a victory for conservatives inside and outside the churches. Although he was later invited back to Barbados by the government of Errol Barrow, he never resumed the editorship of *Contact.*

The strengthening of the regional right brought renewed pressures on the CCC to temper its commitment to the poor. For instance, the Grenadian Archdeacon Huggins commented:

> [The CCC] seems to preach only liberation theology and theology of the poor. I don't think that Christ was the Christ of the poor alone. He is also the Christ of the rich. So there must be a happy balance. [15]

The ten-year anniversary of the CCC's founding was celebrated amid both joy and sadness in November 1983. "Little did we know that the end of ten years would mark the end of an era," wrote the Rev. Kirton. The era which ended was that of the seventies, with its enthusiastic commitment to ecumenism and opening to new ideas. Today, there is determination to push ahead with the ecumenical project, but also an awareness that the CCC must frequently swim against the political tide.

The controversy over its values and direction prompted the CCC to undertake an internal reflection at the beginning of 1984. It resulted in a clear reaffirmation of the CCC's commitment to a theology of solidarity with the poor. At the same time, it was made clear that *Caribbean Contact* was not the official voice of all the churches but rather an open forum for dialogue. Under its new editor, Colin M. Hope, *Contact* has continued to speak out on poverty and social injustice and on such issues as South African apartheid and the lack of democracy in Haiti and Guyana.

At a gathering of CCC officials in March 1988, the Rev. William Watty, chairman of the Methodist Church in the Caribbean and the Americas, strongly urged the CCC to continue its option for the poor. He advised his listeners not to be surprised when they are called "fools," subversive, or out of step with the realities of the world, for advocating solidarity with the poor. Those motivated by Christian values—"the children of light"—follow a different morality than the "children of the world," and "necessarily the one is subversive of the other."

The Rev. Watty reminded the gathering that those committed to maintaining the status quo also exist within the churches. Referring to the spread of the right-wing sects, he charged that some "children of the world" were "masquerading as children of light" and using religion as a weapon to oppose social change. In this context, said the Rev. Watty . . .

> I don't see that the CCC, if it understands its mandate at all, has any choice but to continue to be a "fool," to insist on being out of step, out of tune and out of touch. That is the light in you which makes you children of light . . . If insisting on social change and solidarity with the poor makes you look idiotic in a world which does not want any change and has no time for the poor, then give God thanks and content yourself to be fools. For the foolishness of God is wiser than men and the weakness of God is stronger than men. [16] ∎

Caribbean Women: Old Burdens, New Voices

In building alternatives from the ground up, Caribbean women have led the way in the 1980s.

They have done so literally, as farmers and traders producing food for the region. And they are doing so figuratively, as grassroots activists dedicated to transforming their societies and women's roles in them.

In the last two decades Caribbean women have raised their voices to protest the double burden carried by women who are members of the working poor. They have denounced unemployment, low wages and the growing problem of violence against women. Women's organizations have won many small and large victories in their struggles. But barriers to empowerment remain daunting in societies historically dominated by men and by forces outside the region.

The Barbados Dance Theatre Company performs at CARIFESTA in 1981.

Courtesy of WAND

Farm to Market: Women in Agriculture

Inna country yuh haffi do some breed a back breaking wuk. Me used to help my faada in de field and me know seh a back breaking wuk. Him grow yam and cassava on fi-him five acres of land and him plant plenty cane. A we haffi wuk it. Yuh haffi bush di land, bun di land, clean it, pack di stone fi buttress it, fork it, plough it, plant it and weed it.

Nobody no count cultivating as a skill and is worse when yuh is a woman cultivator. Dem hire man fi dig yam hill and fi dig di land, but di woman always haffi weed di grass and dem pay cheaper fi dat.[1]

Since the slavery era, women's labor has been central to economic production in the Caribbean. On the plantations women predominated in the "field gangs" which did the heaviest work. The more skilled jobs such as driver were reserved for men. To cut their costs, the plantation owners gave slaves small plots of land on which to plant food crops. Women worked these "provision grounds" and sold the surplus in the market, beginning their role as the main producers of food crops throughout the region.[2]

Women today make up from 30% to 50% of the agricultural labor force in Caribbean countries. They are small farmers (working land by themselves or with husbands), traders, and agricultural wage laborers. The rural woman's day typically starts between 5 and 6 a.m. She prepares breakfast for the family and cares for children before heading for the fields, where she weeds, hoes, plants, and reaps. She returns to care for livestock, fetch water and prepare dinner. She may also sell produce by the roadside or in the market.[3]

The constraints all small farmers face are even more severe for women farmers. They typically own or rent very small plots of land, and have little access to capital or credit. Most have only a few years of formal schooling. Extension officers and aid agencies often ignore female farmers in programs offering training, credit or new technologies.

This is in part because planners typically focus on export crops, and pay little attention to production for local consumption. Women dominate the growing of the vegetables and fruits which make up the basic Caribbean diet: yams, cassava and dasheen; squash, cabbage and eggplants; beans, okra, hot peppers, onions; plantains and sweet potatoes; melons, tamarinds, papayas, mangoes, guavas and much more. Women traders, known as hucksters or higglers, buy this produce from farmers and transport it to town markets and even between countries. Hucksters from Dominica, for example, regularly sell produce in the neighboring French Antilles and as far away as the U.S. Virgin Islands.

While women farmers and traders work hard for little return, women who work as laborers on land owned by others are the most exploited. Wages for field hands are at the bottom of the pay scale, and are usually lower for women than for men. In St. Lucia, for example, the hourly minimum wage for female farm workers is equal to US $0.39 for women and $0.44 for men.

"Miss Beryl" works on a government-owned sugar estate in Jamaica. She earns J$17.25 (US$3.14) for an eight-hour day of heavy manual labor in the cane fields. During the out-of-crop season which lasts for three months, there is work only three days a week, making her weekly pay J$51.75. Out of this she pays rent of J$50 a month for a two-room shack with a latrine and a charcoal stove outside, plus food, clothing, school uniforms and books for her two children.

Survival would be even more difficult if not for the help from her sister, who has emigrated to New York and found a job as a nurse's aide. The small remittance Miss Beryl receives every few months has enabled her to continue sending her children to school. But her older daughter is talking about moving to Kingston to work as a maid.[4]

The hardships of rural life, combined with rising educational levels, has prompted a large-scale migration of younger women to the towns. Often leaving children in the care of grandmothers and aunts, they enter the urban ghetto, ready to take any job. Those lucky enough to find one typically wind up as poorly paid domestic servants or factory laborers, permanently joining the ranks of the urban poor.

Women's Wages, Women's Work

The most common experience of young women leaving school or migrating from the rural areas is unemployment. Unemployment rates for women are everywhere higher than for men, often twice as high. In response, many women have turned to the burgeoning "informal economy," earning money as market vendors, craftswomen, dressmakers, and so forth.

Women earn less than men at every rung of the class ladder. They are concentrated in occupations thought of as "female," which tend to be semi-skilled, low-status and poorly paid. Domestic servants are among the most exploited, reflecting the low social value attached to housework. In many Caribbean countries minimum wage laws and other protections do not apply to domestics. Where they do, the wage is very low—$40 a month with meals is not unusual.

Because of the individual nature of domestic service and because there is an endless pool of women who need work, it is very difficult for domestics to organize. There have been a few successful attempts, notably the National Union of Domestic Employees in Trinidad and Tobago.

Educated women have wider choices. But the schools still steer girls into "female careers" as teachers, nurses and secretaries, which tend to be lower-paid than white-collar occupations for men. A number of projects have trained women in non-traditional occupations such as auto mechanics and carpentry. These efforts have been very successful, but remain small-scale.

Where women and men are employed in the same industry, women often are paid at discriminatory rates. In St. Vincent, for example, the legal minimum wage for industrial work is equal to US$3.92 per day for women and US$5.10 per day for men. Many Caribbean countries have a similarly split wage scale.

This injustice is not merely a relic of bygone days. Cheap female labor is the basis of what has come to be called the "global assembly line," the network of transnational manufacturers who locate their factories wherever labor costs are lowest, often in "free trade zones" exempt from taxes and most regulation. As in Mexico, the Philippines and other low-wage havens, the workforce in assembly factories in the Caribbean is predominantly female.

Corporate managers say they hire women because they are "better suited" to delicate work such as assembling electronic components and stitching garments. The real reason is that women, disadvantaged in the job market, can be exploited more easily than men. Wages and conditions vary, but the hallmarks of the assembly factory are low pay, job insecurity and the absence of trade unions. Workers can lose their jobs abruptly for reasons such as pregnancy, refusing to work overtime, or talking back to a supervisor. Managers are usually male and foreign, and sexual harassment is common.

Employers also say women are "docile," meaning they are less likely than male workers to attempt to organize. But this is changing, as female factory workers increasingly demand the right to unionize. It is a difficult struggle, since governments, anxious to create jobs, often tacitly promise investors a non-union work force. Where unions do function, their power is limited by the companies' ability to shut down and even leave the country on short notice rather than meet labor demands.

Pico Ltd. is a New York-based transnational company with plants in St. Vincent, St. Kitts and South Korea. Its St. Vincent factory employs about 100 women assembling cable TV parts for export to the United States.

After a prolonged struggle, Pico workers won the right in 1982 to be represented by the Commercial Technical and Allied Workers Union. The union confronted management over wages, unfair dismissals and harsh disciplinary practices. In 1984, following a dispute over the firing of a union shopsteward, Pico locked out its workers. Company officials left the island, demanding as a condition for reopening that the union no longer represent the workers.

A month later, the St. Vincent government mediated a settlement in which Pico agreed to rehire 90% of the workers in return for a "cooling off" period in which an internal grievance committee would replace the union. The ink was hardly dry on the agreement when it became clear the company had effectively busted the union. It rehired only 60 workers, excluding union activists. The grievance committee became a

Women's Construction Collective

Jamaican construction worker trained by the Women's Construction Collective (above).

(Right) Grenadian women training as auto mechanics.

Division of Women's Affairs, Grenada

229

permanent "Workers' Council," a company-sponsored alternative to a union. Pico now employs a paternalistic approach to maintaining worker loyalty and enjoys labor peace. Should new disagreements arise, however, the women at Pico have no support from a union and are isolated from other workers' struggles.[5]

Barriers to unionization in industries where women work, combined with the image of trade unionism as a male domain, has meant that a relatively low percentage of women workers are organized. Female union members, moreover, are often relegated to a supportive role, such as catering union functions, while men handle management, arbitration and negotiation. There have been prominent exceptions—among them Ursula Gittens of the Trinidad & Tobago Public Services Association; Yvonne Francis Gibson of the St. Vincent Teachers' Union; Marva Phillips of the Trade Union Congress in Jamaica; and Nelsida Marmolejos of the Majority General Workers' Central in the Dominican Republic. Overall, however, unions have not dealt specifically with problems faced by women workers. And women have not been able to use trade unionism as a route to political power in the same way as have men.

Women in Families

The practice of underpaying women for their labor rests on a prevalent myth. Women are not breadwinners, it is said, but are supported by husbands, so their wages are merely supplemental. This has never been true for a majority of Caribbean women. A great many are single heads of households. Many others who have partners must work to supplement the meager earnings of men who are themselves unemployed or underemployed.

The nuclear family, consisting of a married couple and children, is just one of the family forms existing in the region. These draw on various cultural roots: the African extended family, with parents, children, grandparents and cousins living in close proximity; the patriarchal East Indian family, with its strict marriage customs: stable, often lifelong, common-law unions, prevalent among older working-class couples; and the nuclear family, favored by the middle and upper classes.

All these family forms and combinations of them offer support systems to women. Child care provided by grandmothers, godmothers and aunts frees young women to enter the work force and even to emigrate in search of wage-earning opportunities. In the absence of social security and welfare mechanisms, the extended family provides a crucial safety net for the individual in need.

But the traditional family forms are no longer as strong as before. Migration to the cities and overseas increasingly separates kin. Unemployment and poverty create pressures which work against stable couple relationships. At the same time, sexual mores are changing, influenced by trends outside the Caribbean and by the foreign media images which saturate the region.

One result is that more young women are forced into unstable, dependent relationships with men. A boyfriend typically provides some financial help while the relationship lasts, especially if a baby is expected. After the birth he often drifts away, leaving the woman with an even greater financial burden and vulnerable to exploitation by a new man.

Few mechanisms exist for securing child support from fathers, especially from young men with few resources. It is the woman who must find a way to provide. It is this reality, not the myth of the second income, which leads women to accept work at very low pay.

Poverty is also the backdrop to the alarming rise in violence against women throughout the Caribbean. In Caribbean cultures, as in most others, there are strong male-dominant, patriarchal and *machista* elements. Wife-beating is accepted, if not approved. But culture alone cannot explain the rapid rise in crimes against women, including rape, assault, incest and even murder.

This is due above all to the escalating economic crisis, in which men's frustration and feelings of powerlessness find an outlet in abuse within the family. Many women fight back or leave such relationships. But many others cannot because they are economically dependent on the man.

Prosecuting rape and domestic abuse remains difficult in the Caribbean, as elsewhere. But awareness of the problem is growing, and women's groups in several countries have recently set up the first rape crisis centers and counseling services.

Shouldering the Debt Burden

Rising unemployment is just one aspect of a growing crisis which has affected Caribbean women. Governments saddled with multi-billion dollar debts are orienting economic policies toward a sole aim: to earn foreign exchange with which to service the debt (since it cannot be repaid). Complying with demands of lenders such as the International Monetary Fund, governments are undertaking "structural adjustment" programs which impact heavily on the poor and on women most of all.

Under structural adjustment, production for domestic consumption becomes the poor stepchild of the economy. Priority is given to cash cropping, manufacturing and tourism, sectors with a high proportion of foreign ownership and control. The position of women as producers becomes more marginal; they may lose their land, leaving only the option of migrating to the city. There their living standard often falls since food, housing, and other necessities cost much more than in the rural areas.

In Haiti, economic policies imposed by the U.S. Agency for International Development called for a large-scale displacement of peasants from the land to work in manufacturing.[6] Hundreds of thousands of peasants have crowded the disease-ridden *bidonvilles* of Port-au-Prince. Young women from these slums provide the major work force for the U.S.-owned assembly factories, where wages are US$3.00 a day.

The IMF usually requires a country to devalue its currency and remove price controls on food and other goods. Women trying to feed families feel the impact of soaring prices acutely. In the Dominican Republic, the cost of basic foods

Inter-American Development Bank

Getting water in village in La Vega province, Dominican Republic. Funds have been cut for rural water systems like this one.

tripled and quadrupled after an IMF agreement was signed in 1984. A pound of rice went from 15 to 85 centavos, a litre of milk from 45 to 95 centavos, and beans rose from 45 centavos to 3 pesos a pound—a more than sixfold increase.[7]

Structural adjustment sharply cuts funding for social services and utilities, including schools, hospitals, nutrition programs, public transportation, water and electricity. Women feel such cutbacks most as they try to raise healthy, educated families. As services are eliminated or become too expensive, women compensate with their own time and labor. A housewife carries water from a public tap after water rates rise, or takes a two-hour trip to a health clinic because the one in her neighborhood has closed. At the same time, cuts in social services increase female unemployment since these categories are overwhelmingly staffed by women.

As bearers and nurturers of human life, women suffer from policies which favor economic growth and debt servicing at the expense of human growth. And by affecting women more than men, such policies further limit women's ability to contribute to national development. What is needed, argues Peggy Antrobus of the University of the West Indies' Women and Development Unit, is "an alternative approach which directs resources *toward* poor women, rather than one which does the opposite."[8] This could help achieve a development model which is self-reliant, sustainable and people-centered.

Women Organizing: From Awareness to Empowerment

Throughout Caribbean history, women have played prominent roles in social struggles, from slave rebellions to contemporary labor protests. Although it is primarily the male heroes whose names are remembered, there are a few exceptions. Ni, often called Nanny, was a Jamaican Maroon leader at the beginning of the 18th century who led prolonged guerrilla warfare against the British. She is celebrated as a military strategist and political leader of Nanny Town, a free community of escaped slaves. A heroine of more recent times is Dona Tingo, a Dominican *campesina* who led her community's resistance when a powerful landowner attempted to take over their land. She was killed by the landowner's thugs in 1974, becoming a symbol of struggle for peasant organizations in the Dominican Republic.

Caribbean women have a history of social activism through community and church groups, trade unions and political parties. In the past, however, this seldom led to national influence or political power for women. Community groups run by women concentrated on social welfare work, such as family planning or aid to the handicapped. In political parties and trade unions, women played a subordinate role. Every major political party had its "women's arm," often headed by the wife of a male party leader, which worked tirelessly at campaigning, fundraising and mobilizing members. But few women ever rose to leadership within the party. Despite this, women identified strongly with the rival parties, making women's cooperation across party lines very difficult.

In 1970 a group of prominent women formed the Caribbean Women's Association (CARIWA), a regional umbrella for non-governmental women's groups. Over the next few years, spurred by publicity surrounding the U.N. Decade for Women (1975-1985), Commonwealth Caribbean governments set up special desks to deal with women's affairs. The Manley government in Jamaica led the way, responding to pressure from the women's arm of the People's National Party. Barbados, Guyana and Trinidad followed, and eventually all 13 CARICOM member states had created a Women's Bureau or Women's Desk.

Working with the women's desks and with the women's program of the Caribbean Conference of Churches, non-governmental organizations held seminars and workshops to raise awareness of issues affecting women. Out of a regional seminar in 1977 came WAND, the Women and Development Unit of the University of the West Indies' outreach division. Based in Barbados, WAND supports women's initiatives through research, training and public education.

Among early victories for the women's movement were reforms in many discriminatory laws. Some governments legislated equal pay for equal work, attempting to abolish the old double wage scale. Other reforms came in family law, including maternity leave laws and legislation giving equal rights to children born in and out of wedlock.

The end of the Decade for Women, marked by an official U.N. conference and a non-official forum in Nairobi in 1985,

231

prompted Caribbean women to look back and reflect on what had been achieved. Gains were evident, but so were limitations. The governmental women's desks had proved weak in many cases, deprived of adequate staff, funding and political support. The two governments most committed to improving the status of women, the Manley government in Jamaica and the Bishop government in Grenada, had fallen from power. Despite an increased number of women ministers and parliamentarians— and one female prime minister—political power structures remained dominated by men.

Non-governmental women's organizations were limited by their largely middle-class base. Professional women had made great gains during the decade, working their way up to senior positions in the public and private sectors. But organizations led by professional and academic women could not always successfully reach out to working-class women, nor did they always try. Groups with members from differing class backgrounds found that issues of class frequently emerged, often in terms of dynamics between middle-class leaders and a grassroots base.

Party tribalism and ideology also continued to divide women. Some women's groups were closely associated with political parties, such as the Organization of Women for Progress, associated with the Workers' Party of Jamaica, and the Antigua Women's Movement, associated with the Antigua Caribbean Liberation Movement. The Federation of Cuban Women was tied to the Cuban Communist Party, and in revolutionary Grenada, the National Women's Organization was a creation of the New Jewel Movement. Such ties, while conveying certain advantages, also carried risks. The NWO in Grenada fell apart as soon as the New Jewel Movement ceased to exist.

The most serious constraint, however, was a fundamental limitation in the definition of "women's issues." The concept of "women in development," popularized during the decade, remained peripheral to real policy-making. While churches and international agencies were funding sewing cooperatives, governments were slashing social services, freezing wages and implementing other policies with drastic effects on women. North American and European feminists did not address these problems consistently, Caribbean women found. Caribbean activists allied themselves increasingly with an emerging Third World women's movement through such networks as DAWN (Development Alternatives for a New Era).

The economic crisis dominates the agenda as the 1980s draw to a close. In part because of its impact, the class base of the Caribbean women's movement has broadened. If the '70s were the "professional woman's time," the focus now has shifted to the creative organizing among urban and rural working-class women.

In the poor barrios of Santo Domingo, the Committee for the Defense of Neighborhood Rights (COPADEBA) has organized to protest rising prices and prevent the eviction of families from their homes. Women make up a majority of COPADEBA's members, notes organizer Elvidia Moronta, because "men spend their time doing other things." In Jamaica, the Women's Construction Collective trains young women

from the ghetto in construction skills, then secures well-paid jobs for them. The collective has also built health clinics, public sanitary facilities and houses for flood victims.

The Belize Rural Women's Association was formed when rural members of the larger Belize Organization of Women and Development decided to form their own group. It links several dozen craft and food processing coops, and includes women from all of Belize's ethnic groups. Through fundraising abroad, BWRA bought a truck to help its members transport farm produce to market. It has joined with other Belizean women's organizations to develop health education programs for rural women.

Some of the most active organizing has taken place in the Dominican Republic, where the National Confederation of Campesina Women (CONAMUCA) has struggled for land rights and to secure better services for rural communities.

"Edita" lives with her husband and four children in the community of Hato Damas in the south of the Dominican Republic. The family owns a small plot of land on which they grow yucca, beans, citrus and papayas, and raise a few cows, chickens and goats. They live in a three-room wooden house with a charcoal stove in the back where Edita cooks the family's typical supper of boiled green bananas and dried fish. At night, from the hill, one can see the distant lights of Santo Domingo.

In addition to farming, Edita's husband works in a factory some miles away. He belongs to the Farmers' Association, a base group of the Independent Peasant Movement. Edita belongs to the Federation of Peasant Women of San Cristóbal (FEMUCA), a base group of CONAMUCA.

The leadership of FEMUCA has worked with a church-supported organization in the capital to develop education programs for its members. The women themselves decide their goals and methods of struggle. They successfully pressured the government to extend electricity to their area and to build a school in the village. But the major problem facing the community—land—has proved more difficult.

The peasants of Hato Damas have sought for years to recover lands expropriated from them by the dictator Trujillo. In 1985, women and men began to cultivate disputed lands. They were arrested and taken away by police. A group of 35 women went to the nearby town of San Cristóbal and occupied a church, demanding the release of the prisoners. Other women supported them, bringing cooked food to the church. Negotiators were brought in, and finally the prisoners were freed. But the land was not returned.[9]

Many grassroots groups such as FEMUCA receive support from international agencies, churches or organizations run by middle-class intellectuals. Increasingly, however, they are emphasizing democratic decision-making and moving away from models dominated by outside sponsors or internal leaders. This has helped the women's movement as a whole begin coming to terms with the issue of class. Organizations such as Sistren in Jamaica show that solidarity across class and party lines is possible when these issues are confronted consciously.

In 1977, a group of 13 women from the Kingston ghetto were working in the Manley government's emergency jobs program as street cleaners and teachers' aides. They asked a dramatist from the Jamaica School of Drama to help them produce a play for Workers' Week. The result was *Downpression Get a Blow,* a play about women factory workers organizing for their rights.

The 14 women became the nucleus of the Sistren Theatre Collective, combining professional theater, popular education, a silkscreen project and a magazine. This dynamically creative group seeks to raise awareness of problems affecting women and their possible solutions. They have scripted and produced many plays, dealing with such topics as domestic violence, teenage pregnancy and exploitation in the workplace. They also carry out educational workshops with women sugar workers and other groups.

Through their work in the collective, the members of Sistren have developed a wide range of skills, including acting, scriptwriting, teaching, graphic arts and accounting. This self-development has made possible a democratic collective process. While oriented toward the experience of working-class women, the collective has integrated several middle-class members, defining roles for them which use their skills in fundraising and documentation.

In addition to its work in Jamaica, Sistren has sent members of the collective to assist newly-formed women's groups in Belize, Guyana and other Caribbean countries. WAND, the Women and Development Unit of UWI, provides similar assistance and linkages. Both have contributed to a growing regional perspective within the Caribbean women's movement, which is reflected in such new networking efforts as Women for Caribbean Liberation, formed by progressive women's groups in 1986.

The victories sometimes seem small against the burdens of past and present. Compared to two decades ago, however, the women's struggle has made enormous strides. A member of Sistren summed it up this way:

So yuh see, all me life ah been working and ah don't have a house or a piece of land to show for it . . . Ah don't save no money, but ah think ah get more enlighten and ah learn and understand more as di years go by. Ah find out lickle more bout history and government and di rest of di world. It open me eye and what ah realize is dat di working class people change a lot even though we still have plenty left to achieve.

Dem have maternity leave for women now, which never exist when ah was working first time. On a whole ah tink dis generation tek things more serious dan we. So ah tink dem will achieve more dan we achieve because we achieve more dan our parents. If dem come togedder and keep on demand what dem want to see change and work hard to get it change, dem will get someweh.[10] ∎

Sistren performing "Trickster and de Muffet Posse," a play about women's struggles against sexual and social violence.

Caribbean Unity, the Distant Dream

The fragmentation of the Caribbean dates back to the origins of modern Caribbean society. The colonial legacy was one of artificial divisions and rivalry—of being "chopped up like a loaf of bread," in the words of Maurice Bishop. Geographic separation, language barriers, and nationalism all play a part in perpetuating these divisions. And as the role of the European colonial powers wanes, the growing influence of the United States has created new obstacles to unity.

Caribbean "unity" is a loosely defined but fundamental part of the progressive vision for achieving greater economic and political independence. The small, weak Caribbean economies would clearly benefit from greater linkages, a fact long recognized if not acted upon successfully. Likewise, political independence has proven weak and vulnerable for the Caribbean micro-states. Sovereignty in the shadow of a superpower, it is realized, will be virtually impossible for the Caribbean countries individually. Only united do they stand a chance.

While official attempts at unity have been dogged by failure, efforts at the popular level have gone forward quietly and with modest short-term goals. Among the major groups involved are intellectuals and cultural workers; women, farmers, and trade unionists; grassroots development workers; and the Church. Through regional meetings and action projects linking different countries, they are building bridges to span the old divisions and work toward a common philosophy of change.

"The Caribbean Man"

Before the arrival of Columbus, the Carib and Arawak Indians settled the entire Caribbean. Although they did not create a unified state, the Amerindians' network of settlements and trade linked the islands to mainland areas which are now Belize, the Yucatán peninsula, Venezuela and Guyana.

The European conquest led to the division of the region into island-states. Spain, Holland, England and France seized individual territories as plunder in the interminable colonial wars. Four empires developed, each locked in an embrace with the colonizer through the monopoly system. The colonial authorities governed each territory separately, although groups sometimes were administered together for convenience. Relations between islands were suppressed in favor of each colony's tie to the "mother country," leading to an insular mentality among the West Indian planters. Later, the Europeanized middle class emulated this attitude.

The plantation system left its legacy in societies stratified by race, color and class. Especially in multi-racial societies, these divisions split the working-class majority to the benefit of those on top. In Guyana and Trinidad, in particular, rivalry between Africans and East Indians frustrated the development of working-class solidarity.

Despite these divisions, the desire for some kind of unity has been a persistent theme of popular Caribbean culture. As the calypsonian Black Stalin put it:

Them is one race - the Caribbean man
From the same place - the Caribbean man
That make the same trip - the Caribbean man
On the same ship - the Caribbean man

On closer examination, however, this concept of unity turns out to be limited in scope. It relates specifically to black Caribbean people, whose shared history includes African origins ("One race from the same place") and the slavery experience ("The same trip on the same ship"). This excludes other groups, notably East Indians and Hispanics, who make up part of the larger Caribbean population. Secondly, the concept of "Caribbean Man" which evolved in relation to the Black Power movement of the 1960s is usually, although not exclusively, defined in terms of the English-speaking Caribbean. This double qualification of race and language—and, perhaps unintentionally, gender—is evident in a calypso by Explainer:

So if you born in Kingston
Or if you born in Bridgetown
If you is Bajan or Jamaican
Once you black you's my brother man
The Vincentian feller
That's my black brother
So if you's Bajan or Vincentian
Once you black, you's my brother man.

The countries named by Explainer—Jamaica, Barbados, and St. Vincent—are all former British colonies. But the non-English-speaking territories also have large black populations. The concept of a black Puerto Rican or Martiniquan as "brother" to a black Jamaican is articulated only rarely, usually in a self-conscious attempt to broaden the concept of unity.

The divisions between the English, Spanish, French/Creole and Dutch areas of the region are the primary obstacle to the development of a broader Caribbean identity. These divisions are reflected above all in language and culture. Due to the regional dominance of English, people in the non-anglophone territories feel language barriers more acutely. While Spanish and French sometimes are taught as second languages, there is no serious attempt to compensate for linguistic diversity. The result is a negligible flow of communication and contacts across the linguistic barriers.

Another hindrance are the immigration barriers between territories with differing extra-regional political ties. Any Frenchman can travel across the Atlantic and enter Guadeloupe, Martinique or French Guiana with scarcely a nod from customs officials; but citizens of non-French islands only a few miles away must have visas to enter. Immigration barriers even exist within subregions. Citizens of the Commonwealth Caribbean states need passports to travel between those countries, while American tourists can enter with nothing more than a

Prime Minister Eric Williams of Trinidad, left, and Fidel Castro. Photo dates from the early '70s, when four Commonwealth Caribbean states established diplomatic relations with Cuba.

driver's license.

Where U.S. politics are involved, the problems multiply. To enter Puerto Rico one must apply for and receive a United States visa. Under the Reagan administration the U.S. State Department denied entry to numerous Latin American and Caribbean progressives seeking to visit Puerto Rico. In one case, U.S. immigration authorities detained and finally deported a young Grenadian Catholic, Suzanne Berkeley, who had arrived in Puerto Rico to attend a "Theology in the Americas" conference as a special guest.

U.S. influence has contributed to breaking down the traditionally strong ties between the people of the Spanish-speaking Caribbean. As U.S. citizens, Puerto Ricans are legally subject to the U.S. Treasury's currency ban that prohibits Americans from travelling to Cuba. In 1982 the

Reagan administration refused to allow Puerto Rican sports fans to attend the Central American and Caribbean games being hosted by Cuba that year. Some 200 fans defied the ban; when they returned to Puerto Rico, U.S. customs officials seized the Cuban books and records they had purchased as souvenirs.

Regional Integration in the Commonwealth Caribbean

*You try a Federation, the whole thing end in confusion
Caricom and then Carifta, but somehow ah smelling disaster
Mister West Indian politician, you went to big institution
How come you can't unite seven million
When a West Indian unity I know is very easy
If you only rap to you people and tell them like me.*

— Black Stalin, "Caribbean Man"

While no one has yet sought to unite the entire Caribbean, the many attempts to unite the English-speaking countries are the subject of Black Stalin's cynical verse. The concept of such a union has emerged repeatedly, in part because the former British colonies—with the exception of Guyana and Belize—are small. Yet despite their common language and history, the countries of the Commonwealth Caribbean have found regional unity an elusive goal.

The principal attempt was that of the West Indies Federation, whose short life span (1959-1962) established a backdrop of failure to the subsequent regional integration movement. Initially pushed by the labor movement in the 1940s, the Federation was to include ten English-speaking territories. But the Federation collapsed when the two largest members, Jamaica and Trinidad & Tobago, pulled out, determined to "go it alone" to national independence [see Part I, Ch. 7].

Convinced that a political union could not work, regional politicians began exploring possibilities for a more limited economic association. In 1969, the Caribbean Free Trade Association (CARIFTA) was established with the original ten countries from the Federation, plus Guyana. Its purpose was to stimulate production in the member territories by lowering trade barriers between them.

A common market alone, however, failed to increase production greatly. The next step was to link production in the various territories so as to cut the costs of industrializing. To this end, the Caribbean Community and Common Market, known as CARICOM, was formed in 1973. In addition to creating production linkages, CARICOM was to promote "functional cooperation" in such areas as tourism, regional transport, health care, and scientific research. It was also supposed to coordinate the foreign policies of member states.

There were achievements in functional cooperation, especially in health and education. But in the area of production linkages, CARICOM's most ambitious projects never got off the ground. One scheme involved building two aluminum smelters which would use Trinidad's natural gas and Guyana's hydro-power to turn Jamaican and Guyanese bauxite into aluminum. But the project became entangled in a dispute between Jamaica and Trinidad, and was abandoned after Jamaica and Guyana pulled out.

The real problem was not that production linkages weren't feasible, but that production under local control and using local resources hardly existed in most of the CARICOM countries. There was little attempt to involve the people who knew most about production—the workers and farmers—in the planning. Key questions of land ownership and class structure were never addressed.

Attempts at production links gradually fell by the wayside, and CARICOM became limited to the common market and functional cooperation. By the late 1970s, CARICOM was frequently reported in the regional press to be "on its last legs" or "merely in need of a decent burial."

The role of Trinidadian prime minister Eric Williams was an additional factor. With its oil-rich economy, Trinidad was a source of aid to weaker CARICOM states and also the largest market for manufactured goods within the common market. Williams had a strong idealistic commitment to regionalism, but became disenchanted with the shortcomings of CARICOM and what he saw as ingratitude for Trinidad's aid. Although he personally had helped to institutionalize the annual CARICOM summits, after 1975 he refused to attend them. From 1976 to 1982 the CARICOM heads of government did not meet at all.

CARICOM was officially revived in November 1982 when the heads of government gathered in Ocho Rios, Jamaica for their third summit. It was the first time in seven years that the Commonwealth Caribbean leaders had come together, and there was an air of optimism and self-congratulation as they affirmed that "the maintenance and deepening of the Caribbean community . . . provides the only certain way for the survival of our States as independent, free and developing societies."[1]

A year and a half later, as the regional heads met for their fifth summit, these words seemed empty. Summing up the dismal state of CARICOM, Trinidadian journalist Jeremy Taylor wrote:

> There is no free movement of labor, no waiving of entry restrictions and no common currency. The Caricom Secretariat, starved of funds, operates in the depressed Guyanese capital of Georgetown with no physical presence elsewhere.
>
> There has been no serious coordination of foreign policy, no attempt to form a parliament, and trading has become a bitter battle against regional protectionism. A regional clearinghouse, established to simplify trade, has been choked with work for two years. More Caricom states are turning to bartering, and the joke is that nothing is left of regionalism except the University of the West Indies—now being decentralized—and the West Indies cricket team.[2]

There have been two major stumbling blocks for CARICOM. One is the low level of trade within the common market, which has never accounted for more than 12% of the total trade of member states.[3] Since the members of CARICOM do not all share a common currency, they have had to

Caricom Perspective

Roderick Rainford, the Jamaican-born secretary-general of CARICOM.

settle their accounts in foreign exchange. A credit device designed to bypass this, the CARICOM Multi-Lateral Clearing Facility, collapsed in 1983 because of debts owed to it by Guyana. Since then, the shortage of foreign exchange has posed a major barrier to increased intra-regional trade.

The emphasis on exporting to and importing from markets outside the region has come at the expense of trade within CARICOM. In the early '80s, to conserve foreign exchange, a number of CARICOM states imposed licensing requirements for imports from within the free trade zone. This turn to protectionism caused bitter disputes. In 1988, the CARICOM members finally resolved to drop all trade barriers within the common market area, a move they hope will revive intraregional trade.

The other problem has been termed "ideological pluralism," but the root cause is really the differing political alliances and agendas of the CARICOM states. After the Grenada revolution in 1979, CARICOM debated the question of ideological differences and their effect on integration. It was the first time such differences had been seen as a problem, even though Jamaica and Guyana had both announced pro-socialist paths in the 1970s.[4] Jamaica, Guyana, Trinidad and Barbados had even established diplomatic relations with Cuba in 1972. They did so not for ideological reasons, but out of conviction that the larger states of the region should have relations—and a willingness, in the optimistic early days of the regional movement, to chart their own independent course.

A decade later, things had changed. Soon after taking power, Prime Minister Seaga severed Jamaica's relations with Cuba. At the Ocho Rios summit in 1982, Seaga and Barbadian prime minister Tom Adams led an attempt to expel Grenada from CARICOM by proposing a "human rights" amendment which would have made "free, fair and regular elections" a requirement for membership.

The invitation to line up with the United States against Grenada raised many embarrassing questions which the leaders would have preferred to avoid. Everyone knew that Forbes Burnham maintained himself in power through fraudulent elections; should Guyana, site of the CARICOM secretariat, be censured? And just what *was* the state of human rights in the other member countries? No leader wanted to open his or her performance to scrutiny. Prime Minister Bishop underscored these doubts by offering a counter-amendment which would have included the right to life, jobs, food, education, electricity and running water—"rights" which if used as criteria for membership would have left CARICOM with no members at all.

A further problem was that no fault could be found with Grenada's behavior within CARICOM. Bishop was an outspoken proponent of regionalism, and Grenada played an active and constructive role in CARICOM and other regional bodies. The authors of the Demas Report, commissioned in 1980 to examine CARICOM's problems, stated they did not view ideological differences as a major obstacle to integration.

In their final communique, the leaders rejected the Seaga/ Adams amendment and affirmed . . .

> . . . the right of self-determination of all peoples including the right to choose their own path of social, political and economic development, and we insist that there can be no justification for any external interference with the exercise of that right.[5]

The communique declared "inadmissible" the "use of force in international relations," and called for conflicts to be resolved "by peaceful means based on respect for sovereignty, independence and territorial integrity."

Less than a year later, the brave ideals of Ocho Rios were thrown to the winds as six CARICOM governments assisted a foreign invasion of one of CARICOM's member states. At the very least, the Grenada invasion marked a failure to coordinate the foreign policies of CARICOM members. At a deeper level, it symbolized the weakness of the commitment to regionalism in the face of pressures for each country to seek extra-regional alliances.

The rift in CARICOM caused by the invasion has largely healed. But the leaders are still often unable to speak with one voice, especially on matters involving United States policies. Meeting in St. Kitts-Nevis in 1985, the CARICOM foreign ministers denounced the U.S. economic embargo against Nicaragua. But after intensive lobbying by U.S. officials, the CARICOM heads of government backed down. When the leaders met for their sixth summit in Bridgetown in July 1985, the resolution was scrapped.

After the bloody election-day massacre in Haiti in November 1987, a shocked Caribbean looked to CARICOM for a strong reaction. Prime Minister Seaga had taken his own initiative, forming a small group of "Concerned Caribbean Leaders" which visited Haiti and held meetings with General Namphy. In a position reflecting that of Washington, Seaga's group endorsed the Haitian army's plan to hold new elections on January 17. Other CARICOM leaders, led by the Barbados and Trinidad prime ministers, argued that such elections could not be free or fair. Meeting to discuss the Haiti crisis, the

CARICOM leaders spent most of the session arguing, and finally issued a confused and contradictory statement.

After Leslie Manigat was installed in an army-controlled fraud, the Barbados government called for suspension of Haiti's observer status in CARICOM. But Seaga and Dominica prime minister Eugenia Charles argued for accepting the results of the poll, stating that flawed elections were better than no elections. Their position successfully headed off a united CARICOM stand against the Haitian army's electoral travesty.[6]

The squabbling within CARICOM has left many people uncertain about the future of the regional movement. But while such disagreements are likely to persist, there remain strong incentives to continue working toward integration. This is especially true for the smaller islands, which feel the disadvantages of their isolation most acutely.

In 1987, the seven members of the Organization of Eastern Caribbean States—St. Vincent and the Grenadines, St. Lucia, Dominica, Antigua-Barbuda, St. Kitts-Nevis, Grenada and Montserrat—began exploring the idea of forming a unitary state. Several leaders were enthusiastic, notably Compton of St. Lucia and Mitchell of St. Vincent. A popular referendum on the idea was planned for early 1988.

The proposal soon ran into misgivings on various sides. The Antiguan government announced it would not participate, and Montserrat was undecided. Opposition parties and some grassroots organizations demanded broader consultation on the plan, some fearing that the proposed unitary state would be a new vehicle for U.S. influence.

As of mid-1988, the referendum was postponed and progress seemed stalled. But the OECS countries have pushed ahead with deepening their cooperation in various areas, including legal and police services, fisheries and education. In 1988 they agreed to drop passport barriers among themselves, so that citizens of OECS states will be able to travel within the subregion using only documents such as birth certificates and drivers' licenses. The gradual strengthening of such cooperation may in time provide a basis for a political linkage. Although previous attempts to unite the Eastern Caribbean have failed—notably the "Little Eight" project in the 1960s—the advantages of unity ensure that such efforts will continue.

Popular Unifiers: Cricket, Carnival, Migration and Music

The majority of West Indians know little about the workings of CARICOM and other regional bureaucracies. The average person in the Caribbean experiences regionalism in a different way: as something based on people-to-people ties and the economic links they promote. These have always existed in the Caribbean and are deeper and stronger than the formal integration mechanisms.[7]

The most important unifier is inter-island migration, rooted in the phenomenon of male migration for employment. Caribbean men have always traveled to take available work: to build the Panama Canal, to cut sugar cane in Cuba, or to work in the oil refineries of the Netherlands Antilles. While away, men marry and have children, creating families with dual-island loyalties. It is entirely normal for a person to have blood relations in several territories and to have lived in more than one. A typical example is George Headley, one of the region's famous cricketers:

> Born in Panama on May 30, 1909, to a Jamaican mother and a Barbadian father, George Alphonso Headley was taken to Cuba at the age of five and to an aunt in Jamaica at nine.[8]

Such kinship networks are the basis for many informal economic ties between countries. A boat leaves Grenada every week loaded with fresh fruits and vegetables which Grenadian farmers send to their relatives in Trinidad to sell on the Trinidad market. The profits return to Grenada, part of the web of informal ties which bind the two islands. Similarly, a man from Dominica who has found work in neighboring Guadeloupe will be likely to send back part of his earnings to his family at home.

Migration is the only unifier which consistently straddles the colonial divisions between the English, Spanish, French and Dutch territories. To cite a prominent example, former Grenadian prime minister Maurice Bishop was born in Aruba to Grenadian parents while his father was employed in the Aruban oil fields. Although Aruba is part of the Dutch-speaking Netherlands Antilles, many English-speaking West Indians have lived there because of the oil industry. Migration sometimes creates enduring cultural links. Around the turn of the twentieth century thousands of West Indians, especially Jamaicans, migrated to eastern Cuba to work in the sugar industry. They left a West Indian cultural stamp on that part of the island, so that Santiago de Cuba, the eastern provincial capital, is now "the most Caribbean city in Cuba"—meaning that it has the most African and West Indian cultural influences and a predominantly black population.[9]

People-to-people ties, of course, are strongest within each cultural/linguistic block. Within the English-speaking Caribbean a number of cultural elements serve as unifiers, of which the most important is undoubtedly the sport of cricket.

"Whoever and whatever we are, we are cricketers," writes C.L.R. James.[10] Cricket was an upper-class British game introduced into the Caribbean (and into Australia, India, South Africa and New Zealand) by the colonial settlers. But class and color distinctions on the cricket field eventually gave way before the growing superiority of black and brown players, who dominated West Indies cricket by the 1940s. The West Indies won its first test series against England in 1935, and since the 1960s has dominated world cricket—the colonized beating the colonizers at their own game.

Cricket is important to unity because the West Indies competes internationally as a single team, although individual island teams also play each other. The West Indies Cricket Team is made up of the best players from each island, and is the focus of boundless regional pride. Moreover, the Caribbean's supremacy in cricket allows it to enforce an anti-apartheid policy against South Africa. All the Commonwealth Caribbean nations are signatories to the Gleneagles Agreement which discourages sporting links with South Africa, and the West Indies Cricket Board of Control has banned South African cricketers from the region. In 1983, however, a group of "rebel cricketers" mainly from Barbados sparked an acrimonious regional debate by going on a lucrative unofficial tour of South Africa. The West Indian governments were unable to agree on action to be taken against the mercenary sportsmen, although the cricket board has barred them from future competition in the Caribbean.

What cricket is to West Indians, baseball is to the Spanish-speaking Caribbean. Cubans, Dominicans, and Puerto Ricans are passionate baseball fans, and the three

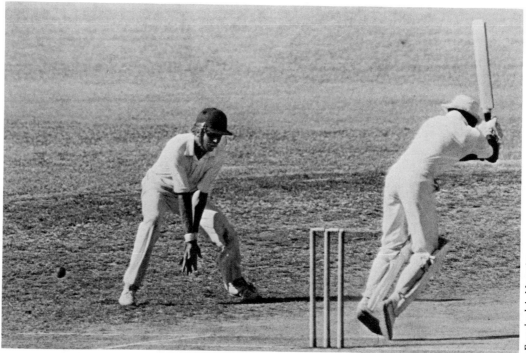

West Indies versus England in a cricket test match.

Everybody's Magazine

countries have produced some of the best players in the world, including many in the U.S. major leagues. Examples include Luis Arroyo of Puerto Rico, Felipe and Matty Alou of the Dominican Republic, "Mini" Minozo of Cuba and many others. The famous Roberto Clemente, centerfield for the Pittsburgh Pirates until his death in 1972, was born in Puerto Rico and is regarded as a hero in his homeland.

Love of baseball not only unites the Spanish-speaking Caribbean peoples; it also builds bridges between the Caribbean and other parts of Latin America where baseball is played, such as Mexico, Nicaragua and Venezuela. National teams frequently play against each other, and all compete in the Pan American games. In this arena, political barriers are bypassed. Puerto Rico competes as an independent nation. Cuba, which is isolated in political and diplomatic settings, participates fully and is highly respected for its sports prowess.

Calypso: Voice of the Small Man

In the eyes of the outside world, two cultural phenomena have come to represent the Caribbean and symbolize the vibrancy of its culture. Both have their origins in the West Indian working class: reggae/Rastafarianism, originating in Jamaica, and carnival/calypso, originating in Trinidad. Although strongest in their countries of origin, both of these cultural "complexes" have spread throughout the Caribbean and are claimed by West Indians as the region's original creations.

Calypso is one of the earliest authentic West Indian art forms. It is rooted in the African oral tradition, in which songs of praise or derision were sung as a form of pointed social comment. In the modern Caribbean, calypso serves as the "voice of the small man," who enjoys a vicarious social protest through the scathing commentary of the calypsonian. The dominant characteristics of calypso are wit (preferably spicy), colorful language, and opinionated reference to social or political events of the day. For instance, a calypso composed in the 1930s commented on the abdication of Edward VIII from the British throne.

Believe me, friends, if I were King
I'd marry any woman and give her a ring
I wouldn't give a damn what the people say
So long as she can wash, cook and dingolay.

Many calypsos were banned by the colonial authorities in the 1930s for being "profane." Although sex was a popular topic, what the authorities actually objected to was the boldness of calypsonians in mocking and embarrassing the ruling class. A 1950 calypso by the Growling Tiger, for example, broke social taboos by denouncing the misdeeds of a British expatriate official in Trinidad:

The Assistant Director of Education
He found himself in confusion
Drunk and driving his motor car
Dangerous to the public, what behavior!

He is a disgrace to my native land
So the public should demand his resignation.

Calypsonians are usually of working-class origins, traditionally from the poor areas of Port-of-Spain. As part of their humorous personae they adopt sobriquets borrowed from British nobility or from the roster of history's great conquerers: The Mighty Duke, King Solomon, King Obstinate, Atilla the Hun, Black Stalin, Lord Nelson, Lord Kitchener (Kitchener, along with The Mighty Sparrow, dominated Trinidad calypso for decades; he is named for the commander of the British overseas forces in Africa and India during the 19th century).

The period during and after World War Two saw the marriage of politics and calypso. This was linked in part to the emergence in 1956 of The Mighty Sparrow, whose career in turn paralleled the political rise of Dr. Eric Williams and his People's National Movement in Trinidad. Sparrow was a strong supporter of Williams, but he did not fail to air popular dissatisfaction when Williams was seen to be breaking his promises:

They raise up the taxi fare
No, Doctor, no

Lord Kitchener and The Mighty Duke, in a photo probably dating from the 1950s.

And the blasted milk gone up so dear
No, Doctor, no
But you must remember
We support you in September
You better come good
Because I have a big piece o' mango wood.

Inevitably, calypso goes beyond mere commentary to become a potent political weapon. By highlighting an issue or scandal it fans the flames of public controversy, often with direct results. The calypsonian's true role is that of a catalyst for mass expression: he gives voice to a vague but widespread sentiment, and in so doing helps to galvanize it into a definite protest. This happened, for example, with the calypso "Boots," which helped make militarization a regional issue. Politicians dread ridicule at the hands of the calypsonians, and within the past few years several calypsos aimed at incumbent governments have been banned from the airwaves in Barbados and Antigua.

Calypso's unifying power comes from its effectiveness as a means of mass communication. The most popular numbers receive air play all over the region, informing people in other territories of current issues in the country where the song originates. While the official version of events is contained in the news media, the average person's interpretation (which may be quite different) is publicized through the calypso.

Calypso is closely linked to Carnival, the festival held in the days leading up to Lent. Carnival is biggest in Trinidad, but also is traditional in Grenada, St. Vincent, Antigua, Aruba, and Brazil. The Carnival season begins in January with the opening of the calypso tents. Here the public gets to hear the season's new crop of calypsos and size up contenders for the title of Calypso Monarch. In the "pan yards," steelbands rehearse for their competition, which in Trinidad's past often took the form of a violent clash. The climax comes on the two days before Ash Wednesday. Sunday night is "Dimanche Gras," when the Calypso King and Queen are chosen. In the dawn hours of Monday morning begins J'Ouvert (*jour ouvert*, or open day), when costumed masqueraders converge on Port-of-Spain for two days of unbroken revelry.

> *Up on the Hill Carnival Monday morning breaks upon the backs of these tin shacks with no cock's crow, and before the mist clears, little boys, costumed in old dresses, their heads tied, holding brooms made from the ribs of coconut palm leaves, blowing whistles and beating kerosene tins for drums, move across the face of the awakening Hill, sweeping yards in a ritual, heralding the masqueraders' coming, that goes back centuries for its beginnings, back across the Middle Passage, back to Mali and Guinea and Dahomey and Congo, back to Africa where Maskers were sacred and revered . . .*
>
> *The music burst forth from the steelband; shouts went up, and the steelband and the masqueraders . . . the robbers and the Indians and the clowns—the whole Hill began moving down upon Port-of-Spain . . .*
>
> From *The Dragon Can't Dance* by Earl Lovelace
> (Essex: Longman Group Ltd., 1969)

Carnival has become more commercialized since the 1960s, losing some of its original spirit of rebelliousness and mock violence. In becoming a major tourist attraction, however, it also has become a Caribbean unifier, as people from the other islands and from Caribbean communities abroad flock to Trinidad for the yearly event.

Reggae and the Sufferer Culture

At the opposite end of the island chain, Jamaica is the birthplace of Rastafarianism and the reggae music it helped inspire. Their evolution is closely bound to the Afro-Jamaican experience. Yet they have taken on significance for people all over the Caribbean, above all for black youth; and they form an important cultural link between West Indians in the Caribbean and those living abroad.

At one level, reggae is an international commercial success, the first Caribbean music ever to make it big in the white music world. "Reggae is a victorious thing for arts in the Caribbean," proving to Caribbean youth that their culture produces something valued by the outside world.[11] This international recognition is closely tied to the ascendency of Jamaican superstar Bob Marley, who dominated the reggae world until his death from cancer in 1981.

It is at the deeper level of meaning, however, that reggae and Rastafarianism take on their true importance. Ironically, this has little to do with reggae's international success, since reggae's popularity with white listeners is almost entirely due to its compelling rhythms and melodies. Nor does the rather voyeuristic interest in Rastafarianism among tourists to Jamaica and others necessarily imply an understanding of the religion's meaning in the Afro-Caribbean context.

Rastafarianism speaks to the historical experience of black peoples in Jamaica and the rest of the New World. As international capital penetrated Jamaica in the 1950s and a materialistic middle class emerged, Rastafarianism gained strength as an alternative creed for those shut out of this process. Rooted in the Pan-African tradition of Marcus Garvey, Rastafarianism promised redemption through repatriation to Africa for black people suffering in the white man's world [see Part I, Ch. 6].

Early Rastafarian music incorporated elements of Afro-American spirituals, hymns, and rhythm and blues, which were popular among poor Jamaicans. When reggae burst forth at the end of the 1960s, these elements were woven into the new music, along with references to Africa, Garvey, Zion (the promised land) Babylon (the white world), and Jah (God). Marley's "Zion Train" is essentially a transformation of an old Baptist spiritual, illustrating how black Christian religiosity is one of the strains feeding into the evolution of Rastafarianism:

Zion train is coming our way
Zion train is coming our way
Oh people better get on board
You better get on board
Thank the Lord, praise Fari
   [Ras Tafari, or Haile Selassie, worshipped
      as divine by Rastafarians]

Everybody's Magazine

The "Peace Concert": Reggae superstar Bob Marley brings together rival party leaders Michael Manley, left, and Edward Seaga, right, for a symbolic reconciliation onstage in Kingston in 1978. With the 1980 election approaching, violence was rising between warring factions of the Jamaica Labour Party and People's National Party. Over 800 persons died in political violence by the time the election was held.

The dominant influence, however, is Pan-Africanism and the Garveyite theme of repatriation.

Africa unite
Cause we're moving right out of Babylon
And we're going to our fathers' land

Although Rastafarianism predates and influenced reggae, reggae in turn has served as a vehicle for the spread of Rastafarianism. There are now Rastas in every country of the English-speaking Caribbean, as well as in West Indian communities abroad. In addition, many youth affect some aspects of the Rasta style but do not fully adhere to it as a religion. Reggae's appeal is nonetheless far broader than that of Rastafarianism. The music's wide popularity among black

West Indian youth reflects its portrayal of the reality they live—the "sufferer culture" in a world of economic hardship, racism and injustice.

They made their world so hard
Everyday we got to keep on fighting
They made their world so hard
Everyday the people are dying
It dread, dread for hunger and
Starvation dread dread, dread on dread
Lamentation dread dread
But read it in revelation dread dread
You'll find your redemption.

Rastafarians traditionally regard political struggle as

241

irrelevant, seeing salvation as possible only through a future "redemption," or repatriation. Reggae, however, departs from this. Marley in particular is forceful in urging the downtrodden to stand up and reclaim their rights. In the song "Wake Up and Live," he echoes Garvey's call for united struggle by those of African descent:

Rise ye mighty people
There is work to be done
So let's do it little by little
Rise from your sleepless slumber

Another theme in Marley's music is the need for black people to triumph over the divide-and-rule tactics of the establishment. He sings of the struggle for the unity and liberation of the African continent ("Africans a liberate Zimbabwe"). Closer to home, he denounces the violence which the political parties have encouraged within the Jamaican working class:

Would you let the system
Make you kill your brotherman
No dread no

While this message is directed especially to Jamaicans, it speaks to youth all over the Caribbean. In one of his last compositions before his death, "Redemption Song," Marley urges black youth to transcend the history of slavery, and voices his faith in the new Caribbean generation:

Old pirates yes they rob I
Sold I to the merchant ships
Minutes after they took I
From the bottomless pit
But my hand was made strong
By the hand of the Almighty
We forward in this generation
Triumphantly

The song goes on to echo the liberation philosophy of Frantz Fanon:

Emancipate yourself from mental slavery
None but ourselves can free our mind

Marley thus articulates for Caribbean youth an activist alternative to the passivity of the "sufferer" or the self-destruction of the ghetto fighter. This has helped shape a new awareness and pride which may in time provide the basis for greater unity. As the calypsonian Black Stalin argues:

A man who don't know his history can't form no unity
How could a man who don't know his history form his own
  ideology
If the Rastafarian movement spreading and Carifta dying slow
Den is something dem Rastas on dat dem politicians don't
  know.

Building Bridges

We broke language barriers and declared them no longer a limitation to our unity. On a very personal, human level we enjoyed with our Caribbean sisters the sameness within our cultures. We enjoyed dancing to Antiguan music in the same way we dance in Cuba. Our foods are also very similar as are our gestures when speaking. We share a common sense of humor. We worked hard and talked about everything that affects us as Caribbean women.

— Cuban delegate at First Caribbean Women's Encounter[12]

The First Caribbean Women's Encounter, held in Antigua in 1984, brought together women from every part of the region. They came from English-speaking Antigua, Barbados, the Bahamas, Belize, Dominica, Guyana, Jamaica, St. Lucia, St. Kitts-Nevis, St. Vincent and Trinidad; from Spanish-speaking Cuba, Puerto Rico and the Dominican Republic; from French-speaking Haiti; and from Dutch-speaking Curaçao and Suriname.

The encounter was organized by the Antigua Women's Movement, the women's arm of the Antigua Caribbean Liberation Movement. Because the ACLM was involved, the government of Antigua responded with paranoid harassment, stationing police in the convention hall to record the proceedings on film and tape.

Progressive political parties and women's groups are two of the sectors working actively to promote contacts between different parts of the Caribbean. Others include academics, artists and writers, development workers, trade unions, and church and ecumenical organizations. These categories are not distinct, but overlapping, with individuals often involved at several levels—a university professor who belongs to a left political party, for example, or a woman working with a church-sponsored development project who also leads a popular theater group.

Regional universities are a key element in this process, both in terms of their own programs and in terms of the informal linkages which have emerged among academics. The University of the West Indies has long been considered one of the few successful examples of regionalism. The CARICOM governments jointly support the university, enabling students from all the Commonwealth Caribbean countries to attend for only minimal fees. UWI's three campuses, in Jamaica, Barbados and Trinidad, are the main academic centers in the region. Its Institute for Social and Economic Research is an important source of original research and thinking on regional issues and policies.

UWI programs in agriculture, medicine, law and other disciplines are a major source of trained personnel and technical assistance for regional development programs. The university has given support to various community outreach and networking efforts. An example is the Caribbean Network for Integrated Rural Development, launched in 1988 by UWI's Social Welfare Training Centre. Working with other regional bodies such as the Women and Development Unit (WAND) and the CCC's CADEC, the new organization will attempt to link and support groups involved in rural development.

Although the UWI system forms the core academic network in the region, faculty at other regional universities participate in exchanges as well. The University of Puerto Rico hosts the Institute of Caribbean Studies, and scholars at UPR have done noted work on regional militarization. A limited exchange program has begun between UWI and the Centre Universitaire Antilles-Guyane in the French Antilles. Barbadian novelist George Lamming received an enthusiastic welcome when he visited the campus in Martinique.

In addition to these academic linkages, an independent movement of progressive intellectuals has come together outside the university structure. A first "Conference on Culture and Sovereignty" was held in Grenada in 1982. From the gathering emerged the Regional Committee of Caribbean Cultural and Intellectual Workers, headed by Lamming, which called for "a sovereign Caribbean nation-state embracing the entire archipelago." Although the network is no longer active, informal ties between its members continue.

Journalists are another group working to strengthen their ties, although this networking has thus far been mainly among English-speaking journalists. Journalists from eight countries formed the Caribbean Association of Media Workers in 1986. Headed by Guyana-born journalist Rickey Singh, the association seeks to strengthen the regional media and its ability to help build an authentic Caribbean identity. One proposal is for Caribbean television and radio stations to jointly produce programs of regional interest to counter the dominance of foreign programming. The United Nations through UNESCO has already funded such an exchange between stations in the Eastern Caribbean.

A dynamic regional network has been that of popular theater groups. The Eastern Caribbean Popular Theater Organization includes the Movement for Cultural Awareness in Dominica; the New Artists Movement in St. Vincent; Harambee in Antigua; the Grenada National Popular Theater Committee; and Teyat Pep La in St. Lucia. It coordinates exchanges and workshops, particularly between French Creole-speaking countries such as Dominica, St. Lucia and Martinique. The network also maintains contact with theater groups in other parts of the Caribbean, such as Sistren in Jamaica and Mofo in Suriname.

One goal of popular theater is to raise consciousness by involving people in a dramatization of their own experiences. Not surprisingly, grassroots development workers and activists have played a prominent role. Dominica's Movement for Cultural Awareness receives support from the Small Projects Assistance Team, a development group working in rural Dominica. The Grenadian theater committee is linked to the Agency for Rural Transformation, and Teyat Pep La to St. Lucia's Folk Research Center. In St. Vincent, a founder of the New Artists Movement, Cecil "Blazer" Williams, has worked with the development group Projects Promotion and with the Movement for National Unity.

Building a cooperative bakery in Dominica.

Small Projects Assistance Team

Probably the most consistent work in regional cooperation is being carried out by the Church, especially the Caribbean Conference of Churches. Through CADEC, its development arm, the CCC funds development projects in most Caribbean territories. Workshops sponsored by the CCC frequently bring together participants from around the region. At an agricultural training seminar held in Jamaica, 40 small farmers from Belize, Jamaica and the Turks and Caicos met to share their common concerns. They came out strongly in favor of greater unity and cooperation among traditionally isolated small farmers.[13]

Long dominated by English-speakers, the CCC has in recent years made a conscious effort to be more inclusive and strengthen the role of its non-anglophone members. In 1981 the CCC held its general assembly in Curaçao in the Netherlands Antilles, and the CCC and the World Council of Churches held a joint workshop there in 1988. Both events had a significant impact in the Dutch-speaking island, focusing new attention on Caribbean linkages.[14] In 1986 Myrtha Leetz-Cyntje of Curaçao was elected as one of the CCC's three presidents.

In the early seventies, the ecumenical movement was the first to call for diplomatic ties between Cuba and other Caribbean states. The CCC's inclusion of the Cuban churches has been important in keeping alive what few ties exist between Cuba and the rest of the region. Cuba hosted a meeting of the CCC's Continuation Committee in 1983.

The CCC's monthly newspaper, *Caribbean Contact,* has an important role as the only regional publication attempting to cover the entire Caribbean. Although its emphasis remains on the Commonwealth Caribbean, the paper includes news from the French, Dutch and Spanish-speaking countries. *Contact's* commitment to broadening its coverage is reflected in the recent hiring of an assistant editor fluent in Spanish and French. The paper already includes one or two articles in translation in each issue.

The churches, both within and outside the CCC structure, have been willing to tackle some of the most difficult problems in regional relations. In 1984 the Conference of Bishops of the Dominican Republic and Haiti called for an urgent solution to the "inhuman and unjust" treatment of Haitian immigrants in the Dominican Republic. The bishops announced the creation of a pastoral center for Haitian immigrants in Santo Domingo, one of the few attempts to bridge the animosity between the two neighboring peoples.

The same sectors working to build regional ties also help to promote links with networks outside the region. The Caribbean Project for Justice and Peace, located in Puerto Rico, convened a gathering of activists and scholars in 1984 to study the militarization of the region. The 70 participants represented four distinct blocs: the Spanish-speaking Caribbean, the English-speaking Caribbean, Central America, and North America/Europe. "Our main objective was to link people from Central America and the Caribbean and enable them to discuss the situation they face," said Awilda Colón, one of the organizers. "We hoped that Puerto Rico, which is presently a springboard for militarism in the region, could become a springboard for communication and peace."[15]

If the perception of shared crisis serves to strengthen the regional dialogue, a weakness of the process is its tendency to take place at the level of conferences and other temporary events. Ongoing, organized cooperation has proved difficult to sustain. Such cooperation takes place most often among grassroots development groups, where projects often span more than one territory. This is also the level at which popular sectors such as small farmers are most likely to participate in inter-island cooperation.

One example is the Farm Youth Regional Exchange Program, organized by farmers' unions in St. Vincent, St. Lucia, Dominica and Grenada. The program involved 36 young farmers, aged 18 to 29, who participated in a three-week rotating exchange. The Vincentian farmers hosted three Grenadians, three Dominicans and three St. Lucians; the Dominicans hosted three Vincentians, three St. Lucians and three Grenadians; and so on. The program, involving islands with similar terrain and agriculture, was intended to help the youths develop leadership skills and a commitment to transforming the small farming sector. It also helped prepare them for a planned exchange with Canadian farmers.

"We need to manage the growth of progressive movements so that the popular base always provides a solid foundation of support," comments Atherton Martin, a development worker from Dominica. Activists increasingly have found that such support comes through purposeful activity at the grassroots level, building a movement from the base up rather than the top down. To some governments, such cooperation is at best irrelevant, at worst a threat. But as the formal integration movement founders, these cautious beginnings may point the way to a new regionalism more solidly grounded in the creativity and strength of the Caribbean people. ∎

NOTES TO PART SEVEN

The Left Debate

1. Interview with Octavio Rivera, member of the Political Committee of the Bloque Socialista, Dominican Republic, in *Intercontinental Press,* April 16, 1984.
2. Fidel Castro, public address in Havana, November 14, 1983.
3. Interview with Kenrick Radix, *Intercontinental Press,* April 30, 1984; interview with Don Rojas, *Intercontinental Press,* Dec. 26, 1983.
4. See for example Richard Hart's introduction to *In Nobody's Backyard: Maurice Bishop's Speeches, 1979-1983: A Memorial Volume* (London: Zed Books Ltd., 1984).
5. *Struggle,* Feb. 10, 1984.
6. *Catholic Standard,* Feb. 26, 1984.
7. Oilfields Workers Trade Union, "Statement Condemning the Invasion of Grenada," Nov. 1, 1983.
8. *Ibid.*
9. *Struggle,* Nov. 11, 1983.
10. George Lamming, address at University of the West Indies, Cave Hill, Barbados, November 17, 1983.
11. Clive Thomas, address at Queen's University, Kingston, Ontario, May 9, 1984.
12. *The Militant,* December 30, 1983.
13. *Outlet,* December 23, 1983.
14. Interview with Octavio Rivera, *op. cit.*
15. Jamaica *Daily Gleaner* interview with Trevor Monroe, cited in *Struggle,* May 1987, p. 5.
16. Letter from WPA to *Catholic Standard,* March 4, 1984.
17. *Caribbean Contact,* December 1983.
18. EPICA interview with Tim Hector, Antigua, May 1984.
19. *Dayclean,* November 5, 1983.

Religious Challenge and Conformity

1. Other important figures include Dale Bisnauth and Mike McCormack of Guyana, Pablo Marichal of Cuba, William Watty of Dominica and Jamaica, Luis Rivera of Puerto Rico, and David Mitchell of Grenada and Barbados—among others.
2. *Caribbean Contact,* September 1981.
3. EPICA interview with Dr. Roy Neehall, Trinidad, August 1982.
4. *Ibid.*
5. *Caribbean Contact,* December 1981.
6. *Caribbean Contact,* May 1982.
7. *Caribbean Contact,* August 1981.
8. *Caribbean Contact,* April 1983.
9. Moises Rosa Ramos, "Analysis of the Church in Puerto Rico," Church and Theology Project of the National Ecumenical Movement of Puerto Rico (PRISA), 1985.
10. Interview by Don Foster with Horace Levy, Social Action Centre Ltd., Kingston, Jamaica, June 1984.
11. EPICA interview with Michael James, CCC, Barbados, May 1984.
12. CCC statement, October 25, 1983, cited in *Caribbean Contact,* November 1983.
13. Conference of Churches of Grenada, "Message addressed to all people in Grenada, Carriacou and Petite Martinique," signed by Rev. Sydney Charles, acting chairman.
14. Dr. Leslie Lett, "Grenada: A Churchman's View," remarks presented to Caribbean Studies Association, St. Kitts-Nevis, June 2, 1984.
15. *Caribbean Contact,* May 1984.
16. *Caribbean Contact,* April 1988.

Caribbean Women: Old Burdens, New Voices

1. Sistren with Honor Ford-Smith, ed., *Lionheart Gal: Life Stories of Jamaican Women* (London: The Women's Press, 1986), pp. 61-63.
2. Pat Ellis, "An Overview of Women in Caribbean Society," in Pat Ellis, ed., *Women of the Caribbean* (London: Zed Press, 1986), p. 4.
3. Lorna Gordon, "Women in Caribbean Agriculture," in Ellis, p. 36.
4. Based on EPICA interviews with women sugar workers in Frome/Petersfield communities, Westmoreland province, October 1987. "Miss Beryl" is a composite.
5. "Profile of a Transnational Electronic Industry in St. Vincent," *Caribbean Dialogue,* December 1986, citing findings of the Women Workers Project of CARIPEDA (Caribbean People's Development Agency) and Center for Caribbean Dialogue in Toronto.
6. Josh DeWind and David Kinley, *Aiding Migration: The Impact of International Development Assistance in Haiti* (New York: Center for Social Sciences, Columbia University, 1986), chapters 3-5.
7. EPICA interview with officials of the Central General de Trabajadores, Santo Domingo, Nov. 1986.
8. Peggy Antrobus, "Gender Implications of the Debt Crisis in the Commonwealth Caribbean: The Case of Jamaica," paper presented at First Conference of Caribbean Economists, Kingston, July 1987.
9. EPICA interview with FEMUCA members, Hato Damas, Dominican Republic, Nov. 1986.
10. Sistren, *Lionheart Gal,* pp. 86-87.

Caribbean Unity, the Distant Dream

1. Ocho Rios Declaration, cited in *Caribbean Contact,* December 1982.
2. Jeremy Taylor, London Observer Service, July 2, 1984.
3. EPICA interview with Dr. Lloyd Searwar, Guyana, March 1988.
4. Dr. Neville Linton, "Facing Up to Ideological Pluralism in CARICOM," *Caribbean Contact,* July 1983.
5. Ocho Rios Declaration.
6. "Haitian Election Issue Exposes Regional Disunity," *Caribbean Insight,* February 1988. "Caricom Delegation Naive," *Caribbean Contact,* January 1988.
7. Rosina Wiltshire-Brodber, "Informal and Formal Bases of Caribbean Regional Integration," presented at Hunter College, Sept. 1, 1984.
8. David Frith, "Salute to George Headley," *Outlet,* April 6, 1984.
9. *Cuba Internacional,* July 1983.
10. C.L.R. James, "Garfield Sobers," in *The Future in the Present* (London: Allison & Busby, 1977), p. 225.
11. EPICA interview with Barbadian artist Omowale Stewart, August 1982.
12. *Outlet,* November 2, 1984.
13. "Cooperation Among Small Farmers Urged," *Caribbean Contact,* January 1988.
14. EPICA interview with Myrtha Leetz-Cyntje, Curacao, March 1988.
15. EPICA interview with Awilda Colon, Puerto Rico, October 1984.

Conclusion: Toward a Constructive Caribbean Policy

Over the past decades U.S. involvement in the Caribbean has been largely negative in its impact on the region. For this to change, two basic preconditions are necessary.

First, an improvement in relations must begin with a dialogue in which we in the United States listen carefully to Caribbean views. People-to-people exchanges between the two regions can serve as a starting point. These must go beyond tourism to encompass contacts with all social sectors, but particularly with grassroots organizations representing working people. Such a dialogue can lead us to a deeper understanding of the Caribbean and the impact of U.S. policies in the region, a prerequisite for any change in U.S. actions.

Such change can only occur, however, in the context of a more fundamental shift in U.S. foreign policy. This shift must reflect a changed concept of the U.S. role in the world, and particularly in this hemisphere. It is basically a change from "master" to "partner," from domination and empire-building to friendship on the basis of equal sovereignty. That in turn requires political changes within the United States, posing a long-term challenge to Americans.

Both of these processes have begun, albeit in modest ways. Grassroots organizations and policy groups in North America and the Caribbean have initiated a dialogue in which a number of essential points have emerged. These are not precise policy recommendations, but broad concepts serving as a guide to policies that we in the United States can support.

One: Support economic aid which fosters Caribbean regionalism and self-reliance.

The failure of the Caribbean Basin Initiative has provided a starting point for considering how economic aid to the region might be made more effective. One set of ideas emerged from symposia held in Barbados in 1987 and 1988, organized by the Washington-based Development Group for Alternative Policies. Six U.S. members of Congress met with a broad range of Caribbean spokespersons, including representatives of regional institutions and grassroots organizations, private sector leaders and government officials.

Central to their critique was the fact that the CBI was designed with minimal input from the region. In planning the CBI, U.S. officials focused on advancing U.S. ideologies and political goals, and thus ended up with a program largely divorced from Caribbean realities. To be effective, the Caribbean panelists stressed, aid programs must be planned in consultation with Caribbean grassroots organizations, political leaders and technical experts.

The participants also pointed out that U.S. aid programs often bypass regional institutions or even create new ones that duplicate the work of existing organizations. They rely on foreign consultants who often do not fully understand local conditions. The result is programs which undermine rather than strengthen regional cooperation and capabilities.

Wherever possible, aid projects should use Caribbean consultants rather than importing foreign "experts." Such expertise is available through institutions such as the Caribbean Development Bank, the University of the West Indies, the Caribbean Food Corporation, and the Caribbean Agricultural Research and Development Institute (CARDI). Outside the Commonwealth Caribbean, national institutions can play a similar role. The United States can encourage the development of local capabilities by granting scholarships for Caribbean nationals to train in scientific, technical and business-related fields.

A major flaw of the Caribbean Basin Initiative is its excessive focus on export production, especially by foreign-owned firms. This has encouraged the proliferation of free trade zones which have no impact on Caribbean economies other than the creation of low-wage, non-union factory jobs. Instead, aid programs should emphasize support to small and medium-sized local producers, especially food producers. With credit, technical assistance and equity investment, Caribbean farmers and manufacturers could increase the region's self-sufficiency in food and other goods, and also produce a surplus for export.

Finally, aid programs must address the crisis in social services. At a time when structural adjustment programs are forcing drastic cutbacks in government spending on health, education and nutrition, aid donors must take up the slack. A program jointly financed by USAID and the Caribbean Development Bank, the Basic Human Needs Project, funds such programs in the Eastern Caribbean and has been very successful.

Two: Respond to the crisis in commodity markets, especially sugar.

Caribbean countries desperately need to stabilize their earnings from basic commodity exports whose prices fluctuate on the world market. The United States should consider creating a stabilization fund modeled on the European Economic Community's STABEX facility. Such a device can provide for a soft loan to cover the earnings deficit when a country's income from a basic commodity falls a certain percentage below average.

The sugar trade, so crucial to Caribbean economies, has pitted subsidized American and European producers against Third World farmers. At a minimum, the United States should hold the line on further reductions in the sugar quotas of Caribbean countries. The U.S. government should provide funding and technical assistance for the long-term transformation of the sugar industry, including the development of industries based on sugar byproducts.

The Caribbean Basin Initiative's trade preferences have been of some help to the region, but they do not go far enough. Tariff barriers could be phased out on most remaining products presently excluded from the CBI. Such preferences should only be extended to goods produced under conditions which protect workers and their right to organize. Trade should favor goods produced by small and medium-sized enterprises with majority Caribbean ownership.

Three: Develop an alternative tourism which strengthens

Caribbean economies and respects Caribbean cultures.

The tourist industry in the Caribbean is largely foreign-controlled. It relies on imported food and merchandise, so that more than half of each tourist dollar leaves the region. A nationally-owned tourism using local foods and handicrafts would help to stimulate other sectors of Caribbean economies. Rather than promoting false cultural images and an irresponsible hedonism—leading to the spread of prostitution and AIDS—tourism should reflect the dignity and values of Caribbean societies.

Four: Respect ideological pluralism and the right of Caribbean countries to experiment with alternative development models.

Beginning with the European colonial powers and continuing today with the United States, outside forces have imposed their economic and social models on the Caribbean. These models are now in crisis, unable to provide sufficient employment, social services or economic growth.

The search for alternatives is not an "either-or" process—either "our" system or "theirs." It is a creative process of experimentation, often drawing on elements from several different models. Socialist currents are an aspect of most social change efforts in the region, but seldom the dominant one. We must dispel the myth that every attempt at change provides an opening for "communism" and threatens U.S. interests.

As sovereign nations, Caribbean countries have the right to choose any economic system. Many regions of the world include nations with varying systems, and there is no reason why socialism in the Caribbean need threaten United States security. It is, rather, U.S. military intervention and support for dictatorships which creates hostility toward the United States and threatens our security.

Five: Develop an alternative policy toward Cuba.

In this context, it is time to take a hard look at our national obsession with Cuba. Whether Americans agree with the ideology of the revolution or not, the Castro government enjoys popular support. The policy of isolating the Havana government has had little success in changing Cuban behavior. And the U.S. vendetta against Cuba is blinding many North Americans to the real causes of the Caribbean's problems.

PACCA, Policy Alternatives for the Caribbean and Central America, has set forth some basic elements of an alternative policy toward Cuba. A first step is to reestablish full diplomatic relations and trade. When these ties are resumed, the two countries can more easily negotiate bilateral issues, such as radio broadcasting and interference, migration, maritime border disputes, response to hijackings, violations of airspace, and the U.S. base at Guantanamo Bay.

Rather than simply blaming Cuba for conflicts in the region, the United States should enter into discussions aimed at resolving regional and global security concerns. One goal of such talks might be mutual Cuban and American compliance with peace accords emanating from the Central American region.

Finally, the U.S. government should immediately lift restrictions on the free flow of information between the two countries, including the ban on U.S. citizens traveling to Cuba. Our goal should be to increase, not prevent, contact and exchanges between the two societies.

Six: Respect Caribbean sovereignty and non-alignment, and make the Caribbean a "zone of peace."

After the Grenada invasion, Senator Barry Goldwater suggested that Grenada, Puerto Rico, the U.S. Virgin Islands and any other Caribbean territories so wishing form an "archipelago state" to be admitted to the Union. Clearly, the old North American dream of a Caribbean empire is not dead.

The Caribbean is not a U.S. appendage, tropical state or empire, but a group of sovereign nations. Trade, aid and tourism will naturally take place between the United States and the Caribbean, but they must take place on a basis of mutual respect, as difficult as this concept may be for a superpower.

This includes respect for the right of Caribbean nations to be non-aligned and to stay out of east-west conflicts. The "zone of peace" concept, initiated by the Caribbean churches and supported by grassroots organizations, deserves the support of Americans as well. The U.S. militarization of the region must be halted, and funds spent on military aid should be largely transferred to economic development programs.

Finally, North Americans must accept the right of Caribbean countries to have diplomatic and trade ties with partners of their choosing. In addition to the traditional partners—the United States, Canada and Europe—these will likely include countries in Latin America, Asia and the socialist bloc. A self-reliant and non-aligned Caribbean, with diverse international ties, would be more in the long-term interest of this country than a dependent and conflict-ridden region, however subservient.

Moving from a relationship of domination to one of partnership is undoubtedly a difficult and long-term process. Such a change, when it comes, will rest on countless initiatives by individuals and groups willing to break the patterns of the past. ∎

Resources for Action

NONFICTION BOOKS

On the history and economics of the region:

Caribbean Story, by William Claypole and John Robottom. Longman Caribbean Ltd., 1980. Two volumes.

Readable, comprehensive history of the region, with excellent illustrations.

From Columbus to Castro: The History of the Caribbean 1492-1969, by Eric Williams. Harper & Row, 1970.

Definitive economic history of the region.

Capitalism and Slavery, by Eric Williams. University of North Carolina Press, 1964.

Classic study of the role of slavery in building modern industrial capitalism.

Empire as a Way of Life, by William Appleman Williams. Oxford University Press, 1980.

Examines roots of U.S. imperialism in the American past.

The United States and the Caribbean 1900-1970, by Lester D. Langley. University of Georgia Press, 1980.

A history of U.S. intervention in the region.

Growth of the Modern West Indies, by Gordon K. Lewis. Monthly Review Press, 1968.

Historical essays on the English-speaking Caribbean.

The Other Side of Paradise: Foreign Control in the Caribbean, by Tom Barry, Beth Wood and Deb Preusch. Grove Press, 1984.

Popular overview of the region focusing on corporate control of resources.

The Poor and the Powerless: Economic Policy and Change in the Caribbean, by Clive Y. Thomas. Latin America Bureau/ Monthly Review Press, 1988.

Comparative survey of development policies in the region, with case studies of Jamaica, Grenada, Guyana, Barbados, Trinidad and Puerto Rico.

On culture and language:

Dread: The Rastafarians of Jamaica, by Joseph Owens. Sangsters's Book Stores, 1976.

Study of Rastafarian philosophy by an American Jesuit who lived among the Rastas in Kingston in the early 1970s.

Rasta and Resistance: From Marcus Garvey to Walter Rodney, by Horace Campbell. Africa World Press, 1987.

Traces the cultural, political and theological roots of Rastafarianism.

Caribbean and African Languages, by Morgan Dalphinis. Karia Press, 1985.

Examines roots and development of Caribbean Creole languages and their social and political usage.

Language and Liberation: Creole Language Politics in the Caribbean, by Hubert Devonish. Karia Press, 1986.

Examines role of Creole languages in national politics and liberation struggles, with examples from around the region.

Kaiso! The Trinidad Calypso, by Keith Q. Warner. Three Continents Press, 1982.

Lively study of calypso's evolution and role in Caribbean society.

Caribbean Contours, edited by Sidney W. Mintz and Sally Price. Johns Hopkins University Press, 1985.

Anthology of essays on topics including race, politics, language and music.

On women:

Lionheart Gal: Life Stories of Jamaican Women, by Sistren with Honor Ford-Smith. The Women's Press, 1986.

Autobiographical testimonies by members of the Sistren Theatre Collective, portraying life struggles of Jamaican working-class women.

Women of the Caribbean, edited by Pat Ellis. Zed Press, 1987.

Essays by 19 Caribbean women on women and work, the family, education, culture and development.

"Nana Yah," from the play by Sistren Theatre Collective. Design by Jean Small.